ESCAPADE

AN EXPLORATION OF AVENGERS CURIOSITIES

**J Z FERGUSON
& ALAN HAYES**

Published by
QUOIT MEDIA LIMITED
www.quoitmedia.co.uk

QUOIT

This edition first published in 2025 by Quoit Media Limited,
Brynmawr, Llanfair Caereinion, Powys, SY21 0DG

For more copies of this book, please email quoit@quoitmedia.co.uk

ISBN 978-1-911537-25-0

Copyright © 2025 J Z Ferguson and Alan Hayes

The right of J Z Ferguson and Alan Hayes to be identified as the authors of this work has been asserted in accordance with the Copyright, Designs and Patents Act 1988.

All rights reserved. No part of this publication may be reproduced, stored in or introduced to a retrieval system, or transmitted, in any form, or by any means (electronic, mechanical, photocopying, recording or otherwise) without the prior written permission of the publisher.

Cover illustration by Robert Hammond,
inspired by René Magritte's *Le fils de l'homme* (*The Son of Man*).
Cover concept, internal design and digital artwork by Alan Hayes.
Memorabilia photos on pages 262, 267, 269, 281, 284, 286, 289 © Alan Hayes.

A CIP catalogue record for this book is available from the British Library.

Quoit Media Limited's authorised EURP is Rick Davy,
contactable at rick@quoitmedia.co.uk

Printed and bound in Great Britain by Clays Ltd, Elcograf S.p.A.

MIX
Paper | Supporting responsible forestry
FSC® C018072

IN MEMORIAM

Wolfgang von Chmielewski
(1940-2021)

Donald Monat
(1928-2018)

Simon Oates
(1938-2009)

CONTENTS

005 – Foreword by Roy Bettridge
007 – Introduction

INNER AVENGERLAND

011 – *This'll Kill You* by Alan Hayes
034 – *Tell Me About It* by J Z Ferguson

OUTER AVENGERLAND

061 – *The Stage Play* by Alan Hayes
120 – *The Radio Series* by Alan Hayes
158 – *The First Avengers Movie* by J Z Ferguson
177 – *Avengers International: Reincarnation* by J Z Ferguson
201 – *Steed and Mrs. Peel* by J Z Ferguson

BEYOND AVENGERLAND

237 – *Las Luchadoras vs. el Robot Asesino* by J Z Ferguson
261 – *Das Diadem / Der Goldene Schlüssel* by Alan Hayes
279 – *Minikillers* by Alan Hayes
308 – *Escapade* by J Z Ferguson

349 – Afterword
350 – Acknowledgements
351 – About the Authors

FOREWORD

How much can one television show give to a fan? The question answers itself – everything. But for me, The Avengers is a gift that keeps on giving.

Back in 1995 – at the tender age of nine – I had no idea what was around the corner when I was introduced to the world of John Steed and his many partners. The whole experience has been a delight to this day, a journey that has been full of fantastic discoveries. Who knew that it was a male partnership in the beginning? Who knew that there were episodes that John Steed didn't even appear in? Who knew that Play School presenter Julie Stevens had been one of Steed's early 1960s partners? Who knew that Hammer film legends Peter Cushing and Christopher Lee had appeared in The Avengers at the height of its success? Who knew that Purdey in The New Avengers could have been a right Charly?

The wonderment I experienced reading about these things in Dave Rogers' amazing books was just the tip of the iceberg. There were books on the series that had been published when the show was at its height, there were videos available, and there were also toys and games that had been specially made and released; many of these are now expensive collector's items. I was like a child in a sweet shop with all of this bountiful information. The collector in me was desperate to obtain these precious items, and I had a voracious appetite to find out more and more about The Avengers. But was there really more out there to learn?

Then along came Alan Hayes' splendid website The Avengers Declassified – a virtual treasure trove of information on my beloved show. Through this fantastic resource, the lid was lifted on the missing first series and the male partnership that started one of the cornerstones of 1960s television. There was also further light shed on the lesser-known spin-offs of the 1970s, such as the Avengers radio series made in South Africa of all places. Not content with imparting information about this radio version, The Avengers Declassified even recovered off-air recordings of a large proportion of the programmes produced – and digitised them, preserving an otherwise lost series!

And now to the present day – is there still more to learn about The Avengers?

The answer to that question lies in the book you're holding: a fantastic collection of articles that tickles the taste buds of a fan like me. For the most part, it looks beyond The Avengers of the television screen, focusing on the unfamiliar and fascinating, the incarnations of the series which are not well known or celebrated. This is something that *The Avengers Declassified* always did well. It is appropriate, therefore, that several of the chapters in this book started out as features for *The Avengers Declassified* and have now been revisited and expanded.

In *Escapades – An Exploration of Avengers Curiosities*, you will read about television and film scripts that didn't make the cut, how John Steed was reborn on stage, radio and the silver screen, how *The Avengers* was intended to develop had it returned in the late 1970s or in the subsequent decades, and bizarre – and mostly unofficial – spin-offs that saw Emma Peel transplanted to Germany and Spain, the Cybernauts to Mexico, and the *Avengers* format to the United States. And this is a mere taster of the ingredients that make up this magnificent title.

I believe that what *The Avengers* can give to me is never-ending. There will always be new people to connect with, new facets to consider, and new adventures to discover, and, as this book proves, just because it is more than half a century old doesn't mean that it's not possible to find new and exciting things to say about *The Avengers* – in its many incarnations.

Roy Bettridge

Roy Bettridge is an *Avengers* fan of nearly three decades' standing. A writer since the age of 15, his first independently published books have been based around his love of the series, with titles including *Look (Stop Me If You've Heard This One...) But There Was This TV Show*, *Split!*, *Love All*, *The Morning After*, *From Venus With Love*, to name but a few. His most recent book is *The Avengers – The Official Quizbook* (tinyurl.com/steedquiz). He has also penned a standalone thriller - *Flood* - and more titles are said to be on the way. He currently resides in Kettering.

INTRODUCTION

Avengerland.

This term has taken on a few different meanings since entering the *Avengers* lexicon. As originally conceived, it refers to *The Avengers*' in-show universe, typically the version of it depicted in the Emma Peel and Tara King episodes: a surreal fantasy world in which diabolical masterminds are around every corner, the streets are devoid of passersby, and deaths are bloodless. Over time, the term has been co-opted by location spotters and used to collectively refer to the areas in southern England that provided exterior filming locales for *The Avengers*, *The New Avengers* and other contemporary film series. Those involved in the production of the 1998 *Avengers* movie restored the "s" in "*Avengers*" and used "Avengersland" to describe the film's setting, a world in which the sixties had been going on for decades. However, for those in the business of film and television production, "Avengerland" means something quite different.

Success.

The projects that we have chosen to examine in this book provide ample evidence of this, though that might come as something of a surprise given that so many of them can be considered, to a greater or lesser extent, failures. The American *Avengers*-esque pilot *Escapade* did not lead to a full series. *Las Luchadoras vs. el Robot Asesino* did not become a classic or fondly remembered entry in the Mexican wrestling movie canon, despite copying large portions of the episode *Return of the Cybernauts*. *This'll Kill You* and *Tell Me About It*, scripts submitted for inclusion in the colour Peel era and *The New Avengers*, respectively, were passed over by the production teams. Mooted revivals *The First Avengers Movie* and *Avengers International* never made it past the script stage. Diana Rigg's participation in the short film series *Der Goldene Schlüssel / Das Diadem* and *Minikillers* was not enough to save the ambitious German film company behind them from going under. The three-issue Acme Press / Eclipse Comics limited comic book series *Steed and Mrs. Peel* was plagued by delays, with issue three appearing over a year after issue two, and remained a one-off until Boom! Studios began publishing new stories under the same title two decades later. The ill-fated stage play based on the series closed after a scant 36 performances. The only bona fide success amongst these projects is the South African radio adaptation of the series, which was not only well made, but extremely popular, only coming to an end when it ran out of Peel and King era scripts to adapt and producer David Gooden was denied permission to commission original stories. Given the fate of so many of these projects, how can they be considered to be evidence of the series and the world it created being synonymous with success?

The answer is quite simple. It is not the rate of success of these projects that matters, but the fact that so many projects were attempted in the first place, that so many people recognised that there was something very special about Avengerland, and sought to replicate it, adapt it, or revive it in order to perpetuate its particular brand of magic. Passed over episode scripts are evidence of writers' desire to write for the series. Mooted revivals in the form of a series of TV movies and episodic television show demonstrate the reluctance of Brian Clemens et al. to let this unique programme be consigned to the history books. Stage, comic and radio adaptations point to the faith placed in the series' formula, signature charm and wit, and iconic characters, all of which were clearly deemed to be strong and distinctive enough to thrive in a new format. Productions in Germany and Mexico that "borrowed" elements of the series did so in the hope that some of *The Avengers*' success would rub off on their efforts, while American production company Quinn Martin believed *The Avengers* was durable enough to be successfully transplanted to the United States. Therefore, regardless of its fate, each project is, first and foremost, an acknowledgement of the series' brilliance and success. At the same time, each project's success, or lack thereof, tells us something about what made the original series tick, and why *The Avengers'* particular brand of magic proved so difficult to replicate.

Whether a success or failure, each of these projects is a fascinating example of an alternate Avengerland or an unseen adventure set in the original series' universe. All should be evaluated as creative endeavours in their own right, independent of *The Avengers'* considerable legacy. Of those projects that did not succeed, none of them is the complete failure that its ultimate fate would seem to indicate. If you have never explored some or all of these projects, we hope that this book motivates you to seek them out. If they are familiar to you, we hope that that this collection of essays encourages you to revisit them with a new perspective. Most importantly, we hope you enjoy our explorations of these weird, wonderful, and varied takes on a beloved series.

INNER AVENGERLAND

**THIS'LL KILL YOU
TELL ME ABOUT IT**

THIS'LL KILL YOU

ALAN HAYES
with thanks to Ian Beard and Rupert Blaise

Project Type: Prospective Television Episode
Date: August 1967

Synopsis

Teaser

Central London in July. A night-time thunderstorm rages. Top meteorologist Sir Basil Austin – his clothes wet from the rain – arrives at his office. Meteorological maps and graphs cover the walls. A large map of the British Isles hangs next to a large glass sheet that has been marked up with a chinagraph pencil, denoting a high-pressure area running behind a weak, occluded front. To the north run the depressions – low pressure areas with narrow isobars and spiked rain fronts.

Sir Basil takes a cigar from the box on the desk, goes to the map of the British Isles, and shoves the glass sheet across it. The high-pressure area is centred over South East England, the weather front reaches Norway, and the low pressure areas run through the Icelandic Gap. He then studies a map of the Florida coast – showing Cape Kennedy – and one of China. He dials a number on a green scrambler phone.

At his apartment, John Steed and Emma Peel are sheltering from the storm. Steed is reading *The Fly Fisher*, and Emma is making Gaelic coffee – into which she cheekily puts demerara sugar, despite Steed's insisting on the raw variety. He comments positively on the flavour, but secretly knows what Emma has done.

The telephone rings. After hearing nothing but squawks and quacks from the earpiece, he pushes the scrambler button. The call is from Sir Basil Austin. Steed complains to the meteorologist that the weather forecasts lately have been wildly inaccurate, and this has spoiled his plans to do a bit of fly fishing.

Sir Basil summons Steed to his office in order to further discuss the weather conditions. Suddenly, his cigar explodes violently and he is thrown back in his chair. When the smoke clears, all that can be seen of Sir Basil are the soles of his shoes, sticking out from behind the upturned chair.

Act One

Steed and Mrs. Peel sift through the remains of Sir Basil's office. Emma selects a cigar from the box, and examines it. Steed, meanwhile, inspects a barometer, the hand of which points to 28.92 millibars. He notes with horror that Emma is slicing into the cigar with a knife, which is no way to treat a good cigar. However, it is a most suspect one – her incision has revealed what appears to be nitro-glycerine.

Steed remarks that the barometer reading – two-eight-nine-two – is the secret combination of the office filing cabinet. He opens it and thumbs through the files held within. He comments that England should currently be gripped by a heatwave, but Emma fully expects snow. She studies the Cape Kennedy map and asks why the country's top meteorologist was interested in launching sites. Has someone found a way to control – or disrupt – the weather? Were that the case, the avengers agree that chaos would ensue – economic disaster, ruined crops, and, worst of all, there would be no pheasant shooting.

Steed retrieves a folder marked 'WRIGHT, David' from the filing cabinet. Its contents reveal that Wright is Sir Basil's second-in-command, and therefore now the top man. Apparently, he was a high diving medallist at the 1964 Tokyo Olympics. Might he be responsible for Sir Basil's death?

The next morning, while driving in the countryside, Mrs. Peel passes a saloon car. Its driver, Corker, starts the engine and follows her, but does not notice when she ducks into a turn-off. As her pursuer flashes past, Emma reverses back out onto the road, and sets off after him. However, she loses sight of the car, and comes to a fork in the road. Not knowing which direction the car has taken, she shrugs and takes the right-hand fork, continuing to her destination at a more sedate pace.

Meanwhile, Steed pays a visit to a joke shop. Janie Upshaw, a bright, confident and pretty young girl of about eighteen, greets Steed. He wants to speak to Mr. Upshaw, who wrote the joke book that he is reading, but Janie – Mr. Upshaw's daughter – tells him that he died three weeks previously. However, she has no wish to follow in her father's footsteps – she has had quite enough of it all after fifteen years of being the victim of his practical jokes. However, she quickly warms to Steed, who is as charming as the day is long.

Steed asks whether it would be possible to make an exploding cigar. She says that it would be straightforward, but that she is selling the shop. Steed asks if Mr. Upshaw – who used to invent practical jokes – had met with a fatal accident, but Janie tells him that he was just old and died of a bad cold, which had been triggered by the awful weather. Steed extends his condolences and the pair exchange farewells. As Steed departs, Janie picks up a pin and starts systematically bursting balloons, one after another.

Later on, Steed drives to a group of isolated, ugly, concrete buildings. A notice on the security fence outside reads: "GOVERNMENT RESEARCH CENTRE – DEPARTMENT OF CLIMATOLOGY – KEEP OUT." Steed drives through the gates, and parks up outside one of the buildings.

Inside, at one end of a laboratory, a series of plate glass windows are inset into a wall. Behind them are chambers that imitate climatic conditions in various environments. Further windows show the effects of cloud cover. Beneath each window is a control panel, accessed via a trolley chair that runs along a rail. The panels are operated by Professor Parto, a scientist who speaks in a staccato rhythm and has a reputation for fanatical dedication.

Steed enters, claiming to represent the Ministry of Science and Technology. Parto whizzes along the rail, complaining that the research centre has to operate on a shoestring budget. Despite his truculence, he shows Steed around. Their first stop is the window marked "ZERO CLOUD COVER", which reveals a sun-blasted scene of bare rock and sand. It would dehydrate a man in minutes, Parto declares. The next window shows the effects of full cloud cover — large toadstools; writhing, white vines; and a steamy atmosphere caused by too much cloud.

Parto warns that the world faces catastrophe should the weather be interfered with — and fears that someone has been seeding the cloud cover with carbon dioxide crystals or CO_2 gas. But, he theorises aloud, the westerly jet stream — with its velocities of up to 200 miles per hour — would make it exceptionally difficult to accurately target controlled weather events.

Mrs. Peel, meanwhile, has located Sir Basil's number two, David Wright. He is diving at an open-air swimming pool. He disrobes down to his swimming trunks at the foot of the diving platform — revealing a healthy, bronzed physique — places his spectacles in their case, and then starts to climb to the top board.

Emma drives in and speaks to the pool attendant, who refuses her entry as she is not a club member. However, he agrees to pass on a message to Mr. Wright, after he has completed his dive. They spy him on the highest platform, where he is carrying out a series of exaggerated warm-up exercises that are entirely for show.

A car coasts up silently and stops some distance behind Mrs. Peel. At the wheel, Corker fixes his sardonic eyes on Emma as he chews on some gum.

The attendant explains to Mrs. Peel that Wright is a former Olympian who likes using this competition-standard pool. He goes on to say that its sluice gates are so efficient that it is possible to very quickly empty the water from the pool — which, coincidentally, is exactly what is happening at that very moment.

Wright — his vision blurred without his glasses — cannot see that the water in the pool is draining away fast. He performs his regular, rather pretentious, last-minute exercises and prepares to dive. Teetering on the edge, he suddenly backs out of the dive — his balance was slightly off — so he starts his ritual once more.

The attendant at last realises that the water has drained away. He tries to attract Wright's attention. After all, he is about to make a terrible mess of the pool.

Finally, Wright is happy with his preparations, and, arms outstretched, he executes a perfect swallow dive. He is guaranteed a very unhappy landing.

Meanwhile, Steed leaves the Ministry of Climatology, driving out through the main gates. He joins the road, changes gear and accelerates. Suddenly, the steering wheel comes away in his hands, and the car veers wildly across the road.

Act Two

Emma rings Steed's doorbell. Once inside, she finds him brushing his suit. He explains that he had ended up in a haystack after his car was sabotaged. Emma tells him what has happened to David Wright, and also that she has been tailed all the way to Steed's by a strange man. Steed suggests that they effect an introduction.

Mrs. Peel has Corker follow her into the park, where Steed overpowers him. They bring him back to Steed's apartment and learn that he is a private inquiry agent. He claims to be working for Mr. Peel, and comments that this should not surprise them as they are living together, "all lovey-dovey". Emma refutes Corker's accusation – she and Steed are just good friends – and pointedly explains that her husband has been dead for seven years.

Corker says that he last saw Mr. Peel only two days ago. Emma and Steed resort to subterfuge – they admit that Corker has caught them red handed. Steed asks him for Mr. Peel's present address, so that they can discuss the situation man-to-man. Corker will only co-operate if he is employed as an intermediary. This proves satisfactory to Steed, and a meeting at eleven o'clock on the following day is arranged. However, when Corker leaves, Steed decides to follow him.

Some while later, Steed arrives at Corker's run-down office. He is faced with a door, the frosted glass panel of which bears the stencilled legend, "WILLIAM CORKER – PRIVATE INVESTIGATOR". The door proves to be unlocked and the room it leads to is empty apart from a battered desk and an old filing cabinet. Steed calls to Corker, but receives no reply. He makes for the inner office, and notices a bucket has been balanced over the door. Steed sighs at the man's artlessness and eases himself through the part open door without disturbing the bucket.

In Steed's apartment, a gift-wrapped box sits upon a table. It is addressed to Mrs. Peel – and a ticking sound is coming from within. Emma enters with a basket of groceries and a bottle of wine. She calls for Steed, drops her coat over the arm of a chair, and wanders through to the kitchenette with the groceries. She returns to the lounge, pours herself a glass of wine and takes a sip. She has not noticed the box or the ticking.

In Corker's inner office, Steed returns to the door – and the bucket. He tries to dislodge it, but it is fixed there and will not fall. Too late, he realises that he has disturbed a trip mechanism beside the bucket. He whirls around as a large sandbag swings across the room towards him. He drops to the floor and the sandbag swings past, splitting the door from top to bottom. He picks himself up and dusts off his trousers. He examines the sandbag, and thumps it playfully. He instantly regrets doing so – it is as hard as nails. He calls out for Corker – again, nothing. He surveys the room. Papers are strewn about everywhere – the office has been ransacked. He works speedily, checking drawers, papers and Corker's desk diary. He finds little of significance bar a yellow balloon. The words "JUMBO'S GIGANTIC FUNFAIR" and the caricature of a happy, smiling elephant can be made out as he inflates it. Steed then makes a further discovery – Corker's dead body stowed in a cupboard.

Steed returns home to find Emma behind the settee. She has taken cover after examining the ticking box. Steed – "JUMBO" balloon bobbing at the end of a length of string – freezes on the threshold as Emma gestures towards the parcel, which suddenly stops ticking...

Act Three

Steed slices through the giftwrap, and gingerly lifts the lid of the box. A Jack-in-the-Box springs up, wobbling wildly. He then reaches into the box, delicately removes a child's nursery clock, and checks it over. He and Emma take stock: a meteorologist killed by an exploding cigar; his replacement plunged into an empty pool; a private detective killed by the bucket-above-the-door trick; and Steed's steering wheel loosened. The clues suggest that the killer is a lethal practical joker. But who sent the Jack-in-the-Box? Steed suggests Professor Parto, Emma thinks a toyshop is more likely...

Later, Emma takes the Jack-in-the-Box to a toyshop. The proprietrix, a woman with a rigor mortis smile, enquires if "Modom" wishes to exchange the gift, which was purchased at the shop. Emma likes it, but says it is unsuitable for "little Luella", her three-year-old chimpanzee. She asks if the buyer left an address. Apparently not, as he paid with cash, and gave his name as Steed. Defeated, Emma goes to leave, only to be faced with dozens of bright yellow "JUMBO" funfair balloons.

Emma then heads to Steed's apartment, carrying one of the balloons. Steed is away, so she records him an answerphone message. She explains that she found a great many yellow balloons advertising the funfair at the toyshop. She says that having a sense of humour is surely a prerequisite for a funfair owner – and this one may well be the practical joker that they are seeking. She further explains that she plans to investigate Jumbo's Gigantic Funfair right away and asks Steed to meet her a hundred yards to the left of the entrance to the West Gate at 9.45pm. She leaves.

Steed returns to Upshaw's Joke Shop. The stock has been depleted considerably since his last visit. Price tags offer reduced prices, and the walls and windows are covered in "CLOSING DOWN SALE" and "PRICES SLASHED" notices. Janie Upshaw has sold the shop to a supermarket and they have no interest in the stock, so it is being sold off at bargain prices.

Steed has been reading Upshaw's book and wants to ask Janie some questions. She agrees – on the proviso that Steed purchases something. He offers to buy a traditional Jack-in-the-Box, but Janie hasn't got one in stock. As Steed doesn't want anything else, he offers her a £5 note as a goodwill gesture. Janie accepts the money and selects four giant hands and cuts them up with a pair of scissors. She has bought them with the five pounds, so he can now ask his questions.

Steed says that the book mentions that clowns and fairground people – "professional practical jokers", in Upshaw's words – used to visit the shop. They would sometimes get him to make things for them. Does she know any of them?

Janie recalls several such characters, whom she describes as she destroys further items that she is buying with Steed's five pounds. There was an 'Uncle Henry' who always used to bounce her on his knee. She was only able to stop this practice when she was fifteen. Mr. Rainey – better known as the clown, Charlie Reindeer – was another, but he now works for a circus in Glasgow. Another man was Mr. Carlton, who, according to Janie's father, possessed the greatest imagination of any practical joker. He last came to the shop three years ago. He owned a scruffy little funfair called Carlton's Carnival, and she thinks he went broke. Finally, there was an unknown woman, who used to visit about six or seven years ago. She apologises for being unhelpful, and, at Steed's suggestion, cuts up a grotesque mask – one and tuppence – to round off his five pounds. He thanks her and departs.

A large man wearing a grotesque mask looms silently behind Janie. She turns, startled, and then regains her composure. She had forgotten all about her other customer, who has taken an age to select his purchase. He has decided to take the mask, which he removes. His face and head are revealed to be totally covered in elaborate and outlandish tattoos. He hands over some silver coins, which Janie counts and confirms to be the correct amount, addressing the man as "Mr. Zebra". He leaves to follow Steed.

***

At the funfair, night has fallen. Music and the barkers' voices join with the illuminations to create a vibrant, carnival atmosphere. The yellow Jumbo balloons are everywhere, but Mrs. Peel has brought her own. She nibbles at a stick of candy floss and spies a giant barrage balloon, emblazoned with the legend, "JUMBO'S GIGANTIC FUNFAIR", floating in the air a short distance away, anchored to the ground by guy cables. She looks ruefully at her little balloon and releases it into the night air.

Meanwhile, Steed has returned to the Government Research Centre. He is having a whale of a time, zipping up and down Professor Parto's trolley rail. When the scientist arrives, Steed asks him what might happen if someone with plenty of money and a warped sense of humour sought to alter the world's climate. Parto remarks that it would be foolish — and quite possibly suicidal — to try. Were the ice caps to be melted, for instance, there would be blizzards, countries like France, Norway, Sweden and Great Britain could be buried under thirty or forty feet of snow, and the seas would freeze. A second ice age would engulf the world.

Steed fishes out a cigar case and offers Parto a cigar. The professor almost takes one, but declines the invitation. Steed smiles and returns the case to his pocket.

At the funfair, Emma checks her watch. A voice booms out from the loudspeakers placed around the fairground. The funfair is closing for the night and all those present are encouraged to make their way home. The lights are beginning to be turned off, and stallholders pull down their shutters. Emma breathes a sigh of exasperation. Steed has not kept their rendezvous. People mill past her and soon — bar the distant barking of a dog — there is total silence. She backs into the shadows, hiding between two stalls, as a roustabout, doubling as nightwatchman, walks slowly by, checking locks and looking for stragglers. Emma is retreating further into the dark alleyway between the stalls when, suddenly, a noise makes her turn. A man with a wolf's face stares at her. She backs away, and turns to face a bearded woman. She runs, but her escape is blocked by a two-headed man! The three figures close in on Emma. She dodges them, darting down another passageway and out into the open. Her freakish foes are just a few paces behind. She makes for the shadows once again and slips away from her pursuers. Her course leads her to a tent with a light coming from inside. Catching her breath, she pushes her way in.

The harsh glare of the overhead light causes Emma to close her eyes and blink. As she grows accustomed to the light, she sees that she is in the presence of a well-built woman, who is in the act of bending a thick iron bar. The Strong Woman notes Emma's arrival and drops the metal bar. Her face breaks into a smile. She is expecting a volunteer and thinks Emma is this person.

Not having heard Mrs. Peel's taped message, Steed is unaware that he has missed their rendezvous. He remains at the Government Research Centre, and has now been introduced to a newcomer known to the professor as Mr. Carlton. He is an obsessive practical joker, who says that Steed may know him better as Jumbo of Jumbo's Gigantic Amusement Parks. He has come to see Parto as the professor is collating some data for him concerning the weather, a topic of vital importance to him. Another bad summer like those of 1962 and 1963 and he could go bankrupt. Steed leaves Jumbo and the Professor talking as he goes to Reception to make a telephone call.

Meanwhile, in the tent at the funfair, Emma is in something of a predicament. She is strapped, spread-eagled, to a target board. A knife thuds into the wood and sticks, quivering, about a yard from her head. The Strong Woman prepares to throw another deadly blade. Emma is concerned that her colleague in this knife-throwing act seems somewhat amateurish.

Mrs. Peel's freakish pursuers – Tom, the Two-Headed Man, Harry, the Wolfman, and Mary, the Bearded Lady – suddenly burst into the tent, and accuse Emma of snooping around. The Strong Woman explains that Emma is to replace Annie in the act, and that they had no doubt frightened her while she was trying to find the rehearsal tent. They agree that this is quite possible. Tom removes his additional head, Harry takes off his wolfman mask, and Mary peels off her false beard. All three are quite normal – they had been tidying up after the fair had closed for the night and hadn't had time to change. The Wolfman explains that they always run late on Wednesdays, and that security is poor, so they take things into their own hands when necessary. By way of apology, Mary invites Emma to pop into her tent for a cup of tea, as soon as the rehearsal is over. They depart.

The Strong Woman resumes practicing. She hurls a knife, but it whistles wide of the target board, disappearing into the shadows beyond. She gripes that she will never get the hang of knife throwing.

Calling his answerphone, Steed now hears the message that Mrs. Peel had left for him earlier, about their meeting at the funfair. He replaces the handset and returns to the laboratory, but there is no sign of the Professor or Jumbo. That is, until he peers into the window marked, "10/10 CLOUD", and sees the body of Professor Parto entangled in a mess of fleshy white vines. Steed runs to the airlock door, spins its wheel-lock mechanism, and hurries inside. As he examines the Professor's body, a sound comes from the next chamber.

He cautiously enters the Zero Cloud environment, only to find it empty. He makes for the next chamber, but its door is firmly locked. He turns to see the door that he entered by swing shut. It, too, is now locked tight. The heat in the chamber, beating off the bare rock and sand, is stifling. Steed gasps, loosens his collar and tie, and tries the doors again.

A hand twists a temperature control in the laboratory. The thermometer reading pertaining to the Zero Cloud chamber starts to rise. The hand moves to another control, marked "ATMOSPHERE", and adjusts that setting also.

Inside the chamber, beads of sweat cascade down Steed's face. He goes to the inset window and hammers at the thick glass. He sees the nightmarish, tattooed face of Zebra staring back at him from the control panel.

Back at the funfair, Emma's ordeal at the hands of the Strong Woman is over. Many knives protrude from the board at untidy angles. Not one of them is close to her spread-eagled form. As the Strong Woman retrieves the knives, she tells Emma that she has known Mr. Jumbo for many years, and that he has a great sense of humour. Emma says she would like to meet him and is told that he went to a meeting and is yet to return.

The Strong Woman says that they should wait for Zebra, the knife thrower. Emma is confused. It transpires that the woman's regular act involves the tearing-up of telephone directories, but she is trying to learn new skills. She expects that Zebra will be along soon, as he is very punctual.

Inside the Zero Cloud chamber, Steed has discarded his jacket. He is covered in sweat and is gasping for air. He grasps his umbrella by the ferrule and swings the handled end at the window, but it simply bounces off. He wilts, exhausted.

In the tent, the Strong Woman lays out an assortment of knives and axes on the throwing table in Zebra's preferred arrangement. She is about to undo the straps holding Mrs. Peel to the board when Zebra finally arrives. He picks up a knife and suggests they begin. Emma doubts that this is a positive development...

Act Four

Zebra stands by the table, a throwing knife in his hand. He throws it into the target board with precision. Mrs. Peel flinches – there are knives all around her body. Boldly, she suggests that Zebra cannot be a real name – it is too funny for words. Zebra says that it is his professional name. Another knife swishes through the air, thuds into the board, and quivers no more than a few inches from Emma's face.

In the Zero Cloud chamber, Steed kneels, panting, beside a ventilator grille. He manages to wrench it off. The aperture, however, is very small. As the temperature gauge rises towards the red "DANGER" mark, his head sags and his breathing becomes laboured. The rock and sand scene dances and shimmers before his eyes.

Zebra is finding that Mrs. Peel is stubborn and obstinate. She asks about his tattoos. Zebra proudly reveals that the work took four years, but Emma declares that they do not hide his Chinese origins. Zebra reacts angrily, throwing a knife that lands touching the side of Emma's neck. He demands to know what her real job is. The sweetly delivered answer? "Housewife." As Zebra turns away to pick up another knife, Emma works at cutting the leather strap on her right wrist by rubbing it against a knife near to it.

A Chinese roustabout enters, salutes "Colonel Zebra", and informs him that the pipes have been connected. The man turns smartly and leaves, while the Colonel returns to the matter in hand. He has two knives left – and he wants answers. Who does she work for? She responds by suggesting – in cod-Chinese – that he can take a running jump. This prompts the throwing of another knife, which lands perilously close to Emma's face. As Zebra turns to pick up the last knife, Emma saws frantically at the leather strap – and her hand comes free! She grabs the knife she had used, and cuts the other hand free.

Zebra turns and notices what is happening. The final knife is thrown. Emma ducks – and the knife lands where her head had been just a split second before. She rapidly cuts an ankle free. Zebra scrambles for another knife, finding one just as Emma frees her other ankle. She rolls to one side as another knife flies through the air towards her, thudding harmlessly into the board. She retaliates by throwing the knife at the overhead light, which shatters. The tent is plunged into darkness. She pulls another knife from the board, and uses it to slash through the side of the tent, whereupon she makes a swift exit into the night air.

A little later, Steed lies huddled against a wall in the Zero Cloud chamber, his jacket pulled over his head. He scrabbles weakly at the sand-covered floor – and then he is still. Shortly afterwards, Emma arrives and calls for him, but receives no response. She notices the "DANGER" reading on one of the temperature dials, which prompts her to check the Zero Cloud chamber. She spots the unconscious Steed, dashes back to the controls, and sets the temperature and the atmosphere to zero and full respectively. She runs to the insulated door, spins the locking wheel and enters. She goes over to Steed – and sees that he has been lying with his face close to the open ventilator grille, through which air is now rushing under full pressure. Steed opens his eyes and smiles weakly, complaining that his nose is beginning to peel.

Emma helps Steed back to the laboratory, where he recovers in the trolley chair. Emma has the perfect remedy for what ails him – a bottle of Champagne and two glasses she has brought from his car's refrigerator. She pops the cork, and fills the glasses, passing one to Steed. He drinks thirstily and holds out his glass for a refill. They exchange notes – Steed recollects seeing a tattooed man; that was Colonel Zebra, a Chinese agent, explains Emma. Steed then tells her about Mr. Jumbo, who used to be Mr. Carlton of Carlton's Carnivals until he went bust in 1963 after two bad summers. Emma remarks that Jumbo is now the owner of three amusement parks and four holiday camps – he has certainly prospered, but she reckons that the last thing he wants is torrential rain. Steed suggests that Colonel Zebra might have different ideas entirely. They leave together.

A short while later, in a large, luxurious caravan at the funfair, Jumbo and a Chinese roustabout sit waiting for Zebra's arrival. Jumbo is feeling frightened. He is also upset that Zebra killed Professor Parto, quite unnecessarily. Zebra arrives and warns that, without his financial backing, Jumbo would still be bankrupt. Zebra owns the business in all but name, and his plan is almost complete – the whole world will be deluged with rain. Zebra suggests that this will be Jumbo's greatest ever practical joke.

Outside, Mrs. Peel places a ladder against the side of the caravan. She climbs to the roof, where she lies flat and squirms toward a mushroom-shaped ventilator from which a yellow light emanates. Placing an ear to it, she hears muted voices coming from within the caravan. Jumbo is protesting that millions of people will die. Zebra is unconcerned – his people are used to such conditions and the world's population can cope with dropping by a few million.

Nearby, Steed looks out from one of the darkened alleys. He spots an anchored barrage balloon. A basket hangs beneath it and rests upon the grass. A guard approaches, patrolling the area. However, everything seems quiet, and he is not anticipating trouble. Consequently, he is easily surprised by Steed, who hooks the man's neck with the handle of his umbrella and drags him into the darkness. Steed emerges and climbs over the rope cordoning off the area around the balloon. He makes a close inspection, and notes that a number of CO_2 gas cylinders are clamped to the sides of the basket. Thin, flexible pipes snake from these cylinders and lead to complex electronic equipment installed inside the basket.

Inside the caravan, Zebra gloats that he had chosen and financed Jumbo as he was bankrupt and advertised himself with balloons. Jumbo contests that Zebra could have launched his balloon from China so much more easily. Zebra disagrees. Should anything have gone wrong, China would have been blamed, and that would have been politically undesirable. The funfair is an ideal launching site, he attests.

Suddenly, a buzzer sounds in the caravan. Zebra goes to the telephone and learns from a Chinese guard that there is an intruder in the grounds. Zebra orders a shoot-to-kill policy regarding this trespasser, and swiftly exits the caravan.

Steed emerges from the far side of the balloon basket. A series of powerful floodlights come on, catching him in their glare. He sees the silhouettes of four guards running towards him, so he advances, umbrella at the ready. He deals rapidly with one guard and turns to face another.

Left on guard in the caravan, the Chinese roustabout covers Jumbo with a pistol, his back to the caravan window. Suddenly, the glass shatters as Emma launches herself from the roof and swings into the caravan. Her flying feet catch the guard squarely in the back – he is thrown headlong into the control panel on the opposite side of the caravan. She quickly follows up with a karate chop, and the unfortunate labourer slides to the floor, unconscious. Jumbo is agape. Emma asks what is going on, and Jumbo explains Zebra's plan to seed the clouds with CO_2 using the balloon outside. Emma suggests they try to stop that happening.

Zebra has reached the launching area and has boarded the basket, where he is making adjustments to its control dials. He notes that Steed is still battling with the guards, and that Emma and Jumbo are arriving on the scene. Zebra takes a gun from his pocket and aims at Emma. She dives and rolls to safety, but Jumbo keeps running. Steed is now dealing with the last guard standing. Zebra takes aim at Emma for a second time – as she runs directly towards him. Jumbo reaches the basket ahead of her – and throws himself in, disturbing the Colonel's aim. The former collaborators struggle with each other, with Zebra coming out the victor when he clubs Jumbo with the butt of his gun. Steed fells the guard and turns towards the basket. Zebra steadies his arm and aims his gun at Steed. It is point-blank range – how can Zebra possibly miss?

Emma warns Steed as she throws her knife. He ducks and the knife flashes through the air, severing an anchor rope. The basket jerks, causing Zebra to lose his balance – he shoots a bullet, but it is wayward. Steed slashes the remaining guy ropes with the sword stick hidden in his umbrella. Released, the balloon and basket lift swiftly from the ground. He and Mrs. Peel hear a series of despairing wails from Zebra, which become fainter and fainter the higher he ascends into the night sky.

Emma cannot believe what Steed has done – in releasing the barrage balloon, with its payload of CO_2 gas, surely it will now never stop raining?

Steed has thought of that – he has severed the connecting pipes and the gas canisters now lie on the ground encircling the footprint of the now rapidly rising basket.

Tag Scene

At his flat the following morning, Steed is dressed to go fishing. He has a rod at his side and is selecting bait from a tray of artificial flies. Emma enters. Steed asks if she is ready for their excursion. He has put the picnic basket in the car and asks if she means to bring the book that she is reading – *A History of Tattooing*. She is ready and she has the book. She remarks that, according to the book, there is a waiter who has a complete wine list tattooed on his body. Steed quips that it would be tricky if you wanted to order a bottle of Zeltigen. He selects an appropriate fly from the tray and looks out of the window. He thinks the good weather will hold.

Emma asks whether there is any news of Jumbo. Steed tells her that Jodrell Bank have lost all trace of the balloon. Emma is a little sad: "Twinkle, twinkle, little Jumbo," she intones gently. Steed reminds her that Jumbo was not exactly innocent – he knew what Zebra was up to, and about the murders. Emma agrees, and thinks that the funfair owner's predicament would appeal to his sense of humour – the Americans send up satellite weather balloons and now Britain has Satellite Jumbo up there, circling the Earth.

They make to leave. Emma remarks that at least they will know that the rain is natural, if it appears. Steed scoffs at the suggestion – it will not rain!

A thunderclap sounds just as they exit his front door – and, suddenly, Emma and Steed are caught in a rain shower. Steed is not happy about this development, but his mood changes as he and Emma exchange glances. They both begin to laugh as they enjoy the feel of the rain on their faces.

Analysis

The foreshortened nature of the Emma Peel colour series (Series 5) has long been a subject of debate among *Avengers* afficionados. Diana Rigg left the show having completed twenty-five episodes, including *The Forget-Me-Knot* (1968), in which she passed the baton of *Avenger* girl to the incoming Linda Thorson. Documentary evidence suggests that Ms. Rigg was contracted to appear in twenty-six colour episodes, and it is often postulated that two 1967 Steed and Peel productions were struck from the schedule.

One of these unmade scripts was quite likely to have been Cyril Abraham's *This'll Kill You* (dated August 1967). The other is generally acknowledged as being *Split!* by Brian Clemens, which was later recycled as an early Series 6 episode featuring Tara King.

There is at least one other candidate, namely *It's Bigger Than Both of Us*, written in July 1967 by Jessie Lasky Jnr. and Pat Silver. This American husband and wife writing team had previously written for *The Saint* (*The Saint Bids Diamonds*, 1965) and *Danger Man* (*Two Birds with One Bullet*, 1966), in addition to a great many credits in their home country. However, despite their apparent suitability and strong track record, their *Avengers* script was reputedly lacking in the wit and lightness of touch expected, and it is believed to have been rejected.

This'll Kill You was commissioned and written during what was without a doubt the most turbulent period in *The Avengers*' history. The truth behind the crisis that visited the series towards the end of Series 5 – during its second filming block – is difficult to fathom, not least because accessible surviving accounts of the events are exclusively from one side of the conflict. The most popular theory is that the managing director of the Associated British Picture Corporation (ABPC), Howard Thomas, considered that their popular series was becoming excessively mired in the fantastic, and that Patrick Macnee's character was being allowed to become too humourous. As such, he reportedly wished for the series to return to a more grounded realism – and this intention was indeed confirmed in the 15th July 1967 edition of the film industry journal *Kine Weekly*.

ABPC's concerns could well have been at least partly instigated by an April 1967 review in the United States *TV Guide* listings magazine. In his regular column, the highly influential television critic Cleveland Amory had compared the colour series negatively to the earlier monochrome Emma Peel episodes, highlighting the preposterous storylines seen in the episodes most recently aired: "(1) the story of a pretty girl named Venus who believes there is life on Venus, but, just to make sure, causes an awful lot of death on Earth [*From Venus With Love*], (2) the story of a 'see-through man' who not only invented a formula for invisibility but goes around disputing, via murder, the fact that seeing is believing [*The See-Through Man*], (3) the story of a Captain Crusoe who flies valuable missile documents out of the country by virtue of the fact that he is a parrot, and also runs afoul of the International Exhibition of Caged Birds, whose organizer is – now get this – Edgar Twitter [*The Bird Who Knew Too Much*], and (4) the story of a professor who not only makes 'duplicate' people but even the kind of people who can't be killed. One of them is run over and killed by a salesman, then escapes and is run over again – whereupon the salesman shouts, 'I've killed him! I've killed him again!' [*Never, Never Say Die*] The producers, it may be said, have done the same with the show. All this plot nonsense has been at the expense of what was once, despite its satiric overtones, a genuinely engrossing adventure story. And for this show to be killed not once but twice is doubly sad because its two principals, Patrick Macnee (Steed) and Diana Rigg (Mrs. Peel) deserved better."

Considering that *The Avengers* relied heavily on its American funding, ABPC would undoubtedly have been made aware of Amory's review – though it almost certainly served only to confirm ABPC management's own misgivings about the direction the series was taking. The timing of the review does appear to chime somewhat with the marked change in style of the final Emma Peel episodes. After a fortnight's break in production, filming resumed on *The Avengers* in May 1967 for what some sources refer to as Series 6 since the transmission of these episodes was delayed for nearly five months (to avoid confusion and to align with official home entertainment releases, we refer to all 1967 episodes as forming Series 5). The eight episodes filmed as part of the second Series 5 production block included *The £50,000 Breakfast*, *Dead Man's Treasure* and *You Have Just Been Murdered*, which were of a notably less fantastic nature than their immediate predecessors. However, if there had indeed been an edict delivered from on high to the producers to the effect that *The Avengers* needed to be more realistic going forward, then other new episodes seemed to ignore this stipulation – particularly *The Positive Negative Man* (with its electrically-charged killer) and *Mission: Highly Improbable* (with its miniaturisation element).

Ultimately, ABPC decided that producers Brian Clemens and Albert Fennell were not the right people to implement the changes they required, or perhaps they met with resistance from them with regard to these editorial revisions. Irrespective of their reasoning, ABPC gave notice to Clemens and Fennell, who were required to clear their desks by September 1967 having completed all episodes in production at that time. Additionally, Laurie Johnson, composer of the series' theme and incidental music, discovered that ABPC were not interested in renewing his contract. The three men were advised that they would be replaced by a new team. The new man was in fact Clemens and Fennell's direct predecessor John Bryce, a man well known within ABC Television and who had previously produced *The Avengers* very successfully during its videotape era between 1963 and 1964.

Were this not change enough, the stars of the series were also feeling disenchanted. Actress Diana Rigg, who had only been persuaded at the last minute to stay on board for a second year by her co-star Patrick Macnee, announced in the British national press on Friday 14th April 1967 that she intended to leave *The Avengers* later in the year. This necessitated a search for a suitable replacement, a process that triggered three sets of actress screen tests, which were staged between July and September of 1967. Executive Producer Julian Wintle was also moving on to pastures new, although by the end of the first colour series, his involvement in the day-to-day running of the production had reportedly become minimal. With a screen partner with whom he shared a great chemistry leaving, and the familiar, trusted team of Clemens and Fennell being ousted, series lead Patrick Macnee seriously considered his own position, before eventually being persuaded to stay for an eighth consecutive year as the dapper John Steed.

John Hough, who had joined the production towards the end of Series 5 as a second unit director, recalled that confusion abounded during this time when interviewed by Dave Rogers in the 1980s. "No one was told why Albert, Brian and Laurie were fired. All we heard at the time was that it was a cost-cutting exercise, which everyone knew to be untrue." The biggest problem facing the new team, however, was adapting to a production process that involved the simultaneous shooting of up to three episodes. "The actual operation that was handed down from [Albert and Brian at] the production office was really a very, very slick machine," commented Hough. "To have somebody else come in and be able to operate something that Brian and Albert had done so well, simply didn't work, so the new series began to run behind schedule."

The new team commenced filming on Monday 23rd October 1967, and allegedly the production descended into chaos soon after, with footage shot per day dropping to an unsustainably low level. However, daily call sheets appear to refute this, revealing that new episodes were actually being completed over fewer filming days than Clemens and Fennell had generally needed for entries in the 1967 series. This suggests that ABPC took issue with the quality of the material being produced on Bryce's watch, rather than the amount of time taken to produce it. Regardless of the reason, ABPC were dissatisfied with Bryce's efforts and attempted to contact Brian Clemens, but Clemens was on a motoring holiday in Wales and in the days before mobile telephones, was consequently very difficult to contact. "Wherever I went," he revealed to Dave Rogers in *The Ultimate Avengers*, "I was preceded by phone calls: would I get in touch with so and so? Would I please contact this person? I eventually did so and they said would I please come back. They asked me first. It's not generally known, but they didn't ask Albert back. They asked me and I said I wouldn't go back without Albert. By this time, they had almost completed three episodes, one of which was virtually unshowable and the other two were pretty awful." There had also been no attempt made to explain Steed's change of partner from Emma Peel to Tara King. "I insisted on writing *The Forget-Me-Knot*. I came back on to the series on a Thursday [7th

December 1967], started writing the script on Friday, finished it on the Saturday and we started filming it on the following Monday or Tuesday." (In actual fact, filming commenced on Thursday 14th December, but nonetheless, a very tight turnaround.)

Amidst all this turmoil, Cyril Abraham's *This'll Kill You* script appears to have become a victim of changing production teams and their requirements. As the script was dated August 1967 – a time when filming and postproduction was in progress for Series 5 episodes *Murdersville*, *The Positive Negative Man* and *Mission... Highly Improbable* – one would assume that it was commissioned by Clemens and Fennell with a view to it becoming the 25th or 26th colour Emma Peel adventure. When production under the auspices of Clemens and Fennell drew to a close on Friday 22nd September 1967, *This'll Kill You* remained unproduced. The orders Clemens, Fennell and Johnson received from above, which indicated that they should conclude production on episodes in progress, no doubt precluded them from setting the wheels in motion on *Split!* and possibly *This'll Kill You*. The script was therefore not necessarily rejected by Clemens and Fennell before they left the series, but simply was not taken up by Bryce, who commissioned seven new scripts instead. Chances are the new showrunner would have been keen to make his mark upon the series by filming scripts that he had commissioned himself, rather than those he had inherited. However, it appears that, when Clemens and company returned to *The Avengers* they did not see fit to have Cyril Abraham tweak his script to incorporate the new characters and direction. This suggests that Clemens was not entirely happy with it. It is, however, entirely possible that a second draft of *This'll Kill You* was asked for and either rejected or not completed. (It is Cyril Abraham's personal script that survives today. It was sold on an auction website – along with other scripts, letters and documents – following the death of Abraham's widow, Joan, in 2014. It was the only *Avengers* item offered, perhaps suggesting that *This'll Kill You* was not further developed.)

One particular element of *This'll Kill You* that feels somewhat out of place in *The Avengers*' film era is the suggestion that Colonel Zebra and his dastardly plot-of-the-week – to deluge the world in rain – is state-sponsored by China. It is very unusual for a real country to be named in *The Avengers*, particularly if that country's involvement in the narrative has negative connotations. Several Series 4 episodes feature fictional countries such as Kalaya (an African nation in *Small Game for Big Hunters*) and Barabia (an Arabian country referred to in *Honey for the Prince*). The scripts for the colour Emma Peel series tended to take a slightly different approach, featuring characters that represented easily identifiable but unnamed nations – in episodes such as *The Correct Way to Kill* and *Death's Door*. A handful of episodes did openly name countries – such as the Series 4 entry *Room Without a View*, which identified both China and North Korea – but it is highly likely that, had *This'll Kill You* entered production, the direct references to China would have been dropped or softened in some way.

On the subject of Colonel Zebra's Chinese heritage, Mrs. Peel's response to his questions and threats – "Plitty ladee say you go takee jumpee" – was undoubtedly meant as a witty riposte intended to anger her opponent, but it amounts to lazy racial stereotyping by writer Cyril Abraham. This practice was not uncommon in television and films of the era, but it *is* unusual for *The Avengers*, which generally tended to avoid cheap digs at foreign accents and characteristics. The exceptions to this rule tended to be if the characters themselves were deliberately comedic – such as Brodny (Warren Mitchell) in *Two's A Crowd* and *The See-Through Man*, or Nutski (Michael Gough) and Olga (Anna Quayle) in *The Correct Way to Kill* – and, even in those instances, the treatment was gentle and inoffensive. As Zebra is most certainly not such a character, it is probable that this line – and Mrs. Peel's description of Zebra as "a Chinaman", a derogatory term – would have been altered prior to filming.

At the time of writing *This'll Kill You* for *The Avengers*, Cyril Abraham had been writing for television for seven years, during which time he had scripted episodes for several television dramas, including *Coronation Street* (1960), *No Hiding Place* (five episodes, 1960-64), *Family Solicitor* (one episode, 1961), *Catch Hand* (one episode, 1964), *King of the River* (one episode, 1966) and *Z Cars* (eight episodes, 1967). Born in Liverpool, England, on 22nd September 1915, Abraham was educated at the Liverpool Collegiate School and, later, on HMS Conway, a training ship, prior to securing an apprenticeship with the Lamport and Holt shipping line, which was based in his home city. During the Second World War, Abraham served as a Marconi wireless operator in the Merchant Navy. He married Evelyn Howarth in 1945, though the relationship later ended in divorce. Upon his return to civilian life after demobilisation, he harboured a desire to become a professional writer, but, not knowing how to break into that particular field, instead gained employment as a bus driver with Liverpool City Transport. During his time on the buses, he met Joan Thomas, a local schoolteacher who would prove to be a major influence on his future career path – and became Abraham's second wife when they married in 1964. She encouraged his literary aspirations and rented him a typewriter. Abraham began by writing short stories and articles, some of which saw publication in Australian magazines and journals, before moving on to submitting story ideas and scripts to television companies. His first commissions came in 1960 from Associated-Rediffusion and Granada Television for police drama *No Hiding*

Place and the northern soap opera *Coronation Street*, respectively. Abraham would meet with his greatest success during the 1970s, as creator of the highly successful BBC Television period drama *The Onedin Line* (1970-1980). The series grew from a December 1970 *Drama Playhouse* pilot written by Abraham, and he would go on to pen a total of twenty-two episodes, a little under a quarter of those recorded. He also turned his talents to writing novels based on *The Onedin Line*, and was responsible for five of the six published. These books were adapted and augmented versions of the television scripts. He also wrote an original novel, *The Blazing Ocean*, published in 1979 by New English Library. Cyril Abraham died of liver failure on 30th July 1979, shortly after completing his fifth *Onedin Line* novel, *The White Ships*. He had planned out a lengthy series of *Onedin Line* novels, seeing his central characters James and Elizabeth Onedin into old age, but with his death, these came to nothing. In terms of his association with *The Avengers*, that proved short-lived and abortive, and *This'll Kill You* represents his only known work for the series.

Trivia Points

- There are some elements of Cyril Abraham's *This'll Kill You* script that will conjure up a feeling of *déjà vu* for *Avengers* fans. Admittedly, many of the colour Emma Peel episodes follow a distinct formula, with one week's adventure acting as a rough template for the next. Abraham's script contains many of these formulaic ingredients, as well as some plot elements that recall particular *Avengers* episodes:

    o It has the requisite number of unfortunate victims, eccentrics, and red herrings, as well as a diabolical mastermind.

    o Steed and Emma enjoy their usual rapport, and work independently before joining forces at the end.

    o The episode's premise seems to draw heavily on that of *A Surfeit of H²O* (1965), specifically the idea that weather could be controlled and rain could weaponised.

    o The funfair setting was original enough for the filmed series, but had been utilised in the videotape era in both *Tunnel of Fear* (1961) and *Man in the Mirror* (1963).

- Practical jokes had featured in *Death of a Great Dane* (1963) and *A Touch of Brimstone* (1966), and the concept would be revisited definitively in Dennis Spooner's 1968 classic *Look - (Stop Me if You've Heard this One) But There Were These Two Fellers...*

- Mrs. Peel receives a gift-wrapped box, which raises concerns as it is ticking. This idea revives memories of *The Danger Makers* (1966), in which Emma receives a potentially boobytrapped box of chocolates.

- By the time Steed loses control of the Bentley in *This'll Kill You*, it has become something of a habit. *Death's Door* and *The Positive Negative Man* – both late Series 5 episodes – feature similar happenings. Steed's repair bills must have been rather costly, to say nothing of his insurance premiums!

- Finally, the knife throwing act that Emma Peel is on the wrong end of in *This'll Kill You* recalls a similar plot device featured in *Conspiracy of Silence* (1963).

• These recognisable features would not necessarily have counted against Cyril Abraham's script, since it was written at a time when the series' producers were refashioning the best of the videotape era scripts as high-budget, colour episodes – *Dressed to Kill* was remade as *The Superlative Seven*, *Don't Look Behind You* as *The Joker*, and *Death of a Great Dane* as *The £50,000 Breakfast*.

• When scripting *This'll Kill You*, Cyril Abraham elected to introduce the series' central protagonists during the teaser sequence, breaking from the generally established formula during the Emma Peel era that dictated that Steed and Mrs. Peel would not appear this early on. Should the episode have gone into production, it is possible this would have been altered to fit the common practice.

• In 1998, the weather control conceit employed in *This'll Kill You* would be explored in more depth as the central theme of the ill-fated Warner Bros. movie, *The Avengers*. Indeed, the weather chambers described in *This'll Kill You* appear to be very similar to the little climate pods on display at Wonderland Weather in the movie.

- Mrs. Peel's freakish pursuers – the funfair's two-headed man, wolfman and bearded lady – are introduced as Tom, Harry and Mary, respectively. We are also told the name of the previous assistant in the knife-throwing act: Annie, who does not actually appear in the episode. However, Cyril Abraham chose not to give a name to the funfair's strong woman, who is referred to throughout as 'Strong Woman'.

- The scene in which the Strong Woman undertakes her knife-throwing practice takes place on a Wednesday night, as revealed by Harry in the dialogue, and it is on this night – going into the early hours of Thursday morning – that Steed and Mrs. Peel defeat Colonel Zebra's plot. It is therefore possible to extrapolate that the events of This'll Kill You begin on a Monday night (when Sir Basil Austin arrives at his office) and end on a Thursday morning (when Steed and Emma reconvene at Steed's apartment and then get rained on). The script also gives the month as July.

Verdict

This'll Kill You is one of the hitherto missing artefacts of The Avengers that has escaped the attention of fans of the series, not its greatest lost treasure by any stretch of the imagination, but a fascinating 'what if'.

It captures the characters of Steed and Mrs. Peel effectively, as one might expect of something written while the series was at its height of popularity, but some characters – particularly the eccentric-of-the-week, Professor Parto – are mere ciphers, and would require clever actors to bring them to life. There is some wit on display, however, notably in the way in which Abraham has the audience and Mrs. Peel initially believe that the funfair's knife thrower is a woman who can barely hit the target board. This proves to be a nice piece of misdirection, as she is later revealed to be a telephone-directory-tearing strong woman who is keen to broaden her skillset.

One scene in particular seems somewhat at odds with the way The Avengers generally worked during this period – that in which Emma leads the private detective, Corker, into the park and Steed manhandles and captures him. It would ordinarily be Mrs. Peel meting out this sort of physical violence, rather than Steed.

Corker himself seems to be something of a prototype for Randall and Hopkirk (Deceased)'s Jeff Randall in that he is not a terribly capable detective, tends to get beaten up quite easily, and has an office that has seen better days. In getting himself killed, he has a touch of Randall's partner Marty Hopkirk about him, too!

In the final reckoning, *This'll Kill You* is a competent script from Cyril Abraham for *The Avengers*, but one which is neither original nor especially distinctive. This isn't a particularly damning criticism, as the same comment could easily be made about many Series 5 episodes. Had it been made, *This'll Kill You* would no doubt have been altered during its journey to transmission, but, even in its script form, it is entertaining and would no doubt have made for a perfectly diverting adventure for Steed and Mrs. Peel. The funfair setting, in particular, would undoubtedly have provided colour, charm and fantasy, and set *This'll Kill You* apart in the memory from the adventures produced around it, at least visually.

TELL ME ABOUT IT

J Z FERGUSON
with thanks to Jaz Wiseman

Project Type: Prospective Television Episode
Date: 1976

Synopsis

At a small private airfield, John Steed watches four soldiers unload a coffin from a plane. The coffin slips while it is being unloaded, and Steed tells the men doing the unloading to be careful, as they do not want to kill the coffin's occupant! Purdey, who is also at the airfield, offers her condolences to Steed for his loss, but is surprised when she hears a voice from within the coffin complaining about needing air.

The coffin is opened in an interrogation room. Its occupant, Lorik, is handcuffed to a chair while Steed and Purdey look on. Lorik repeatedly insists that he will tell them nothing, having held out against torture in the past. Steed, Purdey, and the interrogator all don masks. Mike Gambit enters, carrying a vase of flowers and also wearing a mask. He places the vase on a table close to Lorik. Steed asks Lorik to tell him about "[t]hat business in Mozambique". Lorik, suddenly cooperative, asks Steed what he wants to know.

Meanwhile, Geoffrey Sanders, a distinguished, elegantly dressed, fiftysomething man, is handed an air pistol by one of his four henchmen, who have pulled stockings over their heads to conceal their identities. Sanders walks down a corridor toward a heavy steel door marked "Restricted Area. Special Intelligence Unit C". A guard by the door aims his gun at the approaching Saunders. Sanders pretends that he has gone the wrong way, then shoots the guard with the air pistol. The guard collapses, unconscious. Sanders' men open the steel door and drag the guard through it.

Back in the interrogation room, Lorik has just finished telling Steed, Gambit, Purdey, and the interrogator everything they want to know. Steed tells Gambit to remove the vase of flowers. Gambit complies, leaving a bewildered and dejected Lorik behind.

Gambit takes the vase of flowers to the room containing Sanders' henchmen, one of whom swings a steel bar at Gambit's head. Gambit dodges the bar, drops the vase, and defeats his attacker. Gambit then passes between two other henchmen, knocking them both out en route, in order to reach a fourth man who is loading a bag with steel cylinders. Gambit dispatches the fourth man, but is shot by Sanders with the air pistol. Gambit loses consciousness and collapses next to the remains of the shattered vase, the breakage of which has revealed that it contained one of the steel cylinders.

Later, at the Special Intelligence Centre, Purdey pours tea on the terrace and offers it and a cucumber sandwich to a moody Gambit to soothe his bruised ego. Gambit ignores her and focuses on Steed and a senior army officer, who are conversing on the sprawling lawn in front of the centre. The officer is concerned about the loss of the cylinders — their contents have not officially been invented yet! While they converse, Purdey tells Gambit that she attributes his defeat by Sanders to him not getting enough sleep, and suggests a siesta. Gambit agrees to take one, and asks when Purdey can join him. She offers him a sandwich instead. The officer, meanwhile, tells Steed that they must get the twelve stolen cylinders back.

Sanders meets with his henchmen. He asks one, Jarret, why they only have eleven cylinders, when he swore that they stole twelve. Jarret replies that he dropped one in the fight with Gambit. On the way to their cars, Barker, another of the henchmen, tells Jarret that he knows they took twelve cylinders. He concludes that Jarett has stolen the missing cylinder. Jarett holds Barker at gunpoint and threatens to kill him if he tells Sanders about the theft, but promises to make Barker rich if he keeps quiet. Barker nervously agrees to take the money, but warns Jarret that Sanders will kill them both if he finds out that they have betrayed him. Jarett is unfazed. He tells Barker that they will try out the substance in the cylinders to see if it works, and sell "truth" to others if it does.

Steed attends a meeting with the senior army officer from Special Intelligence, a general, a minister, the PPS to the prime minister, and a man from MI5 (known as "Q"). They discuss how dangerous the substance in the cylinders is, and the higher-ups argue about who is to blame for the theft. Purdey enters and reminds Steed that they are due at the embassy. Steed tells her to go on ahead, as he will be stuck in the meeting for awhile.

Purdey attends the embassy function, which is in aid of the Brotherhood of Nations. Various ambassadors, diplomats, and other dignitaries voice their hope that the newly formed Brotherhood will help them achieve peace. Jarret is also there, disguised as a waiter. He sneaks into the cloakroom and fills a balloon from the pilfered cylinder, then returns to the soiree. Purdey moves to the balcony just before Jarret enters, releases the gas from the balloon, and makes a swift exit. The dignitaries start insulting each other. Jarret peeks in and watches as the dignitaries begin to get physical. Purdey returns from the balcony and is shocked by the pandemonium. Steed and the minister arrive, and take in the scene. The minister is horrified, but Steed looks thoughtful, pronouncing the display "odd". The minister calls for silence and the dignitaries settle down, bewildered by their own behaviour. To re-establish a sense of normality, Steed proposes a toast to "brotherhood", and the dignitaries chime in enthusiastically.

Gambit visits a Ministry of Defence research centre, where a supervisor shows him a number of monkeys using typewriters. The supervisor is convinced that they will write something brilliant given enough time. Gambit pretends that one of the monkeys has typed out a quotation from Shakespeare, then quips that it is in code when the supervisor discovers that the monkey has typed gibberish. The supervisor takes Gambit to Wetherby, a scientist, for a briefing on the contents of the stolen cylinders. A white-coated, masked figure in the background listens with interest as Wetherby tells Gambit that the cylinders contain PX400, an airborne virus that affects the brain by blocking inhibitions, causing people to tell the truth. Its side-effects include aggression and hypertension. Gambit asks who knew that the virus was being used at the Special Intelligence Centre. Wetherby replies that only Dr. Sanders and himself knew. Sanders, the masked eavesdropper, confirms this. When pressed, Wetherby admits that the supervisor and Barker, the supply officer who delivered the gas to the Special Intelligence Centre, also knew. Gambit asks to speak with Barker, but Wetherby replies that he is on leave. Gambit asks Wetherby to get Barker's address, and the two depart. Sanders makes a call and tells someone that Barker has become a problem.

Barker is indulging in some archery practice. When he moves to the target to remove his arrows, a masked figure shoots arrows at him, pinning him to the target. Before the figure can make the final, fatal shot, Gambit appears and fights the figure. Gambit's opponent lands on an arrow during the fight and is killed. Gambit pulls the man's mask off, revealing one of Sanders' henchmen. Gambit asks Barker if he knows the man, but Barker lies and claims he does not.

Maitland, a successful architect, takes a meeting with Jarret after Jarret claims that Maitland is involved in a scandal. Jarret dons a mask and gases Maitland, then asks him what the scandal is about. Maitland tells him.

Elsewhere, town clerk Lowther and MP Jeffreyson receive threatening telephone calls from someone requesting a very large sum of money.

Steed and Gambit are at Barker's home on the pretence of providing security after the attempt on his life. They suggest that Barker was attacked because of his connection to PX400, but a nervous Barker dismisses their theory. The doorbell sounds and Barker is unable to prevent Gambit from answering the door. The visitor is Jarret, who recognises Gambit and pretends to be an insurance salesman. Gambit tells him to call another time and Jarret departs. Purdey arrives with PX400, which the trio use on Barker. He tells them that Jarret has PX400 and is using it to blackmail people. Jarret shoots him through the window before he can say more, then flees. Gambit gives chase, but loses him. Gambit tells Steed that he would recognise the killer again, as he was the insurance salesman. They now know someone is about to be blackmailed.

Jarret meets Lowther and uses the gas on him. Lowther states that he has the money Jarret asked for and a gun that he hopes to kill Jarret with. Jarret kills Lowther instead.

The trio examine Lowther's body the next day, and discover his gun. They discuss the ten thousand pounds he took from the town hall vault. Purdey finds an unmailed letter addressed to an MP named Jeffreyson on the body. In it, Lowther says he is being blackmailed and urges Jeffreyson to see Maitland. Steed tells Purdey to pay Jeffreyson a visit.

Jeffreyson claims that he is not connected with anyone in a way that would make him susceptible to blackmail. Purdey uses the truth gas on him, and he tells her that he has to pay someone ten thousand pounds to keep quiet about dodgy building contracts that he, Maitland, and the other blackmail victims used to illegally make money.

Sanders meets with Maitland, and shows him a picture of Jarret. Maitland, under the influence of the gas, says that Jarret visited him and asked for a list of names. Sanders asks for the same list, then exits before he is seen. Steed arrives and realises that Maitland has recently been under the influence of the gas. He surmises that Maitland had a visitor who asked for a list of names. Steed asks for the same list, then uses the gas on Maitland when he refuses.

Sanders meets with his henchmen. Jarret is on the run, but Sanders believes the list of names Maitland provided will help them to locate him. Steed, Gambit, and Purdey also have the list, and split up to find Jarret.

Jarret meets another blackmail victim, Paxton, on a golf course. He and Paxton pretend to bet ten thousand pounds on Jarret's ability to make a hole in ten shots as a way of legitimising the blackmail money. Purdey arrives, posing as a fellow golfer. Jarret pretends that he has won the bet, but Purdey intervenes when the money is handed over. Jarret pulls a gun on her, but is killed by Keller, one of Sanders' men. Purdey returns Paxton's money. After Jarret's body is taken away, Purdey shows Gambit the key to Jarret's hotel room. Keller also sees the key.

Purdey and Gambit search Jarret's room, which is somewhat messy. Gambit speculates that someone may have searched it already. In the bathroom, Purdey spots the shower curtain moving and attacks the person behind it: Keller. Purdey defeats Keller and takes Jarret's stolen cylinder, which Keller had found in the hotel room, from him. Gambit wonders where the other eleven cylinders that were stolen are. The trio attempts to question Keller, but he has amnesia after his fight with Purdey. They surmise that Jarret was one of the people involved in the robbery, and kept a cylinder for himself to use for blackmail. They also infer that Keller was involved in the robbery, and was sent to kill Jarret for his treachery. They wonder how they can help

Keller to remember why the cylinders were stolen in the first place. Steed suggests word association. Through this, Keller tells them about a conference at the International Hotel. They look up the conferences taking place at the hotel, and settle on the World Peace Conference as the likely target. The trio ponders what the consequences could be of politicians telling the truth – it could start a war!

Sanders and four of his henchmen arrive at the hotel and go to its conference room, where they install cylinders under the delegates' tables. A master control is also installed to allow Sanders to open all of the cylinders at once.

The trio arrives at the hotel. Steed tells Purdey and Gambit to go to the conference room, while he stops to speak to the minister. Purdey and Gambit interrupt Sanders and his men's preparations in the conference room and a fight ensues. Sanders sneaks away in the commotion, knocking out a guard along the way and taking up his post in order to avert suspicion.

Purdey and Gambit conclude their fight just before Steed enters the conference room. One man recovers and attacks Steed with one of the cylinders. Steed defeats him, but the cylinder is damaged in the process and the man crashes into the foyer containing the delegates while clutching it. The delegates are cleared out, but the minister picks up the cylinder and receives a large dose of the gas. Steed warns him not to say anything, as, having inhaled the gas, they are all security risks. Steed surveys the remaining onlookers while Sanders tries to sneak away, and asks who is behind the operation. The gas breaks down Sanders' defences, and he confesses.

Purdey joins Gambit at his flat. He puts on music and pours drinks, clearly in the mood for romance. He asks Purdey how long she thinks the effects of the gas will last. Purdey replies that they will probably be under the influence for some time, as they received heavy doses from the leaking cylinder. Gambit asks Purdey if she is attracted to him. Purdey confirms that she is, then "remembers" that she promised to meet her brother for dinner. Gambit replies that he did not know she had a brother. Purdey says that if she does not, then the gas must have worn off. She exits, leaving Gambit wondering whether she was telling the truth.

Analysis

In 1975, a commercial made for Laurent-Perrier champagne featuring Patrick Macnee and Linda Thorson as John Steed and Tara King led to an offer by French backers to bankroll new episodes of *The Avengers*. By January 1976,

Brian Clemens, Albert Fennell, and Laurie Johnson had also acquired some British funding, and set about defining the form that this new version of *The Avengers* would take. Recognising that times had changed since the series had last been in production, and that evolution was an essential part of *The Avengers'* DNA and success, the creatives opted to make the new series a sequel to the original, dubbing it "The New Avengers" to signal that change was the order of the day (and also to avoid rights issues that prohibited the use of the original series' name). In keeping with this nominative mission statement, numerous modifications were made to the series' formula, which included expanding the main cast from two people to three, increasing the amount of location filming and number of action sequences, and putting an accent on drama, rather than humour. Clemens ensured that these changes were properly instituted by taking on a role that, today, would best be described as "showrunner", which eventually extended to him solely or jointly penning 17 of the series' 26 episodes. This was, obviously, a heavy workload for one individual, and critics of *The New Avengers* often suggest that the series suffered creatively from having too few contributors. However, what the critics often fail to note about Clemens' heavy involvement in the majority of the scripts is the coherence and richness it lent the series. The recurring themes of loss, betrayal, friendship, loyalty, and how the past affects the present tie the series together by offering a unified perspective on life that no other season of the series possessed. The inclusion of these themes also made the series more realistic, as did other aspects of the scripting. The leads were depicted as being affected by the losses and betrayals of friends and colleagues. The characters' biographies and personal traits were not mentioned once and then forgotten; instead, elements of the leads' backstories garnered mentions across multiple episodes, while personal traits also surfaced repeatedly. Conversations between the leads returned to the same topics on multiple occasions and were peppered with in-jokes. As well as increasing the series' realism, these ingredients helped the leads to become well-defined characters made of, in Clemens' parlance, "thicker cardboard", and also established a modicum of continuity between episodes that had largely been absent from the original series. Such continuity also extended to Steed's department — often dubbed "The Ministry" — which was better defined in the new series due to the majority of the scenes set in it being shot in the rooms and corridors of Pinewood Studios' Heatherden Hall. This meant that, for the first time, the organisation had a recognisable base. As well as establishing its own internal continuity, the new series made a habit of referencing original series events and characters, and combined these two continuity strands in order to flesh out a broader *Avengers* universe that stretched beyond the story of the week.

In essence, Avengerland had never been imbued with so much emotion, realism, continuity and character work, and these elements, which greatly enriched The New Avengers, are undoubtedly a product of Clemens having so much direct creative control over the series.

It seems likely that, rather than being driven to take on the bulk of the series' scripting duties by circumstance, Clemens chose not to use a large pool of writers in order to maintain this level of creative control. Supporting this hypothesis is the fact that Clemens made a conscious decision to write the first few episodes of the series himself, an exercise he used to help define the series' identity: "I had to discover 'The New Avengers' for myself. That's why I wrote the first three or four scripts, because I couldn't explain it to anybody." (Shirley Davenport, "Why Brian picked Joanna as a girl in a thousand", The Glasgow Herald, October 19, 1976) It is therefore probable that, once he had produced those first few stories, Clemens determined that it was necessary for him to continue to be heavily involved in the scripting in order to ensure that his vision for the new series was maintained throughout. However, Clemens clearly also realised that he could not feasibly write every single episode of the series, even if he wanted to, and set about finding others to assist him with his task. It is unknown if the few other writers who contributed scripts to the series were specifically sought out by Clemens, or if he fielded submissions from interested parties and selected those writers whose work best adhered to his vision for the new show. However, his selections suggest a mixture of the two methods. He likely approached his good friend Dennis Spooner, as well as Terence Feely, who had co-written the ill-fated Avengers stage play with him and contributed to his series Thriller. John Goldsmith, in contrast, likely had to propose a story idea for consideration before being asked to write a script. Regardless of how they were recruited, it is notable that Clemens did not select writers who were Avengers stalwarts. John Goldsmith had never written for the original series, while Dennis Spooner had contributed four scripts – two in each of the David Keel and Tara King eras – and Terence Feely had only two Keel scripts to his name. Clemens therefore seems to have actively attempted to avoid bringing the original series' most prolific contributors onboard, perhaps because, as he told Avengers writer and researcher Dave Rogers, he wanted to prevent the series from feeling like a rehashed version of the Peel / King era: "Don't forget, this was called The NEW Avengers, so we had to stay true to that, otherwise the critics would have hammered us for just serving up a new batch of the old Avengers." (Dave Rogers, The Ultimate Avengers, Boxtree, 1995) It is also notable that Spooner and Feely's Avengers contributions had been partially or fully confined to the Keel era. As The New Avengers was a mix of the grittier,

Cold War espionage-tinged Keel / Gale era and the bizarre / surreal aspects of the Peel / King years, the selection of Feely and Spooner suggests that Clemens was looking for people who could inject some of the grittiness of the series' earliest incarnations into the new show, as well as those who had experience writing for a male avenger other than Steed, something that would prove useful with the addition of Gambit.

This seeming desire to bring in writers who were either new to the series or had experience writing for a grimmer Avengerland could explain why Tony Williamson, a writer who had contributed nine scripts across the Peel and King eras, had his *New Avengers* offering, *Tell Me About It* (also referred to as *Tell Me About It?* in the script), rejected. However, Williamson indicated in 1991 that he had been reluctant to contribute to *The New Avengers*, which suggests that Clemens and co. approached him (Michael Richardson, *Bowler Hats and Kinky Boots*, Telos, 2014). Further muddying the waters is the fact that Williamson wrote to Albert Fennell on 18th December 1975, suggesting that the plot of the series' pilot episode involve the kidnapping of the Queen, an idea that was ultimately rejected (Michael Richardson, *Bowler Hats and Kinky Boots*, Telos, 2014). Whether Williamson wrote in at Clemens and co.'s request, or the series' producers responded to his letter with an invitation to submit further ideas, *Tell Me About It* seems to have been written because there was at least some belief on the producers' part that Williamson could be a good fit for the new series. This is supported by indications that, as will be discussed later in this analysis, Williamson was given a production brief about the new series that had been prepared by Clemens and Fennell for use by writers and directors working on the series. However, despite being given access to this document, Williamson was at something of a disadvantage from the start, as there are indications that he wrote his script early in the show's (pre-)production, when its identity was still being hashed out. Though the script is undated, references to elements of Purdey's character that were ultimately dropped before, or in the early days of, production allow for a rough estimate as to when the final draft was submitted: likely sometime between the announcement of the casting of Gareth Hunt and Joanna Lumley as Steed's new partners on 8th March 1976, and the commencement of filming of *The Eagle's Nest* in April. Another indication that the script was written in the early days of the series' (pre-) production is that it styles the series' title as "The new Avengers", with an all-lowercase "new". This is likely Tony Williamson's attempt to replicate one of the series' initial logos – either one featuring the "new" scrawled, graffiti style, on one of the original *Avengers* logos, or one depicting the "new" as being held above the words "The Avengers" by the thumb and forefinger of a hand – with his typewriter. With the series being in something of a state of flux at the time of the writing of the script, it is entirely possible that, when Clemens finalised his vision for the series, it became clear that what Williamson had produced was not quite what he had in mind, and, as a result, it was rejected.

Other potential reasons for the script's rejection emerge when delving into the text itself. The plot finds Steed, Purdey, and Gambit investigating the theft of several cylinders of a gas that forces people to tell the truth, which the thief intends to use to sabotage the World Peace Conference. The truth gas itself is a very *Avengers*-ish concept. Indeed, Williamson had made another gas – one which froze people in place and rendered them oblivious to everything occurring around them – the basis of his Tara King story *Super Secret Cypher Snatch*. Similarly, *The New Avengers* used a sleeping gas as the basis for the first season episode *Sleeper*. However, the gas in *Tell Me About It* is used differently than in the two produced episodes. In *Super Secret Cypher Snatch* and *Sleeper*, it is the villains of the piece who use the gas (as a means to steal secret documents and rob banks, respectively). *Tell Me About It*, in contrast, finds not only the villains deploying the gas, but the leads as well. This is a strange creative choice on Williamson's part. Even though Steed, Gambit, and Purdey are administering the gas in the interests of national security, and the people they are using it on – dishonest individuals, criminals, etc. – are hardly upstanding citizens, their use of it casts them in the uneasy and sinister role of interrogator. While it is true that the leads work in espionage, a cutthroat business which calls upon its operatives to perform many unsavoury acts in order to get results in high-stakes situations, *The Avengers*, particularly in its more fantasy-oriented incarnation, generally allowed its leads to remain aloof from unpleasant acts, such as formal interrogation. (Steed did participate in interrogation and perform other morally questionable actions in the Keel and Gale eras, behaviour that often caused him to clash with his more strictly ethical partners.) Instead, such roles were allocated to the likes of the titular Ministry interrogator in *The Wringer*, who was revealed to be a traitor, or Colonel Mannering in *The Interrogators*, who pretended to be a Ministry-sanctioned interrogator heading up interdepartmental security in order to extract information from unsuspecting agents. Even those interrogators who were not villainous still shouldered the moral implications of their work – by passing on the information they extracted, they allowed the leads to keep their hands clean and retain the moral high ground. *Tell Me About It*, in contrast, features an official interrogator the first time the gas is administered by the leads, but, after that, the leads dispense it and question the subjects themselves. While the implication is that Steed, Purdey, and Gambit would prefer not to physically torture anyone – and, indeed, Purdey expresses sympathy for Lorik when he reveals that his fingers were broken in a previous interrogation session, implying that she does not approve of such methods – the fact that they personally and repeatedly administer the truth gas in order to deprive people of their will and force them to talk – while calmly donning masks to prevent themselves from being affected – unquestionably lends them a sinister air. Even in *The New Avengers*' more realistic, consequentialist take on Avengerland, the leads' actions feel like a step too far, and may have left viewers wondering whether their heroes were at best morally ambiguous, at worst sinister operators who would use any means necessary to achieve their objective.

Oddly enough, while Williamson seems keen to cast the trio in a sinister light, he also seems to want to evoke sympathy for unsympathetic characters. The script finds Purdey expressing sadness at Barker's death, and treating Paxton with kindness when returning the money he would have paid to the blackmailing Jarret. And yet, Barker is part of Sanders' robbery crew and is willing to perform criminal acts for money, while Paxton is only blackmailable because he is corrupt. As they are not blameless victims, one wonders why the script seems determined to evoke sympathy for their plights.

Turning from unsympathetic characters to outright antagonists, we find that there are actually two separate threats at work. As the mastermind behind the theft of the gas cylinders, Sanders is initially set up as the archvillain. However, the focus soon shifts to Sanders' henchman, Jarret, who pilfers one of the cylinders and uses it to blackmail people. As the trio pursues Jarret and makes his actions the focus of the investigation, Sanders becomes something of an afterthought, rarely appearing or doing anything of note. By the time Jarret is killed and the trio realises that he was not behind the theft of the cylinders, one has almost forgotten that Sanders exists and has ceased wondering what his plans for the cylinders are. Further muddying the waters is the fact that Jarret tests his cylinder on the Brotherhood of Nations, while Sanders' target is the World Peace Conference. The similarity of these two organisations makes them easy to conflate in the reader's mind, making it appear as though Jarret is somehow aiding his boss by testing the gas at a meeting of the Brotherhood. At the very least, when Sanders arrives at the World Peace Conference to set his plan in motion, there is a definite sense of déjà vu. Things are further confused by the addition of Barker. The man in the middle, he originally works for Sanders, but is intimidated into collaborating with Jarret. This makes it difficult to keep track of why he is doing what he is doing and who he is doing it for. Further confusion is added when Sanders sends his men after Jarret for betraying him, while the leads pursue Jarret at the same time by following the same clues, believing he is the mastermind behind the cylinder theft. This criss-crossing of the leads' and villains' motivations would undoubtedly have made it hard for viewers to follow the plot as the episode wore on. Overall, it would have been better if Williamson had settled on one villain. As it is, it feels like there are two separate plots, with Jarret leading the trio on a merry dance in what seems like an effort to pad out the running time, before his death returns Sanders to centre stage and the initial plot thread receives a belated wrap-up that the audience long ago forgot it needed – and, given that Sanders' motivation for sabotaging the conference is never revealed, is not worth the wait.

Turning to the script's tone, Williamson chose to seed the original series' sense of the bizarre throughout his story. The most notable example of this is the scene in which a supervisor at the Ministry of Defence research centre explains to Gambit that she is running an experiment to prove the hypothesis that a group of monkeys with typewriters could eventually turn out something profound if given long enough. This is an endeavour that one could easily imagine one of the original series' scientists pursuing for their own eccentric reasons – albeit one that would be unlikely to reach the screen, as acquiring and wrangling the monkeys would undoubtedly have been more trouble than the scene was worth – though Gambit's decision to gently mock the supervisor for embarking on such a ludicrous experiment runs counter to the bemused acceptance that characterised Steed, Emma, and Tara's reactions in similar situations. Gambit's reaction is perhaps an acknowledgement by Williamson of the less frivolous attitudes of the seventies. Another bit of bizarreness comes in the episode's opening scene, in which Steed tells the occupant of a coffin to keep quiet and instructs the coffin bearers to be careful with their load, lest they kill the occupant! Again, Williamson seems to intentionally offer a counterweight to this touch of whimsy in the form of Purdey's solemn demeanour and condolences to Steed in the moments before she grasps the full, bizarre reality of the situation.

Along with bizarreness, there is also humour to be found in the likes of Keller's amnesia, which turns him from ruthless killer to confused-yet-helpful interrogation subject – learning his name, he enthusiastically exclaims that he likes it, after earnestly asking "What is soap?" when Purdey mentions slipping on it during their fight. Humour is also injected into Purdey and Gambit's climactic fight scene via the minister's query as to whether Purdey and Gambit can sort out Sanders' men and negate the need to cancel the conference, and Steed's understated reply: "I'm sure they're doing everything they can." Even the names of the organisations holding conferences at the same hotel as the World Peace Conference raise a smile, as they range from the likes of the National Bird Watchers Society to the delightfully offbeat Association of Brass Rubbing.

While the humourous and bizarre elements are appropriately (*New*) *Avengers*-ish, other aspects of the script are odd inclusions on Williamson's part, particularly since he had written for the original series. One such oddity surfaces in the scene in which the various ambassadors and dignitaries representing the Brotherhood of Nations are exposed to the truth gas and begin insulting each other. While the image of these dignified statesmen acting in such an undignified manner is generally in keeping with the series' predilection for the bizarre and penchant for mocking politicians and their ilk, the fact that the insults doled out are based on race, political affiliation, national stereotypes, and the like violates the series' tendency to remain aloof from such matters. Indeed, the show generally avoided referring to real countries, opting instead to hint at their identities or invent fictional nations. Similarly, direct references to political events were generally avoided, so a reference to Watergate is a strange inclusion by Williamson. Though *The New Avengers* made more overt references to real countries and events than its predecessor, it is more than likely that, if the script was filmed, all of its insults and political references would have been toned down or removed entirely.

Another oddity comes in a scene in which Steed meets with various higher-ups regarding the theft of the gas. While the higher-ups squabbling amongst themselves about who is responsible for the theft is in keeping with *The Avengers*' delight in skewering those in power, and *The New Avengers*' emphasis on inter-departmental politics, the name of one of the men at the table seems an odd choice. Described as the man representing MI5, the script refers to him as "Q", clearly a winking reference to James Bond's quartermaster, who provided Bond with his espionage paraphernalia. This gag works better on the page than it likely would have on screen, where it would have drifted into outright parody. While *The Avengers* was not averse to parody, such an overt reference would have sat uneasily against *The New Avengers*' more grounded, sober tone. In addition, it is unlikely that the series' creative team would have allowed the reference to "Q" to stand, as it would have not only invited legal issues, but also suggested that Steed and Bond occupied the same universe, despite being distinct properties. Of course, it is entirely possible that Williamson was only using "Q" as a shorthand to give a rough idea of what the character was like and indicate the organisation he was representing, and did not intend for him to ever be referred to as "Q" onscreen. If that was the case, "Q" would probably have passed muster in print, but certainly any mention of that particular letter would have been unlikely to reach the screen.

The Characters

Steed

Given that Steed was, by the time of The New Avengers, a well-established character who had been on television for nearly a decade during the series' original run (and appeared in several re-runs after the series went off air), it is unsurprising that he appears in Williamson's script with his characterisation intact. Indeed, Williamson had previous experience writing for Steed, so a certain amount of muscle memory was likely at work while he was producing the script. As a result, Steed's sense of humour and ability to calmly accept bizarre or serious events are present and correct. For example, he responds to the sight of the Brotherhood of Nations dignitaries attacking each other by merely commenting that the display is "odd", and reacts to the death of a town clerk with unruffled concern, to the point of making a quip about town clerks "living dangerously this year" that one can easily imagine coming from Patrick Macnee's lips. Similarly, when Steed enters the conference room after Purdey and Gambit's energetic fight with Sanders' thugs and finds it in complete disarray, he merely queries whether his younger colleagues are going to tidy up after themselves. Steed's habit of keeping things from his colleagues is also retained in this script, with Purdey only realising that the coffin she and Steed are escorting contains a living occupant when said occupant begins to complain about his lack of air.

In addition to the familiar elements, there are some small tweaks to Steed's character in the script that are in keeping with his New Avengers status as a senior agent accorded more responsibility and a place among the decisionmakers. While Steed continues to report to those above him, the script finds him hashing things out with a general, a minister, a senior army officer, the PPS to the prime minister, and a man from MI5 on a much more equal footing than before. Indeed, when the higher-ups require an assessment of how serious a matter the theft of the truth gas is, Steed is the one they ultimately look to for answers. At the same time, despite his new position, Steed has retained some of his inherent mischief and healthy disrespect of authority, and cheekily tells the assembled men that the stolen gas could result in a catastrophe or no problems at all. The glares he receives in response fail to make him repentant for his subtle nose-thumbing. Later, Steed plays peacemaker in the aftermath of the hostilities that break out between the members of the Brotherhood of Nations due to exposure to the truth gas. When the confused delegates regain their senses and find themselves in complete disarray, Steed allows them to save face by reestablishing a sense of normality, proposing a toast to "brotherhood" in which the dignitaries gratefully participate. In spite of his newfound position and influence, Steed's cynicism about politicians and politics remains intact, and has, in fact, strengthened over the years, as evidenced by his critical quips about everything from world affairs to the state of the nation's economy in *The New Avengers*. In the script, it comes through in his assertion that, if politicians started telling the truth, they could start a war, the implication being that he believes they are rarely honest and hold more inflammatory opinions than their diplomatic language would suggest. Williamson also acknowledges that he is writing an older Steed by giving the chief avenger an untaxing action scene, requiring him to dispatch one of Sanders' men with a series of blows, while otherwise leaving the fisticuffs to Steed's younger partners. Overall, the script, like the series, strikes a nice balance between evolving Steed as a character, and keeping him as the recognisable figure that audiences know and love.

Gambit

Before composing his script, Williamson clearly read the description of Gambit's fighting style in Clemens and Fennell's production brief, which stated that Gambit "should be shot – from great stillness – into a blur of close shots – a blur of fast movement – and out again to the stillness we will come to associate with him before and after vigorous action." (Dave Rogers, *The Ultimate Avengers*, Boxtree, 1995) This dictate translates to the script via fight scenes that describe Gambit as "a blur of motion", "[flying] into shot", "moving so fast we can barely see what he does", unleashing "a rapid series of blows", and moving "with incredible speed". As Gambit's onscreen fights were presented in a similarly rapid-fire, high-action manner, the combat sequences penned by Williamson feel true to the character. Other elements of Gambit's characterisation in the script are also in keeping with his onscreen persona. His joke at the Ministry of Defence research centre supervisor's expense – he pretends that one of the monkeys participating in her experiment has produced a Shakespeare quotation – is a classic piece of Gambit mischief, akin to him getting the target range dummies to shoot at Bradshaw in *Target!*. His suggested means of curing Keller's amnesia – knocking him out again – also sounds like the sort of half-joke he might make to lighten the mood when facing a frustrating situation. The sometimes-grim tone of his humour also comes through, with Gambit suggesting that Lowther did not post a letter because of the "rising cost of living" while looking at the man's corpse and commenting that the investigation has reached a "dead end" after Jarret's death, lines that recall his "very dead" comment after the death of an opponent in The Eagle's Nest. Gambit's quip upon seeing a soaking-wet Purdey after her fight with Keller in a shower – "I'm all for showering with a friend, but that's ridiculous." – meanwhile, is the kind of comment he would make as part of his and Purdey's onscreen campaign of gentle, teasing one-upmanship.

However, in other ways, Williamson's seeming lack of opportunity to see Gareth Hunt's portrayal of the character or read any completed, filmed scripts is evident. While Gambit's Shakespeare / monkey practical joke is in keeping with his personality, the fact that he makes it at the expense of a female supervisor seems rather out of character. Gambit would typically try to charm and flirt with a woman – particularly if she was an attractive woman – rather than antagonise and annoy her by mocking her research. It is true that Gambit did gently irritate or discombobulate attractive women, such as Jane, Coldstream's bemused secretary in Angels of Death, but such instances are rare and reserved for individuals that Gambit perceives as hostile or an obstacle to doing his job – Jane, for example, is holding a gun on him and working for a man he believes may be a traitor. The supervisor, in contrast, is someone Gambit wishes to receive assistance from, so it makes no sense for him to give her reason to dislike him. This uncharacteristic interaction may, however, be explained by handwritten addendums to the script that indicate that the supervisor was originally intended to be a man, before Williamson changed his mind during the writing process and opted to make the character a woman. This makes Gambit's abrasiveness toward the supervisor much more in keeping with his personality, as he often made a point of puncturing the egos of officious or arrogant male characters who treated him with disdain – see his irreverent interactions with the snobbish Brown-Fitch in The Eagle's Nest, and his liberation of files from a controlling file clerk in Target!. The quip Gambit directs at Wetherby in the script about the lab rabbit that has not slept for a month – Gambit queries whether Wetherby has given it sleeping pills – is in the same vein. As scripted, therefore, Gambit's interaction with the supervisor would be in character if he was speaking with an overly serious man, but the last-minute switch to a female character would have required some retooling of his dialogue and actions to make the scene ring true. Also speaking to Williamson's unfamiliarity with Gambit's character is his decision to have him use the exclamation "Fancy", which was the signature catchphrase of another seventies telefantasy hero, Jason King. Williamson wrote for King in five Department S scripts and six Jason King stories, which perhaps explains why this particular exclamation sprang to his mind. While this response perfectly suits Jason King, it is a completely un-Gambit-like reaction – a quip or raise of the eyebrows would be much more his style. Another small moment that seems to run counter to Gambit's characterisation is when he is shown drinking brandy. Brandy is Steed's tipple; Gambit preferred scotch. However, given that Gambit is at Barker's house when he is drinking it, Williamson perhaps intended for Barker to offer Gambit the brandy, and Gambit to accept it out of politeness.

Purdey

While the script is undated, the fact that the name "Purdey" features in it tells us that it was penned, or at least finalised, after the casting of Joanna Lumley. Purdey was originally to be called "Charly", but Lumley suggested that the character be renamed "Purdey", after the expensive brand of shotgun, as there was a perfume on the market called "Charlie". Just as Purdey was known as "just Purdey", sans any "Miss" or "Mrs." honourific, a draft of the script for *The Eagle's Nest* dated 16th March 1976, seems to indicate that "Charly" was intended to be the character's only name. However, the *Tell Me About It* script appears to indicate that, for a brief period, the series' creatives considered making "Purdey" the character's surname, using it in addition to, rather than as a replacement for, "Charly". While all of the character's lines are labelled "Purdey" in the script, she is referred to as "Charlie / Charley" (Williamson uses both spellings interchangeably and in place of what appears to be Clemens and co.'s intended spelling of "Charly") by other characters on several occasions. This might lead one to believe that the script was originally written when the character was known as "Charly", and, once the character was renamed "Purdey", the labels for the lines were amended, with a few references to the old name in the dialogue simply overlooked. However, this theory is undercut by the fact that Purdey is called "Miss Purdey" by one character, and responds with "Purdey" – rather than "just Purdey", as in *The Midas Touch* – when another character prompts her for her surname by saying "Miss-er...?" All uses of "Charley / Charlie" in the script, in contrast, are sans honourific. It therefore seems that the intention, however briefly, was for the character's name to be "Charley / Charlie / Charly Purdey", with "Charley / Charlie / Charly" her first name and "Purdey" her surname (as indicated by the fact that she uses it when she is being called "Miss"). Of course, it is entirely possible that, as Williamson was not part of the production team, he simply misunderstood when he was told that the character would now be called "Purdey", and assumed that this was the character's surname. However, it is intriguing to think that the production team considered calling the character "Charley / Charlie / Charly Purdey".

Another sign that this script was written early in the series' (pre-) production is the line "Purdey strips for action". Instead of the leather outfits and catsuits worn by Cathy Gale and Emma Peel, or the trouser / culotte ensembles preferred by Tara King, Purdey's fighting outfits were originally going to consist of wrap-around skirts that she could remove before engaging in combat. However, this aspect of Purdey's character was discarded — likely because it was deemed impractical or time-consuming — and was only featured in *The Eagle's Nest*, in which she removes her wraparound skirt to reveal a green leotard before engaging in her first fight.

In terms of characterisation, Purdey describes herself as a "confirmed feminist" in the script, and wonders why the "Brotherhood of Nations" could not be referred to as a "Sisterhood" instead. This is in keeping with her comments in *The Last of the Cybernauts...??*, in which she tells Steed that he does not need to be so gallant because women are "liberated". However, the series generally stopped short of having Purdey, or indeed any of the *Avengers* women, describe herself as a "feminist" onscreen. Aside from the series' creatives likely not wanting to stray into the political implications of the word, Purdey and her predecessors tended to be women of action rather than words, preferring to simply get on with doing what they wanted and coolly deal with anyone who attempted to interfere with or criticise their actions. As a result, the onscreen Purdey would be unlikely to feel the need to describe herself as a feminist, and would instead cut to the chase by asking why the word "sisterhood" could not be used. Similarly, Purdey reasserting her feminist credentials later in the script by referring to her search for a person as "wizard hunting" instead of "witch hunting" gives the impression that both Purdey and the script are trying too hard to make a point, and runs counter to both the series' and Purdey's penchant for cool subtlety regarding such matters.

The script also gives Purdey a new skill, depicting her as being at least reasonably competent at golf, just as Emma Peel was in *The Thirteenth Hole*. While Steed was shown golfing on many occasions, and Gambit claimed not to be a fan of the sport in *Dead Men are Dangerous* — rather ironically, since Gareth Hunt was an avid golfer — Purdey's opinion of golf and her ability to play it were never referenced onscreen.

As in the series, Purdey is depicted as a proficient fighter in the script, performing her signature high kicks and doling out a devastating left hook akin to the punches she lands in the likes of *House of Cards*. However, the script also has her unleashing some karate chops, suggesting that Williamson envisioned her as being a karate practitioner like Emma Peel. In the series, however, Purdey was depicted as primarily relying on her particular brand of high-kicking, ballet-influenced combat, and a mere trainee in the art of karate, taking instruction from both Spence (*House of Cards*) and Gambit (*Dead Men are Dangerous*).

Other elements of Purdey's characterisation are completely in keeping with her onscreen portrayal. Purdey's love of food, as referenced in the likes of The Eagle's Nest, The Tale of the Big Why, and Three Handed Game, is present and correct, with Purdey telling Gambit that it motivates her and expressing a desire for oysters and pheasant. Purdey's gentle, humanitarian touch, displayed when conversing with the likes of the forgetful Hara in The Eagle's Nest, is channelled in her sympathetic reaction to Lorik's revelation that his fingers were broken during a previous interrogation, and her sad response to Barker's demise. As in the likes of Angels of Death, in which she offered her condolences to Steed for the death of his friend and suggested he take time off to grieve, she expresses her sympathies to Steed when he is escorting a coffin, assuming someone close to him has passed away. When she begins hearing a voice from within the coffin, however, she displays a touch of a callous streak – also a trademark of her character in the filmed episodes, as evidenced by her flippant suggestions as to the cause of death of fellow agent Stannard in The Eagle's Nest – assuming that Steed is indulging in ventriloquism with his dead friend. Overall, the picture painted of Purdey in the script is of a character that is recognisable, but still evolving toward her onscreen depiction.

The Purdey/Gambit Relationship

As in the case of his characterisations of Purdey and Gambit, Tony Williamson's take on the pair's dynamic demonstrates that he had not had the benefit of seeing it play out onscreen or of reading scripts written to correspond with the onscreen dynamic. As a result, while Gambit's attraction to, and pursuit of, Purdey is heavily featured, the pair's relationship in the script feels very different from their onscreen one. The episodes find Purdey and Gambit engaging in petty bickering and debates on various topics, with a certain amount of one-upmanship characterising their verbal fencing. In addition, Purdey has a habit of taking pleasure in Gambit's discomfort in embarrassing situations, such as when she catches him posing nude for an artist (Three Handed Game). However, their relationship was also characterised by a great deal of warmth. Whether quietly enjoying each other's company during a stake-out (Forward Base), playing Scrabble while discussing work (The Last of the Cybernauts...??), or spending their leisure time together by playing tennis or dancing at the disco (Trap), there is never any question that Purdey and Gambit are friends. In addition, their concern for one another's well-being and distress when they believe that the other is dying or dead (Faces, Target!) are evidence of their deep affection (and, possibly, love) for one another, while their effortless working relationship demonstrates their complete synchronicity and willingness to trust one another with their lives.

The pair's dynamic in the script, in contrast, not only lacks warmth, but gives the impression that they barely tolerate, let alone like, each other. While the onscreen Purdey might enjoy having the upper hand when it comes to Gambit or revelling in his embarrassment, and tosses out the odd critical barb about his bachelor lifestyle – Dr. Leparge: "Total degeneration." Purdey: "Gambit's speciality." (*K is for Kill: Tiger by the Tail*) – she never indicates that she dislikes him. The script, in contrast, frames Purdey as perceiving Gambit as nothing more than a tiresome pest that she would be happy to be rid of. Over the course of the story, she implies that the idea of defecting is appealing because she would get away from him; describes him as "fragile" and "sensitive" because he does not get enough sleep; criticises him or grimaces when he jokes about the case reaching a "dead end" and the "rising cost of living" after someone expires; gives him an unimpressed look when he suggests knocking Keller out again to cure his amnesia; and flashes him a "frozen smile" when he quips that he hopes she has more interesting vices than opening other people's mail. Gambit, in turn, has registered her low opinion of him, wryly remarking, when Purdey claims that she was worried about him, that he "didn't think [she] cared". They also do not seem to be on the same wavelength professionally, even in dire situations. When Purdey engages in a very physical fight with Keller in a hotel room bathroom, turning the shower on in the process, Gambit tells Purdey that "this is no time to take a shower", not registering that this is a sign that she is in trouble. Similarly, when the pair fight Sanders' men at the episode's climax, they do so separately, without engaging in any of the collaboration that marked their joint fights in the likes of *The Last of the Cybernauts...??* – in which they reveal that they have a "party trick" move that they use to defeat villains – and *Dirtier by the Dozen*.

In spite of this apparent mutual animosity, Gambit pursues Purdey in the script. When she suggests that he ought to have a siesta to catch up on his sleep, he asks her to join him. When she tells him to search under a hotel room bed, he responds that he has a "better idea". When he asks what "motivates" her ego, and her answer is "food", he offers to call room service. In order to foil him, Purdey intentionally asks for food that is out of season. Gambit sighs resignedly in response because, as the script states, he is "used" to being rebuffed, but this reaction makes it difficult to understand why he thinks Purdey is worth the trouble of chasing at all, since they barely seem to get along well enough to work together. (Perhaps the scripted Gambit's physical attraction to Purdey is the only thing that makes working with her tolerable for him!) Matters are made worse by Purdey's comment that, the last time she went into a hotel room with Gambit, "I had to fight my way out." This statement runs completely counter to the mutually respectful relationship the pair shared in the series. While Gambit repeatedly made his attraction to Purdey clear, he made very few physical overtures toward her, and, when those were rejected, made no attempt to force the issue or make her do anything she did not want to do. In turn, the onscreen Purdey certainly never indicated that she had to fight off Gambit at any point, and, indeed, the fact that she is shown spending time alone with him off-duty demonstrates that she trusts him completely. The situation described by Purdey in the script therefore bears no resemblance to how the characters related to one another in the series, and further indicates Williamson's lack of familiarity with the pair's dynamic.

The sole moment that suggests any affinity between the two comes in the tag scene, in which Gambit asks Purdey if she is attracted to him while they are under the influence of the truth gas. The fact that they are spending time together at Gambit's flat and Purdey's claim that she returns his affections (which she immediately undermines by implying that she is no longer under the influence of the gas) suggest that there might be something between them. However, this scene still lacks the warmth and affinity that characterised the pair's onscreen relationship, and, after their borderline indifference and hostility toward each other throughout the script, comes off as too little, too late.

The Triumvirate

The script regularly splits the three leads up, but, when they are together, there are occasional glimmers of their onscreen dynamic. One moment, in which Steed chastises Purdey for hitting Keller hard enough to give him amnesia – Steed: "What did you hit him with? The bath?" Purdey: "I slipped on the soap!" – anticipates filmed scenes in the likes of *Forward Base*, in which Purdey tells an incredulous Steed that the man she was following walked into Lake Ontario and re-emerged dead from a bullet wound, and Gambit informs Steed that he found a man on dry land wearing a wetsuit. In both instances, Steed treats his younger colleagues like wayward, misbehaving children. Elsewhere, Purdey's expression of her sympathies when she believes that Steed has lost a friend, and her understanding smile when Steed tells her that he will be late for their embassy function, infuse their relationship with a little of its onscreen warmth. Overall, however, there is a general lack of fellow feeling amongst the trio. This is partly due to the fact that they are afforded very few opportunities to collaborate, the most notable examples being when they use word association to jog the amnesiac Keller's memory, their examination of Lowther's body, and their interrogation of Lorik. However, they feel strangely disconnected in these scenes, the dialogue they exchange mostly impersonal or, in the case of Purdey and Gambit, sometimes vaguely hostile. Matters are not helped by the fact that Gambit and Steed barely interact in the script, and are rarely even in the same place – the sole moment they share sans Purdey occurs while they are protecting Barker, but, rather than talk to each other, they direct their dialogue toward Barker. Purdey and Gambit form the combination that receives the most attention, followed by Purdey and Steed, but a surprising number of scenes find the characters working solo. Overall, there is a detached, distant feeling amongst the triumvirate that runs counter to the strong friendships and working relationships depicted onscreen.

Other Characters

Rather than feature a single villain, *Tell Me About It* divides the antagonist duties among a few characters. Geoffrey Sanders (mistakenly referred to as "Paul" at one point in the script) is, ostensibly, the diabolical mastermind of the piece. The script paints a picture of him as a distinguished, nattily dressed man – clad in a smart grey suit with a rose in his lapel, wearing gloves, carrying a walking stick, and with a silk handkerchief in his pocket – who is in his early fifties. Between his debonair attire, stick (in place of an umbrella), and age, one cannot help but assume that he is intended to be a villainous version of Steed. Even his modus operandi is very Steed-like: rather than attacking and killing an armed guard, Sanders pretends to be lost, then shoots the man with a tranquiliser gun, a subtler, less violent approach that is in keeping with Steed's preference to avoid outright combat. At the same time, Sanders' use of the tranquiliser gun cleverly differentiates him from Steed, who generally avoided guns, and highlights his villainous nature. Sanders' look and introduction hint that the senior agent may have finally met his match, and set the audience up to expect a climactic battle between Steed and his villainous doppelganger. Unfortunately, this showdown never occurs. Sanders and Steed do not meet until the end of the episode, when Sanders, under the influence of the truth gas, confesses his crimes. Along with this anticlimactic defeat, Sanders' other actions are fairly pedestrian – he orders his henchmen about and uses the truth gas on Maitland in scenes that do little more than move the plot along. Nothing he does matches up to the flair and intrigue of his introduction or casts him as a criminal genius on par with Steed's cunning agent, nor does his debonair sense of style seem to feed into his dealings – indeed, his actions could be performed by any nondescript villain.

Sanders' henchman Jarret, meanwhile, relieves Sanders of some of the antagonist duties by getting in on the villainy of his own accord. Unfortunately, Jarret is even less interesting than Sanders, lacking even his natty aesthetic. Instead, he is simply a cutthroat mercenary out to earn money by criminal means, willing to ruthlessly threaten or kill anyone who interferes with his plans. Jarret himself is ultimately killed by Keller on Sanders' orders, but, as he is not a particularly interesting character, his death is no great loss and only serves to move the plot along in a utilitarian fashion.

Turning to the more minor villains, Barker is rendered slightly memorable due to his archery skills and predilection for women's hats. Ultimately, however, he only adds to the body count and is easily forgotten. Keller, ironically, is rendered somewhat memorable by his memory loss. However, Keller's memorability has less to do with his characterisation, and more to do with erasing what little characterisation he has to humourous effect. Sanders' other henchmen, meanwhile, are so generic as to not even be given names.

The villains' lack of distinctiveness and memorability extends to other characters. Lorik, the first person upon whom the trio uses the gas, is rendered slightly interesting via his unusual mode of arrival – he is transported to the interrogation room in a coffin – and tales of holding firm in the face of torture, but all of his scenes occur pre-titles, so he is quickly forgotten when the plot takes off in earnest. The senior army officer who lectures Steed about the loss of the gas, the MI5 man, the general, the minister, and the Prime Minister's PPS are all generic authority figures used to having their way. None of them lingers in the mind. Instead, they blend into a single entity that the audience solely remembers for being deftly handled by Steed. The ambassadors and diplomats are also equally interchangeable. Despite representing different nations, they all spout similarly diplomatic lines when not under the influence of the gas, and equally offensive insults when they are. Purdey's civil servant acquaintance at the Brotherhood of Nations soiree has a mildly superior demeanour, but does not even warrant a name. The supervisor teased by Gambit about her monkeys-with-typewriters experiment is rendered slightly entertaining by her mild pique, but, ultimately, it is Gambit's joke at her expense that is the most memorable aspect of her scenes. Wetherby, one of the developers of the truth gas, is somewhat amusing because of his inability to recognise that his claim that no one knew the gas was at the Special Intelligence Centre is undermined every time he confirms that another person did know about it. He also takes on a "classic

Avengers eccentric scientist" vibe when he shows Gambit the results of some of his experiments — including a rabbit that has not slept for a month and a hamster that has bent its wheel out of shape — but lacks the idiosyncrasies that characterised the best examples of those characters in the original series. Blackmail victims Maitland, Lowther, Paxton, and Jeffreyson, meanwhile, are generic and uninteresting, serving as little more than plot propellers who provide further leads for the trio to follow.

Given *The Avengers'* penchant for including interesting and memorable guest and incidental characters in its stories — and Williamson's history with the series — it is odd that none of Williamson's non-lead characters leaps off the page. Though *The New Avengers* was more grounded than the later seasons of its predecessor, it still included interesting guest roles. Perhaps the right actors would have breathed life into *Tell Me About It*'s players, but, as originally conceived, very little of note makes any of them stand out.

Similarities to Other Avengers and New Avengers Episodes

There are several similarities between this script and episodes of both the original and sequel series. As has been previously discussed, two produced episodes revolve around the use of a gas: Williamson's *Super Secret Cypher Snatch* — which also features a character named "Jarret" and in which, perhaps not coincidentally, the villains don masks to prevent themselves from being affected by the gas, just as the trio and villains do in *Tell Me About It* — and *Sleeper*. The truth gas premise is also the inverse of that of *False Witness*, which features a substance that forces people to lie. The attempted sabotages of the Brotherhood of Nations and World Peace Conference are reminiscent of the plot to bomb a peace conference in *They Keep Killing Steed*. One of Sanders' henchmen dying by falling on an arrow anticipates Mullins' demise in *Faces*, while Barker having arrows shot at him while he is standing in front of a target recalls Steed's perilous situation in *The Master Minds*. Lorik emerging from a coffin is reminiscent of Perov doing the same after faking his death in *House of Cards*, and also recalls *Bizarre*, in which a host of lively "corpses" live it up beneath their graveyard.

Verdict

Tony Williamson had his work cut out for him when penning *Tell Me About It*. All signs point to it being written early in *The New Avengers*' (pre-) production, meaning that Williamson likely did not have the opportunity to watch completed episodes or read any finalised scripts to get a sense of the characters and feel of the series. Making things doubly difficult was the series' ongoing evolutionary process. This continued through the production of the first few episodes, which feature a grimmer tone, more intense violence, and a more abrasive Gambit, elements that were all ultimately toned down. As a result, the series' feel and characters were something of a moving target, nearly impossible for a writer to hit.

Williamson's effort should therefore be assessed with these difficulties in mind, and praised for the ways in which it succeeds. Williamson's familiarity with Steed was obviously a boon to him, as he writes him perfectly in character — still devious, still charming, still a master of the spy game. At the same time, he adeptly depicts Steed at a different stage of his life and career, writing him as a senior agent with the authority and gravitas to cross swords with the higher-ups, and the wisdom to instruct his younger colleagues. Likely at Clemens' request, Williamson also keeps Steed out of the fights and reduces his share of the legwork, but does so in a way that never makes the character feel sidelined. Indeed, Steed's contributions are as important as those of his younger colleagues, and consist of a mixture of traditional investigation and deftly dealing with the higher-ups, a combination that makes Steed's more senior role a multi-dimensional one and keeps him actively engaged in the plot. Patrick Macnee often complained that he was "put out to pasture" in *The New Avengers* — a complaint that was largely unwarranted, as Steed played a substantial role in the vast majority of the episodes — but it would be difficult for him to argue that Steed does not get his fair share of screentime in this story.

The premise itself is also suitably *Avengers*-ish, and would have suited this era of the show well — a truth gas is no more outlandish than a giant rat or sleeping gas, and the sight of various characters donning masks would have added menace to the story. However, outside of the general premise, it seems that Williamson took the brief that the series would be a more dramatic, grim, gritty take on Avengerland a little too seriously. The casting of the leads as interrogators who regularly use the gas on unwilling subjects is an uncomfortable one, and frames them as morally ambiguous players who are difficult to relate to or root for. Similarly, the general lack of warmth and camaraderie amongst the trio, particularly between Purdey and Gambit, means there is little pleasure in watching them interact. Perhaps Williamson was aiming for a Steed / Cathy Gale or Steed / David Keel antagonistic dynamic between Purdey and Gambit, and was seeking to revive the moral ambiguity that Steed displayed in the show's early seasons with the trio's use of the gas. While some of the character traits and relationship dynamics depicted in *The Avengers*' earliest seasons would be incorporated into *The New Avengers*, the leads' onscreen relationships with one another were generally warm and trusting, and the leads themselves possessed more of a moral compass than in Williamson's take.

Williamson's more serious mindset is also reflected in his take on the occupants of "New Avengerland", who lack *The Avengers*' guest characters' distinctive brand of quirkiness. *The New Avengers* had fewer eccentrics, but it still had them, and what its players lost in quirkiness, they made up for in humanity, fallibility, and feeling. In the case of Williamson's guest characters, the eccentricities are toned down, but not replaced with anything of substance.

In essence, Williamson's premise is a good one, but his take on the show's tone, characters, and universe fails to capture *The New Avengers*' mixture of realism and the bizarre, warmth and richness, light and shadow. As a result, the script would have required considerable reworking to make it suitable for filming, a reality that undoubtedly contributed to the decision to reject it.

The authors recommend The Morning After's paperback reproduction of Tony Williamson's Tell Me About It *script, which is available to buy from Lulu.com (tinyurl.com/2s3bh67r).*

OUTER AVENGERLAND

THE STAGE PLAY
THE RADIO SERIES
THE FIRST AVENGERS MOVIE
AVENGERS INTERNATIONAL
STEED AND MRS. PEEL

THE STAGE PLAY

ALAN HAYES
with thanks to John Buss and Elizabeth Feely

Project Type: Theatrical Production
Staged: July to September 1971 (United Kingdom)

Synopsis

Curtain Raiser

The audience take to their seats to the strains of the British national anthem. A foreign anthem succeeds it as a spotlight picks out the Royal Box, in which a visiting dignitary – a large, silver-haired man – steps forward to acknowledge those present. Suddenly, an arrow hits him in the chest and blood spreads across his snowy dress shirt. He drops from sight as the audience and his entourage scream. The opening chords of the *Avengers* theme ring out. A telephone rings.

Act One

Scene 1: John Steed's Penthouse Apartment – morning

John Steed's penthouse apartment is rather plush. Doors lead to servants' quarters, a bedroom and a dining room, and Steed's front door is at the top of a short, curved staircase with metal railings. The decor reveals his eccentric tastes – a turtle carapace is on display by the stairs, an Egyptian Mummy case is positioned against the back wall, and an Allen Jones hatstand in the shape of a female figure stands near the bedroom door. However, the apartment is in disarray. A party that lasted into the small hours of the morning has left bottles, glasses, and items of clothing strewn everywhere.

A loudspeaker telephone rings and pulses red. Steed's attractive blonde butler, James – wearing a shirt, striped waistcoat and black shorts – answers the call. Mother is on the other end, asking to speak to Steed about "top urgent" business. With immaculate timing, Steed returns from the newsagent, where he has purchased a copy of *The Times*. He asks James to go off and iron it. Steed picks up a discarded bowler hat, but finds it does not fit him. He surmises that it "must belong to the other fellow".

He sits down cross-legged, removes a bra and a pair of tights from a fruit bowl, and picks himself some grapes. Mother tells him that a foreign minister has been assassinated in a London theatre – the third such killing in a month. Most embarrassing for the British government. Mother has sent MI5 agent Bobby Carruthers to brief Steed, and has also alerted Mrs. Wild. Mother ends the call.

James returns with *The Times* and Steed's breakfast – an orange juice and three aspirin. Steed downs the tablets and notes that an iron-shaped hole runs through the newspaper. He asks James to make a cup of coffee for Mrs. Hannah Wild, whom he is expecting at ten.

Prompt as always, Hannah rings the doorbell as the clock strikes the hour, and Steed admits her. She is a tall, striking brunette, and wears a golden leather ensemble – jacket, dress and boots – lined with chains. She extricates a pair of knickers from a cigar box, lights a long, black cigar, and confesses that her Cuban holiday was disastrous. Her flight got diverted by illiterate Cuban hijackers, who had got on the wrong plane. They all ended up in the jungle of New Guinea.

Steed, meanwhile, has kept busy. He lost money at Ascot, won a girl's heart at Lady Frimpling's soiree, ran into Jerry Potter, ran over Jasper Miserly on Park Lane, killed Anton Rovitsch with a corkscrew, threw a party, and hired a new manservant called James, whom he suspects might actually be a girl.

Steed tells Hannah about the killings, the panic in high places, and that World War III is a distinct possibility – this could be their most challenging assignment yet. Hannah is simply pleased that their services are required.

A sudden groan comes from Steed's Egyptian Mummy case. It swings open and Melanie, a good-looking, dark-haired girl staggers out, completely naked. She says that Freddy Pitt-Miller had told her that it was the toilet. Steed asks James to cover the girl up. James conducts Melanie to a bedroom. Hannah remarks that Steed certainly throws good, old-fashioned parties.

Bobby Carruthers arrives. He is a public school type, as stiff as a poker, and is humming a tune. Steed and Hannah can't quite place it. They soon realise that the MI5 agent repeats everything they say, parrot-fashion, as if his mind has gone.

Carruthers' back-up man, Tom 'Snipper' Parsons, arrives. He is dressed as a frogman, with flippers and breathing apparatus. He hums the same tune and gabbles about mermaids and the sea. Before he can pass on any useful details, he inhales cyanide secreted in his breathing tube and dies.

The agents' behaviour seems somehow familiar to Steed. Hannah reminds him about an experimental mind-altering machine that they came across at Stanford.

Jack 'Chummers' Cholmondleigh, Parsons' back-up, arrives, humming the tune. Spacesuited, he carries a helmet, and walks as if in zero gravity. He says that he is just back from the Moon, where he saw Carruthers and the moon maidens. He offers to fly Steed and Hannah to the Moon, communicates with Ground Control and puts his helmet on. It seals – cutting off his oxygen supply. Steed tries to twist the helmet off, but to no avail. Hannah hits at the visor with an ice hammer, but it will not break. They rip at the suit, but it will not tear. Chummers claws at his helmet, but he dies.

Steed asks Carruthers about the Moon, but Carruthers just repeats the question. This is just as well as the other agents destroyed themselves as soon as they tried to reveal where they had been, acting on an implanted instruction.

The next agent arrives, humming the tune and moving like a bird. Randy Maitland believes that he is a pigeon. He last saw Chummers at the Great Bird Cage, a community project with a decent coop, good food and a bevy of desirable female birds. Maitland offers to arrange an introduction for Steed, and dashes to the open window. He flaps his arms and launches himself into the air, believing that he can fly. His scream is silenced only when he hits the ground below.

Steed and Hannah depart to see if there is anything that can be done for Maitland. Carruthers remains in the apartment.

A Whitehall man arrives soon after, and announces himself as Walters, the Minister for Internal Security. He talks to Carruthers, who he thinks is either communicating in an unfamiliar code or is just plain insolent. Walters telephones Mother, who assures Carruthers that Walters is trustworthy. However, Carruthers' strange response inspires Mother to ask his secretary for the latest code book.

The avengers return. Walters introduces himself, but Steed and Hannah have not heard of him or his Ministry. Walters admits it is a newly created role. Unconvinced, Steed asks if Walters has come from the Moon or the Great Bird Cage. Walters protests that he has come from Whitehall. Steed plays along: "The Great White Hall. And how are the Great White Maidens these days?" Walters laments that he doesn't know the code.

Hannah wonders whether Walters is Maitland's back-up man. Walters maintains that he is no such thing – and hands over his identification as proof. He wishes that he had not been moved from the Ministry of Agriculture and Fisheries – or from Technology before that. Steed and Hannah at last realise that they have made a mistake.

Walters explains that he has come from the Cabinet to brief them. STRAPTIT – the Government's Extrapolation Unit – has concluded that revolutionaries are trying to discredit Britain in the eyes of the world, hence the assassinations. Once confidence has been shattered – both at home and overseas – the revolutionaries will install themselves as an alternative government. Walters warns that, because of his reputation, Steed and anyone with whom he is connected will be in extreme danger. Steed considers this to be business as usual.

Walters wants Steed to attend a BUMFREEZE security meeting at the Government's underground bunker in the Scottish Highlands. He feels that

Steed will be able to advise the Chiefs of Staff on the unorthodox aspects of the situation. As he departs, Walters tells Steed to be there at 9.00pm.

Steed then receives a telephone call. A seductive, bewitching, female voice warns Steed not to go to the bunker – and to expect a gift. The voice breaks into a sinister, yet feminine, chuckle, and then the line goes dead. Steed makes up his mind not to go to the bunker, as the caller was surely daring him to attend. As for the gift, an answer comes soon enough.

The doorbell is rung. Steed's latest visitor is Melanie, now fully clothed. She hands Steed an extravagantly wrapped hat box, which she says has something to do with Freddy Pitt-Miller. She makes her apologies as she is due at a party where everyone will be topless. She departs.

Hannah starts to unwrap the box, thinking that it may contain Freddy's Victorian bowler hat, which Steed covets. However, Steed is suspicious of Melanie's highly coincidental arrival and departure. He takes over, and delicately probes the wrapping. A car backfires outside in a heart-stopping fashion. Steed removes the lid entirely and he and Hannah recoil in horror at the sight of Freddy Pitt-Miller's severed head! Melanie must have been corrupted by the revolutionaries.

Steed decides to go to the BUMFREEZE meeting. He is sure that it is a trap, but it will be an opportunity to meet the enemy. Once he has left, with Hannah in close pursuit, James makes a telephone call to 373-1686 and reports that "Steed's on his way, ducky." The same sinister, feminine laugh drifts from the loudspeaker...

Scene 2: A Helicopter, Somewhere in Scotland – that night

A female helicopter pilot contacts her control centre, identifies herself as Gerda Von Metz, and reports that she is flying over the bunker in Scotland. She will land in one minute and it will take her ten minutes to penetrate the thick concrete walls of the bunker, two hundred feet underground. She demands full power in order to break through. Control confirms full power.

Gerda tests her transmitter unit, removing her leather gauntlets to reveal a large ruby ring on her left hand. As she twists it, it glows – an effect that spreads to cover the whole of the helicopter – and emits a weird electronic pulsing sound. Satisfied, she twists the ruby again and the effects subside. She laughs, telling Control that she cannot wait to meet John Steed. Control – addressing Gerda as "Baroness" – wishes her good luck.

Scene 3: Steed's Bentley – that night

Steed is at the wheel of his vintage Bentley, with Hannah seated beside him, her hair blowing in the wind. They are nearing their destination when Steed upsets Hannah by saying that he wants to enter the bunker alone. She resents his over-protective nature. Steed remarks that being protective towards her makes as much sense as cuddling a barbed wire teddy bear – and that it is better that she is there as back-up should anything go wrong in the bunker.

Scene 4: Top Secret Operations Room, Somewhere in Scotland – that night

The bunker resembles a members' club, furnished with leather-backed armchairs, side tables, and a long conference table, on which sits a red telephone. On a low table to one side is a large, illuminated tropical fish tank. There is only one entrance to the bunker – a sliding, tubular elevator door made of burnished steel.

The room is empty, and yet a voice can be heard, singing about Steed to the tune of *Greensleeves*. Gerda's sinister chuckle and the chants of Melanie and other girls arise from other parts of the room – voices without bodies. Melanie finds this unnerving and complains. Gerda twists the ruby, triggering the attendant visual and aural disturbances. Soon, Wanda, Victoria, Prunella and Melanie – all decked out in kinky black PVC fighting gear with silver trimmings – appear from thin air.

Gerda stands to the fore, imperious in thigh boots and figure-hugging black vinyl with red piping. She tells her acolytes that when Steed arrives, she wants him to see them – at first. There is no point in just killing him, as Steed is more than a man and his influence would live on. He must be disgraced, his legend destroyed. Only then can they achieve their objectives.

The lift door slides open and Steed enters cautiously. He sees Gerda and the others and is sad to register Melanie's presence. Five guns are trained on him. He quips that it is rude to point – especially with firearms. Reaching into his jacket, he bluffs that he will give them no trouble and would like a cigarette. Gerda presses her pistol into his ribs, and removes a gun from his pocket. Steed gets a whiff of her perfume – Patou's *Joy* – and whispers that he wears Lusty-Puff, which comes in a plastic, mock-simulated toad-skin replica of a Turkish tram-driver's jockstrap.

Gerda despises Steed's masculine arrogance, and boasts that she will enjoy destroying his reputation by killing Steed's superiors in his presence. She possesses a machine – the Giant Computer Brain, or "George" for short – that can twist the human mind and erase people from the minds of others, effectively rendering those people invisible. She and her girls will soon appear to vanish, but Steed alone will still be able to hear them.

Gerda twists her ruby ring at the sound of the elevator descending. The girls disappear. Steed chases their voices and their laughter, grasping at the air like a blind man. He is tripped up by an invisible girl, prompting a wave of feminine giggling.

The laughter subsides as General Bull, Admiral Drake and Air Marshal Striker disembark the lift, with Walters in tow. Steed warns them about Gerda and her acolytes, but the military men wave him away. Steed recommends that they all leave the bunker as there are assassins present – delectable, deadly and invisible. A giggle arises that only Steed hears. Bull, though, smells perfume, which Steed attributes to the invisible assailants. The military men believe that Steed has gone stark raving mad. It is such bad form on his part, so terribly un-English.

The Chiefs of Staff commence their meeting, first discussing the security of visiting foreigners. Drake notes that such visitors are vulnerable because of their fondness for sightseeing. Steed remarks that it is their fondness for girls in kinky leather outfits that puts them at risk. Bull advises briefly confining dignitaries to their embassies to ensure that a full security screen can be put in place.

An ashtray rises from a nearby table and hovers in mid-air. Steed alerts the meeting, but the item is immediately returned to its original position. The discussion resumes, exploring the nature of the security arrangements. A chair slides across the room, but is stock still by the time Steed mentions it. The military heads now talk of internment for known dissidents, though Bull notes that the usual subversive organisations appear not to have been involved in the wave of assassinations. Another ashtray and a cigarette lighter dance around in the air, but are swiftly returned to their places when Steed grabs Bull and forces him to look.

Gerda is amused by this little game, and begins counting down from ten. Steed protests further, but a flustered Walters asks him to leave. Nine... eight... Steed pulls a gun from a concealed holster, fires blindly, and orders everyone to leave. Walters goes for help. Suddenly, Steed receives an unseen blow to the stomach and the gun is invisibly twisted from his hand. He grapples with his attacker, takes a blow to the head, and sinks to his knees.

The invisible assassins make quick work of Drake, whom they force backwards onto the conference table. A knife appears to thrust itself into his chest, killing him instantly. Striker – his arms twisted up behind his back – is drowned in the fish tank. The last survivor, Bull, choking from a stranglehold, weakly calls for help. Steed struggles to his feet, but is again felled. Moments later, Bull lies dead.

Hannah – summoned by Walters – bursts from the lift and rushes over to Steed. She surveys the carnage and asks what has happened. "Would you believe... mice?" Steed quips.

Scene 5: Whitehall Communications Centre – next day

Walters sends a Most Secret telex message to Mother. It details STRAPTIT's analysis of the BUMFREEZE fiasco, stating that Steed has suffered a mental breakdown and may be a traitor. He will be further examined at home and, should the diagnosis prove positive, he must be dismissed from the Service. Walters schedules a general conference for 0800 hours on the following day, to be attended by STRAPTIT, BUMFREEZE, FATCHOPS, FUTTOCKS and CRUD. Walters ends the message by stating that rain has stopped play in the Gloucestershire versus Yorkshire cricket match, with the score at 230 runs for five wickets.

Mother subsequently telephones Walters, who is listening to the cricket commentary when the call comes through. Asked about the "crisis", Walters says that Gloucestershire are in a right pickle. Mother agrees, and enquires about the situation with Steed and the revolutionaries. Walters' opinion is that Steed has either defected or gone insane as his explanation for the murder of the Chiefs of Staff is nonsensical. Mother promises to send Mike Johnson, a psychiatrist friend of Steed's, around to Steed's flat – he can be relied upon to give an unbiased diagnosis. In the meantime, Steed will be kept under house arrest – and if he *has* gone over to the other side, then Mother sees only one solution... to kill him!

Scene 6: Steed's Apartment – later

Two military policemen and Mrs. Wild watch over Steed as he is psychoanalysed by Johnson, an eccentric with more tics and twitches than a dog with fleas. The psychiatrist concludes his check with a word association test. Steed's answers are predictable for the most part, until Johnson says "White", to which Steed responds "Slightly chilled", and "Red" which garners "Room temperature" in reply, betraying Steed's love of wine. However, Steed becomes distracted by a smell, and asks Johnson if he can detect *Joy* by Patou. He opens the Mummy case. It seems empty, but it contains the invisible Gerda. Steed concentrates – and suddenly he can see her, though to the others she remains invisible. She expects the psychiatrist's report to be most entertaining.

Hannah calls for Walters, who enters and asks Johnson for his diagnosis. The psychiatrist's verdict leaves Gerda thunderstruck: Steed is in rude health – stable, confident and normal to the point of eccentricity. However, Gerda is not defeated.

Steed suddenly draws a gun and shoots the psychiatrist three times in the chest. Gerda is thrilled. Johnson collapses to the floor.

There is a moment of shock, and then Hannah pounces upon Steed, forcing him to drop the gun. She motions to the military policemen, who level their rifles at Steed. Hannah warns Steed that she is arresting him, though it pains her to do so.

The party and escort march to the door. Steed appears listless, so Gerda blows him a kiss. As the others exit, Gerda chuckles, twists her ruby ring and vanishes. The apartment is now empty other than for the sound of Gerda's sinister laughter, as she celebrates the downfall of her greatest enemy.

Act Two

Scene 7: An Office at the Ministry of Internal Security – next day

The following day, a meeting is convened in Walters' office at the Ministry of Internal Security. The desk and all other furniture, fittings and equipment are decked out in the red, white and blue of the Union Jack – even the wastepaper bin.

Steed stands stiffly to attention, flanked by the two military policemen. Hannah is also present.

His tone solemn, Walters reads aloud from an official document. "John Wykeham Beresford Gascoigne Steed, for cowardice in the face of the enemy, for mental instability, and for the unauthorised slaughter of a Department employee without the necessary permissions, you are sentenced to be dismissed from the Service with dishonour and to be stripped of your insignia according to precedent. Have you anything to say before sentence is carried out?"

Steed does indeed. He objects to the way in which Walters has mispronounced "Wykeham".

At Walters' instruction, Hannah operates the gramophone, which starts to play the *Colonel Bogey March*. She apologises and has to move the needle three times before she homes in on the correct track. Snatches of *Good-bye-ee* and Vera Lynn singing *We'll Meet Again* emanate from the speaker before, finally, *The Stripper* plays softly.

In time with the music, she removes Steed's bowler, crushes it and throws it in the waste basket. She takes his carnation, tears off its petals, and tosses it in the bin. She then tells Steed to empty his pockets. He hands her his Licence to Kill card, several gadgets, a key, a Buckingham Palace garden party season ticket, a blade of grass from the Queen's Lawn at Ascot, a telephone number, and his Old Etonian tie. She drops them all into the bin and then lifts the needle from the record.

Walters orders an inquiry into Steed's collusion with Britain's enemies. In the meantime, Steed is placed under house arrest. Mrs. Wild will act as gaoler and has orders to kill him should he attempt an escape. She handcuffs herself to Steed and drags him off. Walters also makes his exit.

The hotline phone buzzes. A military policeman answers the call. It is from Mother, but the Ministry chief finds the man's strong Geordie accent incomprehensible and entreats his secretary to pass him the code book...

Scene 8: Steed's Apartment – later that day

James, convinced that Steed is innocent, delivers refreshments to the handcuffed pair. Steed and Hannah find that their manacles make it very difficult to pour cups of tea, a situation that amuses Steed. He remarks that it is hard to tell which of them is the captor and which the captive. He also makes an allusion to Charles Baudelaire's 19th century poem *The Cat*, reminding Hannah of a time when they were together. She warns him that she is not susceptible to nostalgia. He twists her attached arm, but she calmly retrieves a gun from her handbag with the other. She has no doubts as to which of them is in control.

Steed turns his attention to the tea tray and entreats Hannah to allow him to butter her crumpet, while perhaps she jams his scone and puts a little marmalade on his muffin. Steed's ribald jesting seems to pay off as Hannah laughs helplessly, but she quickly regains her composure and asks what made him crack.

Steed contests that it is all true: the invisible Amazons, the mind control, everything. As for the psychiatrist, he had alerted his friend, knowing that invisible eyes were watching, and fired three blank cartridges to make the supposed killing look convincing. He advocates opening the Egyptian Mummy case as the psychiatrist is probably still waiting inside and can confirm what he has said. However, when they open the case, the psychiatrist falls out, dead. There is a large bloodstain on his chest. Steed is aghast and Hannah has had her worst fears confirmed.

Steed enquires how many bullet holes Hannah can see on the body. There is just the one, whereas he had fired three shots at point blank range, suggesting a fourth shot has been fired by someone else.

Carruthers unexpectedly appears from a military chest in which he has been sleeping. Steed asks him if he saw who shot the psychiatrist. As before, Carruthers' responses come in the form of repeated phrases that he has recently heard. He then hums the tune of *Greensleeves*.

James enters, about to go out shopping. She spots the psychiatrist's corpse, complains that she has just hoovered, but promises to tidy up when she returns. She leaves, imparting a "Goodbye, ducky" to Carruthers, who resumes his imitations. He mumbles quietly to himself, mimicking Maitland as a pigeon, and then Parsons as a frogman. But then Carruthers says something that strikes Steed as odd: "Steed's on his way, ducky." This is a phrase that neither Steed or Hannah have heard, meaning that Carruthers must have heard it after Steed and Hannah had left for the bunker. Hannah points out that James has a habit of addressing people as "ducky" – and they have just let her stroll out from under their noses.

It occurs to Hannah that James might have said the telephone number aloud when she called the enemy. If she did, Carruthers could well have heard it. Hannah and Steed attempt to prompt Carruthers to repeat the number by saying again what they had said before they had left for the bunker. This has the desired effect on the befuddled agent, who even imitates the sound of the dial spinning and returning. "Three... seven... three. One... six... eight... six... Steed's on his way, ducky," he recites. Steed congratulates Carruthers, who reverts to his impression of Maitland.

Steed dials the number on the loudspeaker telephone. The call connects and he hears a snatch of *Greensleeves*, which he recognises as the tune that Cholmondleigh and the others had been humming. "Greensleeves Finishing Academy for the Daughters of Gentlefolk. You bring them in, we bring them out. Can I help you?" chirps a young-sounding female voice at the other end of the line.

Hannah introduces herself as Mrs. Chaddersley-Corbett and arranges a visit to the Academy in order to check its suitability for her niece, who is coming out. She is invited to go to Maidenhair Manor at Hymen-on-the-Green, near Maidenhead, later in the day. The receptionist ends the call by singing the Academy's jingle: "There's naught so sad as an English rose left where the lower-class daisy grows."

Hannah determines to go to the Academy alone. She is beginning to believe Steed's story, but he could have had a live round among those blanks and, after the court martial, must remain under house arrest. She swiftly removes the handcuff from her wrist and then locks it around one of the banisters, high on the stairs, leaving Steed strung up like a puppet. She exits.

Fearing that Hannah will not tell Mother of her movements, Steed decides to employ Carruthers – who Steed observes is dancing a jig like Nureyev – to contact their superior on his behalf. He trains Carruthers to dial 000-1111 using the payphone on the street outside as his own phone line has "probably got more taps on it than Fred Astaire." He must tell Mother that Mrs. Wild has gone to Maidenhair Manor at Hymen-on-the-Green and is in danger. Mother should send help immediately. "St. George for England!" shouts Steed as the hapless agent exits.

One-handed and with considerable dexterity, Steed pours himself a glass of Burgundy and raises it in a toast: "And Nuits-Saint-Georges for France!"

Scene 9: Conversation à Deux

A couple of giggly girls are using the telephone box. Carruthers knocks on the glass, but they ignore him. He opens the door and repeats a phase he heard earlier: "May I butter your crumpet?" The girls scream and run away. Carruthers enters, dials the number that Steed gave him and drops some coins in the slot.

The telephone rings on Mother's desk. He answers the call as his secretary, Miss Lacey, watches on.

Bubbling over with confidence, Carruthers delivers his message, but in a muddled fashion: "Hello, my name is Fred Astaire. I've got more taps on me than a telephone box. My hymen is green and it's in danger from Nureyev."

Mother has Miss Lacey pass him the code book. He rifles through it as Carruthers blurts out further nonsense. Before long, Mother believes that he is speaking to the American Vice President, Spiro Agnew, who is drunk and is being indecently assaulted by an insane Russian who refuses to take precautions.

Mother instructs Miss Lacey to put him through to the CIA.

Scene 10: Madame Gerda's Academy for Young Ladies – late afternoon

The Georgian-styled drawing room of the Greensleeves Academy is airy and sunlit. Two sets of French windows overlook the terrace and a large portrait of the proprietor, Baroness Gerda von Metz, hangs above an ornate fireplace.

Gerda, every inch the country gentlewoman dressed in tweeds and pearls, is instructing six girls in micro-mini school uniforms in the arts of combat. Wanda and Victoria are engaged in a hand-to-hand battle, Prunella and Nicola are fighting with knives, and Jasmine and Emma are cleaning revolvers while humming *Greensleeves*. Gerda delivers instructions and advice on technique and how to exploit the weaknesses of the male. She asks the girls a series of questions: "Who are we?" The future. "What do we want?" Absolute power. "How do we get it?" By terror. "Who are our allies?" All women. "What is our god?" The machine!

Melanie enters from the basement. Electronic noises from below are silenced when she closes the door behind her. She has come up as the thing down there frightens her. Gerda reassures her that it loves them all and can only hurt their enemies. Melanie returns to the basement on the promise that Prunella will relieve her shortly. Gerda worries that Melanie needs more time to adjust to their ways.

The doorbell chimes *Greensleeves*. An eighth girl, Miranda, soon enters, also in uniform. She announces that Mrs. Chaddersley-Corbett has arrived, having telephoned earlier. Gerda bids Miranda show the visitor in and the girls switch from combat training to embroidery, flower arranging and deportment.

Hannah enters, dressed in riding clothes, hat and ponytail wig, and introduces herself as Jane Chaddersley-Corbett, playing it very horsey and hearty. She declares that she has come to talk about her niece, who needs "finishin' properly".

Gerda has a nagging feeling that she knows this woman and asks if they have met. Hannah thinks it unlikely, unless Gerda hunts, engages in point-to-point or rides horses – and notes that Gerda is not English. "No, Swedish," Gerda confirms before revealing that the Academy is an exclusive establishment. It sports a small number of girls and an exclusively female staff since she considers that women are more conscientious than men. Gerda dismisses the girls, who curtsey and exit demurely through the French windows.

Gerda enquires about Hannah's niece and is told that the girl is 17 and has anti-establishment tendencies that she hopes the Academy will eradicate. Hannah spies the door to the basement and, keen to investigate, she asks to see the Academy's prospectus. Gerda leaves to pick up a copy.

Finding that the basement door is locked, Hannah turns her attention to a Regency writing desk and forces the lock with a device hidden in her riding crop. However, she finds nothing of interest inside. Next, she breaks into the drawers of a circular library table, unaware that Gerda is watching from behind her portrait, which gradually turns transparent. Hannah returns to the basement door, meaning to try once more to open it – and it opens. Melanie enters and recognises Mrs. Wild, who quickly knocks her unconscious and hides her body behind a sofa. Moments later, Gerda returns and declares that she now knows who Hannah is.

Hannah makes for the French windows, but three of Gerda's students appear in the threshold of the first and another four in the second, and advance on Hannah. She deals with three of them with a series of karate moves, but another throws a gold mesh net over her that tightens around her. Gerda delivers a withering verdict: "The famous Hannah Wild... The girl who fights like a man – on the side of men. You're a traitor to your sex, my dear."

Wanda wants to torture Hannah, but Gerda means to hand Hannah over to George, a machine that will twist her mind and turn her into an ally and a great asset to the cause. One minute's exposure to the machine will be enough for Gerda's present purposes. As three of the girls carry the struggling Hannah down into the basement, Gerda reassures her that the treatment is painless and causes no physical damage. Wanda follows to supervise.

James arrives to warn Gerda that Steed is proving more resilient than they had expected. She reports that she had found the psychiatrist alive and had to kill him herself. She also remarks that Mrs. Wild is close to believing Steed's story. Gerda is unworried – George will soon have dealt with the troublesome Mrs. Wild. Gerda waves James away, ordering her to ensure that the mind-processed Hannah carries out her instructions.

As James exits, Hannah enters, zombie-like, flanked by two girls. She announces that she serves the cause and John Steed is her enemy. "What must you do about him?" inquires Gerda. A savage mania suddenly overtakes Hannah as she roars "Kill him! Kill him! Kill him!"

Scene 11: Ministry of Internal Security – early evening

In Walters' office, a grey-haired secretary taps away at an electronic shorthand machine as a nurse gives Carruthers an injection and then departs. Carruthers complains that Mother has been talking gibberish and seems not to understand that Steed and Mrs. Wild are in danger. However, Walters realises that the injection has not worked when Carruthers burbles that Fred Astaire, a Russian named Nureyev, and a furrier called Hymie Green have kidnapped Mrs. Wild. "They want to get their hands on her muffin," he says, earnestly.

Walters summons the nurse and instructs her to lead Carruthers away. Before they exit, Carruthers remarks that a light on the world map on the wall has just been extinguished. This marks an agent's death on foreign soil. Walters grabs a hat to hold across his chest in a gesture of respect, and declares: "Soon they'll be going out all over Europe... France may no longer call us perfidious Albion and our gunboats may have all become bijou residences on Chelsea Reach, but while those lights burn there are still some corners of a foreign land where brave, ex-public school men still perjure, corrupt, blackmail, cheat, stab, shoot, strangle and disembowel for the honour of England... Rule Britannia!"

Hannah enters as Carruthers and the nurse depart. Resisting the mind control, she tenders her resignation in order to stop herself from killing Steed. Walters refuses her request, even when she tells him that she is a security risk. Walters scoffs at the suggestion. Undeterred, she surrenders her gun, only for Walters to return it and propose that she takes a few days off to recover from the hurt and disappointment she must feel about Steed. He will send someone to take Steed off her hands. Hannah exits, defeated. Once she has left, Walters telephones Mother to tell him that he is most concerned about Mrs. Wild.

Scene 12: Steed's Apartment – minutes later

Steed remains handcuffed to the banister in his apartment. He somewhat awkwardly pours himself another glass of Burgundy. As he does so, Hannah enters silently, still attired in her riding outfit. She closes the front door, at which point Steed registers her presence. Her facial expression is blank.

Steed asks about the Greensleeves Academy, but Hannah claims not to have heard of the place. She slings a scarf around Steed's neck, and begins to strangle him. He resists with his free hand, gets a nerve hold on her wrist, and propels her to the floor. She leaps up and snatches a rapier from the wall. Steed grabs a furled umbrella and a fencing bout ensues. Steed tells Hannah that she is being controlled somehow – and knocks the rapier from her grasp. This merely inspires Hannah to fight even more fiercely, but finally Steed manages to send the weapon flying.

Torn between wanting to kill Steed and save him by breaking her conditioning, Hannah retrieves a gun from a drawer. Steed takes one last sip from his glass and warns Hannah that she will regret it if she shoots him. She apologises in a choked whisper – and fires three bullets into him. The glass drops and shatters on the floor. Steed hangs limp from the banister, a blossom of red spreading across his shirt front. Hannah screams his name, the evil influence broken by her murderous act. She frees him from his bonds, and cradles him tenderly in her arms on the floor.

Steed weakly tells her that he has little time left. Hannah begs him not to talk. Steed, fading away, asks for one last kiss – a proper one. As she kisses him on the lips, his arms encircle her in a powerful embrace, and he kisses her hard. He then rolls over so that he is on top of her. She surrenders for a moment before furiously rejecting his advance, realising she has fallen prey to an underhand trick.

Steed is not dying. The blood is in fact Nuits-Saint-Georges Burgundy, the gun was loaded with blanks once again – and Steed doesn't even have the good grace to be fatigued. Both angry and relieved, Hannah whips him with a cushion, an assault that Steed repels like a boxer, letting the blows bounce off his raised arms.

Steed protests that Hannah had to be made to think that she had killed him – to break the spell. There were three more blanks in the gun and he had prayed that she would use it. Rather that than an axe – it could have been very nasty. Hannah tells Steed that there is a machine at the Academy that permits Gerda to process and control people's minds. "It... takes you over. It's horrible!" she breathes.

Steed feels that they should pay the Academy a fresh visit – together this time – and since he is now supposed to be dead, they will have surprise on their side.

Hannah goes to change into a more appropriate outfit – "something uncomfortable" she jokes – and Steed asks for a clean shirt.

There is suddenly the sound of a key in the front door lock. Steed quickly lies down and pretends to be dead.

James enters, gun at the ready. She spots Steed's body, smiles and then visibly relaxes. She crosses to the telephone and dials a number.

Steed crawls towards James, but accidentally makes a noise. James spins round and trains her gun on Steed. James is disappointed to learn from Steed that he has killed Mrs. Wild as she seemed keen on doing the same to him. On reflection, James sees the advantages – she can kill Steed herself and make it look as if Mrs. Wild had killed him and then had taken her own life.

Hannah, now attired in a red leather fighting suit, enters silently and creeps towards James while Steed distracts his treacherous butler. About to strike, Hannah is unexpectedly intercepted by Steed's pop art hatstand, which springs into life. Its womanly shape twists to grab at Hannah, taking her very much by surprise.

This development distracts James and gives Steed an opportunity to attack. Within seconds, two fights are in progress: Hannah versus the all-too-animated hatstand to one side of the room, and Steed and James to the other.

Steed chops James in the midriff, resulting in a clanging sound and a sharp pain in Steed's hand. Steed realises that he is fighting a robot! The pair disappear from view over the back of the sofa. Restraining the struggling robot, Steed exclaims that "This is a great new experience. I'm about to unscrew a girl!"

Hannah, meanwhile, grasps at an empty Burgundy bottle and breaks it over the hatstand's head. The unfaithful furnishing crashes to the floor, immobilised. Pleased with her handiwork, Hannah asks if she can lend Steed a hand.

Steed has no need of a hand – he has James', which he throws to her, followed by a leg and two arms. A short while later he appears from behind the sofa holding a tangle of wires, a foot and James' head and quips that his butler has gone to pieces. Finally, he presents the torso, which sports two large breasts. "Somebody boobed," he remarks. Hannah groans at the cheap joke, but Steed is actually referring to the fact that, just above the navel, he has seen the wording "Ministry of Technology, Experimental Division," and the initials H.W.

Somebody has indeed boobed, as Steed and Hannah know somebody with those initials, the erstwhile Minister for Technology, now at the Ministry of Internal Security – Horace Walters!

Steed comments to Hannah that it is high time that they paid a visit to Walters' office in Maidenhead...

Scene 13: Ministry of Internal Security – that night

Carruthers, dancing a jig and singing *Tiptoe Through the Tulips*, enters Walters' office. The nurse is in hot pursuit. Carruthers invites Walters to join in, but Walters ignores him and asks the nurse about Carruthers' condition. She explains that the more injections she administers, the worse Carruthers becomes. Walters gestures that the nurse should take Carruthers away. She leads the unfortunate agent from the office, crossing paths with Steed and Hannah as they arrive to see Walters.

Steed gets straight to the point. "Hello, Walters. Made any good robots lately?" The Minister calls for security, but Steed and Hannah have dealt with the guards.

Hannah and Steed accuse Walters of having created James and recommended her as a servant, saying that she had maximum security clearance. Walters recalls that a backroom boffin had made some prototype robots, but he himself had very little to do with them. Steed and Hannah persist, suggesting that Walters had turned traitor after becoming fed up with being shuffled between departments.

Walters calmly lifts a red, white and blue tea cosy and grasps a red, white and blue gun that was hidden beneath it. Steed and Mrs. Wild's suspicions were correct. Walters had tired of his professional – and personal – status and put his time at the Ministry of Technology to excellent use, having them develop robots, the Mind Machine, and some other little surprises.

Walters gestures towards a door concealed in the Union Jack mural. A secret room lies beyond. However, Walters is distracted by the unexpected reappearance of Carruthers, whom he shoots in the arm. Steed reacts quickly and chops at Walters, who falls to the floor. Once again, there is a clang and Steed's hand smarts.

Carruthers exits, clutching his wounded arm, while Steed and Hannah bend down next to Walters. "I told you I changed my personal status," says the Minister weakly, his voice sounding like a tape recorder running down. He reveals that the woman they know as Gerda was formerly the real Walters. "Marvellous what doctors can do... today." Walters expires with a twang.

Steed and Hannah kick the concealed door open and disappear through it.

Scene 14: Brain Room of the Master Computer

Steed and Hannah advance cautiously into the computer room. Around them, banks of lights wink and data tapes spin. They find a throne-like chair and a circular table, both fitted with metal restraining straps. Hannah recognises it as the place she had been taken to to be processed.

Steed flicks a switch. The computer twinkles into life. It has a sort of face — eyes, a nose, and a mouth. From its mouth comes a voice not unlike that of the urbane English actor George Sanders. It introduces itself as George, "your friendly neighbourhood threat to mankind," and warns Steed not to play with its switches. Steed shakes hands with a convenient protrusion. Hannah declines to do likewise until she is sure that it is a hand.

The computer reveals that it was made by Gerda, and that its function will be to help run things once her plan is enacted. In case the nature of the plan is in any doubt, it sings a little of *If I Ruled the World* in a very decent baritone. The avengers raise their guns and Steed advises Hannah to aim for the transistor banks. George delivers a low pulsing sound which paralyses them both, their guns clattering to the floor.

George raises the alarm. This meets with an immediate response from Gerda, who enters with four of her Amazons — wearing black vinyl fighting suits with silver piping and each carrying a gun — and a hefty brute called Scarman. The pulsing sound ceases and the girls overpower the intruders.

Hannah asks Gerda if it is true that she is actually the real Walters. Gerda looks herself up and down and says, "More or less. You see, it's women who are in the ascendant today. I thought I'd join them rather than try to beat them. Tomorrow the world will be ruled by women."

Steed points out that Scarman is a "fine, big lass". The henchman moves to respond — violently — but Gerda dissuades him from such action. Scarman is tolerated because the girls need something to play with. There is also the mind machine, notes Steed — another male. Gerda comments that George is a special case. He adores women and loves the feel of their hands on his switches. They are building him a mate. Steed finds this most amusing: "How sweet. You'll be able to listen to the patter of tinny feet," he wisecracks.

The girls strap Steed to the throne and Hannah to the circular table. Gerda taunts Steed that in half an hour George will destroy the mind of every person of above average intelligence quotient in London. Steed is relieved that at least the British Government will be unaffected. Gerda barely notices the witticism and continues. The population will be putty in her hands with London robbed of its leaders and her conquest of Mankind will have begun.

Steed points out that there is a device that is programmed to respond automatically to this kind of attack — The Doomsday Weapon. "The moment you start to send out your radiations, it will seek you out and destroy you," warns Steed.

George confirms that such a device could well exist. It would be a reasonable precaution for any government to take. However, George believes that Mother, the Prime Minister, and Steed would have a deactivation code word.

Since only Steed is to hand, Gerda connects him with electrodes to George, who will pluck the override code from his mind. For starters, though, she wants to know what plans are in place for an alternative regional government, something that only Steed's "small and arrogant department" knows. However, Steed has no intention of making this easy for George, whom he dubs a "nasty little plucker".

A humming sound starts and grows in intensity. George's screen lights up and a faint image of a document starts to appear on it. Gerda recognises it as the document she wants to see, but Steed concentrates hard and the document disappears – to be replaced by a series of images of events that Steed recalls from his past. He is proving a difficult subject.

As time is short, Gerda resorts to more expedient methods, attaching electrodes to Hannah's head. Gerda warns Steed that, unless he talks, George will empty Mrs. Wild's mind, leaving her a mindless idiot. It is his choice.

Steed holds his nerve. Gerda orders George to proceed and a humming noise commences – different this time. Hannah writhes in pain. Steed focuses his mind on thoughts of Hannah. A close-up image of Hannah's face appears on the screen, causing Hannah's discomfort to subside. Steed is protecting her from the process.

Gerda realises that she will have to break Steed's concentration. She snaps her fingers. The Fantasy Sadist enters and approaches Steed. She brandishes a whip and is dressed in a corset, shoulder-length gloves, and thigh boots – all in black leather. For a moment, the image of Hannah disappears, causing Steed's friend to cry out in pain, before Steed reasserts his mental control. Hannah calms.

Gerda calls in the Fantasy Maid, one of her Amazons dressed as a French serving maid. She wears a short satin dress with frilly lace decoration, black stockings and suspenders, with the effect being rounded off with a feather duster. Steed struggles to keep his concentration, but resists temptation.

Next up, Gerda summons a girl who combines Steed's two greatest delights – women and horses. The Fantasy Masochist trots in, bridled and bitted like a horse, wearing boots and spurs, and with a long mane hanging from her head and ponytail attached to her rear. Steed agrees that she has a "lovely pair of fetlocks," but manages to keep his cool.

At this point, Melanie strolls in. She wears a skimpy, sexy outfit, and carries a cricket bat that she has found in a cupboard upstairs. She thinks it once belonged to the Archbishop of Canterbury as it has the word "Grace" painted on it.

Steed is gobsmacked, not by the sight of the near-naked Melanie, but by the bat, which belonged to the great cricketer W.G. Grace – an heirloom lost to posterity for nearly a century. He is momentarily in heaven – a state not reflected in Hannah's face, which contorts in agony as her image again fades from George's screen. Steed realises his mistake and regains his focus, as does the image of Hannah before him. "Sorry, Mrs. Wild," he laments. "Just a batty moment."

Gerda is furious with George and warns that he will suffer for his failure. Steed invites George to study his screen as the computer could do with some excitement. A moving image of Hannah resolves. To begin with she is fully dressed, but then she begins removing items of clothing, in the style of a stripper. As she discards each garment, it becomes apparent that her body is covered with mathematical equations and formulae. George begins to overheat. All those quadratics! The calculus! The logarithms! And then, Hannah is down to her knickers, beneath which is hidden the final equation. Hannah protests. Steed reassures her that a gentleman would never tell. "*But you're no gentleman!*" Hannah complains. On screen, fraction by fraction, Hannah begins to slide her knickers down.

Gerda wants Hannah to stop. George wants the knickers to drop. He is experiencing the very peak of sensual excitement in his circuits. An explosion rips through one of his computer banks, and instantly Steed and Hannah's restraints snap open. A loud hum rises.

Scarman throws himself at Steed. In the same moment, Hannah lunges for a gun on the floor, grabs it and keeps Gerda and the others covered. Steed and Scarman struggle, breaking items of furniture over each other's heads, exchanging blows, sending each other crashing into the computer banks. There is a small blast every time that George takes an impact in the tussle. Sparks fly. Smoke rises. Lights wink ever more insistently. Data spools spin faster and faster. The humming noise grows louder, more distressed sounding, until finally Steed defeats Scarman, who slams into the centre of the computer with one last, great thud – and George explodes. In the melee, Gerda escapes to fight another day, catching a ride in a waiting helicopter, but her Amazons all go limp and collapse.

Steed and Hannah survey the devastation. They suddenly find themselves speaking in unison and realise they have become telepathically linked, a side effect of their having been wired up to George. They wonder what their next step ought to be. Since they can read each other's minds, they realise that they have a romantic assignation ahead of them.

The pair are just about to slip off together when they are interrupted by Mother, who has just arrived at the Academy. He calls out for Steed and Mrs.

Wild as he enters the Brain Room. He is positively beaming with delight and remarks that they have done a splendid job. Suddenly a loud gunshot rings out, and blood spreads across Mother's chest. "I just want to say that... that I've just been shot," he blurts before breathing his last.

"Well, here we go again!" say Steed and Hannah in a single voice as they run off to investigate.

Performances

Regional: Birmingham Theatre (now Birmingham Hippodrome)
Hurst Street, Birmingham, West Midlands B5 4TB, United Kingdom
Auditorium Seating Capacity: 1,850 seats

Thursday 15th July to Saturday 24th July 1971
at 7.30pm (Mondays, Tuesdays, Thursdays and Fridays)
and 5.00pm and 8.00pm (Wednesdays and Saturdays)
A total of 12 performances (greatest possible attendance: 22,200)

London West End: Prince of Wales Theatre
31 Coventry Street, London W1D 6AS, United Kingdom
Auditorium Seating Capacity: 1,133 seats

Monday 2nd August to Saturday 21st August 1971
at 8.00pm (Mondays to Thursdays)
and 6.00pm and 8.50pm (Fridays and Saturdays)
A total of 24 performances (greatest possible attendance: 27,192)

Cast

Simon Oates (John Steed), Sue Lloyd (Hannah Wild), Kate O'Mara (Gerda Von Metz, the leader of the Forces of Evil), Jeremy Lloyd (Bobby Carruthers, an MI5 agent), Anthony Sharp (Horace Walters, the Minister for Internal Security), Julie Neubert (James, Steed's butler), Wendy Hall (Melanie, one of Steed's ladies), John F. Landry (Mother, MI5 chief / Randy Maitland, an MI5 agent / General Bull) (*), Mary Llewellin (Miss Lacey, Mother's secretary), Kenton Moore (Tom 'Snipper' Parsons, an MI5 agent / Scarman, Gerda's bodyguard) (**), Paul McDowell (Jack 'Chummers' Cholmondleigh, an MI5 agent / Military Policeman), Lisa Collings (Victoria, one of Gerda's gang), Gail Grainger (Prunella, one of Gerda's gang / Nurse / a Fantasy Maid), Gypsie

Kemp (Wanda, one of Gerda's gang / a Fantasy Sadist), Joanna Ross (Nicola, one of Gerda's gang / a Fantasy Masochist), Kubi Chaza (Jasmine, one of Gerda's gang / a Fantasy Cricketer), Helen Gill (Emma, one of Gerda's gang), Heather Kyd (Miranda, one of Gerda's gang), Derek Tansley (Air Marshal Striker / Johnson, a Psychiatrist), Tim Buckland (Admiral Drake / Military Police Sergeant)

Members of the cast were also called on to play various dignitaries, wives, guards, secretaries and passers-by.

(*) A publicity photograph exists of Jeremy Lloyd in the role of Mother, suggesting that John F. Landry was either a late addition to the cast or was simply not available for the photocall.

(**) A publicity photograph exists of Paul McDowell in the role of Scarman.

Production

Script – Terence Feely and Brian Clemens
Producer – John C. Mather
Director – Leslie Phillips
Set Designer – Michael Young
Lighting – Nick Chelton
Sound – Anthony Horder
Sound and Lighting Equipment – Theatre Projects Ltd.
Fight Sequence Arranger – Tim Condren
Stage Manager – Peter Charles

Scenery and Props
Scenery built by Victor Mara Ltd.
Helicopter by Hall Stage Equipment Ltd.
Bentley by Holywell Displays
Hatstand Model by Rootstein
Typewriter by British Olivetti Ltd.
Hamlet Cigars by Benson & Hedges Ltd.
Cigarettes by Dunhills Ltd. (Birmingham) / Rothmans Ltd. (London)
Lighters by Ronson Ltd.
Champagne by Moet & Chandon
Furniture by Mooredan Ltd., Old Times Furnishing Co. Ltd., J.C. Farley and The Trading Post

Costumes
Mr Oates' Suits by Benson, Perry and Whitley
Miss Lloyd's Costumes designed by Berkeley Sutcliffe and made by Atomage Ltd.
All Other Costumes designed by Ronald Cobb
and made by Atomage Ltd., Isolyn Ltd. and Brian Reed
Wigs by Wig Creations
Frogman Suit by Breakaway at Simpsons (Piccadilly) Ltd.
Uniforms by Bermans Ltd.
Tights by Berkshire International
Boots by Sacha (International) Ltd.
Girls' Hairstyles by Bruno of Birmingham (Birmingham) / Vidal Sassoon (London)

Film Sequences
Directed by Don Sheldrop
Produced by R.L.S. Productions Ltd

Foyer Photographs by Tom Hustler of Mayfair
Poster / Flier Design (London) by Russell / James Associates
Technical Advice by Xirot Productions
Presented by The John Mather Organisation by arrangement with Bernard Delfont

For The John Mather Organisation Ltd.
Production Manager – John Rothenberg
Manager and Stage Manager – Peter Charles
Deputy Stage Manager – Bill Clancy
Assistant Stage Managers – Tom Dolby and Myles McMahon
Sound Controller – Cordelia Mansall
Wardrobe Master (Birmingham) – John Bowen
Wardrobe Mistress (London) – Kay Gilbert
Master Carpenter (Birmingham) – John Jones
Publicity Representatives – Fred Hift Associates, The Carlton Theatre, Haymarket

For The Birmingham Theatre
Proprietors – Moss Empires Ltd
Chairman – Prince Littler CBE
Managing Director – Louis Benjamin

Resident Musical Director – Gwyn Davies
Manager and Licensee – Wilfred May
House Manager – Barry Hopson

For The Prince of Wales Theatre
Licensed by the Greater London Council to Bernard Delfont
Lessees – Prime Presentations Ltd.
General Manager – Brent Maxfield
Box Office Manager – Ken Limbrey
Master Carpenter – Tom Povey
Chief Engineer – George Fleck
Property Master – Jimmy Hinchcliffe

Analysis

The Avengers ceased to be a going concern at the end of 1969, by which time all the ITV regions had worked their way through the first run of Series 6 starring Patrick Macnee and Linda Thorson. Further episodes would not be forthcoming (at least not until 1976 and *The New Avengers*) as a result of American sponsorship being withdrawn. This money had been in place since 1964 and made the production of the filmed episodes possible. However, the series remained popular in the United Kingdom, as evidenced by ITV launching itself into a series of regional repeats of Series 4, 5 and 6 between May 1969 and December 1971. Consequently, despite the fact that fresh episodes were no longer being produced, *The Avengers* remained in the consciousness of the British public in the early years of the 1970s. One result of this enduring popularity was that *The Avengers* was revived as a theatrical production in 1971.

Hugely ambitious and technically challenging, *The Avengers* on stage was hailed by its producer, John Chartres Mather (1923-2004), as the show which would "blast the British theatre into the seventies". In a July 1971 edition of the *Birmingham Evening Mail*, Mather further extolled its virtues: "It is a very big venture. I first had the idea two years ago, but at the time I hadn't the money or the backers. It's a great piece of hokum and there will be helicopters, cars, explosions and glamorous girls. It will be a very fast moving production and scenes have been written in a sort of filmic way."

Mather had been involved in theatre since the age of 14, when he staged his first play in his native city of Edinburgh. His early experience included a year as a stagehand at the Dundee Repertory Theatre, similar work in London, and then troop entertainments during the World War II. After the war, he staged musical extravaganzas – to varying degrees of success – before forming Chartres Productions in 1951 with partners George Routledge and Gordon White. Although they were primarily involved in musical theatre, their most notable production – at least in hindsight – was a British theatrical tour featuring famed horror film star Bela Lugosi in his signature role of Dracula. Lugosi performed *Dracula* on 229 occasions between 30th April and 13th October 1951 – and yet the production still lost money. Mather would go on to work with the Danziger Brothers, producing 26 episodes of *Mayfair Mysteries* principally for the American market. In 1954, Mather supplied the script for the Danzigers' *Devil Girl from Mars*, a somewhat turgid affair that has become a cult movie. This production would prove important for *The Avengers* stage play, as it was during the making of this film that Mather first became aware of the Atomage fetishwear manufacturer that costumed the film's star Patricia Laffan in a striking black polyvinyl chloride (PVC) outfit. In the mid-fifties, Mather set himself up as a talent agent and based himself in Rome, catering to the many American movie companies filming in Italy at that time due to the attractively low production costs. John C. Mather International proved to be a great success, expanding by 1960 to Madrid, Paris and Munich. It was eventually merged with the William Morris Agency of America, at which point Mather was put in charge of their European offices. He left the company in 1970 to return to theatre production.

Several British newspapers carried brief interviews with Mather in April 1971, in which he claimed that the groundwork was done for the £35,000 production (approximate comparative value in 2024 according to the Bank of England: £423,530), licensing had been confirmed with EMI, and that a script by old hand *Avengers* scribes Terence Feely and Brian Clemens was in place.

Liverpool born Terence Feely (1928-2000) initially entered the field of journalism after studying English and psychology at the city's Jesuit College. He secured a small job on a Middlesborough local newspaper prior to moving to London, where he joined the editorial team of the *Sunday Graphic*. As a sideline, Feely began writing submissions for film scripts, one of which – *Heartbeat*, written in 1955 – attracted the interest of legendary film director Alfred Hitchcock. These endeavours led to Feely scriptwriting for television from 1959, when he was commissioned to write the first of several episodes of the Associated-Rediffusion crime drama *No Hiding Place*. Feely's contribution to *The Avengers* came in the early days of the series, when Ian Hendry was the star and Patrick Macnee the support, and was limited to two 1961 episodes – *Nightmare* and *Dragonsfield*. (He would go on to contribute two scripts to *The New Avengers* in the mid-seventies.) He would later return to ABC Television in 1965 as story editor on their flagship anthology series *Armchair Theatre* and *Armchair Mystery Theatre*. He was also involved in developing an *Armchair Theatre* production – James Mitchell's *A Magnum for Schneider* (1967) – into a full-blown series, *Callan*. At around the same time, Feely also contributed two scripts to Patrick McGoohan's game-changing espionage series *The Prisoner* – *The Schizoid Man* (1967) and *The Girl Who Was Death* (1968). When Feely came to collaborate with Brian Clemens on *The Avengers* stage play script, he had recently supplied two well-regarded scripts for Gerry and Sylvia Anderson's *UFO* – *The Man Who Came Back* and *Timelash*.

Brian Clemens OBE (1931-2015), born in Croydon, Surrey, initially worked as a messenger boy at the J. Walter Thompson advertising agency. Previously, during national service at Aldershot, he had been a weapons training instructor in the Royal Army Ordnance Corps, a role which would hold him in good stead for his eventual career writing thrillers. Having risen to the position of copywriter at J. Walter Thompson, Clemens began submitting story ideas and scripts to television companies and, in 1955, had one accepted and produced by the BBC – *Valid for Single Journey Only* – which led to employment as a staff writer with independent film and television producers the Danziger brothers. The Danzigers had a reputation for producing 'B' movies and film series television in a perfunctory, cheap and cheerful style, but this was an excellent grounding for Clemens, who wrote dozens of 'quickie' scripts for them and others in a short period. Between 1955 and 1959, he wrote 38 scripts for the Danzigers' anthology drama *The Vise*, as well as contributing multiple scripts to *Dial 999*, *Man from Interpol* and *The Cheaters*. Many of these were supplied under the pseudonym Tony O'Grady, a name which employed his mother Suzanna's maiden name. Clemens also branched out in 1959 to write for ITC film productions, initially supplying two scripts for H.G. Wells' *Invisible Man* before penning the first episode of *Danger Man* to go into production – *The View from the Villa* – and 1963 episodes of *Man of the World* and *The Sentimental Agent*. Clemens' episode for the latter series – *A Very Desirable Plot* – witnessed the television debut of Diana Rigg, who would of course join *The Avengers* a short while after. Clemens' own association with *The Avengers* was already well underway by this point. Indeed, it dated back to *Brought to Book*, the second episode transmitted in January 1961. In total, Clemens wrote or co-wrote an unequalled 32 episodes of *The Avengers* (49 including *The New Avengers*) and, from 1965, acted as associate producer and then producer on the series. Clemens contributed scripts to several other series during the 1960s, including *The Baron*, *The Champions* and *Adam Adamant Lives!*, and, at the time of his involvement in *The Avengers* stage play, was writing scripts for ITC's *The Persuaders!* and the Hammer Film feature film *Dr. Jekyll and Sister Hyde* (1971).

Terence Feely later reflected on his and Clemens' approach to *The Avengers* stage play when talking to David Richardson (*TV Zone* issue 47, Visual

Imagination Ltd., October 1993): "We had a wild story, far wilder than anything that appeared on television, because we said that if we were going to do it for theatre we had to be further out than anything the audience had seen on television, otherwise why should they come to the theatre?"

When his new *Avengers* production was first announced to the press, John Mather was still in the process of casting the show, or, as he described it, "the difficult task of finding the stage equivalents of the Patrick Macnees, the Honor Blackmans and the Diana Riggs of this world". He had, in fact, approached Patrick Macnee to reprise his role of John Steed, but the popular *Avengers* star – an experienced stage performer – had declined the offer as he felt strongly that *The Avengers* was suited only to television. "The stage is a place that should look dazzling and beautiful, but basically remain a place for the exchange of ideas, dialogue and characters – and not whiz-bang-wallop," said Macnee when interviewed for Dave Rogers' *The Complete Avengers* (Boxtree, 1989).

Mather was not disheartened by Macnee's decision and announced in the Saturday newspapers of 1st May 1971 that actor Simon Oates (1932-2009) would be taking to the stage as the production's youthful and dashing John Steed. Although not a household name in quite the same way as Patrick Macnee, Oates was familiar to audiences in the United Kingdom for his roles in several television series. These included *The Mask of Janus* (1965), *The Spies* (1966) *The Three Musketeers* (1966-67) and, most notably, *Doomwatch*. From 1970 to 1972, he co-starred in this successful BBC drama series about a government department investigating environmental and technological concerns. He had also starred in the science fiction 'B' movie *The Terrornauts* (1967).

Speaking to the author of this chapter in November 2008, Simon Oates described how he had become an actor. "I was at drama school and we were invited to be in a mystery play at the Everyman with Robert Eddison. I was seeing a girl at the time who was actually a pro actress. She was working at Chesterfield for Gerry Glaister, who became a big television producer and director, and she met me and saw this, knowing I wanted to turn pro. Her father, who was very wealthy, had arranged for her to have her own repertory company for a period of time. She said, 'I'll tell you what, you were my leading man in my company, and I'll give you a list of the plays that you did', which of course I hadn't done at all! She went back to Chesterfield, where she was a juvenile lady, met Gerry and recommended me to him. He took her word for it and so I started in Chesterfield on 18th July 1954 in a play called *Someone at the Door*. I went up there as a fully fledged actor only having done amateur stuff before, but I blagged my way through it and that's how I started. Fortnightly rep at Chesterfield, York, Birmingham and all over the place in various rep companies. You had a week to learn your lines and moves, then you played them. When you were playing them, you were rehearsing the next week's play. You were in rehearsal at ten o'clock until five o'clock, and then on stage at half past seven. When you went home, you learned the next day's act, which used to take me until about one in the morning. It was hard, but if you could do it, you could do it. But it was, obviously, great experience for a young actor. If you've done four years or so in rep, nothing can happen on stage that you hadn't already had to deal with in that learning curve. As for television, I treated it exactly the same, except I didn't have to talk so loud to reach the back of the gallery! I wasn't a method actor, I was a *me* actor. I remember doing one rep show and I went on and tried to play myself. When you went to see the stars, they were who you wanted to see. If you saw John Wayne, you wanted to see John Wayne. The character they were playing may have been interesting, but you went to see the man. So, I realised that if I'm the leading man in the rep, the audiences are coming to see me in this, playing this part, so I thought it was a good idea to play myself and as far as possible, that's what I've always done.

"I can't really remember a lot about my early television work. I came down South and it kind of happened. I did a couple of *Armchair Theatre* plays. Sydney Newman really had a grip on television drama. Single plays like those were so beautifully done. They had the choice of who they wanted because they were so well thought of. They were very, very professional and I loved every moment of them. I also look back on [*The Mask of Janus* and its sequel *The Spies*] with enormous gratitude. They were very important for me. At that time, I first realised just what fame meant. You've got a company of regular actors including Peter Dyneley and Dinsdale Landen, and you're rehearsing at the Acton Hilton – as we called the BBC's rehearsal rooms in Acton – and recording them. You're walking about and someone might recognise you from something, but once the programmes go out on air, you just can't go out. You can't go on the Tube, can't get on a bus because suddenly it's instant recognition – 'ooh, it's 'im!'. It became very embarrassing. People would come up to you, want to talk, want autographs. I was in the Army & Navy Stores at one point, buying something, and all the girls I could see had sussed me, but the woman who was in charge of the department knew my face and thought she knew me – but of course, she didn't! We had this long conversation – I asked her how her mother was. She thanked me for asking. I enquired if her mother had the same old trouble, because all mothers have the same old trouble, don't they? So, she told me about that and said how nice it had been to see me. I said it was nice to see her too, asked her to give my love to her mother, and walked out. I stopped for a moment and saw the girls were telling the woman who I actually was. That was quite good fun."

Oates' character in *Doomwatch*, Dr. John Ridge, was an intelligent and dapper ladies' man – and this facet of the character may well have drawn Mather's eye. The 'ladies' man' aspect was particularly pertinent to *The Avengers*, as the Steed character had been redefined for the stage as something of a womaniser – his partner, Hannah Wild, was apparently the only woman with the willpower to hold out on his advances. As Michael Billington, writing in *The Times* on Wednesday 4th August 1971, opined, "In the past, one always felt Steed regarded sex as something likely to spoil the cut of his suit, but here he lusts comically and ineffectually after his sophisticated sidekick". Oates had also previously appeared twice opposite Patrick Macnee – ten years his senior – in *The Avengers*, in *You Have Just Been Murdered* (1967) and *Super Secret Cypher Snatch* (1968). Six years after the stage play, Oates would be seen for one last time in Avengerland, playing Spelman in *Hostage* (1977), a second series episode of *The New Avengers*.

Simon Oates admitted to having had a particular concern when he was approached to play Steed: "I was totally delighted to get the role. However, when they asked me to do it, I made a point of ringing Patrick Macnee, not least because Pat is a great friend of mine. I was thinking that there might have been something devious going on. Were they trying to blackmail Pat into accepting the role, using me against him? Were they saying to him that if he wouldn't do it, we can easily get someone to take the role off you – we don't really need you. I was concerned because, after all, it was his show. So I rang him and explained the situation. 'I just couldn't do it,' he said. 'It's too energetic for me, so do it with my blessing and thank you so much for ringing.' So I did it... and Pat was right, it was a pretty energetic show. But Patrick Macnee – what a hard act to follow..."

The press release of 1st May 1971 that confirmed Simon Oates' casting also revealed that another important role had been filled, that of arch-villain Madam Gerda von Metz. It was to be the sultry Kate O'Mara (1939-2014) who would squeeze herself into the character's striking black jumpsuit. Born Frances Meredith Carroll to an RAF flying instructor, John F. Carroll, and the actress Helen Bainbridge, O'Mara was encouraged into acting from a young age. She made her earliest 1950s film and television appearances as Merrie Carroll, before quickly adopting the Kate O'Mara moniker. It would become a household name in a glittering career that included a sojourn in the hugely popular US soap opera *Dynasty*. Blessed with an exotic appearance and distinctive high cheekbones, O'Mara was rarely out of work following her graduation from the Aida Foster drama school, though initially she gained employment as a speech therapist at a Sussex girls' school. Gradually, she worked her way into small, uncredited roles in television and film during the early 1960s, making her stage debut as Jessica in a 1963 production of *The Merchant of Venice* at the Flora Robson Playhouse, Newcastle upon Tyne. Her London debut followed five years later, when she played Elsa in *The Italian Girl* at the Wyndham's Theatre. By this time, she had established herself on television and had featured in series including *Danger Man*, *Adam Adamant Lives!* and *The Saint*. Further roles in the genre would follow in quick succession between 1968 and 1970, including parts in *The Champions*, *Department S*, *Codename* and *Paul Temple*. In terms of her previous *Avengers* experience, O'Mara had appeared in the 1969 episode *Stay Tuned*, alongside Patrick Macnee and Linda Thorson.

Although the actors to play these two roles had been decided, other characters were not cast until later in the month. Actress Sue Lloyd (1939-2011) was announced as Steed's new partner, Hannah Wild, at a press photo call in London on Monday 24th May 1971. Born in Aldeburgh, Suffolk, the daughter of a general practitioner, Lloyd was trained in dance as a child, attending Sadler's Wells Ballet School – something that Sue mentioned as being a useful skill in coping with the demands of *The Avengers* stage production (*Daily Mail*, Tuesday 25th May 1971). However, her prospects as a dancer diminished when she grew to a height of 5 foot 8 inches (1.73 metres), although she featured in Lionel Blair's dance troupe for a short while. She also found employment as a showgirl and photographic model, with the latter leading to uncredited "decorative" on-screen appearances in films such as *Go to Blazes* (1962) and *Nothing But the Best* (1964). This work led to acting roles of growing significance in television series such as *The Sentimental Agent*, *Armchair Theatre*, *Love Story* and *The Saint*, before her breakthrough role came alongside Michael Caine in the 1965 movie thriller *The Ipcress File*. Lloyd's first encounter with *The Avengers* came soon after, in the Series 4 episode *A Surfeit of H$_2$O*. Her success in *The Ipcress File* led to her first regular television role, alongside American star Steve Forrest in the ITC thriller series *The Baron*, as Cordelia Winters. Lloyd's role in this series had originally been intended to be a one-off appearance, but pressure from the American ABC Television Network led to her being drafted in to replace Forrest's male sidekick, so as to introduce more glamour into the series. Lloyd went on to appear in 23 of the 30 episodes made. Other work prior to the *Avengers* stage play included the feature films *Corruption* (1968, with Kate O'Mara) and *Percy* (1970), and guest appearances in episodes of *Department S*, *Randall and Hopkirk (Deceased)* and *Hadleigh* on television. *The Avengers* would mark Lloyd's professional stage debut.

The remaining principal roles were awarded to Jeremy Lloyd (1930-2014), Anthony Sharp (1915-1984), and John F. Landry. Jeremy Lloyd (who was not related to fellow cast member Sue Lloyd) was booked to play Bobby Carruthers and was a veteran of two *Avengers* episodes – *From Venus With Love* (1967) and *Thingumajig* (1969) – and was at the time known internationally for his role in *Rowan & Martin's Laugh-In*, which, ironically, was the series credited with causing the demise of *The Avengers* television series. Anthony Sharp (1915-1984), who would portray Horace Walters, the Minister for Internal Security, would later feature in *To Catch a Rat* (1976), a first series episode of *The New Avengers*, and was a familiar face on British television, often playing government types and other officials. Finally, the Nairobi-born British actor John F. Landry would fill Patrick Newell's shoes as Steed and Mrs. Wild's superior, Mother. Landry worked under two names in the business – John Landry as an actor and birth name Francois Landry as a director. He graduated from RADA in 1960 and is arguably best remembered as Turtle in *The Hanged Man* (1975), a role which he reprised four years later in *Turtle's Progress*, both series coming from the pen of Edmund Ward. Landry was unique among the central cast in that he had never featured in *The Avengers* on television. Interestingly, early publicity photographs that came to light in 2022 show Jeremy Lloyd in Mother's wheelchair, suggesting perhaps that he was initially under consideration for the role.

As part of the stage play's publicity drive, Sue Lloyd was interviewed – along with television *Avengers* stars Honor Blackman, Diana Rigg and Linda Thorson – by James Green for the Friday 2nd July 1971 edition of the *London Evening News*. Each actress spoke about their respective *Avengers* character, with the report describing Hannah Wild as "Unmarried, 5 ft. 8 in., reddish-gold hair". Lloyd furnished Green with further details: "I see Hannah as a highly intelligent girl with a certain hardness. Practical, yet with a lot of warmth. She's fond of Steed, but otherwise there's no man in her life. On the action front, her accomplishments will include shootings, half-nelsons and the occasional karate chop. Since Kate O'Mara as the villainess is in black shiny leather, they've given me a crimson leather fighting outfit. I also wear a golden leather suit and dusty pink costume. Obviously, having had so little stage experience, the first night will be doubly tense for me. What must help is that I did face a studio audience while making *His and Hers* [a 1970-72 Yorkshire Television situation comedy, the first series of which featured Lloyd as Kay Sherwin]. Some people think I'm a toughie... rather like Hannah Wild... but I don't agree. If I seem hard, that's a cover. Because actually, I'm a big softie. What I've discovered is that the really dangerous girls who need watching are the wide-eyed innocents!" A few weeks later, she spoke to John Hemsley of the *Aberdeen Evening Express* (27th July 1971) and shared her hopes for the production: "I'm excited about it. If it's a success I think they'll probably do a film of it. The play is going to have more comedy than the TV series, though it will retain the tremendous *Avengers* theme."

The somewhat onerous task of realising Mather's grandiose ideas for *The Avengers* fell to the experienced and much-loved comedy actor Leslie Phillips (1924-2022), who described the show as a "marvellous comedy with a lot of splendid hokum" (*The Birmingham Post*, 19th June 1971). Phillips is best known for his roles in the early *Carry On...* and *Doctor...* film series, in which he regularly played likeable, if often louche, romantic leads. He had started out at the age of 11 in 1935 playing a wolf to Dame Anna Neagle's Peter Pan at the London Palladium. However, Phillips, speaking to Judith Cook in *The Birmingham Post* of Saturday 19th June 1971, was keen to stress that acting was not the only string to his bow, and that he had been directing plays for about fifteen years, "but nobody seems to know about it – I'm rooted in everyone's minds as a comedy actor." In his autumn years, Phillips appeared in a succession of prestige films and television series such as Steven Spielberg's *Empire of the Sun* (1987), *Chancer* (Central Television, 1990-91), *Love on a Branch Line* (BBC, 1994) and three *Harry Potter* films between 2001 and 2011, marking himself out as one of Britain's most admired veteran actors. He was made a Commander of the British Empire (CBE) in the 2008 New Year's Honours, to mark an incredible seventy-five years in showbusiness.

As they sought to transfer *The Avengers* to the stage, Mather, Phillips, Feely and Clemens endeavoured to preserve its light-hearted adventurousness. However, they decided on – or were pushed towards – a tone that was far more racy than had ever been possible under Independent Television Authority regulations. 'Kinky' and 'sexy' were plainly among the buzzwords kept in mind when writing the script, hence Kate O'Mara's character came to be kitted out in a shiny black PVC suit with red decoration, gauntlets and wide-topped thigh boots. Her 'Forces of Evil' – a bevy of attractive young women, also referred to as 'Amazons' – wore similar figure-hugging outfits in black vinyl with white piping. In order to provide a different type of amusement for the audience, a succession of MI5 agents arrived at Steed's apartment convinced they were, respectively, a frogman, an astronaut and a giant pigeon, and John Steed – as on television – was given a succession of one-liners and quips. The difference here is that many of them were rather low brow, risqué and arguably below Steed's dignity.

Sue Lloyd's costumes were designed by Richard Berkeley Sutcliffe (1918-1979) and made in the workshops of fetishwear manufacturer and publisher Atomage Ltd. Sutcliffe was recognised as one of the leading British stage designers of the mid-20th century. He is best remembered for his dazzling and colourful stage scenery and for designing vibrant costumes for musicals, revues and pantomimes. He also created costumes and settings for Shakespeare productions at the Bristol Old Vic. Sutcliffe combined his theatrical work with regular employment as the resident designer for Fortnum & Mason, for whom he designed the ornate, animated clock which is situated above the department store's main entrance in Piccadilly to this day. It depicts William Fortnum and Hugh Mason, who appear from inside it and turn to acknowledge each other every hour, on the hour. Sutcliffe also designed costumes and sets for the celebrated drag queen Danny La Rue and George Mitchell's Black and White Minstrels. Another string to Sutcliffe's bow was that he designed costumes for the female performers at Soho's Raymond Revuebar – and it does seem likely that it was this work that brought Sutcliffe to mind as an appropriate designer for Mrs. Wild's wardrobe.

Atomage also produced a large number of costumes for other characters in *The Avengers*, again with an emphasis on the sexually suggestive, working from designs by Ronald Cobb (1907-1977). Cobb had started out as an actor before moving into set and costume design, working long-term for Murray's Cabaret Club on Beak Street, Soho, and being most prolific between the mid-1940s and the early 1960s. With costumes to design for characters like Fantasy Masochist, Fantasy Sadist and, of course, Gerda and her kinky gang of terribly tempting nubiles in *The Avengers*, Cobb was hardly heading into conventional territory – but, having many years of experience designing for showgirls at Murray's, Cobb was well qualified to come up with the goods. A feature in a 1972 edition of the *Atomage* magazine suggested that "the costumes drew more attention almost than the acting or the script. One critic said: 'The cast was clad in enough rubber, leather and vinyl to satiate the most avid student of [German psychiatrist and author of *Psychopathia Sexualis* (1886)] Krafft-Ebing'."

Isolyn Ltd and Brian Reed also produced several costumes for the production, including those for Simon Oates as John Steed and the more conventional characters, such as Mother and Walters.

Atomage's involvement was not without its problems. The company did not regularly make costumes for theatrical use, their chief line of manufacture being for customers of a sexually adventurous nature, principally sado-masochists. The upshot of this was that, unfortunately, the costumes made for *The Avengers* were visually striking but somewhat heavy and hot to wear under stage lighting. They were also often impractical in other ways, notably in the case of Kate O'Mara, whose vinyl jumpsuit reputedly creaked terribly, in time with every shift in position that the actress made, conspiring to make even simple movements, such as sitting down, exceptionally difficult.

The show was technically very demanding. More than a dozen highly complex sets were built for the show, ranging from a suspended helicopter cockpit with a dangling rope ladder, to Steed's lavishly furnished apartment, his Bentley on the road, an underground bunker, government offices (one of which was bedecked in Union Jack-inspired designs), and the Brain Room of the Master Computer. Most of these constructions included tricky props and operational parts. Back projection of pre-filmed backgrounds was also employed for a number of scenes, as well as a filmed sequence for the final scene showing Sue Lloyd stripping off to her underwear. In her autobiography, *It Seemed Like a Good Idea at the Time* (Quartet Books, 1998), Lloyd revealed that the show's technical requirements far exceeded the norm at their provincial venue in England's West Midlands, The Birmingham Theatre: "The sets were so complicated that, on the first night, we had to borrow all the stagehands from Birmingham's other theatre, the Alexandra, to help out." Simon Oates, meanwhile, commented in *The Birmingham Post* of Saturday 19th June 1971 that "if you started thinking of all the things that could go wrong – in cold blood – you'd give the whole thing up."

Following rehearsals at London's Victoria Palace Theatre, the cast and production team arrived in Birmingham on Monday 12th July 1971 for three days of set-up and technical run-throughs. The show opened at The Birmingham Theatre in the city's Southside area (today dubbed the Chinese Quarter) on Thursday 15th, playing there – as planned – for ten days, with its twelfth and final performance taking place on the evening of Saturday 24th.

Contemporary accounts of the brief run at the Birmingham Theatre were not particularly complimentary. Although provincial 'try-outs' were common prior to a London theatrical run, 'D.I.', writing in the *Coventry Evening Telegraph* (Saturday 17th July 1971), questioned the practice of charging provincial audiences to see productions that were, in some aspects, not ready to be seen: "At one point in the stage version of *The Avengers*, Jeremy Lloyd, that excellent gangling fugitive from TV's *Laugh-In*, says: 'Things have been going very badly wrong.' And that about sums it up. The show is being tried out for ten days at the Birmingham Theatre before opening in London and a 'try-out' it very badly needs... I hope *The Avengers* works in London because it has been executed in the right spirit... The one real sin has been to bring it to Birmingham as an unfinished product. Very few of the gimmicks are working at the moment and the stage staff just cannot cope with the problems which arise. If [the provincial audience] are only to be there to watch unsuccessful experiments with complicated stage props, it seems a little hard to ask them to pay for the privilege."

The premiere performance was particularly beset with problems. Kate O'Mara fell painfully from the helicopter's rope ladder during Act Two, when a stagehand accidentally put a winch into reverse. This had the unfortunate effect of lowering the ladder as O'Mara attempted to climb it. 'F.N.', writing in the *Birmingham Evening Mail* of the following day, noted that "In the final scene, Kate O'Mara as Madam Gerda, leader of the Forces of Evil, should have attempted to escape by climbing a rope ladder to a waiting helicopter. But she did not go up. Instead she came down with a thump. And so did the curtain." The report recorded that Simon Oates had addressed the audience afterwards to say "Come back tomorrow and see how it really ends."

The problems seemed to be endless. Interviewed in August 1987 for the BBC2 programme *On Stage*, Sue Lloyd remarked that "Kate O'Mara was supposed to be invisible at certain times and special effects allowed her to vanish into special props which would part to let her inside. There was this trick sofa which had been designed to swallow her up. Unfortunately, what happened one night was that she pressed the button and nothing happened. After several uneasy moments, she tiptoed off the stage. In the next scene, Jeremy Lloyd came on for a straightforward tea scene. He no sooner sat down when – wham! – the sofa opened up and poor Jeremy disappeared into it." Sue Lloyd recalled the audience being in fits of laughter, not least because her co-star's head and shoulders remained stuck out from the malfunctioning sofa at an odd angle, his outstretched hands still clutching the cup of tea. "Normally, I'm good at ad-libbing," Lloyd later confessed in her autobiography, "but the killer sofa was too much for me. I couldn't go on. I stood there, rooted to the spot, shaking with laughter. All I could think was that Jeremy looked exactly like Archie Andrews, the ventriloquist's dummy [of the radio comedy *Educating Archie*]. I tried to pull him out, but it was no use. In the end, they had to bring the curtain down and send in a couple of strong stagehands to release him."

Another memorable, if equally unwelcome, mishap, also related by Sue Lloyd in her autobiography *It Seemed Like a Good Idea at the Time*, again concerned the serially unfortunate Kate O'Mara: "[One] set included a number of decorative columns which appeared solid, but which were in fact elasticated. Kate had only to lean against the column, part the hidden seams, slip inside and the seams snapped shut behind her, completely concealing her inside. On this particular night, as she disappeared into the column, the elastic snapped shut, biting off Kate's hairpiece in the process. The evil Kate had gone, leaving behind her, dangling in mid-air, what appeared to be an outsize tarantula spider. The tarantula stubbornly refused to move, and remained dangling throughout the scene, bristling alarmingly at the other actors, who had to pretend to be extremely short-sighted every time they passed it."

With the Birmingham engagement completed, the cast and crew travelled down to London. The production's new home was to be The Prince of Wales Theatre on Coventry Street in Westminster, where they undertook preparatory work and further rehearsals ahead of a hoped-for extensive West End run. It was a frenetic period as the West End premiere was scheduled to take place a mere nine days after the final Midlands performance.

Unfortunately, the problems encountered in the provincial run at Birmingham were not sufficiently ironed out by time the show opened in London after an insufficient rehearsal period on Monday 2nd August 1971. *The Avengers* remained a greatly troubled production, impractical from a technical standpoint, at least within the limitations of its budget and available technology.

Writing in *Plays and Players* in September 1971, reviewer Michael Coveney was not impressed. He bemoaned the practice of adapting television series for the stage, which he found to be "the crummiest of ideas," particularly as "here we don't even get the TV stars, and in fact the whole ambiguity of the relationship between Steed and (in this case) Hannah Wild is coarsened. Steed can apparently get his oats with anyone except Hannah. She alone holds out on him. As if that were not sacrilege enough, he wears flared trousers and moves about with about as much grace and style as a flowerpot man on hot coals. He also drinks wine of doubtful vintage straight from the bottle and drives a Bentley which looks like a disused dodgem car." Coveney did at least express sympathy for Oates' co-star: "I felt a twinge of sadness that the beautiful Sue Lloyd and the talented Jeremy Lloyd should be inflicted with this rubbish, though it never quite managed to defeat their optimism. But the rest of the performances were lamentable. People bumped into furniture in the black-outs, only to be seen still bumping into furniture when the lights came up... It was only out of a masochistic sense of duty that I stayed to the end. And then I remembered that many people in the audience had given the impression that they were enjoying themselves. They wore that harmless look of moderate satisfaction which is to be seen on the faces of spectators at cricket matches. Only a leather ball struck firmly into their faces would convince them that they were not having a good time. The producer responsible for this woeful epic announces it in the programme as only the first of a series of unusual, wayout plays. What next? Perhaps *Crossroads* or *The Best of the News at Ten*? He could do worse. On second thoughts, he couldn't."

In a similarly outspoken review, Arthur Thirkell slated the production as "a sorry disappointment. It is obviously meant as entertainment for the whole family, but will appeal only to the very young. It comes across as an inferior version of *Doctor Who*. Simon Oates as John Steed and Sue Lloyd as Hannah Wild are got at by a gang of sexy girls in kinky leather gear – they are a sort of women's lib organisation who are going to rule the world. The show has plenty of special effects, but these are all done so much better on film. Compensations? Well, the girls are very pretty and there's an amusing performance from Anthony Sharp at the Minister for Security. There's a computer on stage that brainwashes humans. I've got a sneaking suspicion it nobbled the authors of this strange mish-mash in which the machines are more interesting than the characters." (*Daily Mirror*, Tuesday 17th August 1971).

The *Daily Mail*'s Peter Lewis seemed to agree with Patrick Macnee that the stage was not the place for *The Avengers*: "The stage is a rotten place to portray science fiction. Illusion on the stage depends on a few visual hints and a lot of word power. The word power here is devoted to shattering whatever atmosphere of menace might have been created. If the original *Avengers* were a spoof, but an acceptable one, then this is a spoof of a spoof."

Fellow critic Helen Dawson felt that *The Avengers* had started off in an audacious fashion, but that what followed had proved a disappointment: "It opens with a *coup de théâtre* of which Hitchcock could be proud, but what follows – despite helicopters, Bentleys, an Egyptian mummy and a James Bond finale – sadly lacks the original's panache. True to the genre, the plot is pretty preposterous... Unfortunately, Simon Oates as Our Hero has none of Patrick Macnee's polished style and, instead, he substitutes a slick, elbow-nudging performance. And Hannah Wild (Sue Lloyd, showing a sizeable amount of cleavage) is a sorry step-down from his other lady accomplices. There are plenty of randy jokes and a bout of all-in leather wrestling, but you'd be better off watching the repeats on the box..." (*The Observer*, Sunday 15th August 1971).

Coveney, Thirkell, Lewis and Dawson's comments were fairly representative of the reviews the play garnered, though a few were more positive, such as Peter Fiddick's in *The Guardian* of Tuesday 3rd August 1971. Fiddick suggested that "If you never knew the series, or never responded to its moderately high camp – it is probably too late to start. Connoisseurs who adored Miss Honor Blackman, accepted Miss Diana Rigg and feel the series went rapidly downhill from then on will indeed find this an example of later period writing. The camp is pitched on the lower slopes, the plotting a matter of female dominators with mind-bending machines, and a lot more sexy double entendres put in now the ITA [Independent Television Authority]'s not around. Only the puns ('He died babbling of Green Shields') have survived. Still, it's solidly cast all through – Simon '*Doomwatch*' Oates as Steed (with not a little resemblance to Patrick Macnee), Sue Lloyd as Hannah Wild, Jeremy Lloyd, John F. Landry and Anthony Sharp having a ball with the bit parts, and Kate O'Mara, ah, filling out the role of the dreaded Baroness Gerda. And, indeed, writers, director (Leslie Phillips) and design team have brought the series' fast episodic flow to the stage better than could have been expected. They even got in the Bentley, a helicopter, a huge mind machine and a parade of fetishes. *Puss in Boots* for grown ups."

Another positive comment came, much later, from the pioneering author of several books about *The Avengers* and other classic British series, Dave Rogers, who attended the play's opening night in Birmingham on Thursday 15th July 1971. In *The Avengers* (ITV Books / Michael Joseph, 1983), Rogers recalled that "Simon Oates, immaculate in his trendy suits, shooting jackets and Cuban heel shoes, made an excellent Steed."

Speaking in 2008, Simon Oates offered an interesting perspective concerning the critics' response to *The Avengers*: "You know what? I never used to read notices until I'd been in something for about three or four weeks. Honestly, with my hand on my heart, I've never read a notice about the *Avengers* show. They didn't affect me because I didn't know. I don't tend to believe them if they say I'm good, any more than I do if they say I'm rotten! I think every critic's column should have a little by-line that says, 'one man's opinion'. There was probably a lot of 'who does he think he is, trying to follow Pat?' – and that's understandable because Pat's a lovely man who gave lovely performances as Steed. So, in a way, I was on a hiding to nothing before I even started, wasn't I? You think of great performances people have given and someone has to try and follow them, and you know they'll never be considered as good as the original."

Co-author Terence Feely put his side of the story when interviewed by David Richardson for *TV Zone* magazine in 1993: "It didn't work because the producer [John Mather] said he could do the effects, and Brian and I suspected he couldn't. But the producer was so plausible and so persuasive that we thought that maybe he could. He said he was a stage manager twenty years ago, and that modern stage managers didn't know how to do it. We had to make people disappear on stage in front of the audience, and he said he was going to get a real magician in. He said: 'It's done with mirrors'. There is an old Edwardian illusion ['Pepper's Ghost'] that can make people disappear, but it's got to be very specially done. We didn't know that. We trusted the guy and it didn't work. In the end the back of a chair was made of slats, and [the actor] simply rolled through the back of it. You can't do that – audiences see it happen." Even the Bentley that Feely and Clemens had been encouraged by Mather to include in the script for Steed to drive ended up being a major disappointment. "It was a cardboard cut-out that was pushed on by two stagehands who just stopped before you [saw] them. It was a mess, and such a shame because it was a great story."

And so the die was cast. Unable to weather the storm caused by the reviews, the persistent technical gremlins, and finding themselves unable to entice sufficient numbers of the paying public into the auditorium each night, *The Avengers* limped to its inevitable early closure at the Prince of Wales Theatre after just three weeks and 24 performances on Saturday 21st August 1971. When Simon Oates was interviewed by *The Birmingham Daily Post* (Saturday 2nd October 1971), he suggested that the closure of *The Avengers* had been "mainly [due] to lack of money."

A replacement production, *Big Bad Mouse*, starring comedians Eric Sykes and Jimmy Edwards, eventually opened at the Prince of Wales Theatre on Tuesday 14th September 1971. *Big Bad Mouse* debuted in the provinces on 28th June 1971 and went on a weekly tour of regional theatres, signing off in Bournemouth three days before its London premiere. It ran in the West End until 29th January 1972. One can only speculate whether a similar arrangement for *The Avengers* might have led to a slicker London production and a longer run.

Brian Clemens held a similar opinion. "It was too ambitious for the time. It should have played out of town for about six months to get it right, iron out the difficulties with the props. There were no difficulties when writing the show. It was just the way they did it. It was some years ago and they didn't do things like that on stage; now they do it all the time. The sets move and things go up and down; it's a whole new art form. It really wasn't the play and it wasn't the cast." (*The Ultimate Avengers* by Dave Rogers, Boxtree, 1995).

Simon Oates also concurred when he spoke to Alan and Alys Hayes in 2008: "[The rehearsal period wasn't] long enough. We couldn't possibly have got the thing together in that time. If I'd been directing, I'd have thrown the furniture about a bit and would have got it right. It needed time, but they'd booked us in and allowed us just this tiddly running-in period in Birmingham – and I knew then that we were on a duffer. Had I been able to direct it as well as play in it, it would have run for a couple of years, I promise you.

"So many things went wrong. I remember pushing that Bentley off stage at one point when it didn't work, and there was a sofa that was designed [to swallow up people so they appeared to disappear]. I remember saying that it could be very dodgy and one night, Jeremy Lloyd got stuck halfway through it. So, I went down and sat in front of him. I told him to keep still. Most of the audience didn't realise... I'm sitting there and he's hiding behind me, trying to work his way through the back of the sofa! Then, in several performances, the rope ladder prop came down and got stuck halfway. It would have been so easy to fix those problems, to make them work. I know all about the stage, presentation, lighting and everything and I knew after four days with the director that we were going to get screwed up – and screwed up we got. We were carrying too much on our shoulders. You weren't only aware of what you were doing and what you were trying to present, but you had your eyes going around wondering what was going to go wrong next. It was like a car that was half finished. Are the gears going to work? The brakes? You're not quite sure. We've not tested that, no, we've not done that either. It was chaotic. I was disappointed, but I sort of expected it really. The flow of the piece was being interrupted all the time by things going wrong. That's my opinion. I think my performance was alright, but then I would think that! But we just kept getting hitches, hold ups, things going wrong. You could feel it coming... It was actually a good fun show with a decent script, but it's like a stand-up going on stage and having audience members falling out of the balcony every ten minutes, or having the microphone or the lighting failing on them... They're not going to get many laughs with all that happening. You're always waiting for the next bomb to go off. I know I was, wondering what was going to happen next and there I am, trying to play John Steed! It wasn't easy. It could have been fantastic, but it was sabotaged from the inside.

"I don't accept The Avengers as a personal disaster because as I say, it could have been avoided. I was stuck in the middle of it, but you can only do your best and try to pull it out of the mire. Had we have had more time, it wouldn't have gone into the mire in the first place, but there you go. It was like being the Captain of the *Titanic*. You can arrange the deck chairs as best you can, but it doesn't make much difference when you're sinking."

The Characters

John Steed

Considering the Avengers pedigree of Terence Feely and Brian Clemens, it is somewhat surprising that the character of John Steed as seen on the stage is quite different compared to that previously established on television during the 1960s. There was, of course, a different and younger actor portraying the character, with Simon Oates substituting for Patrick Macnee, and this will have had an effect. It is almost certain that, had Patrick Macnee accepted John Mather's offer of employment, the Steed of the stage would have been closer to the Steed familiar to television audiences.

Feely and Clemens' script was, according to press reports of April 1971, already in place by that time, whereas casting was not. Producer John C. Mather's comment that he was looking for "the Patrick Macnees, the Honor

Blackmans and the Diana Riggs of this world" suggests that Macnee had already declined the possibility of reviving Steed for the stage and that the script quite possibly post-dates his decision. It seems likely, therefore, that the changes to the character were designed to offer audiences a 'new' Steed, subtly redefined for a new decade.

Most notably, Steed is demonstrably more lustful in his stage persona, more driven by sex than Steed had been on television. Arguably, this harks back to before the 1965-69 film era of the series, to a time when Steed was arguably less the perfect gentleman and would occasionally make plays for the favours of his then-partner Cathy Gale. In common with the stage Steed, the television Steed was always rebuffed in such situations. Here, though, Steed is more direct, making distinctly unsubtle double entendres and even at one stage taking advantage of Hannah when she thinks that she has killed him. Feigning weakness and impending death, he entreats Hannah to give him one last kiss. When she complies, "His arms come round her in a powerful clasp. He kisses her hard, twists her round and rolls over on top of her." These are not actions of the television Steed, not even in the series' videotape era. Rather, they bring to mind the Sean Connery James Bond of *Goldfinger* (1964) infamously forcing himself on Pussy Galore (played by *The Avengers*' Honor Blackman).

Steed, as established on television, was no stranger to one-liner quips, and that characteristic is very much carried across to the stage play. The difference here is that, in general, the jests are distinctly low brow and lack the sophistication of the television scripts. Whereas the television Steed might make witty, if suggestive, remarks such as "I asked the chief predator where to find you and he said, 'Our Mrs. Peel is in ladies' underwear.' I rattled up the stairs three at a time." (*Death at Bargain Prices*, 1965), similar dialogue in the stage play disappointingly relied heavily on double entendres...

> HANDCUFFED TOGETHER, STEED AND HANNAH ARE TRYING TO SERVE TEA.
>
> STEED: May I butter your crumpet?
>
> HANNAH: No, you may not.
>
> STEED: Then would you mind jamming my scone? And putting a little marmalade on my muffin?

...and even jaw-dropping, *single* entendres, such as this example, which plays on the term "rose-coloured [or rose-tinted] spectacles", which suggests that the wearer views the world in an unrealistic way and sees only the favourable aspects...

> STEED: You sit there in your big chair
> (to Mother) viewing the world through rose-
> coloured testicles.

A contemporary press review by Michael Coveney (*Plays and Players*, September 1971) notes that Steed uncharacteristically "drinks wine of a doubtful vintage straight from the bottle". This presumably refers to the scenes in which Steed is handcuffed, under house arrest, and drinks Nuits-Saint-Georges Burgundy. This wine hails from the Burgundian town of the same name in Eastern France and is generally well-regarded for its structure and flavour, so it would seem that Steed knew more about its quality than Coveney did. However, the criticism that Steed drinks straight from the bottle would seem to be more justifiable – the Steed of the television series would not dream of such a crime against sophistication. He would select the correct glass, ensure that the wine was stored at between 57 and 60° Fahrenheit, and uncork it an hour before drinking so as to allow it to breathe. The script contains no reference to drinking from the bottle, so it would appear that this was a move introduced during rehearsals, possibly due to difficulties encountered by Simon Oates when manipulating the bottle and the glasses with one hand while the other was manacled.

Also worthy of note is that, when we are introduced to him in the stage play, Steed has recently engaged a manservant, James, who buttles, acts as a secretary and performs cleaning duties. Steed pretends – for Mrs. Wild's benefit – to be unaware of the fact that James is female and highly attractive. It is only later that he realises that she is not only an enemy agent but also robotic. The Steed of the television series never employed a manservant. However, he did on occasion engage household cleaners such as Elsie in *The Mauritius Penny* (1963) and Mrs. Weir in *The Last of the Cybernauts...??* (1976).

The word association test that Steed undergoes following the debacle at the Government bunker reveals many of his predilections (Steed's responses are in italics): Bacon-*Eggs*, Knife-*Fork*, Mother-*Father* (perhaps referring to Mother's Department colleague Father, seen in *Stay Tuned* [1969]), White-*Slightly chilled*, Red-*Room temperature* (both referring to the storage of wines), War-*Evelyn* (a play on the name of the author, Evelyn Waugh [1903-1966], pronounced 'war'), Wet-*Fish*, Dry-*Martini* (a cocktail made with gin and vermouth, and garnished with an olive), Boy-*Girl*, Girl-*Girl*, Dash-*Verve*, Verve-*Clicquot* (Veuve Clicquot, a highly-regarded Champagne), Shoot-*Pheasants* (a sporting pursuit of the gentry), Die-*Abolical* (a diabolical pun!), Tent-*Camping* (the term 'camping' has a double meaning connected to theatricality and male homosexuality), Marquee-*De Sade* (Donatien Alphonse François, Marquis de Sade [1740-1814], infamous philosopher and author, whose perverse sexual proclivities and erotic writings gave rise to the term sadism), Trade-*Rough*, Craft-*Ebing* (a nod to Richard Freiherr von Krafft-Ebing [1840-1902], a German psychiatrist recognised as an authority on deviant sexual behaviour), Flanders-*Trenches*, Mons-*Veneris* (Flanders and Mons were both sites of World War I battles, though mons veneris is the fatty cushion of flesh providing protection at the junction of the female pubic bones), Cervix-*With a smile* (a play on the term 'service with a smile', again related to the female reproductive system, further illustrating the authors' low aim approach to humour in this production).

Steed's military background is not referred to in the stage play, possibly due to the Steed presented being much younger than his television equivalent. It would not have been plausible to paint Simon Oates' version of the character as a World War II veteran, as the actor had been a wartime child evacuee and was just 13 when the conflict ended (Patrick Macnee was 23 at this time and served in the Royal Navy from 1942-1946). Interestingly, Oates was attached to the Army Intelligence Corps during his term of National Service in the late 1940s, and became the Army's heavyweight boxing champion. In fact, Steed's military career is not consistently reported during the television series, suggesting at various junctures that he served in all three British military forces: *Brief for Murder* (1963) establishes that Steed served as a Royal Navy motor torpedo boat commander in World War II (in common with Macnee himself); *The Hour That Never Was* (1965) reveals that Steed was posted at Royal Air Force 472 Hamelin, where agents were based in-between missions, during the early years of the war; *The Murder Market* (1965) links Steed to the Coldstream Guards, a regular Army regiment; *Game* (1968) reveals that prior to joining the Ministry in 1945, he gained the Army rank of Major and served on courts-martial (in the stage play, Steed experiences this process as the accused party); and, finally, *Take-Over* (1969) suggests that Steed was imprisoned at some point during the war in a Japanese concentration camp. It is perhaps a blessing that the writers of *The Avengers* stage play chose not to further muddy the waters in this respect!

Hannah Wild

Whereas the character of Steed arguably suffered in the transition from television to the stage, Hannah Wild appears to have fared somewhat better. Speaking to James Green in the *London Evening News* (Friday 2nd July 1971),

Sue Lloyd supplied a potted biography of her character: "I see Hannah as a highly intelligent girl with a certain hardness. Practical, yet with a lot of warmth. She's fond of Steed, but otherwise there's no man in her life. On the action front, her accomplishments will include shootings, half-nelsons and the occasional karate chop." The script certainly paints Mrs. Wild as a strong character – she seems bright and sophisticated (somewhat more so than Steed himself). The "hardness" that Lloyd spoke of is certainly there to be seen, particularly when it appears that Steed has turned traitor and is placed in her custody. When he tries to escape, his attempts are efficiently and coolly rebuffed, as are Steed's often unsubtle amorous advances.

Mrs. Wild is, like Steed, a fully-fledged member of the Service. This sets her apart from the "talented amateurs" who once assisted Steed – Dr. David Keel, Cathy Gale, Venus Smith, Dr. Martin King, Emma Peel and others. Walters' comment that "I've never known such a security pedigree" when referring to Hannah suggests that she is a senior agent on or approaching Steed's level. This seems to set her several rungs in the Ministry hierarchy above Tara King, who was a fledgling agent still learning the ropes while teamed with Steed, the organisation's top man.

If Mrs. Wild has one particular characteristic in common with Tara King – and one which is arguably a weakness in their respective armour – it is that she is headstrong and prone to leap into situations that could put herself in danger. When she and Steed find a way to inveigle themselves into the villains' lair – the Greensleeves Finishing Academy for the Daughters of Gentlefolk – she determines to go there alone as Steed has been put in her custody, under house arrest. Steed points out that her course of action is foolish, but she handcuffs him to the staircase banister and heads off. Her visit to the Academy ends with her being captured by Gerda and her Amazons and brainwashed into an assassination attempt on Steed. In defence of Mrs. Wild, Steed is also inclined to go it alone against his partner's better judgement, such as when he insists that Hannah hangs back when he goes into the underground bunker in Scotland – with equally disastrous consequences.

The stage play witnessed a return to the classic *Avengers* combat style of Cathy Gale and Emma Peel, with karate included among Hannah's combat skills. Tara King had deviated from the norm by employing whatever was to hand to overcome her adversaries – in *The-Forget-Me-Knot*, that was, unexpectedly, a handbag with a brick inside it!

Reference is made in the script to Hannah Wild being a widow (much in the same way that Steed's former associates, Cathy Gale and Emma Peel, had been), but precious little detail is provided in this regard. The mention comes when Steed and Hannah are discussing James, Steed's female butler, who is on trial. Hannah asks what James must do to win her spurs, suggesting a sexual nature to the arrangement. Steed remarks that Hannah must be confusing him with her late husband – presumably Steed is aware of his dalliances with other women. Hannah takes exception to the comment and Steed quickly apologises. The exchange appears to have been written purely to establish that Hannah is a widow. Intriguingly, the brief character description given in the *London Evening News* report (alluded to earlier) two weeks prior to the first night in Birmingham states her marital status as "unmarried", so possibly this exchange of dialogue was dropped from the final script to the effect that Hannah was no longer intended to be a widow.

The character and Sue Lloyd's portrayal was generally well received, with several critics singling her out for praise, as in this instance. "[Simon Oates] is matched in the humour of the play by Sue Lloyd, who puts behind her the appalling TV *Baron* series with which she was associated and proves herself a comedy actress of some considerable potential." ('D.I.', *Coventry Evening Telegraph*, Tuesday 17th August 1971)

The Steed/Wild Relationship

Steed and Hannah's relationship is shown as being one of great friendship, though Steed wishes it to be more intimate. They holiday separately, with Hannah just returned from a trip that went horribly wrong. She regales Steed with her story, cursing the illiterate Cubans who had hijacked her flight, taking it to the wrong destination. Steed follows up by documenting his quiet time while she was away, which of course was wildly eventful. They converse with obvious warmth, but Hannah makes it abundantly clear that she has no desire to enter into a deeper relationship with Steed.

When Steed is under house arrest, handcuffed to Hannah, he tries to play on feelings of nostalgia that she might hold concerning a past experience that they had shared. He reminds her of the time when they were together – the venue is not revealed – and she translated a French poem entitled *The Cat* by Charles Baudelaire (1821-1867), which posits that cats and women are similarly enigmatic. Steed repeats part of her translation: "Fervent lovers and austere scholars equally love, in the season of maturity, sweet strong cats, the pride of the house..." He says that those cats bring to mind his relationship with Hannah, but she is unmoved and tells him that this ploy will do him no good. Steed brings up Baudelaire's assertion that it is difficult to know who is patronising who with a cat, suggesting that it is equally questionable whether Hannah is his captor or captive. He tries a twist of her handcuffed arm, but she easily fends off his unimaginative attempt at escape by reaching for the gun in her handbag, demonstrating that she is fully in control of the situation and is not easily swayed by her emotional connection to Steed.

The script is unhelpful regarding the past event that Steed alludes to, stating simply that Steed and Hannah were "together" at this time. Whether "together" means that they were then lovers or just literally together as friends is ambiguous, but the situation would likely have been made clearer in the performance by the two actors concerned.

Mother

We learn very little about Mother in the stage play beyond what had already been established on television during the Tara King series, the character having been introduced in *The Forget-Me-Knot* (1969). In fact, Mother seems to take a back seat in the action of the play compared to the Minister for Internal Security, who officiates at Steed's court-martial when one might have expected Mother to have done so. In the main, Mother is used mainly for exposition and for comedic purposes, as witnessed in his regular need to consult the latest code book when talking to other characters in the play.

Mother is assassinated at the end of the play, paving the way for a sequel production that never arrived.

Horace Walters

Minister for the seemingly newly formed Ministry for Internal Security (sometimes referred to in the play script as the Ministry for Universal Internal Security), Horace Walters is an intriguing character. He is apparently wildly patriotic – if the Union Jack-themed adornments and furnishings in his office are anything to go by – but, as the play unfolds, it slowly becomes clear that he is in league with Great Britain's enemies. He has grown embittered at the way in which he has been shuffled between government departments, being variously put in charge of the Ministries of Agriculture and Fisheries, Technology, and, ultimately, Internal Security. In the latter two roles, he has exploited his position, particularly at the Ministry of Technology, where he has encouraged the scientists to design and build experimental robots and "George", the supercomputer installed in the basement of Madame Gerda's finishing school in Maidenhead. And, even then, he is not what he seems. It transpires that he is a robot himself, and that it is Gerda who is his true embodiment.

Madam Gerda von Metz

Madam – or Baroness – Gerda von Metz appears at first glimpse to be more of a pantomime villain than an archetypal *Avengers* diabolical mastermind. The character appears to be rather one-note, more *Snow White*'s Evil Queen than *Return of the Cybernaut*'s Paul Beresford or *The Joker*'s Max Prendergast. She is Swedish, was played "heavily-accented" (*The Sunday Telegraph*, 8th August 1971) by Kate O'Mara, and is at the forefront of what she perceives as a battle of the genders. She hates men and what they stand for and favours the company and cause of women. In keeping with the diabolical masterminds, she takes this obsession to extremes and intends to conquer the world. The first phase of her plan involves having her supercomputer, George, send out a signal that will melt the minds of Britain's leaders: of government, the forces, commerce and other fields – in fact, all those of above average intelligence. Gerda and her girls would then establish a new British government, a first stepping stone towards a new world order.

Dressed in a tight-fitting black jumpsuit, thigh-length leather boots and surrounded by a bevy of young women in similar gear, Gerda seems every inch the strong Alpha female. She seems to have no need of or regard for men, but a revelation in the penultimate scene twists this perception almost entirely, for it is revealed that she was formerly a man herself: Walters. This narrative twist alters the character's motivations significantly and adds depth where there was previously precious little. Suddenly, the audience realises that Walters – as a man – desired to be a woman and abhors his own sex, which makes both him and her (as one person) a more intriguing creation. However, at least in the script, little is made of the development in the remaining action.

The idea of a matriarchal society was one exploited often in pop culture of the time, such as in the feature films *Devil Girl from Mars* (1954), *Fire Maidens from Outer Space* (1956) and *Zeta One* (1970) and, on television, in the *Doctor Who* adventure *Galaxy 4* (1965). These specific works were all written from the male perspective, arguably take a dim view of women's liberation, and suggest that women should not be trusted with power. *The Avengers* also touched upon the subject in the Brian Clemens scripted *How to Succeed... at Murder* (1966). In this episode, a group of women are trained to hate men, kill male company bosses and take control of their companies, but they are unknowingly working for a man. However, In the case of *The Avengers* stage play, the revelation about Gerda's past suggests that Terence Feely and Brian Clemens were keen to make their protagonist's motivations more complex than those displayed in other works exploring similar themes. Considering that *The Avengers* was very much in the vanguard of female emancipation, bringing strong women characters to the fore in a spirit of equality then otherwise unseen on British television, it is appropriate that its stage incarnation seeks not to undo that work.

Similarities to The Avengers TV Series

When the play opens with the assassination of a foreign dignitary in one of the theatre's private viewing boxes, this recalls Brian Clemens' earlier *A Touch of Brimstone* (1966). In that episode, a visiting Sheikh – in Britain to sign an oil treaty – was humiliated in front of the assembled opera house audience when his seat collapsed as he sat upon it. This practical joke impelled him to return home without signing the treaty.

Gerda refers to the Giant Computer Brain as "George". The script notes that the computer's voice sounds like the actor George Sanders (1906-1972), suggesting the likely thinking behind its naming. However, *Whoever Shot Poor George Oblique Stroke XR40?* (1968), written by Tony Williamson, also anthropomorphised a computer by giving it that same moniker, and this may also have influenced the writers.

The incorporation of robots in this story perhaps owes a debt to *The Cybernauts* (1965) and *Return of the Cybernauts* (1967), two standout *Avengers* episodes which featured cybernetic adversaries of Steed and Mrs. Peel. Notably, in these stories, the avengers hurt their hands when attempting to strike these metal foes, and this is something that also occurs in the Feely-Clemens stage play script.

Hannah Wild is a character name recycled from *The Superlative Seven* (1967), a fifth series *Avengers* episode written by stage play co-author Brian Clemens. However, in the previous usage, the forename had been spelled 'Hana'.

The name Carruthers – figuring here as that of a Ministry operative – is an alias used by Steed in the videotape era entries *The Big Thinker* (1962) and *Killer Whale* (1963). Since these episodes were respectively written by Martin Woodhouse and John Lucarotti, it is most likely a coincidence that Brian Clemens and Terence Feely used the name for the stage *Avengers*. However, Clemens later utilised the name in a script that he hoped would lead to an early-1980s revival of *The Avengers*. In *The First Avengers Movie*, Clemens planned to introduce a new female central character to replace the absent Purdey and chose to call her 'C.C. Carruthers' – the 'C.C.' standing, somewhat ludicrously, for 'Carruthers Carruthers' – suggesting that he was quite fond of the name!

Trivia Points

- The action of the play takes place over three days, with Day One comprising the opening scene in Steed's apartment and the action in and around the government bunker in Scotland. Day Two comprises Steed's court-martial and his house arrest, leading up to the shooting of his psychiatrist friend, Mike, which brings Act One to a shocking climax. The action of Act Two takes place entirely on Day Three, with the final scenes at the Ministry of Internal Security and in the Brain Room of the Master Computer being set after dark.

- When we first meet Simon Oates as John Steed in Act One, he tries on a bowler hat that has been discarded in his apartment after a wild party, but finds that it does not fit him. He comments "That's funny. Must belong to the other fellow." While this works within the narrative as meaning someone else at the party, it is a gentle nod to the television Steed, Patrick Macnee. It also brings to mind an almost identical line of dialogue in the James Bond film *On Her Majesty's Secret Service* (1969), in which the incoming Bond, George Lazenby, quips "This never happened to the other fellow," at the end of the pre-titles teaser sequence, referencing Sean Connery's portrayal of the character. In a nice *Avengers* link, Lazenby's comment regarded the fact that a beautiful woman had seemingly resisted his charms and left without him – and that woman was Diana Rigg (playing Teresa 'Tracy' Draco di Vincenzo). It also seems quite possible that Steed's line was a knowing reference to the Bond film.

- Similarly, when Steed announces that he and Hannah should go outside to check out Maitland's dead body and Hannah asks if he needs her to hold his hand, Steed remarks that "I never had this trouble with Mrs. Peel."

- When the succession of mind-mangled agents arrive at Steed's penthouse apartment in the first scene of Act One, they each hum the famous *Greensleeves* tune. This is because they have each investigated Madame Gerda's Greensleeves Finishing Academy for the Daughters of Gentlefolk and have fallen victim to George, the Master Computer in residence. *Greensleeves* is recognised as a medieval composition, and is often attributed to English monarch

King Henry VIII (1491-1547), who purportedly wrote it for his lover and future queen consort, Anne Boleyn. However, historical facts almost certainly disprove this popular accreditation. The song has been said to be at odds with the prevalent style of English music of the 16th century, being based on an Italian compositional style that did not reach England until after Henry's death. A ballad version entitled *A Newe Norther Dittye of ye Ladye Greene Sleves* was registered at the London Stationer's Company in September 1580 by Richard Jones, and, while *Greensleeves* is thought to have originated prior to this date, it is almost certainly a composition of the Elizabethan era.

- The script suggests that the audience might well have thought that the character Melanie was completely unclothed when she appears for the first time, staggering out of the Mummy case in Steed's flat. Actress Wendy Hall was no doubt relieved to see the note that she would be "wearing a body-stocking and nothing else" in this scene and was not actually required to perform the scene nude.

- Likewise, although the script suggests that the pre-filmed sequence featuring Hannah Wild's striptease (to be projected onto George's screen during the finale) would progress to the point where Sue Lloyd was wearing only her knickers, it seems highly unlikely that the actor would have gone topless for this scene. It is very probable that this filmed insert would have been rethought prior to it forming part of the show. A body-stocking, as employed for Wendy Hall, would seem the solution most likely arrived at.

- The Government's underground bunker was originally to have been located under the South Bank of the River Thames. This line of the script was scored through and replaced with a handwritten annotation by Terence Feely to the effect that the venue was to be changed to the Scottish Highlands. Coincidentally, the Ministry of the Warner Bros. feature film *The Avengers* (1998) is located under the Thames in a similar geographical location, with vehicle entry via the Kingsway tramway subway on Southampton Row in Bloomsbury, central London.

- The underground bunker set was designed in such a way that it lent itself to as total a black-out as possible, with dark areas against which invisibility effects – such as the moving of objects and disappearances

– could be achieved as seamlessly as possible. The script also noted that the dark set would make it possible for the 'invisible' actresses to enter and leave the stage without being seen by the audience.

- When audiences went to see *The Avengers* performed in Birmingham and London, they witnessed Steed being guarded by two military policemen during his court martial and when under house arrest. However, in the original script, these characters had been described as Royal Navy Marines. It does seem more conceivable that a government department in Westminster would call on the land-based Army for its security personnel, and this is very likely why the change was made.

- As part of Steed's court-martial, he is instructed to empty his pockets, permitting the writers to pay a flippant homage to the gadgetry of James Bond. Steed extricates the following: his Licence to Kill card (which has two endorsements on it, one for careless knifing and another for parking a corpse on a zebra crossing); bulletproof credit cards; radio tie-pin (which is unable to receive Radio Luxembourg, one of the first commercial radio stations to broadcast to the United Kingdom); invisible ink; four-inch fountain-pen gun ("Fires four-inch fountain pens"); cigarette lighter camera ("For photographing cigarette lighters"); cuff-link pistols ("For shooting one's cuffs"); poison scent spray ("One sniff and you're stiff"); key to the men's washroom at the Treasury; season ticket to Buckingham Palace garden parties; blade of grass from the Queen's Lawn at Ascot; Alvaro's ex-directory telephone number (very likely referring to Alvaro Maccioni [1937-2013], an Italian restauranteur who famously introduced Mediterranean cuisine to 'Swinging Sixties' London); and his Old Etonian tie (which doubles as a garrotte). Steed confirms this to be the extent of the possessions on his person, apart from his vaccination scar and a lock of Yul Brynner's hair (Brynner [1920-1985] was an internationally renowned Russian-born actor with a completely shaven head, best known for his starring roles in feature films such as *The King and I* and *The Three Commandments* [both 1956] and *The Magnificent Seven* [1960]).

- It is revealed during the court martial scene in Act Two that Steed's full name is John Wykeham Beresford Gascoigne Steed, a fact not previously established on television. We also learn that Walters mispronounces "Wykeham", so presumably it should be pronounced "wikkerm". A further disclosure was noted in Dave Rogers' book, *The Ultimate Avengers* (Boxtree Ltd., 1995), to the effect that Steed was one of a family of eight, the other seven siblings being female. This comment is not included in the surviving script and was most likely an addition that post-dated the document that exists today.

- During the final showdown with Madame Gerda, Steed warns that as soon as she launches her attack, she will fall victim to "The Doomsday Weapon", a device which will respond automatically, seeking out and destroying her. Gerda enquires of supercomputer George whether such a deterrent actually exists, since she suspects that Steed is bluffing. George responds that it would be the sort of reasonable precaution that a Government might take. When asked if a deactivator code for such a device would exist, George suggests that, if it did, it would be known to people in positions of trust, namely "Mother, a certain notable yachtsman, and Steed." The unnamed individual is plainly a reference to Sir Edward Heath (1916-2005), then the current British Prime Minister, leader of the Conservative Party, and a keen yachtsman.

- After Steed is connected to the computer, George's screen reveals the pictures in Steed's mind. Initially, he thinks of the Government document that Gerda wishes to view, but manages to turn his thoughts to other things, causing the document to vanish from the screen. Instead, it shows a succession of Steed's memories, which are described in the script as follows: "Ladies' Day at Ascot, the Oxford versus Cambridge Boat Race, a Rolls-Royce picnic with a girl in the country, Steed in a punt with a pretty girl in a romantic dress doing the punting." It is likely that the Rolls-Royce picnic refers to the tag scene of *All Done With Mirrors* (1968), in which Steed enjoys a dinner with Tara King in the middle of a field, having cooked a fillet steak on the engine block of his 1923 Rolls-Royce Silver Ghost (the script, though, refers to the girl as Rosemary). The punting reference would seem to relate to *Silent Dust* (1965), which includes a scene in which Steed relaxes under a parasol aboard a punt on a river while the craft is piloted by Mrs. Peel. However, in this episode Mrs. Peel is attired in a black t-shirt with an "E" over her left breast, black hipster slacks, and a straw boater hat, rather than a romantic dress (the script refers to the girl in this image as being called Jane, who Steed holds in some affection and regards as "such a lovely little punter").

- The *Avengers* stage production could well have marked Joanna Lumley's *Avengers* debut, as she auditioned for the role of Hannah Wild, but was not selected. When interviewed by Dave Rogers for *Look Who's Talking*, an *Avengers* interview-based fanzine published in April 1986, Lumley recalled that "I was turned down because I was an unknown at the time and, because the male lead they'd chosen also wasn't very well known, they decided to go for someone more famous and, in fact, they chose Sue Lloyd." Lumley's own date with *The Avengers* came along five years later in *The New Avengers*, and, since that time, she has become one of the United Kingdom's best-loved personalities.

- *The Avengers* stage play script that is known to survive today is Terence Feely's own. It would appear to be a draft version as the "Pony Girl" in Act Two Scene 14 had been renamed "a Fantasy Masochist" by the time that the Birmingham Theatre souvenir programme went to press. A more significant change to the same scene was the insertion of a Fantasy Cricketer (played by Kubi Chaza) by the time of the Birmingham premiere. As scripted, the character of Melanie (Wendy Hall) performed the same function. In the absence of documentation concerning how this substitution worked, we have elected to follow the action of the script in our synopsis rather than resort to speculation.

- The script is unclear on the reason for the Amazon girls' collapse following the destruction of the Master Computer. There would seem to be three possibilities here. First, that the mind control processing that they have received requires continued control signals being sent by George. Secondly, they are in some way connected to George and they have been rendered unconscious or killed due to the shock of his destruction. Finally, there is the possibility that this is a sign that they, like James and Walters, have been recreated as robots, though this would raise the question of what was done with the bodies of the originals.

- On this subject, it is not openly explained whether Gerda's girls are with her out of choice or have been subjected to George's mind control. From Steed's comments about Melanie and his past knowledge of her relationship with Freddy Pitt-Miller, it would seem that she at least has been "got at".

- Likewise, the mode of Gerda's escape at the end of the play is not explained clearly in the script – which just says "Gerda conspicuously escapes" – but contemporary press reviews suggest that she escapes via a rope ladder that leads to a waiting helicopter. It is not clear how this worked since the script suggests that the play's denouement plays out underground in the Brain Room of the Master Computer, beneath the Academy. Our synopsis alludes to the method of escape but, to avoid guesswork, does not attempt to explain it beyond mentioning the helicopter.

- A further potential twist to the finale is that Gerda's escape and Mother's arrival and assassination could possibly have been staged on a final, additional set – possibly depicting the grounds of Maidenhair Manor. This is perhaps not as speculative a suggestion as it may appear, as the script lists 14 scenes / settings, and yet, in press interviews, producer John C. Mather referred to the play being comprised of "15 different scenes" (*Birmingham Evening Mail*, July 1971).

Verdict

With the exception of the 1998 Warner Bros. feature film, it is probably fair to say that the 1971 stage play is the most reviewed production in the history of *The Avengers*, certainly in terms of press reaction. It is unfortunate, then, that contemporary critiques were overwhelmingly dismissive and, at times, very cutting in nature, but it would be churlish to suggest that the critics got it wrong. There is a great deal about *The Avengers* stage play that should have been better – and, sad to say, that starts with the script.

One would think that screenwriters of the calibre of Terence Feely and Brian Clemens, both well versed in *The Avengers* (particularly Clemens), would have hit the bullseye with their script, but it barely hits the board. These men were responsible for some of the most imaginative, groundbreaking television of the sixties and seventies, so what went wrong in transferring *The Avengers* to the stage?

Although it may well have been an idea imposed on the writers by producer John Mather, the tone of the piece is, in my opinion – at least in the cold light of a script reading – too comedic, and the comedy on show too unsophisticated. The work appears to have been influenced as much by the seaside postcard humour of the *Carry On* films as it is by *The Avengers*. At times, the one-liners plumb depths to which those films would not sink.

Certainly, *The Avengers* on television relied on laughs almost as much as it did on thrills, but the quips and comedic content were sophisticated and witty, if sometimes whimsical. They were never crass or low brow. Therefore, it is frustrating that *The Avengers* play script is often crass and low brow:

STEED:	The Scots? Sex mad! You don't really believe *The Campbells are Coming* is a war song, do you?

+

WALTERS:	When you've finished with Carruthers, take my little doggie for a walk, would you — the little fellow hasn't been out all day.
NURSE:	Very well, sir. Come on, Mr. Carruthers.
CARRUTHERS: (to NURSE, hopefully)	My little fellow hasn't been out all day, either.
NURSE:	Mr. Carruthers!

+

Government departments with juvenile acronyms such as STRAPTIT, BUMFREEZE, FATCHOPS, FUTTOCKS and CRUD, and place names like Maidenhair Manor, Hymen-on-the-Green.

Thankfully, however, there are occasional flashes of wit:

MOTHER:	It's serious — the British Government is being deliberately compromised.
STEED:	Very serious. That's something they usually prefer to do for themselves.

+

WALTERS:	There they were, all dead, nobody there but Steed and he's babbling about invisible girls in leather drawers.

| MOTHER: | If they're invisible, how does he know what kind of drawers they're wearing? Sorry to be a bore, but it's the kind of question the P.M. always asks. |

+

| STEED: | I would face up to anything, but I have very cowardly legs. A hero is merely a coward manqué. I have always considered that bravery is a triumph of vanity over fear. |

There are also fleeting reminders that Steed is a sophisticate with a love of the good things in life:

| STEED: | St. George for England! And Nuits-Saint-Georges for France! |
| | ...AS HE SIPS AT A GOOD BURGUNDY. |

And glimpses of whimsy:

> The mind-altered agents who believe they are, respectively, a mimic, a frogman, an astronaut and a giant pigeon.

+

> Mother's misunderstanding various people and futilely resorting to the Ministry code book.

It's as if there is genuine *Avengers*-ish material struggling to make itself heard. Unfortunately, the lines that jar *do* tend to grab the attention more than those that fit in nicely.

The best one can say about this aspect of the production is that the script was written in different times and may have appealed more to the sensibilities of a 1971 audience than it does to one of more than fifty years later. It is telling that the *Avengers* television series has not dated in this respect to anything like the same degree.

Leaving the subject of humour behind, the script disappoints on other levels too. To begin with, the opening scene in Steed's apartment seems to go on forever and is of a very repetitive nature, with agent after agent arriving to report to Steed, only to behave strangely and either be killed, commit suicide, or lose their mind. Perhaps it worked better as a performance. Fortunately, the narrative ticks along much more pacily after this scene is out of the way.

Additionally, there are a couple of portions of the script that defy narrative logic. The first of these is when Steed tries to convince Hannah that he has not shot and killed his psychiatrist friend Mike by suggesting that she check the Egyptian Mummy case. Steed expects that Mrs. Wild will find Mike inside, safe and well. Considering that this scene is set on the day following the shooting, and Steed's court martial has taken place in the interim, it seems something of a stretch to expect the man to have remained inside the Mummy case all that time (in fact, he has, but that is only because he has been killed by James). Secondly, Steed and Hannah visit both the Ministry for Internal Security and Gerda's finishing school for young women, and yet don't notice that both these places are in Maidenhead, Berkshire – and are close enough to each other to be connected by tunnels. The geographical location of Walters' office at the Ministry is not revealed until near the end of the play, despite visits in earlier scenes. The twist may well have wrong-footed theatre audiences, but it makes Steed and Mrs. Wild look like amateur hour fools. Additionally, there is no attempt made to explain the homicidal hatstand that attacks Hannah in Steed's apartment. Presumably it is controlled by Gerda / George and has been acquired for Steed by James, but no clues are provided in the script.

A further leap of faith required of the audience comes when Gerda is revealed to be transgender. We learn from the Walters robot that the original Walters has undergone surgery and is now known as Gerda. This in itself is not a leap of faith, as audiences will have been familiar with the concept of gender transition – after all, the first sex change operation in the UK had been carried out in 1951. However, the idea that a 56-year-old, approximately 5 foot 8 inch tall, officious, ex-public school type man like Walters could reinvent themselves (with the surgeons' help) as a 32-year-old, 5 foot 4 inch, forceful and sexy Swedish baroness is faintly ridiculous. However, it must be taken into account that the stage *Avengers* is resolutely a comedy (more so than *The Avengers* television series) and, as such, it is easier to accept this improbability than it would be in an ordinary drama.

Furthermore, Feely and Clemens' decision to reveal that both James and Walters are robots is a touch unsatisfying, particularly in James' case. She is in Gerda's thrall and the fact that James is a robot gives rise to the question "How many of Gerda's Amazons are actually robots?" Additionally, the fact that Melanie appears to have been "got at" prompts one to ask "How many of

Gerda's Amazons are collaborating with her only because George has processed their minds?" The script does not supply answers to either of these questions. The play performance might have made all this clearer.

In tandem with writing partner Terence Feely, Brian Clemens appears to have broken the rules that he himself had established for *The Avengers*. For instance, the writers show blood (when the dignitary at the beginning is shot, on the psychiatrist's body, and when Mother is killed), passersby, female characters being killed (even if they *are* robots) and do not allow for both risqué and innocent interpretations of the material. One cannot help but wonder just how much these innovations were the choice of the writers and how much they were due to the requirements of the producer. Certainly, the comments made in interviews by Feely and Clemens seem to be heavily focused on the plot and the special effects, suggesting that these elements formed their primary interest and focus. It is telling that the pair appear to have made no remarks about how being freed up from the jurisdiction of the Independent Television Authority made it possible for them to be risqué. It is quite possible that those influences came from elsewhere. If that was the case – and Feely and Clemens were working to a strict brief that maybe deviated from *The Avengers* 'series bible' – then perhaps this could explain why the stage play script doesn't feel authentically *Avengers*-ish despite its seasoned authors.

Beyond the script, the major fault with the play was arguably in its overambitious nature. John Mather strove to present a spectacular experience for audiences that would "blast the British theatre into the seventies", but the reality was – at least on the budget secured to stage it and with the technology available – that the production got off the launch pad in an embarrassing fashion. In many ways, the blame should not be laid at the door of the designers, set and prop builders, and stagehands, but at that of the people who made the decisions about what was possible – presumably Mather and director Leslie Phillips. A rethought production that pushed less hard at the boundaries of what was possible under the proscenium arch would have put *The Avengers* on a surer footing, with the added benefit that the actors could work without a constant expectation of calamity.

On the subject of the actors, with no visual or auditory evidence of the play surviving beyond photographs, it would be unfair to dismiss any or all of them purely on the basis of contemporary reviews. Simon Oates received positive and negative notices for his performance as Steed, but he was clearly passionate about the play and understood the responsibility inherent in taking over from the much-admired Patrick Macnee. Seeing his Steed-ish performances as Ridge in *Doomwatch*, he seems to me to have been good casting, and while perhaps some choices were a little off target, the script did him few favours. By comparison, Sue Lloyd, Kate O'Mara and Anthony Sharp attracted more positive responses, and they too seem to have been good choices for their roles.

The shining positive from the production would seem to be the character of Hannah Wild, who works as a strong *Avengers* woman and is worthy of comparison to her predecessors: Cathy Gale, Emma Peel and Tara King. Mrs. Wild comes over as highly capable, cool, intelligent and stylish, if somewhat headstrong.

In all, *The Avengers* stage play is an ambitious, fascinating, if fatally flawed entry in the series' canon. With a mere 36 performances across two venues and a greatest possible viewership of fewer than 50,000 people, it must go down as one of the least seen *Avengers* stories. Its reputation as a bit of a stinker is unfortunate, as clearly those making it went into it wanting to revive *The Avengers* in an extravagant and amusing way, but... End of Play report:

<u>GRADE:</u> D.
<u>COMMENT:</u> Could do better. See Mother.

THE RADIO SERIES

ALAN HAYES

Project Type: Radio Series
Transmission Dates: January 1972 to December 1973 (South Africa)

Series Guide

The information that follows is more of a guide to the surviving South African *Avengers* radio serials than to the series as a whole. This is due to the lack of any surviving production information at the SABC or Sonovision Studios, and the scant detail published in newspapers and magazines of the time. As a result, it is possible only to make educated guesses regarding what was actually broadcast, but it is relatively safe to say that the vast majority – if not all – of the 83 television episodes of *The Avengers* filmed from 1965-1969 would have had a radio equivalent.

Using clues from the off-air reel-to-reel tapes, such as the regular Friday evening cast announcements – which were absent on other weeknights – we have attempted to construct a transmission order for *The Avengers* on Springbok Radio. We have done this by following the recording order across the multiple tracks of the surviving quarter-track tapes.

The following listing should be read with these considerations in mind:

- All serials featured Emma Peel as Steed's partner, regardless of their source. Tara King does not appear.

- Mother features occasionally, and is even referred to in some serials based on television episodes that were made before the character was created.

- *The Fantasy Game* appears to be the earliest surviving *Avengers* serial. The off-air recordings comprise a near-unbroken run from *The Quick-Quick-Slow Death* to *From Venus with Love*, omitting only *Pandora*. Following an indeterminate break, three further, consecutive serials were committed to tape: *A Case of Interrogation*, *Too Many Olés* and *Train of Events*.

- Springbok Radio was very resistant to repeating recorded programmes. However, it was sometimes necessary to make a second recording of an earlier script when, for instance, deadlines were looming large. Character names, story elements and dialogue would be subtly changed and occasionally the serial would be transmitted under a new title. We know that this recycling of scripts was in force on *The Avengers* as *Escape in Time* is confirmed to have been produced twice. *The Avengers* debuted with an adaptation of this story in January 1972, written by Tony Jay. However, the three *Escape in Time* episodes that survive feature Mother, a character Jay swore that he never used, suggesting that the surviving recordings were from later in the series' run and were adapted by Jay's successor, Dennis Folbigge. To distinguish between the productions, they are referred to in this guide as *Escape in Time* and *Escape in Time (Remake)*. It is likely that there were several such remounts across the full run of the series.

- Dave Rogers' book *The Complete Avengers* (Boxtree, 1989) devoted a brief section to the radio series and revealed that *A Sense of History* and *Who's Who???* were among the episodes adapted and that scripts for *The Correct Way to Kill*, *The £50,000 Breakfast*, *Wish You Were Here* and *Killer* were among those sent to Sonovision, implying that these were also likely to have been adapted for radio. Several missing serials have also been confirmed as having been made and transmitted thanks to annotations made to original television scripts.

- When we compare the titles of radio episodes to those of their television equivalents, we ignore the dropping or adding of definite articles. For instance, we would not comment that *Quick-Quick-Slow Death* became *The Quick-Quick-Slow Death* when it was adapted for radio.

The Serials

Escape in Time (5 x 15 minute episodes)
Based on: The 1967 episode of the same name, written by Philip Levene
Recorded: c. Wednesday 6th December 1971
Transmitted: Monday 3rd to Friday 7th January 1972 (series debut)
Archive: Does not survive

Plotline: John Steed and Emma Peel investigate a series of mysterious disappearances of criminals, embezzlers and corrupt politicians, who are wanted by the authorities in connection with their crimes. Our heroes follow a series of leads and find the missing people end up in the distant past – before winding up there themselves!

Production Notes: This *Avengers* story was the first to be transmitted on Springbok Radio. The number of episodes that form this story has been confirmed via the broadcast listings magazine *SAUK-SABC Bulletin*.

Escape in Time was later remade during Dennis Folbigge's tenure as writer.

10th January to 27th March 1972:
Transmission continued but only one serial during this period can be identified

---

The Return of the Ripper (5 x 15 minute episodes)
Based on: The 1968 episode *Fog*, written by Jeremy Burnham
Transmitted: At some point between 10th January and 27th March 1972
Archive: Does not survive

Plotline: Members of the world disarmament committee arrive in London and face thick fog and an historic killer named the Gaslight Ghoul, who picks them off one by one.

Production Notes: No details are known about this serial, the production of which has been confirmed via an annotated television script of the episode, which states the episode title change for radio and the number of episodes.

The script also confirms that the radio serial had the working title *An Old Fashioned Murder*.

The number of episodes (5) places this serial firmly in the early days of the series when Tony Jay was adapting and directing *The Avengers*. His replacement Dennis Folbigge favoured serialisations over six or seven episodes.

The Fantasy Game (7 x 15 minute episodes)
Based on: The 1966 episode *Honey for the Prince*, written by Brian Clemens
Transmitted: Tuesday 28th March to Wednesday 5th April 1972
Additional Cast: Rex Garner as Arkadi, Bruce Millar as Prince Ali, Kerry Jordan as Grand Vizier
Archive: Off-air recording by John Wright

Plotline: There are suspicious goings on at Quite Quite Fantastic Inc., where it is claimed that fantasies can be turned into reality. Two agents end up being shot when they investigate. One manages to warn Steed and Mrs. Peel before he expires. Steed opts to pay QQF a visit and Emma takes a different line, ending up at the honey shop of one B. Bumble. Before long they realise that they are faced with an assassination plot, the target being Prince Ali of Bahrain, who is in London, complete with his harem.

Production Notes: This serial, broadcast on Springbok Radio in late March and early April 1972, is thought to be the only surviving *Avengers* serial adapted and directed by Tony Jay, though it is possible that this is actually a very early Dennis Folbigge serial and that Jay had left the series earlier than suggested. The usual Friday announcement of central cast and crew at the end of Episode 4 was instead given over to a special announcement by Hugh Rouse, recommending that listeners tune in on Monday night at 10.00pm for a new series, *The White Oaks of Jalna*. This programme premiered on Monday 3rd April 1972, so *The Fantasy Game* can be dated based on that information. This is the only existing episode that features such an announcement for another programme.

19th May to 23rd October 1972:
The run from *The Quick-Quick-Slow Death* to *Take Me To Your Leader* is thought to be consecutive. Where a transmission date is a best guess based on data available, the entry is marked as (estimated)

The Quick-Quick-Slow Death (6 x 15 minute episodes)
Based on: The 1966 episode of the same name, written by Robert Banks Stewart
Transmitted: Friday 19th to Friday 26th May 1972 (estimated)
Archive: Off-air recording by John Wright

Plotline: When a foreign agent is apprehended whilst attempting to get rid of a corpse, Steed and Mrs. Peel find that the clues point to a dancing school that proves to be a cover for an organisation introducing enemy spies into British society.

Production Notes: The Quick-Quick-Slow Death is thought to be the earliest surviving *Avengers* serial adapted and directed by Dennis Folbigge (please see *The Fantasy Game*'s Production Notes).

Love All (6 x 15 minute episodes)
Based on: The 1969 episode of the same name, written by Jeremy Burnham
Transmitted: Friday 29th May to Monday 5th June 1972 (estimated)
Additional Cast: Stuart Brown as Mother
Archive: Off-air recording by John Wright

Plotline: Highly respected and reliable government civil servants are suddenly falling head over heels in love with an unremarkable office cleaner - and they can't help but pass all their secrets to her. Just what is this woman's secret?

Production Notes: This serial is notable for featuring Stuart Brown in the role of Mother. The role was usually – perhaps subsequently – played by Colin Fish, and was also portrayed on occasion by Anthony Fridjhon.

Getaway (6 x 15 minute episodes)
Based on: The 1968 episode *Get-A-Way!*, written by Philip Levene
Transmitted: Tuesday 6th to Tuesday 13th June 1972 (estimated)
Archive: Off-air recording by John Wright

Plotline: A trio of Russian assassins is under lock and key at Oldhill Monastery, a strange, supposedly escape-proof prison staffed by monks. Somehow, two of the three manage to evade all the security and regain their freedom. They do this by making themselves invisible to the human eye, by drinking Lizard Vodka. The two escaped assassins both succeed in killing their target. The third assassin is about to make his getaway... and his mission is to eliminate John Steed.

Production Notes: It appears that, judging from narrator Hugh Rouse's delivery, the serial's title should be written as *Getaway* (the television episode's on-screen title is *Get-A-Way!*).

A Deadly Gift (6 x 15 minute episodes)
Based on: The 1965 episode *The Cybernauts*, written by Philip Levene
Transmitted: Wednesday 14th to Wednesday 21st June 1972 (estimated)
Archive: Off-air recording by John Wright

Plotline: Steed and Mrs. Peel investigate a series of murders of businessmen, all of whom have been bidding on a new circuit component. Each appears to have suffered a fatal, superhuman Karate blow to the neck, so Mrs. Peel visits a Karate school. Steed's own inquiries lead him to United Automation, where he finds an ex-Ministry scientist, Dr. Clement Armstrong, who is developing an electronic brain. Unbeknownst to Steed, Armstrong also has a secret sideline – he has invented and is building Pabulum Robots.

This serial was unofficially animated using Muvizu software in 2012-13 as The Cybernauts, *a non-commercial fan-produced project by Paul Farrer of Fazz68*

Productions. The animations remain on the animator's YouTube channel (www.youtube.com/user/fazzman1968).

The Super Secret Cypher Snatch (6 x 15 minute episodes)
Based on: The 1968 episode of the same name, written by Tony Williamson
Transmitted: Thursday 22nd to Thursday 29th June 1972 (estimated)
Additional Cast: Colin Fish as Mother
Archive: Off-air recording by John Wright

Plotline: Cypher Headquarters is leaking secrets at an alarming rate. It seems impossible that this couldn't be happening without someone breaking in, but all those working at the establishment claim that nothing of any note has happened. Every day has been perfectly normal. However, Steed and Mrs. Peel prove that there is a connection between the stolen information and a seemingly innocent window cleaning service.

Production Notes: There is some debate over the title of the television episode, with some sources claiming that it is *Sepet Sucpre Cncehc Sypare (Super Secret Cypher Snatch)*.

Dial A Deadly Number (6 x 15 minute episodes)
Based on: The 1965 episode of the same name, written by Roger Marshall
Transmitted: Friday 30th June to Monday 10th July 1972 (estimated – no episode broadcast on Monday 3rd July 1972)
Archive: Off-air recording by John Wright

Plotline: Company chairmen across the city are dying unexpectedly of heart attacks, though apparently due to natural causes. Can Steed and Mrs. Peel discover who is making a killing in big business... and how?

Not to be Sneezed At (7 x 15 minute episodes)
Based on: The 1968 episode *You'll Catch Your Death*, written by Jeremy Burnham
Transmitted: Tuesday 11th to Wednesday 19th July 1972 (estimated)
Additional Cast: Anthony Fridjhon as Mother
Archive: Off-air recording by John Wright

Plotline: Steed and Mrs. Peel look into the goings on at the Anastasia Nursing Academy, which is developing a deadly germ that causes the victim to sneeze so incessantly that they die. The Academy aims to sell it to the highest bidder and the avengers must protect the doctors who can provide the antidote and are therefore the most at risk.

Production Notes: Colin Fish, the actor who regularly played Mother was not available for the recording of this serial, and was replaced by Anthony Fridjhon.

Pandora (6 x 15 minute episodes)
Based on: The 1969 episode of the same name, written by Brian Clemens
Transmitted: Thursday 20th to Thursday 27th July 1972 (estimated)
Archive: Does not survive

Plotline: Emma Peel is drugged and kidnapped in an antiques shop. When she comes to, she finds it's not a matter of where, but when she has ended up. The answer to that would appear to be '1915', but then she has another question forming in her mind: who is she? Everyone she encounters calls her 'Pandora'. Could they be right? Meanwhile, an elderly former agent, Lasindell, who is on the verge of departing this world, has promised to reveal the whereabouts of his hidden treasure to a couple of untrustworthy nephews who tell him they have revived his dead love from the grave. That'll be you, Mrs. Peel! Should Lasindell fail to co-operate then Pandora, alias Mrs. Peel, will come to harm.

Production Notes: This serial is known to have been produced because the events that take place in it are mentioned in the subsequent story, *Who Shot Poor George / XR40?*

Who Shot Poor George / XR40? (7 x 15 minute episodes)
Based on: The 1969 episode *Whoever Shot Poor George Oblique Stroke XR40?*, written by Tony Williamson
Transmitted: Friday 28th July to Monday 7th August 1972 (estimated)
Additional Cast: Colin Fish as Mother
Archive: Off-air recording by John Wright

Plotline: George is the most important and brilliant computer in the country, but somebody seems to have it in for him. He has been shot at, had acid poured into his workings and been shut down. He manages to call for help via a print-out, but Steed and Mrs. Peel remain uncertain regarding the identity of the saboteur and call upon his creator, Sir Wilfred Pelley, for assistance.

Production Notes: A line in this serial reveals that the previous story was the non-extant *Pandora*. Emma Peel complains that she has "only just finished impersonating Pandora."

A Grave Charge (6 x 15 minute episodes)
Based on: The 1969 episode *Bizarre*, written by Brian Clemens
Transmitted: Tuesday 8th to Tuesday 15th August 1972 (estimated)
Additional Cast: Colin Fish as Mother
Archive: Off-air recording by John Wright

Plotline: Discovered wandering in a snowy field, Helen Pritchard attests to having seen a dead man walking. This leads Steed to pay a visit to the Happy Meadows funeral parlour where he meets the cheery undertaker, Mr. Happychap. Unfortunately, the funeral parlour seems unable to keep its corpses from going for a wander. Steed decides to arrange his own funeral so that he may learn more.

All Done by Mirrors (7 x 15 minute episodes)
Based on: The 1968 episode *All Done with Mirrors*, written by Leigh Vance
Transmitted: Wednesday 16th to Thursday 24th August 1972 (estimated)
Additional Cast: Colin Fish as Mother
Archive: Off-air recording by John Wright

Plotline: Someone is leaking vital secrets from the Carmadoc Research Establishment. Mother explains to Steed that as a precaution he must put him under arrest. Steed, having worked covertly at Carmadoc to find out how secrets are leaking, is suspected by the staff there. Mother assigns Mrs. Peel to the case with the assistance of Watney, a somewhat incompetent 'green' agent. The unlikely pair must unmask the real traitor.

The Morning After (6 x 15 minute episodes)
Based on: The 1968 episode of the same name, written by Brian Clemens
Transmitted: Friday 25th August to Friday 1st September 1972 (estimated)
Archive: Off-air recording by John Wright

Plotline: Having been gassed and knocked unconscious while pursuing rogue agent Jimmy Merlin, Steed awakes to find that London is deserted. Soon he realises that the area is subject to an evacuation and martial law, imposed by a Brigadier Hanson. In reality, the Brigadier is furious that he is to be pensioned off from the Army and has planted an atom bomb with which he plans to destroy the city. All Steed has to do is find it and get it defused!

Production Notes: Some of the incidental music used during this story is remarkably similar to the theme of the ITC series *Department S*, composed by Edwin Astley.

The Joker (6 x 15 minute episodes)
Based on: The 1967 episode of the same name, written by Brian Clemens
Transmitted: Monday 4th to Monday 11th September 1972 (estimated)
Archive: Off-air recording by John Wright

Plotline: Mrs. Peel has received an invitation to the house of Sir Cavalier Rousicana on Exmoor. Sir Cavalier, a 75-year-old recluse, is a renowned Bridge player and has asked Emma over for the weekend after seeing an article she has written. She accepts, but when she arrives, she soon realises that she has been lured there by a dangerous man known as 'The Joker'. She had once helped to put him in prison, but he has now escaped and, with his two unhinged accomplices, subjects her to a succession of lethal tricks and traps.

Production Notes: The television version of *The Joker* was a revised remake of an earlier episode, *Don't Look Behind You* (1963), also written by Brian Clemens and featuring Honor Blackman as Cathy Gale instead of Diana Rigg as Emma Peel.

Episode Five of this story is the only episode which exists with its original Springbok Radio continuity announcement.

The record that Prendergast plays to remind Mrs. Peel of their rendezvous in Paris is *Mam'selle*, written by Edmund Goulding (music) and Mack Gordon (lyrics). The version heard in *The Joker* was a 1947 recording by The Pied Pipers, released by Capitol Records as catalogue number 396. This varies from the television episode, in which an original Laurie Johnson composition, *Meine Leibe, Meine Rose*, was used for this purpose.

Straight from the Shoulder (6 x 15 minute episodes)
Based on: The unaired 1968 episode *Invitation to a Killing*, written by Donald James
Transmitted: Tuesday 12th to Tuesday 19th September 1972 (estimated)
Archive: Off-air recording by John Wright

Plotline: When three thousand FF70 rifles – a brand-new rifle not yet off the secret list – are stolen, Steed suspects the visiting Colonel Aristedes, who is planning a coup d'état in his home country. However, the scheming Adriana Beardsley actually has the guns, which she intends to auction off to the highest bidder – but not before she stages a demonstration for her potential buyers, with Mrs. Peel as an unwilling human target!

Production Notes: Straight from the Shoulder is based on *Invitation to a Killing*, which was reputedly intended to be a movie-length introductory episode for the sixth series of *The Avengers*. It was one of four episodes that were at least partially completed when key production personnel were suddenly replaced by the ABPC management. The original television script was written by Donald James, and was redrafted (without on-screen credit) by Brian Clemens and Albert Fennell as *Have Guns – Will Haggle* – a standard length episode.

Stop Me If You've Heard This (6 x 15 minute episodes)
Based on: The 1968 episode *Look – (Stop Me If You've Heard This One) But There Were These Two Fellers..*, written by Dennis Spooner
Transmitted: Wednesday 20th to Wednesday 27th September 1972 (estimated)
Archive: Off-air recording by John Wright

Plotline: Directors of the Capital Land and Development Company, a business involved in a secret government project, are being murdered one by one. Steed and Mrs. Peel are called in to investigate. A clown's nose at the scene of the crime leads them to suspect Merry Maxie Martin and his partner Jolly Jenkins, retired music-hall artists residing at Greasepaint Grange, a home for ex-vaudeville acts. It seems they may be part of a campaign against the Company, in retaliation for its policy of buying up and closing down old music-hall venues – a campaign orchestrated by the leader of the Greasepaint Grange residents, Mr. Punch...

From Venus With Love (6 x 15 minute episodes)
Based on: The 1967 episode of the same name, written by Philip Levene
Transmitted: Thursday 28th September to Thursday 5th October 1972 (estimated)
Archive: Off-air recording by John Wright

Plotline: Members of the British Venusian Society, an organisation set up to observe the planet Venus, are literally and fatally turning white while on watch at night! A phone call from Mother sends Steed and Mrs. Peel off to investigate this phenomenon. Is the BVS involved or is the cause something even more bizarre: a Venusian invasion?

Take Me to Your Leader (7 x 15 minute episodes)
Based on: The 1968 episode of the same name, written by Terry Nation
Recorded: Thursday 5th October 1972
Transmitted: Friday 13th to Monday 23rd October 1972 (estimated)
Archive: Does not survive

Plotline: A red suitcase containing a hefty sum of money, not to mention a bomb as a security device, is giving people orders about where to take it and when. Believing it is headed for 'Mr. Big', Mother puts Steed and Emma in charge of tracking the case – which leads them straight back to Mother!

Production Notes: No details are known about this serial, the production of which has been confirmed via an annotated television script of the episode, which notes the number of episodes in the serial plus recording and transmission dates.

It is presumed that a five-part serial preceded *Take Me to Your Leader*, possibly a new version of an early Sonovision production from the pen of Tony Jay, running from Friday 6th to Thursday 12th October 1972.

Tuesday 24th October 1972 to Friday 28th December 1973:
The Avengers transmissions continue to their conclusion.

It has not been possible to date the transmissions of the following serials:

A Case of Interrogation (7 x 15 minute episodes)
Based on: The 1969 episode *The Interrogators*, written by Richard Harris and Brian Clemens
Transmitted: A Friday to a Monday in 1972 or 1973
Additional Cast: Colin Fish as Mother
Archive: Off-air recording by John Wright

Plotline: Two men are sitting outside a room where interrogations are going on. One of them goes in and a man named Colonel Mannering violently demands to know the names of his contacts, but he gives nothing but his name – Caspar – rank and serial number. Mother is worried because Caspar, one of his important intelligence men, is missing. It seems Mannering is actually a foreign agent who has struck upon an ingenious method of extracting secret information from British agents.

Production Notes: In addition to the Friday evening episodes (Episodes One and Six), the concluding episode – aired on a Monday – also carries a 'Friday-style' credit announcement, presumably because it was the last instalment of the serial.

Too Many Olés (6 x 15 minute episodes)
Based on: The 1968 episode *They Keep Killing Steed*, written by Brian Clemens
Transmitted: A Tuesday to a Tuesday in 1972 or 1973
Additional Cast: Colin Fish as Mother
Archive: Off-air recording by John Wright

Plotline: Steed and Mrs. Peel are given an assignment with a difference – they are to observe at a peace conference, but for once it is not in Britain. In fact, it is being held in Tarragon, Spain, a place near Zaragoza. The two agents look on the trip as something approaching a holiday. However, what they don't know is that a man called Arcos is waiting for them, or, more precisely, Steed. Arcos and his co-conspirator Markin have developed a process to literally mould a man's features into those of someone else, and Steed is the man whose features they are copying.

Production Notes: A long section of Laurie Johnson's *Symphony (Synthesis)* cue is heard at the end of Episode One as the actors' performance underran significantly.

This radio version transposes the action to sunny Spain – hence the title. *They Keep Killing Steed* was originally to have been set in Spain (budget concerns caused the fallback to a British setting), so it is likely that the script that Sonovision received from EMI was an early draft version.

Episode 1 of this serial was unofficially animated using Muvizu software in 2013 as Too Many Steeds, *a non-commercial fan-produced project by Paul Farrer of Fazz68 Productions. The animation remains on the animator's YouTube channel (www.youtube.com/user/fazzman1968).*

Train of Events (6 x 15 minute episodes)
Based on: The 1967 episode *A Funny Thing Happened on the Way to the Station*, written by Brian Sheriff
Transmitted: A Wednesday to a Wednesday in 1972 or 1973
Archive: Off-air recording by John Wright

Plotline: Journeying on the railway in order to locate a missing agent, Steed and Mrs. Peel uncover a plot to assassinate the British Prime Minister, who is travelling on the same line. The perpetrator proves to be a disgruntled and murderous ticket collector. The avengers enlist the help of Mr. Crewe, the eccentric owner of an abandoned railway station.

Production Notes: The original television script – *A Funny Thing Happened on the Way to the Station* – was credited to Brian Sheriff, a pseudonym. The original story by Roger Marshall, entitled *Overkill*, was substantially re-written by Brian Clemens. The thinking behind the nom de plume is obvious.

The Curious Case of the Countless Clues (7 x 15 minute episodes)
Based on: The 1968 episode of the same name, written by Philip Levene
Transmitted: 1972 or 1973
Archive: Does not survive

Plotline: Men of the aristocracy are being implicated in murders through damning evidence – too much evidence, as a matter of fact – courtesy of a creative blackmailer with a weakness for fine paintings.

Production Notes: No details are known about this serial, the production of which has been confirmed via an annotated television script of the episode, which also confirms the number of episodes.

Split! (6 x 15 minute episodes)
Based on: The 1968 episode of the same name, written by Brian Clemens
Transmitted: 1972 or 1973
Archive: Does not survive

Plotline: A murder takes place within the Ministry of Top Secret Information, but the level of security makes it quite impossible for an outsider to do such a thing. Then a handwriting expert confirms that documents written by Ministry personnel match that of an enemy agent slain by Steed many years ago!

Production Notes: No details are known about this serial, the production of which has been confirmed via an annotated television script of the episode, which also confirms the number of episodes.

It seems likely that this serial was retitled for radio, perhaps to *Split Personality*.

The Rotters (7 x 15 minute episodes)
Based on: The 1968 episode of the same name, written by Dave Freeman
Transmitted: 1972 or 1973
Archive: Does not survive

Plotline: Forestry and timber experts are being murdered. It seems they all know a bit too much about a powerful form of dry rot – which a madman will release on the country if he is not paid the modest sum of one thousand million pounds.

Production Notes: No details are known about this serial, the production of which has been confirmed via an annotated television script of the episode, which also confirms the number of episodes.

Can You Ever Trust A Woman? (7 x 15 minute episodes)
Based on: The 1968 episode *Who Was That Man I Saw You With*, written by Jeremy Burnham
Transmitted: 1972 or 1973
Archive: Does not survive

Plotline: While carrying out orders to infiltrate a top-security defence site, Emma is identified as working with an enemy agent. It's an elaborate frame-up, of course, but by the time she can prove it, the damage is already done. Were it not for Steed and his lip-reader, it would be raining missiles any minute.

Production Notes: No details are known about this serial, the production of which has been confirmed via an annotated television script of the episode, which also confirms the number of episodes and the title change for radio.

Force of Evil (7 x 15 minute episodes)
Based on: The 1968 episode *Thingumajig*, written by Terry Nation
Transmitted: 1972 or 1973
Archive: Does not survive

Plotline: Something is killing archaeologists working on a dig beneath a Norman church, and this something has a voracious appetite for energy. Had the diabolical mastermind who invented it not let two of them escape by accident, Britain would awake one morning to see thousands of the little devils running around – killing everybody!

Production Notes: No details are known about this serial, the production of which has been confirmed via an annotated television script of the episode, which also confirms the number of episodes and the title change for radio.

Escape in Time (Remake) (5+ x 15 minute episodes)
Based on: The 1967 episode of the same name, written by Philip Levene
Transmitted: 1972 or 1973
Additional Cast: Colin Fish as Mother

Archive: Studio recording (Episodes 1 and 2); off-air recording by Barbara Peterson (Episode 3); subsequent episodes do not exist

Plotline: John Steed and Emma Peel investigate a series of mysterious disappearances by criminals, embezzlers and corrupt politicians, wanted by the authorities in connection with their crimes. Our heroes follow a series of leads and find the missing people end up in the distant past – before winding up there themselves!

Production Notes: Sonovision produced two versions of *Escape in Time*. The first adaptation was transmitted as the series opener in January 1972, while this version was produced later in the series, rewritten by Dennis Folbigge. The original version was adapted and directed by Tony Jay and did not feature the character of Mother.

A Sense of History (5+ x 15 minute episodes)
Based on: The 1966 episode of the same name, written by Martin Woodhouse
Transmitted: 1972 or 1973
Archive: Does not survive

Plotline: An economist with a vision of a new Europe, who goes to meet someone opposed to his ideas, is killed with an arrow fired by 'Robin Hood'. The clues lead Steed and Mrs. Peel to St. Bode's College, where headstrong students defy traditional schools of thought. Could one of them be the killer? All becomes clear at a fancy dress party where everyone plays a part from the Robin Hood legend.

Production Notes: No details are known about this serial, the production of which has been confirmed via an annotated television script of the episode.

Who's Who? (5+ x 15 minute episodes)
Based on: The 1967 episode of the same name, written by Philip Levene
Transmitted: 1972 or 1973
Archive: Does not survive

Plotline: Mad scientist Dr. Krelmar has devised a machine that will swap people's minds. Enemy agents Basil and Lola use it – swapping their minds into the bodies of Steed and Mrs. Peel – in order to infiltrate the British spy network and destroy it. Basil goes first, exchanging personalities with Steed, but Mrs. Peel is suspicious that the man who looks like Steed is acting out of character and has to persuade the real Steed of what is going on.

Production Notes: No details are known about this serial, the production of which has been confirmed via an annotated television script of the episode.

The Correct Way to Kill (5+ x 15 minute episodes)
Based on: The 1967 episode of the same name, written by Brian Clemens
Transmitted: 1972 or 1973 (production unconfirmed)
Archive: Does not survive

Plotline: Someone is systematically eliminating foreign agents. Steed declares a truce and calls on his Russian opposite, Nutski. Along with Soviet agents Anna and Ivan, Steed and Mrs. Peel discover SNOB, a quintessential English gentlemen's club with members who are both patriotic and exceptionally well-versed in murder.

Production Notes: No details are known about this serial, the likely production of which has been confirmed by a statement in *The Ultimate Avengers* by Dave Rogers (Boxtree, 1995) noting that a script of this episode was sent to Sonovision by EMI.

The £50,000 Breakfast (5+ x 15 minute episodes)
Based on: The 1967 episode of the same name, written by Roger Marshall
Transmitted: 1972 or 1973 (production unconfirmed)
Archive: Does not survive

Plotline: Steed and Mrs. Peel find that the clues point to canines when £50,000 of stolen diamonds are found in the gut of a murdered man. Mismatched Borzoi hairs lead Steed and Emma to a pet cemetery where they must determine whether the villain's bite is as bad as his bark.

Production Notes: No details are known about this serial, the likely production of which has been confirmed by a statement in *The Ultimate Avengers* by Dave Rogers (Boxtree, 1995) noting that a script of this episode was sent to Sonovision by EMI.

The television version of *The £50,000 Breakfast* was a revised remake of an earlier episode, *Death of a Great Dane* (1962), written by Roger Marshall and Jeremy Scott, and featuring Honor Blackman as Cathy Gale instead of Diana Rigg as Emma Peel.

Wish You Were Here (? x 15 minute episodes)
Based on: The 1969 episode of the same name, written by Tony Williamson
Transmitted: 1972 or 1973 (production unconfirmed)
Archive: Does not survive

Plotline: A holiday hotel that Mrs. Peel goes to spend a break at proves to have a strict 'no check out' policy for certain guests. Mrs. Peel finds that getting away from it all could end up being permanent as she seems to be one of the guests for whom returning home is not on the holiday menu.

Production Notes: No details are known about this serial, the likely production of which has been confirmed by a statement in *The Ultimate Avengers* by Dave Rogers (Boxtree, 1995) noting that a script of this episode was sent to Sonovision by EMI.

Killer (5+ x 15 minute episodes)
Based on: The 1969 episode of the same name, written by Tony Williamson
Transmitted: 1972 or 1973 (production not confirmed, but highly likely)
Archive: Does not survive

Plotline: A succession of British agents have been eliminated, their corpses dumped in a graveyard, carefully wrapped in plastic sheeting. Steed and Mrs. Peel investigate a sinister factory that houses the deadly computer REMAK – Remote Electro-Matic Agent Killer – which they must destroy.

Production Notes: No details are known about this serial, the likely production of which has been confirmed by a statement in *The Ultimate Avengers* by Dave Rogers (Boxtree, 1995) noting that a script of this episode was sent to Sonovision by EMI.

Cast

Principal Cast (all serials)
Donald Monat as John Steed
Diane Appleby as Emma Peel
Hugh Rouse as The Narrator

Known Guest Cast (occasional appearances)
June Dixon, Terrick Fitzhugh, Anthony Fridjhon, Gillian Garlick, Rex Garner, Shelagh Holliday, Annabel Linder, Michael Mayer, Don McCorkindale, Bruce Millar, Gordon Mulholland, Hal Orlandini, Erica Rogers, Joe Stewardson and Lynda Stuart

Announcers
Denis Smith – Opening / Closing Announcer (various serials)

Malcolm Gooding — Opening / Closing Announcer (various serials)
Tony Jay — Announcer ("The Avengers" — all serials)

Production

Principal Production Personnel
David Gooden — Producer
Tony Jay — Adaptor / Director (1971-72)
Dennis Folbigge — Adaptor / Director (1972-73)

Analysis

Three years after the original Avengers television series drew to a close, John Steed and Emma Peel were revived for a new audience in an unexpected locale: South Africa. By arrangement with rights holders EMI in the United Kingdom, The Avengers was adapted for radio from the original television scripts and recorded at Sonovision Studios in Johannesburg. This licensing was actioned without any recompense to those involved in making the television series, as Brian Clemens divulged in The Ultimate Avengers (Dave Rogers, Boxtree, 1995): "Neither Albert [Fennell] or myself — nor Laurie Johnson — knew anything about this, until someone sent us a recording of the show. EMI licensed the radio thing themselves."

Throughout its run from Monday 3rd January 1972 to Friday 28th December 1973, the series was a mainstay of the South African Broadcasting Corporation's English language service, Springbok Radio. It ran in prime time, five nights a week, between 7.15 and 7.30pm. This fifteen-minute timeslot dictated that the South African radio Avengers would stray from the show's traditional format. On British television, it had always been presented as weekly fifty-minute stand-alone dramas, but, for radio, Sonovision would serialise the stories over five to seven consecutive weeknights.

However, serialisation proved not to have as major an impact on plot structure as one might think. The original television series had been designed for sale to commercial broadcasters around the world, with an abundance of 'cliffhangers' written into each episode to allow for commercial breaks. Many of these 'cliffhangers' were successfully transformed into climactic radio episode endings. As a result, the serialisation of the episodes is, rather than a hindrance, one of the most endearing aspects of the radio series.

Other deviations from the original scripts stemmed from the requirement for all production houses to submit the programme, two copies of its script and music clearance forms to Springbok Radio a week before transmission. The programmes would be reviewed and censored, as Donald Monat explained during a question-and-answer session at The Avengers Forum in April 2001, "If some words or lines were not acceptable they were usually edited out by the Service Department. If major surgery was required they would contact the production company who might then have to re-edit or even re-record. However, most producers were well aware of the acceptance code and tended to steer clear of anything that might be rejected. Things that were unacceptable were rather like the BBC in the old days – bad language, explicit sex, anything that might be construed as sacrilegious, or an attack on the government. I don't think *The Avengers* ran into many major problems as the original TV scripts already reflected the acceptance policies of British and American commercial television [in the 1960s], which were not all that different."

A further stipulation imposed upon the series was that each episode had to accommodate two 45-second commercial breaks: one directly after the opening theme and one prior to the closing music. Allowing for station announcements and the like, about thirteen minutes of material were produced for each episode. The commercials transmitted during the *Avengers* broadcasts – for beauty products, household detergents, deodorants and iced lollies – suggest that a family audience listened to the series, with the South African housewife being the major target of advertisers between seven and eight in the evening.

In addition to the regular commercials that aired on Springbok Radio, many timeslots on the station were held by sponsor advertisers, who would finance specific programmes in return for publicity. "When Springbok Radio started in 1950, many programmes were fully sponsored," Donald Monat revealed when interviewed for *Avengers on the Radio* in 2000. "The sponsors bought the time and directly commissioned and paid for the programmes. This gave them the right to approve all scripts and recordings and insert their own commercials, subject to the rules and practices of the network. This was in the style of American commercial radio. However, by the time *The Avengers* took to the air in the seventies, things had changed. Most programmes were selected, approved and paid for by the network and advertisers simply bought commercial spots within them. But there was also a form of limited sponsorship which gave the advertiser the right to a 'presented by' type of credit. To the best of my recollection, Lever Brothers had held the daily 7.15pm strip since the days of full sponsorship and then simply carried on with the more limited form permitted. But... although they could and did make suggestions (particularly when new series were being developed), this did not give them the right to approve or reject actual scripts or individual programmes in the seventies – that was the sole prerogative of the network. All any unhappy advertisers could do was to withdraw their advertising, rather like the situation in network television today in the US and, presumably, the UK."

It is believed that the idea for the *Avengers* radio series came from the Lever Brothers advertising agency. It was not uncommon for sponsors to decree which programmes were to be produced, based upon what they wished to associate their brand and products with. Quite why the washing powder Cold Water Omo – Lever Brothers' major detergent of the day – and *The Avengers* were seen as a match made in heaven is anyone's guess, but this didn't stop each episode from being introduced with the announcement (by Denis Smith and later Malcolm Gooding), "Now, from the makers of Cold Water Omo..."

Though *The Avengers* took Britain by storm, and gained regular network transmissions in the United States (a rare achievement for a British series), it was not a household name in South Africa prior to the launch of the radio series. With no national television service until 1976, there was no way to show television programmes to mass audiences. However, as a film series, *The Avengers* was able to gain a modicum of exposure in South Africa through film rental libraries. Though film prints were often seriously damaged by projector breakdowns or misuse, and reputedly had an average life of no more than two years, they were better than nothing. Donald Monat recalled seeing the series on film at home with his wife June: "Yes, we did have the pleasure of seeing many of the TV episodes, long before the idea of doing the radio series came up, and we thoroughly enjoyed them. They weren't shown in cinemas in South Africa, but you could rent 16mm prints of the films – in fact, we saw many British and American TV series that way. We, like many of our friends, owned a 16mm projector and, at the time, there were film rental libraries in every suburb, much like the video stores of today." Monat also suggested that others involved in the Sonovision productions, notably Dave Gooden and *Avengers* directors Dennis Folbigge and Tony Jay, would have been exposed to the series in this way.

Once the radio series premiered in its prime time slot, *The Avengers* very quickly became a hit show and its stars, expatriate British actors Diane Appleby and Donald Monat, found themselves the centre of attention, as Monat later recalled: "Diane Appleby and I were asked to make personal appearances from time to time and we would pop up in character at department stores and big events, chat to fans of the show and autograph pictures for them. The famous photo of Diane and myself was one of a bunch of publicity shots that were taken at the time. That particular one was printed up as a postcard and distributed widely when we made any promotional public appearances. We used to sign hundreds of them. I think Springbok Radio may have also distributed the pictures to fans. The show was certainly very successful and attracted a large prime time audience."

Monat had carved out a career in acting, writing and directing prior to his time on *The Avengers*, working in South Africa, Canada and his native Britain. "I was born in London, but grew up in South Africa, went to school and university there, and started acting for radio when I was 16," he told *Avengers on the Radio*. "I went back to England in 1949, where I first met my wife, June Dixon, when we were working together in a stage play in London. When the SABC commercial service, Springbok Radio, began in 1950, we went back to Johannesburg and started one of the first radio production companies, personally producing about 15 shows a week. After two years of hectic work, we went back to London and worked extensively in theatre doing plays and revues. We also worked in radio and television and made a couple of short movies. One of them, *Five Guineas A Week*, was nominated for the Royal Command Film Performance and opened at the Odeon Leicester Square with *The Spanish Gardener* (1956). We also created one of the first original musical comedies for British TV. It was called *The Straker Special* [transmitted on 22nd November 1956, a part of the *Jack Hylton Presents* strand] and starred June Whitfield and Dennis Quilley. All this was way back in the fabulous fifties.

"In 1960, we went to Canada, where we worked mainly in radio for CBC, and occasionally in theatre and documentary films. After two years, we went back to South Africa in 1962 for family reasons after the sad death of my brother there. Originally, it was only going to be a visit for a few months, but we were asked to do a stage revue, then a radio comedy show... and then one thing led to another and fairly soon we were working morning, noon and night on our own weekly programmes – *The ABC Show*, *Dr. Livingstone – I Presume?*, *The Loudspeaker Show*, *Stop The Tape – I Want To Get Off!*, *Son Of Livingstone* and *Cool* – doing our best to support ourselves and our five young children. Most of them were done in front of live audiences, with live orchestras or groups, very much in the style of the classic BBC comedy shows. Of course, we both also worked as actors (and directors) for dozens of other shows. During this period (1962–82), I'm guessing that I must have played in well over 2,000 radio programmes. Needless to say, I never counted them!"

The period from the mid-1950s to the mid-1970s is generally considered the golden age of South African radio. Donald Monat remembered it as an exciting but extraordinarily hectic period: "The South African radio networks were producing an astonishing volume of programming, broadcasting full services in English, Afrikaans and several African languages including Xhosa,

Zulu, Tswana and Sotho. In English alone, they were turning out some forty-five hours a week of original drama and comedy programmes – which was probably considerably more than the total output of BBC Radio Drama at the time. The extraordinary thing was that this was done with a very small pool of actors. Ninety percent of the work was done by a group of less than forty of us who went from studio to studio all day long, recording everything from Shakespeare to soap opera and, on a good day, a few commercials, which were much better paid. Some actors were on the staff of the South African Broadcasting Corporation (SABC), but most were freelance. Many might also be working in the evening in stage productions. Budgets were tiny – and so were the fees, which meant that you had to do a great volume of work to make a living."

Consequently, while playing John Steed in *The Avengers*, Donald Monat found himself having to supplement his income by writing, directing and playing in several other programmes: "After all these years, it's hard to remember the details of other shows I was doing at the same time but, looking up an old magazine article from 1973, it seems I was directing a drama series about two truck drivers called *Wheels*, playing regularly in *Medical File*, *Personal Column*, *Max Headley – Special Agent* and *The White Oaks of Jalna*, hosting a musical panel game called *Going for a Song* and June and I were writing and starring in a weekly satirical comedy show called *Stop the Tape – I Want to Get Off!*"

This period of South African radio's popularity came at a time when the country was an international pariah due to its apartheid system, under which the white minority enjoyed all the power and wealth, while the black majority was subjugated. Those working in the arts, who were generally more liberal-minded than those in authority, made efforts to rail against the inequalities and injustices they saw around them whilst adhering to the law. "Many of us were deeply affected by [the political unrest and racial inequalities in South Africa]," Donald Monat reflected in 2000. "In 1962, [June and I] ran into major problems with our stage revue in Cape Town, *Party Lines*, which had a multiracial cast – and we were always having hassles with the censors over our radio comedy shows which frequently ridiculed the appalling policies of the nationalist government. However, in all fairness to the SABC, they did let us have a surprising amount of freedom to do this and, in fact, I think it's fair to say that many artistes and writers made major contributions in pressing for the reforms that ultimately brought about the collapse of apartheid and the emergence of the new South Africa. At that time in South Africa the various media – print, films and radio – came under censorship from different boards or bodies.

"Springbok Radio programmes were censored (or what the station considered 'approved for broadcast') only as finished recordings. The people who did this were not really a government department, they were employees of the SABC, which (at the time) was rather like the BBC, i.e., an independent body, but ultimately responsible to a minister of the government. Our own comedy shows were in a different situation. They ran into problems on Springbok Radio all the time, although we did manage to slip some pretty nifty stuff through, mainly because some of the overworked servicing people were not always paying full attention and sometimes missed the more subtle jokes. However, on the non-commercial English Service (where many of our best series were broadcast) there was no specific censorship. Each producer was held responsible for the programmes he or she put out. Nearly all of them were on the staff, of course, and so were not inclined to risk their jobs – but I was in the fortunate position of being one of the very few freelance producer / directors who also worked directly for the English Service. Our shows were designed to be topical, and they were usually written and recorded only a few days before transmission. I did all the editing personally, often delivering a programme tape to the continuity suite only an hour or two before broadcast. Generally, the first time anyone in senior authority ever heard them was when they were broadcast. As a result of this, we got ourselves into deep trouble on several occasions!"

Although *The Avengers* ended up being made at Sonovision Studios, it had actually had a couple of false starts elsewhere. Two pilot programmes had previously been recorded at AFS Studios (which took its name from that of its owner, A.F. Stanley), another busy production house near the SABC's studios on Commissioner Street. Aside from Sonovision – which had recently moved from its initial location on Kirk Street to a new state-of-the-art facility on Plein Street – and AFS, there were also studios at CRC (Commercial Radio Corporation), AKA (Audio-Kine-Africa) and MvN (Manley van Niekerk), among others. The majority of Springbok Radio's output and many programmes and commercials for other stations were produced in these production houses.

It was during 1971, several months before the first Sonovision recordings, that the first pilot version of *The Avengers* was performed and recorded at AFS Studios. Coincidentally, Donald Monat was also involved in this production, but in a quite different capacity to the one that he would later enjoy. "I do remember that the idea for the series didn't originate with Sonovision. I did an *Avengers* pilot with another production company called AFS. As far as I can remember, I played the chief villain. Someone else played Steed, and there was a different director. In fact, I have a vague memory that we did it twice, with two different Steeds," Monat recalled when speaking to *Avengers on the Radio*.

Neither version was deemed satisfactory, either by the broadcaster, commercial sponsor, or both. For this reason, they were never broadcast and no tape recordings are known to have survived. Consequently, very little is known about them. The actors who might have played the Steed role in the unbroadcast pilot or pilots are Rex Garner, John Boulter and Angus Neill (who was strangely credited as the television Steed in a January 1972 *SAUK / SABC Bulletin* feature). Donald Monat recalled that the "different director" responsible for at least one of the two pilots was his colleague Colin Fish, who would go on to play the character of Mother on a regular basis in the Dennis Folbigge era *Avengers* episodes at Sonovision.

Donald Monat moved on to other work, but soon received some unexpected, yet very welcome, news about *The Avengers*. The production was to be recorded at Sonovision Studios, under the auspices of its owner David Gooden – and Monat was asked to play John Steed. Monat was keen to make the role his own: "I'm sure Patrick Macnee's great performance had become embedded in my memories, but I didn't actually study the TV episodes at the time. I guess I was aiming to interpret the script in the spirit of the TV series, but in my own way – as my voice is quite different to Patrick's. While it's generally true that every actor brings his or her own interpretation and personality to a part – and I hope I managed to do that with Steed – our opportunities for revision were very limited. In South African radio, daily serials such as *The Avengers* were recorded at sight without rehearsal or even a read-through. While I might occasionally change a line or two in order to get a more comfortable phrasing or even drop in an occasional ad lib, there was certainly no time for any serious revisions [as] we had to complete five (and sometimes six) episodes in an afternoon! I'm sure that spending many years in comedy was a big help in keeping a light touch in *The Avengers*."

Once the production had been moved to Sonovision, Gooden, who had received a large number of *Avengers* television scripts from EMI, engaged Tony Jay to adapt them for radio. Jay, a British actor, writer and director of a multitude of South African radio productions, would later come to international acclaim for his work in America as an actor and commercial voice artiste. His brief on *The Avengers* was wide-ranging – in addition to his scripting duties, Jay was also in charge of casting and directing the productions.

"My association with the wonderful Dave Gooden was very close," said Jay, when speaking to *Avengers on the Radio* in 2001, "and I produced and acted in innumerable series and one-off plays at Sonovision over a period of about six years, during which time I had virtually carte-blanche as to how I wished to proceed and whom I wished to cast."

The situation with *The Avengers* was no different. Tony Jay's first job was to cast the role of Steed – but his first choice, the legendary British-born South African actor-entertainer, Rex Garner, proved unavailable. In his place, and "with the late Dave Gooden's approval, I cast Donald Monat immediately as Steed... [He] did very well in the role, as did Diane Appleby as Emma Peel," said Jay. Garner would go on to guest in the series from time to time.

While today movies and television shows can be in development for months or years before being realised, a programme commissioned for South African radio could go from a germ of an idea to being broadcast in a matter of weeks. Consequently, after being given the go-ahead to produce their new series, Sonovision, and Tony Jay in particular, found themselves with little time to spend in pre-production: "The time-frame for pre-broadcast development was not long at all, that being the normal routine in South Africa in those days," Jay recalled. *The Avengers* was no exception: "I had about two weeks to prepare the first two serials – each comprising five fifteen-minute scripts – prior to recording and broadcast. That was nothing unusual, as most radio jobs were facilitated at lightning speed. Subsequent scripts were usually prepared only one or two weeks ahead, as I had to spend much time sorting through the pile of available TV scripts in order to decide which ones were less 'visual' than others."

Early on, Jay decided that some of the content would need to be replaced with material more suitable for radio. In some instances, the problems posed by adapting scripts written for television into sound-only productions could be solved by a simple and expedient innovation: "I soon realised that I would need a narrator, which the late Hugh Rouse did marvellously well. But I wanted a narrator with a point of view and more than a touch of irony, a kind of interested, but sceptical observer, and those interpolations were created by myself, adding a very attractive twist to the programme."

If the turnaround was frenetic for the scriptwriter, it was no less so for the performers, as Donald Monat recalled: "The principal and most successful radio actors became very skilled – and so did the technicians, which was essential as rehearsal time was minimal. A major, ninety-minute play-of-the-week had to be rehearsed and recorded in one day – and serials like *The Avengers* were recorded at sight, with no rehearsal or read-through, five or six episodes in one afternoon. Normally, you didn't even get the scripts in advance. The first time you saw them was when you walked into the studio for the recording. All live effects – such as footsteps, doors opening, drinks being poured, etc. – were done by the actors and all recorded effects and music were normally incorporated as we recorded so that there was very little editing or postproduction to be done."

The company of players that made *The Avengers* would usually number no more than eight for a serial, mainly to save on costs. As a serial might have twenty character parts in it, this meant that actors would often have to play two or three roles. For this reason, full casts were rarely announced during either *The Avengers* or other Springbok Radio productions. Donald Monat notes that "this wouldn't have sounded too good... In fact, it was extremely rare for even the leads to get credited [in anything under half an hour in length]." In the case of *The Avengers*, the two lead actors and the adaptor / director and producer received an on-air credit once a week, at the end of each Friday night episode. Over the full length of the series, the majority of the pool of actors who worked regularly for Sonovision would have appeared in *The Avengers* at some point.

The only ever-present performers in the series, aside from Donald Monat, were Diane Appleby, cast as Steed's indispensable partner Emma Peel, and the narrator, Hugh Rouse, a familiar voice on Springbok Radio due to the news broadcasts he had been delivering since 1950. The sole semi-regular character, Mother, played in most instances by Colin Fish, appeared mainly in serials based on scripts from the Tara King era of *The Avengers*, in which the character featured as Steed's department head. However, Dennis Folbigge, who would eventually take over as writer from Tony Jay, liked Mother so much that he introduced him into adaptations of episodes that had not featured the character.

Recording studios are pretty much the same the world over, and Sonovision was no exception. In one part of the studio, the actors would perform their lines into the microphones, while in the other – a small, sound-proofed control room – the technical side of the recording session would have been overseen by a director, a producer and a controller. These roles often varied considerably from organisation to organisation – for instance, in some Johannesburg production houses, the roles of director and producer were amalgamated and carried out by a single person. For this reason, it is sensible to explain what these jobs entailed at Sonovision during the production of *The Avengers*.

The director – initially Tony Jay, and later Dennis Folbigge – was responsible for the artistic side of the production. His brief would have included the oversight of sound effects and music to be included in the programme, and liaising with, and directing, the actors. The latter task would be achieved visually, through the control room window, and via 'talkback', with which he could communicate directly with performers over their headphones.

The producer's role in South African radio was essentially administrative and organisational. Producers approached programme making in different ways. As David Gooden, the producer of *The Avengers*, came from a technical background, he would regularly supervise the sound engineering side of the production in addition to dealing with his organisational tasks.

Donald Monat was experienced both as a director and producer, in addition to being an in-demand performer, and told *Avengers on the Radio* that, "In some production houses, the producer and the director were often the same person. I, myself, frequently did both jobs [simultaneously]."

The controller – who would be called a sound mixer or engineer today – sat at the mixing desk, adjusting the levels of the various channels in the mix. Paul Wright was often the controller on *The Avengers*, but there were others who filled this role throughout the run of the series.

One of the major operations within the control room would be the playing in of any recorded sound effects and incidental or theme music. These would generally be fed into the mixing console from long-playing vinyl discs and be combined with the microphone sources from the actors' area. "Incidental music would almost certainly have come from library material," Donald Monat recalled. "Any regularly used themes [such as Laurie Johnson's theme to *The Avengers* or his *Symphony (Synthesis)* cue, which was heard in most episodes] would usually be transferred to [reel-to-reel quarter-inch] tape to avoid disc wear." Copyright clearances on tracks from library discs were relatively inexpensive, and each producer would normally have his or her favourite libraries of theme and background music. For instance, Dennis Folbigge seems to have favoured the works of composer Eric Siday for *The Avengers*, regularly utilising tracks from his 1971 Berry Music Co. library long-player *Sounds of Now 1*. Specific pieces of music used in *The Avengers*, such as Laurie Johnson's series theme and *Symphony (Synthesis)* composition, were licensed through EMI.

The control room would also be the setting for postproduction work, if any was needed. "In general, radio postproduction was, primarily, cutting to time – but also tightening up and removing any goofs," commented Donald Monat. "Most of the actors' mistakes (which we used to call 'fluffs') were removed during recording by simply going back and 'picking up' (what we now call 'punching in') at a suitable point just before the fluff [at a point on the tape where an edit would be imperceptible]. However, there were always some minor goofs which would be taken out afterwards. Cuts, in those days, were nearly always made by physically cutting and splicing the tape. When there were too many splices in a tape for broadcast safety – more than say four or five – it would dubbed in its entirety onto a fresh tape." This was to guard against a splice breaking apart while a programme was being broadcast, which would cause a break in transmission. Postproduction would also occasionally be performed on recordings to tighten up gaps between actors' lines or sound effects for dramatic effect.

On Monday 3rd January 1972 at 7.16pm, Springbok Radio premiered *The Avengers*, transmitting the first episode of a five-part adaptation of the 1967 television episode, *Escape in Time*. This is thought to have been recorded on Wednesday 6th December 1971.

Through a combination of slick production work, witty writing and a talented and experienced cast, the series quickly found a regular audience. Listeners were entranced by the bright, fast-moving combination of action and tongue-in-cheek humour that Tony Jay had devised. However, from the outset, Tony Jay had known that his involvement with the series would be a relatively short engagement: "When Dave Gooden approached me to instigate the series, I had already made plans to re-locate back to London, so I stayed on in South Africa for a further six months in order to get the show established on the air." By May 1972, Jay had indeed stepped down and returned home as intended. His role on the series as adaptor / director was taken over by Dennis Folbigge and the transition was handled seamlessly.

"This kind of thing was quite common in South Africa in those days," Donald Monat remarked. "Those of us who wrote and directed often took over other colleagues' writing and production work when someone was away doing a movie, a theatrical tour or was just unavailable."

The main changes during Dennis Folbigge's tenure were that the Mother character was introduced (Tony Jay did not utilise Mother in any of his scripts and later admitted to not liking the character); and the episode count per story was extended beyond the five that Jay had generally favoured. Folbigge also rewrote some scripts from Tony Jay's time with the series, including a new version of *Escape in Time* that incorporated Mother, and these were re-recorded and broadcast. This was not something unique to *The Avengers*, however, and was a common 'get out' ploy resorted to when writers were struggling with impending deadlines or script shortages. The practice was not encouraged by broadcasters, but, if kept to a minimum and changes were made, it would be tolerated.

As the radio episodes were adapted from scripts, they differ in some instances from the transmitted television programmes. To begin with, any television episodes that had featured Linda Thorson as Tara King were rewritten to feature the Emma Peel character instead. In addition, the scripts used as source material for the serials were occasionally early drafts that were heavily revised before being filmed. This meant that stories like *They Keep Killing Steed* (1968), which was originally to be filmed in Spain before budgetary issues caused that idea to be abandoned, were adapted for radio from their original intended form. *They Keep Killing Steed* was, therefore, set in Spain in the radio series and broadcast under the title *Too Many Olés*. Likewise, the radio serial *Straight From The Shoulder* is based, not on the television equivalent, *Have Guns... Will Haggle* (1968), but on the script of the filmed but aborted *Invitation to a Killing*. This troubled production was intended to opener the Tara King series, but a sudden change of production team personnel meant that *Invitation to a Killing* was rewritten, partially reshot, and broadcast as *Have Guns... Will Haggle*. The original cut of *Invitation to a Killing* is lost today, but the survival of the radio adaptation gives an insight into what might have been. It is entirely possible that *The Great, Great Britain Crime*, the other abandoned Tara King episode – parts of which were eventually incorporated into *Homicide and Old Lace* – was also produced for the radio in its original scripted form. In addition, we can reasonably ponder whether the Cybernauts were originally called Pabulum Robots (as they are referred to in *A Deadly Gift*), and whether the eleven surviving serials that have different titles than their television forebears bear the working titles for the television episodes.

By the end of 1973, there were very few scripts left from the bundle received from the UK which had not been adapted for radio. Anxious to continue making his popular series, David Gooden approached EMI and asked for permission to commission original stories. He also investigated the possibility of releasing tapes of *Avengers* serials commercially. Unfortunately, EMI refused permission in both cases. For this reason, the last episode of *The Avengers* was broadcast on Friday 28th December 1973. The series had run for two years and it is believed that as many as eighty-three serials, adapting every episode of the film era of *The Avengers* (Series 4, 5 and 6), were made and transmitted in this time.

The Avengers was replaced from 1st January 1974 by another famous Lever Brothers serial, *The Mind of Tracy Dark*, which ran until 1979. However, there was one last, brief, decidedly tongue-in-cheek hurrah for Donald Monat and Diane Appleby as Steed and Mrs. Peel. Monat and his wife, June Dixon, were commissioned to write a celebratory programme to mark Springbok Radio's Silver Jubilee. This programme eventually aired live in prime time on Wednesday 30th April 1975, directed by Monat himself and entitled *The Great Gong Robbery*.

Donald Monat later recalled that it was quite a tough assignment. "*The Great Gong Robbery* was performed live in front of a studio audience at the SABC Variety Theatre, Broadcast House, Johannesburg, at the time of transmission. This was quite a challenge, as none of us had done a drama or comedy programme literally live on the air for decades!" The accent was on comedy and the plot was straightforward – someone had stolen the famous Springbok Gong (a distinctive xylophone-style instrument upon which station announcers would play call signs at regular times on Springbok Radio), and it was down to a succession of Springbok characters, past and present, to recover it. Two bumbling South African policemen (lifted from Sonovision's legendary *Squad Cars* and played by Michael Mayer and Hal Orlandini) were assigned to the case and formed the linking device, whereby they would call on characters from other Springbok successes, such as *The Mind of Tracy Dark* (which was by this time well established in the timeslot relinquished by *The Avengers*), *Taxi*, *Jet Jungle* (starring Diane Appleby) and many others.

The spoofery was not restricted to radio drama sources, also taking in variety and quiz shows, such as *Pick-A-Box* (a development of British television's *Take Your Pick* from the 1950s) and *Going for a Song* along the way. Since there was such a large cast, it was possible to include characters from two or three series that were no longer on the air. *The Avengers* was one of these, made possible as both Donald Monat and Diane Appleby would be appearing in the broadcast in any case. When we meet Steed and Mrs. Peel in the show, the crime-fighting pair state that they are retired (obviously referencing their absence from the airwaves) and, perish the very thought, are living together.

The Great Gong Robbery proved immensely popular, as did the whole two-hour commemorative programme, so much so, in fact, that the whole two hours, including *The Great Gong Robbery*, were issued on SABC Records (Catalogue No. UKBC 1) some months later, distributed by Trutone. By all accounts, the record - a double album - sold in great numbers and contains the only material from the South African *Avengers* ever to have been released commercially.

When Springbok Radio's broadcasting hours were severely cut back to just six hours a day in its autumn years, it was the beginning of the end for the station. It had long been the most popular of the radio stations run by the SABC, but its fate was sealed in the mid-1970s, when South Africa finally launched itself into the television age with the introduction of the country's first television service – a single channel offering initially. Test transmissions started on 5th May 1975, and the official service was launched on 5th January 1976. This had serious repercussions for radio, which came under increasing pressure due to the new service. Springbok Radio saw its audience steadily decline and, despite protests from many loyal listeners, the station was finally closed down at midnight on 31st December 1985. The SABC replaced it with Radio South Africa – later renamed SAFM. This new station effectively continued the work of the old 'English Service'.

Sonovision Studios still exists, though it moved first to new buildings on Wessell Road in the Rivonia district of Sandton, a northern suburb of Johannesburg, and has since relocated once more to Ballyclare Drive in the Bryanston area, also in Sandton. The studio was, until recently, owned and run by John Culverwell and Louis Van Ass, a former colleague of the late David Gooden.

Donald Monat and June Dixon enjoyed further success later in their lives, as Donald explained during a question and answer session at The Avengers Forum in April 2001: "In the seventies and early eighties, we moved into films and television in South Africa. Our first feature, *Fraud!* (1974), was a low-budget thriller which June and I wrote. I directed the movie and June played one of the leads. We also did a prime time comedy TV series called *The Saturday Show* and wrote and produced an original TV musical based on O. Henry's famous short story, *The Gift Of The Magi*. Finally, in 1984, we moved to Los Angeles – where we have lived ever since, working mainly as writers and producers of corporate multi-media presentations, although I still do quite a lot of voice work for narration, commercials and books-on-tape." He also enjoyed the revival of interest in *The Avengers* radio series and was open to reprising the role should he have been approached. "In general, I thoroughly enjoyed playing in *The Avengers* because the stories were great fun, Steed was a wonderful role and, for me, a special bonus was that I didn't also have to worry about all the responsibilities of production, which I had to handle in a great deal of my radio work. Until I came across Alan Hayes' original essay about the series by chance last year, I had absolutely no idea that there were people outside of South Africa who had ever heard of our radio programmes, let alone fans who collected copies of them. It was quite a surprise! It would be perfectly possible to create new recordings with new scripts, if (a) the necessary funds were available, and (b) the present copyright holders of the original stories and characters would agree to it. Radio production is still very inexpensive compared with almost any other medium of entertainment, so the costs would be relatively modest. If any company or organisation was interested in so doing, I would rather enjoy tackling it. I think it's pretty unlikely – but who knows?"

Archive

In April 2002, John Wright, a crime and western novelist and old-time radio enthusiast living in Port Elizabeth, Eastern Cape, South Africa, contacted the *Avengers on the Radio* website to say that he had recorded some of the *Avengers* radio series off-air in the 1970s and still retained the tapes. It soon became abundantly clear that, without John's endeavours, Donald Monat's fine radio portrayal of John Steed would have been almost entirely lost, as, only three 15-minute episodes from outside of his archive survive today.

Starting in the 1960s, John – an avid listener of Springbok Radio – began recording programmes off-air on quarter-inch, quarter-track reel-to-reel tape. Among these were series such as *Address Unknown*, *The Creaking Door*, *SF-68*,

Consider Your Verdict, Taxi, Lux Radio Theatre, Medical File and the South African adaptations of the Sherlock Holmes adventures... and nineteen complete serials of *The Avengers*! This number included the thirteen that were already known to exist (offered by Old Time Radio dealers in their catalogues) plus another six that had been unheard since 1972-1973 – representing an additional eight weeks of daily *Avengers* broadcasts – that were previously thought missing.

These serials – *The Fantasy Game, The Quick-Quick-Slow Death, Love All, Getaway, A Deadly Gift, The Super Secret Cypher Snatch, Dial A Deadly Number, Not to Be Sneezed At, Who Shot Poor George / XR40?, A Grave Charge, All Done By Mirrors, The Morning After, The Joker, Straight From the Shoulder, Stop Me If You've Heard This, From Venus With Love, A Case of Interrogation, Too Many Olés* and *Train of Events* – were all recorded off-air from the original Springbok Radio transmissions and arrived in the UK complete with Wright's own recording log sheet. Eighteen definitely hail from Dennis Folbigge's tenure as adaptor / director, with the other, *The Fantasy Game*, seeming to be – possibly – the sole surviving example of Tony Jay's work on *The Avengers*. The overwhelming majority of these recordings are completely uncut and include the original Springbok Radio jingles and commercials.

There is clear evidence that the thirteen serials that were previously available were, in fact, sourced from Wright's recordings. Episodes on the OTR retail tapes feature several recording glitches that appear on Wright's tapes, and John recalled making his *Avengers* recordings for the benefit of Ron Baron, a partially sighted radio enthusiast living in America. Ron – "a truly nice guy," as John remembered – was the only person that he ever copied his *Avengers* tapes for. Ron clearly passed along copies to others, and they eventually leaked onto OTR lists.

When questioned on the subject, John could not say quite why he recorded so much of Springbok Radio's output. He professed to a long love affair with radio and the desire to capture some of it for posterity, fearing – correctly, as it transpired – that the heyday of radio drama would not last forever. His recordings of *The Avengers* and other South African productions are all the more valuable when the sorry state of South African radio archiving is considered.

So why does so little remain from the output of one of South Africa's most popular radio stations? The answer is straightforward. Sonovision were supplied the blank recording media by the series' sponsors, Lever Brothers, and, due to the high cost of tape – and the SABC's policy of airing programmes just once – it was very common to record new programmes over previous productions. "Most programme tapes were wiped after broadcast. The reason was simply economic. They could be re-used and the cost of the blank tape was a significant factor in the production company's budget," Donald Monat later recalled.

The SABC Sound (Radio) Archives had been in existence since 1964, after the corporation identified a need to preserve South African broadcast history. The collection focuses mainly on news and current affairs, sport, drama and music from South Africa, in all South African languages, but also includes some international material. *The Avengers* unfortunately slipped the net, along with huge swathes of South African radio drama. The Radio Sound Archive is keen to fill in gaps in its collection, and regularly benefits from donations from private collections.

John Wright generously donated his recordings to the *Avengers on the Radio* website for digitisation and restoration in May 2002. The tapes are mostly 1800 foot (548 metre) reels, with some being of 1200ft (366m) and 2400ft (731m) lengths. Each tape is divided into four separate monaural tracks (two per side of the reel), each of which was recorded at 3¾ inches (9.5 centimetres) per second.

Originally, Wright recorded these tapes in two-track mode (permitting the recording from stereo sources and a marginally better recording quality), but the scarcity and expense of reels of blank tape – this at a time when the compact cassette format was making significant in-roads on the home recording market – meant that he eventually chose to record over the inner tracks of many of his tapes. This practice preserved the original recording as a single- rather than double-track recording, and allowed the taping of another programme over the arguably redundant track (the broadcasts being monaural). The great majority of Wright's off-airs of *The Avengers* serials were recorded in this way, taping over the inside tracks of earlier recordings. Wright made his recordings on Sony equipment – most regularly on a Sony-O-Matic, with the remainder taped on a Sony 260 stereo recorder, which he still had in working order in 2002.

Most recordings were made via a direct patch connection to the radio, giving an excellent frequency response and a warm sound that lacked extraneous sounds. Occasionally, when Wright was away from home, recordings had to be made by placing a suction-cup style microphone over the speaker of a portable radio. These recordings are not of a studio quality, but the results are perfectly audible.

The tapes, in general, were well preserved. The recordings were thirty years old in their year of recovery, and the tapes themselves even older. Inevitably, they had developed dropouts – where the frequency response dips for a time before returning to normal – with some reels more affected than others. However, the overall sound quality was robust, with minimal background noise, good frequency response and clear sound. The fact that they were recorded using a direct connection to the radio means that these are close in quality to the original master recordings, the slow recording speed being the fly in the ointment, if one is ultra-critical. By way of comparison, the 3¾ inches (9.5 centimetres) per second recordings are significantly slower than the average tape speed of 15 inches (38 centimetres) per second that the recording studio masters would be recorded at. However, Wright's recordings proved to be generally very impressive, and represented a marked improvement over the multi-generational copies previously in circulation on the collectors' circuit. It was a pleasure to have been involved in their recovery and to have restored them.

In addition to the nineteen serials recorded by John Wright, the first three instalments of the second version of *Escape in Time* (again from the Folbigge era), also survive – Episodes 1 and 2 as recordings taken from the original studio masters and 3 from an off-air cassette recording. The latter came to light soon after John Wright's tapes had arrived in England. Searching the web for information about *The Avengers* radio series, Barbara Peterson found and contacted the *Avengers on the Radio* site to say that she too had recorded a single episode in the early 1970s. It transpired that the *Escape in Time* episode in question was one for which no other recording existed. Peterson lived in South Africa as a child while her father flew food into famine-struck Mozambique. She made the recording on compact cassette shortly before moving to Lobatse, Botswana (unfortunately out of range of Springbok Radio transmissions) in 1973. She now lives in her native America.

In common with John Wright before her, Barbara Peterson sent her original master recording for digitisation and restoration. The recording was missing the very first few seconds, but, as this was simply a reprise of the climax of the preceding episode, it was possible to patch it relatively seamlessly. It was another piece of the jigsaw, but sadly no further complete serials or individual episodes have surfaced since that time. Despite being a major success in South Africa, the fact that the majority of these serials no longer exists leaves the Sonovision series as an oft-forgotten footnote in *The Avengers* history. However, it did achieve some international exposure. While conducting research for *Noon: Doomsday*, Mike Noon happened upon mentions of international transmissions of the series in a mid-1980s *Avengers* fanzine, *With Umbrella, Charm and Bowler*. In an article about the radio show, Thomas Kralik noted that, "the radio show achieved success in South Africa, New Zealand, Australia and even in the United States, where it aired on WBAI 99.5FM. More episodes are expected to be aired in the near future."

While the broadcasts in New Zealand and Australia are still shrouded in mystery, much more is known about the American broadcasts. WBAI 99.5FM is a non-commercial, listener-sponsored station in New York, staffed in the main by volunteers. At the time that The Avengers aired on the station, it had no programming budget to speak of, so specialist producers tended to share their collections over the air. In the case of The Avengers, episodes were transmitted Mondays to Fridays as part of The Daily Serial strand, which ran from 1977 up until the early 1990s in a variety of timeslots, varying from early evening to six o'clock each morning! The recordings were sourced from old time radio collectors in the States and cleaned up for broadcast by Max Schmid, who often presented the programmes. The recordings that Schmid worked with were sourced, indirectly, from the home recordings made by John Wright, so, unfortunately, WBAI did not air any serials believed to be lost. However, the poor-quality recordings that circulated in Avengers fandom before Wright's master tapes came to light are known to be multi-generational analogue recordings from the WBAI broadcasts.

Verdict

Radio is a difficult medium. On television, characterisation, setting and narrative are disseminated to viewers through dialogue, action and a wealth of visual pointers. Radio has only the voices of the actors and narrator, sound effects and music with which to impart equal detail. The consummate ease with which The Avengers succeeded in an audio medium is a testament to the experience and skill of the radio performers and backroom staff.

Donald Monat simply excelled as Steed, and his performances are arguably the nearest anyone has come to equalling Patrick Macnee's definitive portrayal. This is perhaps a result of Monat interpreting and creating Steed from the pages of the radio scripts, rather than letting Macnee's take on the role strongly inform his approach. From the very first scene that the listener hears, Monat immediately convinces in the role, giving the impression that his Steed is, perhaps, a little older than Macnee's version. Monat's style of delivery also lends John Steed an instant authority – a highly desirable piece of radio shorthand. Just as with Macnee before him, Donald Monat *is* John Steed – no question about it. Monat's portrayal is particularly impressive considering the way in which radio programmes were produced in South Africa during the 1970s. Actors involved in the Avengers recordings would have been dashing from one production house to another, participating in several different productions at any given time. In common with most other shows of the time, *Avengers* programmes were recorded at a frenetic pace, with little or no rehearsal time being set aside in the schedule, and the scripts being performed 'cold'. That Donald Monat was able to build and maintain an identifiable, well-liked character in this working environment is the mark of an actor working at the top of his game.

Diane Appleby's Emma Peel pales somewhat when compared to her television equivalent, Diana Rigg. However, to be fair to Ms. Appleby, the character of Mrs. Peel was never going to be as simple to transfer from television to radio as that of her partner in crime detection. Steed is an archetypal figure, whereas Mrs. Peel was something very new, and much of her character was communicated on television in visual shorthand. In addition, in the surviving recordings, Emma Peel often appears to be Steed's assistant, rather than the equal partner she should be. This may be partly due to societal norms in South Africa and also to the fact that, in adaptations based on the Tara King series, the character is not rewritten to be consistent with her characterisation in the Emma Peel stories, but simply renamed. This does, though, have the side effect of promoting Mrs. Peel from "talented amateur" to an official agent, working for Mother, which, in turn, subtly redefines her relationship with Steed and their work together in those particular serials – the cases that Emma and Steed investigate form a part of Tara-Emma's work, whereas for Emma-Emma they are a sideline to her life and Steed must, on occasion, endeavour to engage her interest before she will become involved. Another product of being an Emma-Tara hybrid is that Emma's characterisation can fluctuate significantly from story to story. For example, in *Train of Events*, Emma is self-sufficient and practical, while in *Stop Me If You've Heard This*, she is unable even to read a map the right way up! Despite being served poorly by some scripts, Diane Appleby always did her level best in the role, and, when required, she could carry the programme single-handedly with great aplomb, as she did in *The Joker*.

The contribution of Hugh Rouse, another regular performer, cannot be underestimated. As the narrator, Rouse provides an essential link between the cast and the audience, keeping the listener up to speed and ably filling the gap left by the absence of visuals. He, every bit as much as Donald Monat, gives a unique and definitive performance. His delivery is superb, dealing with descriptive, dramatic or comedic passages with equal aplomb, even on occasion delightfully breaking the fourth wall and acting as an unexpected advisor to Steed. Narrators have been used in radio programmes since the medium's inception, often with mediocre results. It is to Tony Jay and Dennis

Folbigge's credit that their narrator character sits at the very centre of the piece, giving the series an off-beat style and humour that is entirely its own, but which fits into the *Avengers* format seamlessly.

It's a crying shame that there appears to have been no archival mechanism in place in South Africa in the 1970s to preserve material such as this for the benefit of future generations. The thirty hours of material that do survive – almost entirely due to the foresight of avid listeners – merely leave the listener hungry for more...

THE FIRST AVENGERS MOVIE

J Z FERGUSON

Project Type: Prospective Television Movie
Date: January 1981

Synopsis

Professor Rambling is digging for Roman artifacts. He hears the sound of approaching marching feet, which are so numerous that they crush trees and bushes. Rambling flees in terror, then falls down a deep, dark hole. The vibrations of the marching feet send earth sliding down the hole after him.

Major Pitt and General Cavalo, decked out in Marxist-esque uniforms, meet in their HQ. Pitt, who moves about while suspended from the ceiling by a wire, informs Cavalo that the Chiefs of Staff are on their way. Cavalo observes that they will be in time for tea, and bites into a cream cake in the shape of Windsor Castle.

A small plane carrying a pilot, three passengers, and a box of cream cakes prepares to land at an airfield. Pitt arrives and watches its approach. Suddenly, the control tower hears the pilot and his passengers cry out in terror and a strange, crunching, rending sound. The plane makes a perfect landing, but the emergency team sent to meet the plane discovers that the autopilot has been activated and everyone inside the aircraft has been reduced to a skeleton.

Mike Gambit arrives at the flat of his partner, Carruthers, with news that they are needed. An ex-trapeze artist, Carruthers swings down the fire escape and lands in his open-top car.

Steed, Gambit, and Carruthers survey the remains of the four dead men who were on the flight. With no cause of death forthcoming, Steed suggests that they follow their only lead: the identities of the dead men. Steed elects to investigate Frank Miller, while Gambit and Carruthers plump for Brigadier Brewster.

At Miller's, Steed crosses paths with CIA agent Suzy Stride. Suzy reveals that Miller was one of the CIA's top agents, and was working undercover when he was killed. She also tells Steed that Miller was on the trail of an arms dealer, and had heard rumours of a military coup. A quick investigation of Miller's home uncovers a number of cookbooks on the subject of preparing food for large groups of people – particularly armies – an assortment of magnifying glasses, and a closet full of artificial limbs. It seems that Miller was not after the type of arms dealer Suzy that had in mind!

Meanwhile, General Cavalo is discussing the deaths of his army's Chiefs of Staff – the passengers on the plane – with his subordinates. He is surrounded by scale model replicas of numerous important buildings, including the House of Commons and Buckingham Palace, all of which are made of cake. With his Chiefs of Staff wiped out, Cavalo passes the training of his troops to Captain Carla, who, like Pitt, speaks to Cavalo while suspended from a wire. Colonel Vance is worried about the possibility of an investigation into the deaths of the men on the plane. Cavalo confidently states that Major Pitt and Sergeant Roden will solve that problem.

At Brigadier Brewster's, Gambit and Carruthers interrupt Roden, who is attempting to destroy the Brigadier's papers. Gambit and Roden fight, with Gambit getting the worst of it, before Carruthers intervenes, putting her trapeze skills to use and sending Roden out the window, killing him. When Carruthers and Gambit make their way downstairs to search the body, they discover that it has disappeared! Before they can return to the house, Pitt mortars it, destroying any evidence within, before making his getaway with Roden's body.

Steed and Suzy continue their investigations by visiting Helmut, the ex-business partner of Pelham, another of the unfortunate plane passengers. Helmut explains that he and Pelham used to run their own flea circus, before Pelham quit the venture to return to his "old job" of training troops, leaving Helmut to run the circus on his own.

Cavalo is furious with Pitt for going to Brewster's with only Roden for backup – he believes Pitt should have brought their troops with him. His reprimand is cut short by Carla, who reveals that Colonel Vance – who was confined to his quarters after "cracking up" – has escaped. Cavalo demands that troops be sent in pursuit of Vance, who has managed to make it to his car. Despite some frantic driving, Vance's car crashes into a bridge. Vance throws himself from the car into the water, just before his car is systematically taken apart by an unseen force.

One Dr. Apple asks Steed and Suzy to pay a visit to his hospital. Vance has been found, but he has been driven completely mad by some traumatic experience. Apple has him in confinement, but Vance is using a trowel and cement to fill in the gaps in his cell's brick walls, a pastime which Apple claims is the only thing that keeps him calm. Vance is also completely covered with tiny red dots, ostensibly caused by some allergic reaction. Apple reveals that Vance has been babbling about troops and arms shipments. When Steed and Suzy attempt to question him, Vance speaks of a mysterious "them", a "master race" set to attack very soon and bring a Marxist society into being. Vance warns them that the world has no chance against such a force.

Gambit and Carruthers are now looking into the pilot of the ill-fated plane, Bob Ware. They pay a visit to his brother, George, who insists on living in a tethered hot air balloon – because "the submarine isn't ready yet"! Carruthers and Gambit persuade him to allow them up for a chat. They question him about his brother, but George is evasive. Nevertheless, they manage to discover that Bob Ware flew as a mercenary in South America during the Matto Grosso massacre. Gambit draws on his extensive military background, and asks whether Ware was in league with the federal troops or General Cavalo. The answer? Cavalo.

Back at the hospital, Dr. Apple informs Suzy and Steed that Vance mentioned an "invisible army". Puzzled, they retreat to Steed's, where they receive a call from Helmut. He has been examining his ex-partner Pelham's papers, all of which are military related. Unbeknownst to him, Pitt is lurking outside. Before he can divulge anything of note, Helmut is attacked, and Steed is left with no choice but to listen helplessly to the man's screams over the phone line. The sounds that accompany the attack remind Steed of the Battle of the Ardennes!

Steed and Suzy hurry to Helmut's, but find that he, too, has been reduced to a skeleton. Pitt reports back to Cavalo, and gives him Pelham's papers for destruction. They discuss the need to eliminate George Ware and the exceptional discipline of their troops, who resisted the well-stocked pantry at Helmut's place. Cavalo orders the guards around their base to be doubled, as the remains of Professor Rambling have been found. Cavalo does not want more intruders on his land. Meanwhile, Spline and Jones, two students of Rambling, are searching for the unfortunate professor. They discover the army's path, and Jones decides to search an old army barracks they can see in the distance. Spline finds Rambling's dictaphone, but soon hears the sound of the army advancing on him. He rushes to find Jones, but he has already been reduced to a skeleton. Spline runs for his life.

Steed and Suzy touch base with Gambit and Carruthers over lunch, and ruminate on the possibility of an invisible army. Steed and Suzy are called away by Dr. Apple. Gambit, convinced the "late" General Cavalo is somehow connected to their investigations, departs to further question George Ware in his hot air balloon. Carruthers is left to ponder the *Cooking for the Masses* book Steed and Suzy found at Frank Miller's home. A waiter sees the title, and comments that the book was his "bible" when he worked for the army's Catering Corps, leading Carruthers to conclude that Miller's undercover work involved feeding the invisible army.

Unfortunately, Pitt beats Gambit to George Ware's. He lowers the balloon to the ground and opens the back of an army truck to allow his troops to disembark. A sleeping George awakes, takes stock of his situation, and then succumbs to panic. He sends his balloon back up into the sky, but he is no longer alone. Pitt watches him frantically move around in the basket and listens to his screams. Gambit arrives just as Pitt is leaving and gives chase. Pitt stops and deploys his troops from the seemingly empty back of his truck before driving away. Gambit attempts to give chase, but his tyres are shredded by what sounds like gunfire. Before Pitt manages a clean getaway, however,

Gambit manages to disable the man's army truck. Undeterred, Pitt radios Cavalo for transport, lamenting that he had to sacrifice a full complement of troops to stop Gambit. He then continues on foot to his next destination, Frank Miller's place, with the intention of burning it to the ground.

Carruthers has beaten him to Miller's, however, and discovers a glass phial concealed in a faux tennis ball made of cream cake. Pitt arrives, and a dangerous fight on the building's scaffolding ensues, which ends with Pitt falling and breaking his leg. Carla arrives in the nick of time with the promised transport, and whisks Pitt away before Carruthers can take him prisoner.

Rendezvousing with Dr. Apple at the hospital, Steed and Suzy learn that Vance has died after encasing his own head in cement in a misguided attempt to protect himself. They return to Steed's, followed by Gambit and Carruthers. Carruthers reveals the contents of the phial: a plan for a strange gun with three handgrips. She has also had a life-size version of the gun made up, and shows it to the others. Steed produces some of the artificial limbs he collected from Miller's, and attaches two arms to each of the gun's grips. The team puzzles on the logistics of such a strange weapon. Steed places a call to Kane, a man who manufactures weapons to order, and arranges to pay him a visit. Kane, in turn, contacts Cavalo, who takes action. By the time Steed and Suzy arrive, Kane, too, has been reduced to a skeleton.

Pitt reports to Cavalo, who demonstrates the power of a set of steel dentures by biting into metal. He informs Pitt that all of their troops will be equipped with the dentures, and that they will attack in 36 hours' time.

Steed and Suzy search Kane's files, but find no evidence of an order for a three-grip gun. Steed notes that the watch on the man's skeletal remains has stopped, and infers that whatever killed him also stopped his watch.

Steed and Suzy return to Dr. Apple, who has conducted a thorough examination of Vance's body at Steed's request. Apple tells them that Vance was covered in thousands of tiny versions of the gun in Carruthers' plan.

Suzy checks in with her CIA superior, Hart, and is told about Spline's discovery of the skeletal Jones while searching for Professor Rambling. Hart tells Suzy that he will supply her with the location of Jones' remains, but orders her not to divulge the information to Steed.

Steed, meanwhile, pays a visit to the very tall miniaturist Bernard Igg, to inquire about the three-grip guns. Igg confirms that he produced fifty thousand miniature laser guns for a client, as well as some tiny steel jaws, all of which he delivered to the 33rd Cavalry army base. Steed is surprised – he knows for a fact that the base has not been in use since World War Two.

Gambit and Carruthers pay a visit to Gambit's ex-mercenary acquaintance, Captain Ferret. They identify Pitt and Cavalo in a photo, and Ferret confirms that the two served together. Ferret insists that Cavalo is dead due to his run-in with the Soldad, the soldier ants of South America, which are notorious for stripping the flesh from the bones of their victims.

Dr. Apple calls Steed with Vance's test results. Vance was covered in "Anteedote", a powerful insect repellent. Apple has also found a dead ant in Kane's wristwatch. Steed, already engrossed in a book entitled *The Ant Kingdom*, seems unsurprised by the discoveries. He tells Gambit and Carruthers to take the strange three-grip gun to a museum exhibit. He then takes a bath – fully-clothed! Suzy stops by Steed's while he is bathing and receives another call from Hart. He provides her with the location of Jones' remains, then reminds her not to share the information with Steed. Suzy gets around this order by leaving Steed a note with the location rather than telling him in person, and makes her exit. Steed discovers it just too late, adds his own note, and follows.

Carruthers and Gambit arrive at the museum exhibit, model gun in tow. They discover a large model of an ant standing upright on two legs, and find that the gun can be "held" by the rest of the ant's legs.

Suzy has made her way to the 33rd Cavalry army base. She searches the barrack huts, and finds one with a door. Behind it, she finds large sacks of sugar and hears shouted army commands. She discovers a trap door and goes through it. She finds herself first in a tunnel, and then in a corridor along which more than a few ants are scuttling. She also sees Cavalo's officers coming and going, all of them suspended from wires to avoid stepping on the ants as they move. Suzy forgoes the wire and proceeds to investigate, leaving a trail of squished ants in her wake. She discovers a laboratory, and attempts to take some photographs of it, but soon finds herself surrounded by masses of ants – enough to turn the completely white room black! Carla soon joins them. Suzy is trapped.

Back at Steed's, Carruthers and Gambit have found Steed's note, which instructs them to make their way to the 33rd Cavalry army base, but not before taking a bath. They find the bathtub full of Anteedote, and proceed to share a quick dip while fully clothed.

Carla delivers Suzy to Cavalo, before departing to search for further intruders. Carla runs into, and is knocked out by, Steed, who has followed Suzy's trail into the underground tunnels. Steed interrupts Cavalo, who is threatening to set his steel-jawed ants on Suzy unless she tells him what he wishes to know. Unfortunately, one of Cavalo's guards puts a gun to the senior agent's back, and Steed winds up a captive alongside Suzy.

With Steed and Suzy acting as a (literal) captive audience, Cavalo explains his plan to achieve world domination using his army of ants, ironically comprised of the very same species that mangled his face and body. He has trained the ants to follow his orders, and has had them practice destroying important landmarks, such as the White House, using model buildings made of cream cake that the hungry ants consume. He informs Steed and Suzy that the ants are invulnerable, capable of surviving anything — even the atom bomb. Steed tells Cavalo that he cannot be killed by the ants, as he has doused himself with insect repellent, but Cavalo informs him that his laboratory is hard at work creating a new strain of ant that will be immune to such toxins. Augmented with guns and steel jaws, the ants will be unstoppable. Impressed by Steed's military credentials, Cavalo asks Steed to join him and save himself from the horrible fate of being eaten alive by his ant army.

Meanwhile, Gambit and Carruthers are hot on Steed and Suzy's trail. Finding their way into the underground base, they opt to travel by wire rather than walk. When they are spotted by the revived Carla, they fight her and three guards, all while suspended above the floor.

Steed pretends to accept Cavalo's offer to join his operation, using it as a pretence to grab a cake bowl and throw it over Cavalo's head. As the bowl is filled with ants, Cavalo is temporarily blinded, affording Suzy and Steed an opportunity to escape. They flee into the corridor, just in time to see Gambit and Carruthers finish off their opponents. Gambit and Carruthers take a hold of Steed and Suzy and fly them down the corridor via wire. They exit through the trap door and make their way to the base's parade ground, but know they have no hope of outrunning the ant army. Steed spots a fuel supply tank on the grounds, and has Gambit pump fuel oil down a nearby air vent, then drops a lit match after it. The explosion that follows destroys the underground base and everyone within it. Crispy, dead ants rain down from the sky, and the four avengers walk off into the sunset with the prospect of some very enthusiastic celebrating ahead of them!

Analysis

After *The New Avengers* ceased production in 1977, *The Avengers* was seemingly consigned to television history. However, producer Brian Clemens was not content to let the series go without a fight. Though *The New Avengers* contended with numerous obstacles throughout its run — including unstable financing, partial networking in Britain, and a much-needed American sale that materialised too late — it also met with considerable international success, proving that there was still an appetite for televisual avenging. Furthermore, though late in the day, the series' American sale was a hopeful sign that there was still interest in the show stateside, and that an American network — CBS — might provide the funding demanded by the show's high production values, just as ABC had done in the case of the original sixties series. Clemens therefore set about attempting to rescue *The New Avengers* from cancellation. Unfortunately, a third season of *The New Avengers* proved to be financially untenable for CBS, but the network did express interest in another *Avengers* project: a series of TV movies. This revival made it as far as a first draft script dated January 1981. The screenplay is credited to Brian Clemens, and the story to Clemens and *Avengers* stalwart Dennis Spooner, who, along with Clemens, produced the bulk of the scripts for *The New Avengers*. Coming in at just under 130 pages, it is unquestionably a feature-length story, but not one that is so ambitious in scale that it would have demanded a massive, feature film-sized budget. Even the billed "cast of thousands" turns out to be a misdirect.

As with any project with a connection to the original series, the first question that comes to mind regarding the movie is whether it is *Avengers*-ish. The answer is, to a large degree, "yes". The script even explicitly expects the reader to understand the series' feel and look, stating that a hospital corridor set's aesthetic should be "*Avengers* style", a phrase that should prompt every *Avengers* fan to conjure up an appropriate mental image even before Clemens elaborates on how it should look: long, completely white, with no adornment save for a single door at the end. The trademark *Avengers* strangeness is also alive and well, with the plot revolving around a diabolical mastermind who commands a vast army of killer ants – the aforementioned "cast of thousands" – who strip their victims to the bone. True to the *Avengers* rulebook, we never see them in (violent) action, just the clean, bloodless skeletons they leave behind. Their leader, one General Cavalo, plans to augment their already-considerable power by equipping them with ant-sized guns and steel jaws. (If this is starting to sound a bit "out there", even for Avengerland, recall that this is a universe in which Steed has already successfully defeated a man-eating plant from space and a giant rat.) Because of the diminutive nature of his army, Cavalo's (human) commanding officers travel around their base suspended from wires, so as not to accidentally crush their troops underfoot. (Cavalo himself exerts complete control over the ants, to the point that they stay out of his way when he moves, enabling him to keep his feet on the ground.) This gives rise to some quintessentially *Avengers*-ish bizarre scenes, with Cavalo's people delivering dialogue while suspended in mid-air. In another quirky touch, Cavalo trains his troops to destroy targets using tiny scale models of important buildings (e.g., Windsor Castle, the White House) constructed entirely out of cream cake, which the hungry ants devour. Adding to the strangeness and intrigue is the fact that the audience is kept (quite successfully) in the dark as to the army's true nature for some time – at one point, the lead characters wonder if the troops are invisible – with music cues and sound effects used to signal its approach. All we actually see of the attacks is the victims fleeing from the ants in terror, akin to the way that the cat and bird attacks were depicted in The Hidden Tiger (1967) and Cat Amongst the Pigeons (1976). The framing of these attacks is one of many elements recycled from the original and sequel series, all of which add further Avengers touches to the mix, albeit at the expense of originality. These recycled elements are explored further in the "Trivia Points" section of this chapter.

The script also provides the requisite supply of Avengers eccentrics. An extraordinarily tall miniaturist by the name of Bernard Igg spends his time crouching as much as possible and lamenting that the sign on his door, which reads "B. Igg", leads to him being repeatedly misidentified as "Mr. Bigg", as the dot after the "B" is too small — but, as a devotee of all things miniature, he cannot bring himself to make it any larger! George Ware, the brother of one of the ants' unfortunate victims, takes to living in a tethered hot air balloon to protect himself from the murderous insects. Helmut, a flea circus trainer, keeps the members of his troupe at bay with whip-wielding skills that would put a lion tamer to shame, and can identify each of them by name.

While the Avengers-ish touches are all present and correct, the most problematic aspect of the script is, oddly enough, the avengers themselves. First of all, there are four of them, one up from The New Avengers' trio. This is a somewhat surprising development, as some people involved in The New Avengers indicated that one of the series' problems was the expansion of the main cast from a duo to a triumvirate. Stunt arranger-turned-director Ray Austin described Gambit as a third wheel, and argued that his presence slowed the episodes' pace down as it was difficult to find things for him to do. Even Gambit portrayer Gareth Hunt, who acknowledged that Gambit's role was reduced as part of the adjustments made in The New Avengers' second series, agreed that "[i]t was very difficult to write for that threesome." (Margaret Baroski, "A Fine Gambit", Starlog, March 1990) Whether Brian Clemens shared that opinion — his reasons for cutting down Gambit's screentime were ostensibly to appease Patrick Macnee, who felt Steed had been "put out to pasture" in Series 1 and wanted his character to play a more active role — is unknown, though unlikely given his decision to include a third character in the first place, and his enthusiasm for Hunt and his performance. Regardless, given that there was some question about the wisdom (and success) of writing for three lead characters, it seems strange that, rather than return to the classic Avengers format of a duo, Clemens would instead go one step further, and expand the movie's cast to four lead characters. Interestingly, in the same Starlog interview, Gareth Hunt suggested that either two or four leads would have been preferable to three: "I agree with Patrick *totally* that it should have been Patrick and another Emma Peel, or Patrick and another Emma Peel and two younger agents." This comment suggests that Hunt had read the script for *The First Avengers Movie* and agreed with its approach, as this is essentially the movie's set-up, with Steed and Suzy Stride working together in a Steed / Emma Peel capacity, and Gambit and Carruthers, the "younger" agents, providing a variation on the Purdey / Gambit dynamic.

While the success of *The New Avengers*' triumvirate is a matter of opinion, any reservations one might have regarding the wisdom of including four main characters are certainly well founded. After Steed, Gambit, and Carruthers initially touch base, they split up for their investigations, with Gambit and Carruthers following one line of inquiry, and Steed branching off on his own. His investigation leads him to cross paths with Suzy Stride, with whom he works for the rest of the movie. The result is that the characters are split into two duos that operate more or less independently of one another. When they reunite, the characters swap information in a mostly perfunctory manner, then revert to interacting within their respective duos – in one scene, Steed interacts mainly with Suzy, while Gambit carries on a completely separate conversation with Carruthers, even though all four characters are seated at the same table. Such scenes increase the sense that the duos are separate entities. While this divisive approach was undoubtedly employed to ensure that all of the characters were given a relatively equal share of the screentime and a part to play in the plot, the fact that it was needed indicates that Clemens found juggling four characters difficult, and its use had the unfortunate side effect of preventing the four leads from gelling as a team. Of course, this splitting up of the cast has undeniable advantages. It is easier for the audience to get to know each new character (Suzy, Carruthers) if she is partnered with a familiar one (Steed, Gambit). Furthermore, the classic *Avengers* format favours a male / female partnership, and dividing the cast up provides us with not one, but two such duos. However, the script's set two-handers prevent us from getting a sense of the relationships between Gambit and Suzy, Suzy and Carruthers, and Steed and Carruthers. Even Steed and Gambit say very little to one another, instead interacting with their respective female partners. Given that they are the only link to the previous *Avengers* series, it is hard not to lament the lack of Steed / Gambit interaction, particularly since Macnee and Hunt had proved to be a good double act in *The New Avengers*. In the script, there is no sense of them having a connection that runs any deeper than the ones they share with Suzy or Carruthers, respectively, which is a shame.

Splitting up the characters also affects the movie's tone. Brian Clemens stated that the movie "was going to be more in the style of *The Avengers*, rather than *The New Avengers* and shot here in Britain rather than in the USA." (Anthony McKay and Michael Richardson, "The Avengers Man", *TimeScreen*,

Autumn 1992, Number 19) In reality, the script oscillates between the lighter feel of the colour Emma Peel episodes in the Steed and Suzy scenes, and the darker, sometimes grimmer shadings of *The New Avengers* in the Gambit and Carruthers scenes. While these two tones are not completely siloed off from one another, they create a degree of dissonance in the movie's feel. A scene may revive the Avengerland of old, complete with requisite eccentrics, and then be followed by one that drives home the grim realities of mercenary life. The result is akin to two separate movies cut together, and reinforces the sense that the two investigative duos are isolated from one another.

The Characters

In addition to the tonal issues and unsatisfactory relationship dynamics resulting from the script's division of the characters, the characterisation of the avenging foursome is also something of a mixed bag.

John Steed

In the script, Steed is, unsurprisingly, Steed. Twenty years after first tackling the character in *Brought to Book* (1961), Brian Clemens could probably write Steed in his sleep, though not every piece of dialogue sounds like the man *Avengers* fans know and love. Still, the steel-rimmed bowler is put to good use in more than one fight, and Steed educates Suzy, in typical Steed fashion, about the three "Champagne occasions" that call for the drink. (Only three?) The umbrella is still present and correct, though it has now been fitted with a .303 calibre gun that fires soft-nosed bullets at Steed's department's behest, despite Steed's continued aversion to firearms. Surprisingly, Steed is also driving the Bentley again, despite it being blown to smithereens in *Dead Men are Dangerous* (1977). Whether this is meant to be the original Bentley (and Clemens has simply forgotten about, or chosen to ignore, that episode) or a new one is never made clear. We get a little bit of backstory as well, with Steed's military career mentioned (he reiterates that he served in the Guards and tells Bernard Igg he got lots of crouching in while dodging shells and gunfire during the war), and the names of his parents revealed (Joshua and Araminta). He also gets some good scenes, the best of which is his conversation with Igg, conducted while both men are crouching. It is an exchange that would have given Macnee the opportunity to feign a sympathetic understanding of his interviewee's area of interest, while simultaneously trying to hide his bemusement (and amusement), something he did with aplomb in countless episodes. The scene could quite easily be transplanted into an Emma or Tara era story without anyone noticing the joins.

Mike Gambit

Gambit is the first avenger to appear onscreen. Four years on from *The New Avengers*, Gareth Hunt was a month shy of 39 and, had the script gone into production, likely would have been pushing 40 by the time he reprised the role. This may have influenced the way that Brian Clemens wrote the character. There is a world-weariness to Gambit that was not present in *The New Avengers*, and it paints a portrait of a man who, at this point in his life, really has seen it all, both on and off the job. When Steed tries to reassure Carruthers about their seemingly impossible assignment by saying, "When a case begins for us in a such a bizarre and mysterious way, it usually...", Gambit cuts in with a knowing, "escalates and starts to get REALLY weird." Gambit's military background also comes to the fore, something which, though sketched out in the character's production biography, was never discussed onscreen in *The New Avengers*. In one instance, Gambit catches out a character's lie when he claims that his brother was a mercenary in Angola. "*I* was in the last detail out of Angola," Gambit shoots back, much to Carruthers' surprise. Later, Gambit pays a visit to an old acquaintance, an ex-mercenary named Captain Ferret. Now blind, Ferret identifies Gambit, not by the fact that Gambit knows that they both served in St. Paulo, but by evaluating the damage Gambit has done to his overenthusiastic bodyguard, who failed to inflict so much as a scratch in return. Gambit's military background also gives him a working knowledge of the Matto Grosso massacre in South America and of Cavalo, whose supposed death he questions as the investigation proceeds. This focus on Gambit's military background lends a grimmer edge to a character who was often serious, but not normally for such a sustained period of time, and definitely not at the expense of the lighter moments that so often typified him (and which Gareth Hunt personally preferred).

This is not to say that Gambit is completely humourless throughout the entire script. He spends the whole of one scene hanging on a ladder just outside the basket of a hot air balloon, and is forced to question the balloon's owner from his precarious position on the pretence that there is only enough room for two in the basket, and Carruthers is taking up the rest! The mental image this conjures up is completely in keeping with the sorts of predicaments Gambit would often find himself in in *The New Avengers*. Later, he shares a bath with Carruthers in one of the pair's best and (funniest) scenes. (Both are fully clothed, though Gambit makes it clear he would not mind if they were not!) He also generally lightens up as the script goes on, but there seems to be a definite push to make his character more serious.

Besides being older, Hunt was also beginning to pay for his *New Avengers* stunt work. By 1983, he was visiting an osteopath (and running into Joanna Lumley, who was also paying for her stunt work, at the same clinic in the process!). How much he was suffering from the aftereffects of his stunts by 1981 is unclear, but, initially, the script seems to take any physical limitations he might have had into consideration, with his action sequences being relatively undemanding. At the movie's climax, however, Gambit has a fairly active fight while suspended from a wire, so perhaps Hunt was still up for the stunts after all. The character, at least, is still portrayed as being extremely athletic and a lethal karate master, as well as an expert shot and, ever the ex-race car driver, a man who likes to drive his open-top Morgan fast.

Carruthers

The first new *Avengers* woman is the daughter of two trapeze artists, and performed in a circus with her parents as part of "The Incredible Carruthers" trapeze team. She wears a necklace with photos of both parents. She lives in a flat a few storeys up – with a kitchen that Gambit thinks is too small – and swings down the fire escape to make a dramatic exit. She works with Steed and Gambit and got a 3-minus in knife fighting during her training. Her combat style relies heavily on her trapeze skills, and she can juggle, too.

The script, to its credit, makes the most of Carruthers' skill set. Carruthers, quite frankly, gets all the best fights, including one on some scaffolding, and she joins Gambit in the wire fight. The latter is one of the best sequences in the script and could have looked fantastic onscreen if executed properly. (Interestingly, it bears some resemblance to a fight in the 1998 *Avengers* movie between Uma Thurman's Emma Peel and Eddie Izzard's Bailey. Whether or not the movie got the idea for that fight from this script is unknown, but it is a notable coincidence.) There is also something to be said for an *Avengers* woman who, when cornered, can simply topple backwards out of the nearest window to escape.

Other than her skill set, Carruthers owes a lot of her character to her immediate predecessor, Purdey. Like Purdey, she is an official agent, as opposed to a "talented amateur". At one point, it is revealed that Carruthers' full name is "C.C. Carruthers", which, improbably, stands for "Carruthers Carruthers Carruthers". This smacks of a twist on Purdey's insistence on being called, "just Purdey", with Gambit, Suzy, and Steed referring to her as just "Carruthers", sans any "Miss" or "Mrs." honourific. Carruthers also participates in a reiteration of one of Gambit and Purdey's exchanges from *K is for Kill: The Tiger Awakes* (1977), although the roles are reversed, with Carruthers taking on Gambit's half of the exchange. For all that Purdey was meant to be a combination of her three predecessors (possessing Cathy's coolness, Emma's wit, and Tara's femininity), she always felt like her own character, with her own personality and quirks. Anything that was borrowed was given a unique twist and modified to the extent that only the germ of the idea remained. She certainly was not given second-hand dialogue to parrot, something no *Avengers* woman had to endure outside of a straight episode remake. Such scenes weaken Carruthers' ability to establish herself as a character in her own right.

Since Carruthers spends the majority of her screentime with Gambit, she has also inherited Purdey's half of the Purdey / Gambit dynamic, albeit a watered-down version of the same. Gambit flirts with her, though fairly infrequently, and while Carruthers keeps him at arm's length, she does not do so with Purdey's biting humour. As a result, their relationship is not very engaging, and neither character seems particularly invested in it, with a definite lack of persistent interest on Gambit's part compared to his long-standing, recurring flirtation with Purdey. (This is difficult to reconcile with the script's closing scene, in which it is unsubtly implied that both Gambit and Steed will bed their respective partners, completely eschewing the series' trademark ambiguity as to what went on between the lead characters once the screen went dark.) It would have been better to create a completely new dynamic between Carruthers and Gambit, instead of occasionally raising, then dropping, the ghost of his relationship with Purdey.

Purdey

For those who are wondering, Purdey does not feature in the script at all, not even in the form of a passing reference or in-joke. When and why the character is meant to have departed is not addressed at all – she is simply no longer working with Steed and Gambit. It is unclear whether Purdey's absence can be attributed to Joanna Lumley being unwilling, or unable, to participate, or if Brian Clemens preferred to have a new female character in the series of movies. Certainly, by 1981, Lumley was involved in the series *Sapphire and Steel* and had been contracted to appear in a lead role in Blake Edwards' *The Trail of the Pink Panther* (1982), which may have made her ability to commit to more *Avengers* difficult.

Suzy Stride

CIA operative Suzanne Amelia Stride, about 38, was born in Philadelphia. Her mother was French, and her father was a fourth-generation American. She was educated at Vassar, and was widowed four years before the events of the script. She carries a gun, and also has some hand-to-hand combat skills. Whether "Stride" is her maiden or married name is not clear, but it hardly matters as Steed, rather uncharacteristically, calls her "Suzy" throughout, something he last did with Tara, though only intermittently. (Purdey, with her one-name alias and preference to be addressed as "just Purdey", does not count.) Carruthers and Gambit follow suit, on the very rare occasion that they speak to her at all. Sadly, other than a handful of inconsequential characteristics, there is not much to distinguish Suzy as a character beyond her nationality, so the script reminds us of this repeatedly, seeding it between other throwaway facts. It tells us that she has beginner's luck at snooker. And that she is American. And that she is beautiful. And that she is American. And that she usually reports to a fellow named Lipsky, who happens to be on vacation for this story, so she has to work with his replacement, Hart, with whom she does not get along. And that she is American...

It is possible that all Suzy needed to transform her from a small collection of myriad facts into a fleshed out, well-rounded character was the right actress to breathe life into her. After all, most *Avengers* characters are, by design, fairly thinly drawn. Reading unmade Emma Peel or *New Avengers* scripts conveys how much the words on the page owed to having Diana Rigg, Gareth Hunt, or Joanna Lumley interpreting them, tweaking their delivery, filtering them through their ideas about the character, and improvising the appropriate accompanying body language. Without an actor in mind to enliven a part, any character seems flat. Perhaps an American actress of the same calibre as the American actors who starred in the ITC series that served as the *Avengers*' cohorts – such as *Man in a Suitcase*'s Richard Bradford, *The Champions*' Stuart Damon, *Strange Report*'s Kaz Garas, and Tony Curtis of *The Persuaders!* – could have turned Suzy into much more than the token American character likely introduced to guarantee American funding. As written, however, there is very little for the reader to latch onto in order to get a handle on her, and her nationality alone is not enough to base a whole character on, certainly not if the reader is meant to become attached to her. To make matters worse, like Carruthers, Suzy also borrows from her predecessors, particularly Emma Peel. She re-enacts the scene from *Too Many Christmas Trees* (1965) in which Emma argues that Steed ought to ditch the Bentley and get himself a new car, and, of course, she is a widow. Aside from being an uninspired creative choice, there is something mildly ridiculous about the idea of Steed being partnered with yet *another* widow. If her availability as a love interest was important (and Steed makes quite clear that it is, at least as far as he is concerned!), then why not simply make her single, like Carruthers? Or, at the very least, give her some other creative marital status? By 1981, *The Avengers* ought to have been progressive enough to introduce its first divorcée. Unfortunately, it appears that the desire to evoke the memory of the widowed Emma (or Cathy Gale) won out, but creating points of comparison between Suzy and her predecessors only serves to weaken Suzy's character.

Trivia Points

- The script features many recycled elements that first appeared in other episodes of the series, as well as the odd reference intended to act as an in-joke for fans of *The Avengers* and *The New Avengers*. Examples of these recycled elements and references include the following:

    o The way that the attacks by the ants are portrayed – with the ants unseen, and the camera closing in on their victims as if from the ants' point of view – is reminiscent of the framing of the cat attacks in *The Hidden Tiger*, and the bird attacks in *Cat Amongst the Pigeons*.

    o General Cavalo's character is an amalgam of previous *Avengers* villains. His encounter with the Soldad has left him with a paralysed arm and leg, an eyepatch, and a wax mask covering half of his face. The mask in particular calls to mind Felix Kane from *The Last of the Cybernauts...??* (1976), who also wore a mask to conceal his burnt and scarred face. Cavalo also possesses the military zeal and mercenary tendencies of Colonel "Mad Jack" Miller (*Dirtier by the Dozen*, 1977), and controls a non-human army like Zacardi in *Cat Amongst the Pigeons*.

    o Gambit summons Carruthers for duty with the words "Carruthers! We're needed!" This is a nod to the colour Emma Peel era's "Mrs. Peel, we're needed" scenes, in which Steed would inform Emma that they had an assignment.

    o Gambit and Carruthers engage in an exchange that is similar to one between Gambit and Purdey in *K is for Kill: The Tiger Awakes* (1977). When Carruthers saves Gambit by kicking his opponent out of a window, Gambit responds, "Thanks, but I think we would have preferred him alive," to which Carruthers retorts, "Conflict of interest. I wanted you alive." The exchange in *K is for Kill* is the reversal of this, and follows Gambit's killing of a Russian soldier who was about to shoot Purdey. "Gambit, we wanted him alive," chastises Purdey. "Conflict of interest. I wanted you alive," Gambit replies. In addition, in the script, Gambit follows this exchange by observing that "Steed isn't going to like this", which was Purdey and Gambit's oft-used refrain in *Forward Base* (1977) whenever their investigation took an unsatisfactory turn.

o Like Emma before her, Suzy is not only a widow, but argues that Steed ought to get himself a more modern car than the Bentley, just as Emma did on the trip out to Brandon Storey's house in *Too Many Christmas Trees*.

o Helmut the flea trainer is found lying dead under a running shower, the same way Winters' corpse is left by his killers in *The Correct Way to Kill* (1967).

o Vance dies by having his head sealed in cement, not unlike Bernard in *Quick-Quick-Slow Death* (1966), who dies after having his face pushed into a bowl of plaster.

o Ferret is blind and lives in darkened quarters, much like those of the blind Tompkins in *Cat Amongst the Pigeons*.

o Steed, Gambit, and Carruthers bathe, fully clothed, in insect repellent, which is reminiscent of the prisoners' method of applying the invisibility potion in *Get-A-Way!* (1969).

o Steed recycles the line "This umbrella is loaded" when holding up Cavalo, which he first used in *Cat Amongst the Pigeons*.

o Steed's line just before he lights up the fuel that will destroy the ant army is borrowed, with a few modifications, from the final lines of the first draft script of *The Last of the Cybernauts...??*. Instead of "Not with a bang – but with a whimper", as in the *Cybernauts* script, in *The First Avengers Movie*, Steed says, "Not with a bang. Or a whimper. But with a match."

o   Brian Clemens' penchant for recycling character names comes to the fore in this script. "Suzy" was the name of both Annette André's character in *House of Cards* (1976) and Morgan Fairchild's character in the American *Avengers*-esque series Clemens wrote the pilot script for, 1978's *Escapade*. "Miller", here the name of a dead CIA operative, was Colonel "Mad Jack" Miller's surname in *Dirtier by the Dozen*. Gambit's ex-mercenary acquaintance Captain Ferret shares a moniker with MI12 investigator Ferret from Tony Williamson's *Super Secret Cypher Snatch*. "Vance", one of Cavalo's officers, may owe something to Ronnie Vance from *Brought to Book* (1961) who, in turn, may have been named after Clemens' former ABC/ABPC colleagues Dennis Vance or Leigh Vance. "Carruthers" was Steed's preferred alias when contacting the police in Series 2 (he used it in both *The Big Thinker* [1962] and *Killer Whale* [1963], though neither of these episodes were written by Clemens). Finally, not only does Cavalo's mask call to mind the mask-wearing Felix Kane, but another character in the script is actually called Kane, though he bears no resemblance to his namesake.

Verdict

The *First Avengers Movie* is something of a mixed bag. The trademark *Avengers* strangeness is alive and well, most notably in the form of the requisite supply of eccentrics and Cavalo's ant army. Unfortunately, some of the *Avengers*-esque touches come in the form of recycled plot points and dialogue, and this hampers the script's originality. The splitting up of the four leads into two duos who mostly follow separate lines of inquiry is also problematic, as they often may as well be in separate movies. In addition, new character Suzy is fairly thinly drawn, and both she and Carruthers at times seem more like tributes to past *Avengers* women than their own characters. The reused plot points can be forgiven – after all, *The Avengers* was known to remake whole episodes, so the script can hardly be faulted for borrowing a bit here and there – but, when combined with the unoriginal character choices and other instances of recycling, the result is a sense of diminishing returns, as though the series' freshness had been stifled in favour of recapturing past glories. *The Avengers* was always about moving forward, about reinventing itself with each new incarnation. Even though it had a habit of circling back on itself –

oscillating from gritty spy drama to far-flung fantasy, and back again — it always approached older concepts from a new angle. *The New Avengers* is often accused of looking too much to the past and not enough to the future, but when it referenced what came before, it did so to establish a sense of history and tie the whole of the series together, as well as to establish an internal continuity amongst its own 26 episodes. *The First Avengers Movie*, in contrast, is not simply looking back fondly on what came before — it is attempting to rehash it in place of developing its own identity. Maybe Brian Clemens had simply been associated with the show for too long, and it needed a pair of fresh eyes. Or maybe *The Avengers*' formula only had so much life in it. Either way, it is probably for the best that this script never made it to the screen. For the most part, we have seen it all before.

AVENGERS INTERNATIONAL
REINCARNATION

J Z FERGUSON

Project Type: Prospective Television Series Pilot
Date: March 1985

Synopsis

Teaser

A man in his twenties lies sleeping in a hospital bed, hooked up to both a saline drip and a heart monitor. He is presided over by Gross, a surgeon, and Topski, an important Russian official. Gross informs the incredulous Topski that the man is Bobby Lomax, a legendary Russian double agent who managed to infiltrate MI5 and rise to the level of deputy controller nine years earlier. Gross reveals that Lomax will awaken soon, and, when he does, he will be provided with his usual accoutrements, which have already been collected and placed on a side table: his trademark black Sobranie cigarettes, his favourite Scotch, and a box of tissues to help him cope with his chronic hay fever.

Gross and Topski depart so that Gross may introduce Topski to his "prototype", Ivan Nevsky, an old schoolmate of the now 60-year-old Topski. Topski is amazed to discover that his friend is now a fit, 19-year-old man. Before the pair can get reacquainted, a nurse hurries over and alerts the men that Lomax has gone. Returning swiftly to the hospital room, they find that a quarter of the Scotch is missing, a handful of tissues has been purloined, and the cigarettes are gone. Gross is certain that Lomax has gone after Steed. He informs Topski that Steed killed Lomax, and suspects that Lomax will want to return the favour!

Act One

A Lotus Elan is racing a speeding train. The driver, Mrs. Samantha Peel, makes it to the station just in time to leap aboard. She quickly makes her way to one of the sleeper cars, only to find John Steed staring into the barrels of a shotgun! Sam engages in a brief scuffle with the man brandishing the weapon before Steed intervenes and informs Sam that her opponent is American agent Christopher Cambridge, to whom Steed was showing the shotgun he plans to use on an upcoming shoot. Chris and Sam exchange apologies, then quickly turn to the business at hand. Both have intercepted messages indicating that someone intends to kill Steed. Unbeknownst to them, Lomax is on the train, sneezing away...

Despite Chris and Sam's best efforts, Steed refuses to believe that anyone has a reason to kill him. Though he is still on the active list, he spends most of his time mixing with various high-ranking officials and dignitaries, not scrambling over the Berlin Wall. Chris is undeterred, and reveals that the would-be killer is Lomax. Steed is now even less willing to take the threats seriously – he killed Lomax five years ago! He leaves the sleeper and makes for the dining car, and it is only Chris and Sam's presence that prevents Lomax from taking a shot at him.

The three agents have lunch in the dining car, and Steed explains that Lomax would be old and grey by now – and still sneezing. A sneeze from another dining car occupant startles them, but the sneezer is a woman. As Steed laughs at the possibility of Lomax returning from the dead as a woman, the real Lomax lurks in the rear of the car, smoking a black Sobranie and biding his time.

Chris and Sam accompany Steed to his hotel, still unsuccessfully trying to convince him that his life is in danger. He makes his way to his room accompanied by Lomax, who is disguised as the hotel porter, while Chris and Sam search the hotel. They find many old, sneezing men, but the real Lomax is in Steed's room, unpacking his suitcase while Steed lays out his things in the bathroom. Lomax finds Steed's shotgun and loads it, carrying on a conversation with Steed about the piece as he does so. When Steed realises that Lomax knows more about the gun than he should, he moves out into the main room, only to find Lomax pointing the weapon at him. A shocked Steed identifies Lomax as his assailant!

Chris and Sam's search of the hotel comes up empty. They rendezvous and decide to search the grounds next, but run into the real hotel porter, who complains that a man asked him to park his car, despite not having a car to park! Chris and Sam twig and race up to Steed's room, bursting in just as Lomax is about to kill Steed. Sam dropkicks Lomax out of the nearest window, and he lands with a piece of glass protruding from his chest. Chris is annoyed – he would have liked to take the man alive. Steed confirms that his assailant was indeed Lomax. The agents agree that, despite his puzzling resurrection, Lomax is definitely dead this time, but when they glance out the window, they discover that the body has vanished! Chris and Sam take off in pursuit of the body snatchers, but are too late to do more than catch a glimpse of a retreating truck.

Inside the truck, Gross and an intern examine Lomax. The intern is certain that Lomax is dead, but Gross detects brain activity. If Lomax's brain is alive, Gross argues, there is hope.

Steed, despite Sam's protestations, is determined to attend his shoot, and refuses all offers of protection. He is convinced Lomax is dead for good now, and leaves it up to Chris and Sam to work out how he came back to life in the first place.

Chris suggests they go back to square one and look into the "original-dead-and-buried" Lomax. They read Lomax's file and view surveillance footage taken of Lomax's death. The film shows Lomax waiting to give a top-secret file to a contact from the other side. He is met by Steed instead, and a fight ensues. Lomax pulls a gun, but Steed grabs it and shoots Lomax in the chest. Lomax seemingly collapses and dies from the bullet wound. Chris and Sam agree that Lomax looks dead, but, before they can screen the film again to be sure, they are interrupted by Dr. Pinner, who has exhumed Lomax's body on their instructions. He confirms that the body is Lomax's, as the fingerprints and dental records match. He watches the film with them, and is surprised to discover that Lomax died of a bullet to the chest. The body he exhumed also had a head wound!

Gross has successfully resurrected Lomax using the body of a young man in his twenties who bears no resemblance to his previous host. Despite his intern's misgivings, Gross asserts that they cannot accord Lomax the recommended post-procedure recovery time, as they need him to deal with an urgent situation. Gross wakes Lomax up, and is rewarded with a sneeze.

Act Two

Lomax is eager to take another shot at Steed, but Gross declares that eliminating Sam and Chris must take priority. Their investigation could endanger Gross' entire project. Reluctantly, Lomax agrees, but not before placing a call.

Chris and Sam pay a visit to Ginger Douglas, a dance instructor and Lomax's ex-mistress. She is certain that Lomax is dead – she attended the funeral and saw them bury the coffin. She also confides that it is the anniversary of the first time Lomax sent her flowers. The florist made a mistake and sent her eleven red roses and one daffodil, instead of the dozen roses Lomax intended. Every year after that, as a private joke, he sent her eleven roses and a daffodil. It was a secret only the pair of them knew. Just then, one of Ginger's dance students interrupts, carrying a bouquet that has arrived for Ginger. It contains eleven roses and one daffodil!

Chris phones the florist, but is told only that the order was placed by a man. Ginger is now convinced that Lomax is alive, but is at a loss as to how that could be possible. Lomax is parked outside Ginger's studio and, after seeing Chris and Sam leave, decides to follow them. Ginger looks out the window as Chris and Sam depart, and catches Lomax's eye. They share a look before Lomax drives away, leaving Ginger ill-at-ease.

Lomax pursues Chris and Sam, gun in hand, and lines up a shot. Before he can take it, Sam receives a message over her car's two-way radio informing her that a man named Weir urgently wishes to discuss Lomax with them. Sam abruptly turns the Lotus around to make her way to Weir's, causing Lomax's shot to miss. He settles for following them.

Steed is enjoying his shoot, and fending off the attentions of the attractive (and married) Lady Laura Cartney. The Labrador he sends to retrieve his game returns with a message instead, which provides Steed with the update he requested on Chris and Sam's investigation. He wonders what they will make of Freddy Weir.

Chris and Sam pay a visit to Weir's home. Weir explains that it was he who uncovered Lomax's treachery. Consequently, Weir believes that if Lomax finds him, he will kill him. Chris and Sam ask how this can happen if Lomax is dead. Freddy reveals that he is a staunch believer in reincarnation. He owns animals that he is convinced are the reincarnations of his deceased friends and family members, and states that he has led many past lives himself. Chris and Sam are incredulous, but Weir insists that Lomax has been reincarnated in a new body. As Chris and Sam are about to take their leave, Lomax shoots Weir through a window. Sam stays with the dying man while Chris gives chase. As he fades, Weir tells Sam not to worry, as he will be coming back again soon – this time, he hopes, as a Pomeranian dog!

Chris loses Lomax, but finds his car. Lomax, hidden inside, launches a surprise attack. Chris' counterattack causes Lomax to accidentally shoot himself. Wounded, Lomax begins to drive away. In a last-ditch effort to catch him, Chris reaches through the car window and grabs Lomax by his hair – which comes off. Chris holds onto the wig, but loses Lomax.

Sam phones the Ministry's clean-up squad to take care of Weir's body before leaving with Chris. As they drive away, Sam is amazed to see a Pomeranian dog running toward Weir's house!

Lomax, grievously injured, only just manages to make it back to the hospital. Gross is annoyed that Lomax has damaged another body, but tries to save him.

Chris identifies the maker of Lomax's wig via a label sewn inside: Thatcher Arkwright. Chris and Sam pay Arkwright a visit. He explains that he uses traditional cottage roof weaves to make his wigs. They show Arkwright Lomax's wig, and he recalls that he made it for a medical man, Professor Wyndham, but does not know where he lives.

With Lomax fading fast, Gross orders his intern to locate a new donor. The intern protests that the only available donor is unsuitable, but Gross brushes off his concerns, declaring that they will operate immediately.

Chris and Sam retreat to her home, where they do some research in an attempt to locate Professor Wyndham. Chris discovers that Wyndham is a distinguished neurologist, but his photograph depicts a man with too much hair to require a wig.

Wyndham, as it happens, is Gross' prisoner and has been forced to act as a consultant for Gross' project. Gross pays the imprisoned professor a visit, and asks if the professor's techniques will work even if the sexes of the mind and donor body do not match. Wyndham confirms that they will. Gross returns to the operating theatre and is told that a delegation of important Russian officials will be coming to the hospital the next day to meet Lomax. Gross is confident that Lomax's recent "death" will not prevent the meeting.

Act Three

Chris and Sam visit Wyndham's hospital posing as a reporter and photographer. They tell the receptionist that they have an appointment to interview Wyndham, and she departs to consult the Russian delegation, which is seated in a glassed-in VIP area off of the lobby. Chris recognises one of the men as Colonel Topski of the KGB. They are soon joined by Gross, posing as Wyndham, who informs them that he cannot be interviewed that day and sends them away. Chris and Sam are not so easily deterred. They drive away, park, and return on foot, intent on breaking in. They split up and take different routes into the building.

Sam finds herself in a room containing the dead bodies of Lomax One and Lomax Two. Further investigation takes her to the hospital room containing Lomax Three, whose face is swathed in bandages. Unaware of the significance of the person in the bed, Sam departs – just before Lomax sneezes! She turns her attention to a room marked "Strictly Private", and finds the imprisoned Professor Wyndham inside. Wyndham tells her that Gross took over the hospital three months ago, and has been holding him prisoner ever since. He also tells her that Gross is performing brain transplants!

Chris makes his way to Gross' office and reads the man's papers. Gross, having unveiled the new Lomax to the delegates, brings them to his office, forcing Chris to hastily conceal himself behind the curtains. He listens as Gross explains the procedure to the delegates. He is performing brain transplants by moving the portions of the brain responsible for memory and personality from a dying or dead body to a healthy donor body. He describes the possibilities of the surgery, which would allow the Russians to keep their great thinkers and leaders alive for more than twice their natural lifespan.

Wyndham had pioneered the science, hoping to use it for the good of mankind, but Gross has hijacked it for his own ends.

News of Chris and Sam's break-in reaches Gross, and he quickly finds Chris in his hiding place. Topski identifies him as an American agent, and people are dispatched to search for Sam. Gross decides to demonstrate his surgery technique to the delegates by using Chris as a donor body for the brain of his henchman Yakoff's brother, Boris. They escort Chris to the operating theatre, but are observed by Sam and Wyndham. Sam leaves Wyndham in hiding and follows Chris.

Chris is taken to a room containing an aquarium filled with human brains, all of which are hooked up via wires and tubes to equipment keeping them alive. Just before he is injected with a sedative for his operation, Chris breaks free and a fight ensues. Chris incapacitates Gross and his colleagues just before Sam arrives. They exit into the corridor, where Yakoff is searching for them. Chris pretends that the operation has taken place, and poses as Yakoff's brother, Boris. He knocks Yakoff out before he can question the deception, while Sam incapacitates an intern. They are soon joined by Wyndham, but are caught by Nevsky. Nevsky is about to shoot them when he suffers a fit and collapses into a coma. Chris sends Sam to find Lomax while he and Wyndham examine the unconscious man. The donor brain has rejected the new tissue. The surgery is not the sure thing Wyndham believed it to be. Sam returns and reports that Lomax is gone. They realise that Steed is in danger.

Chris and Sam fly out to the manor where Steed is enjoying his shoot. They ask where to find him, and Lady Laura Cartney informs them that Steed drove back to the house with someone who sneezed...

Steed is busy lighting the black Sobranie cigarette of the third incarnation of Lomax, this one an attractive woman. The moment his back is turned, Lomax pulls a gun, but Steed whirls around and throws his drink in Lomax's face before knocking him out. The combination of the cigarettes and hay fever tipped him off. Chris and Sam arrive a moment later, in time to assure Steed that he has not broken his cardinal rule against hitting women. Despite his new donor body, Lomax does not count.

Chris and Sam return to Steed's for a spot of riding. Steed reveals that the powers that be wish for Chris and Sam to continue to work as a team. Their remit will include investigating cases in Britain, Europe, and the United States. The new teammates ride off together and the scene fades.

Analysis

By 1985, it had been nearly eight years since *The Avengers* had ceased production for television, the last episode of *The New Avengers* having wrapped in Canada in the autumn of 1977. Meanwhile, the series of TV movies that Brian Clemens had mooted as the next incarnation of the franchise, which would have kicked off with *The First Avengers Movie*, had failed to materialise. The movie series was, at least, in good company, joining a lengthening list of failed *Avengers* television ventures that included the third series of *The New Avengers* and the American take on the series' formula, *Escapade*. Despite this string of failed projects, Clemens was persistent, and conceived yet another show in an attempt to return *The Avengers* to the small screen. For his next proposed take on the property, he discarded the television movie concept and returned to the episodic format that had served the show well for 187 episodes.

Avengers International was the result, a proposed new series for which a pilot script was commissioned by the Taft Entertainment-Lawson Group. Dated March 1985, written by Clemens, and entitled, quite fittingly, *Reincarnation*, the plot centres on Bobby Lomax, a Russian double agent killed by Steed during an operation intended to catch Lomax in the act of passing on state secrets. Unbeknownst to Steed, the Russians preserved Lomax's brain, and have now perfected a surgical procedure capable of transplanting the brain's essential components – those holding memory and personality – into a new body. Bent on exacting revenge, Lomax, now unrecognisable in his new body, sets out to kill Steed. Word of Steed's impending assassination reaches the ears of both Steed's new partner, Mrs. Samantha Peel, and American agent Christopher Cambridge. Though both urge Steed to take care, Steed is, understandably, disinclined to believe that he is being targeted by a dead man – until Lomax makes an attempt on his life. Steed is saved by Sam, and Lomax is killed in the process, but that does not stop Lomax from returning from the dead two more times, even as Chris and Sam attempt to get to the bottom of how Lomax has acquired the ability to "reincarnate".

It will be apparent to long-time fans of the series that elements of the plot are reminiscent of those of other episodes. The basic concept echoes the transference of Boris Kartovski's consciousness into other people in *Split!*, and the use of the mind-swapping device in *Who's Who???* and brain-draining machine in *Three Handed Game*. Lomax hates Steed for causing his death and wants revenge, just like Mark Crayford in *Dead Men are Dangerous*. Like Lomax, Crayford and Kartovski were both presumed to have been killed by

Steed, but, in each case, the presumption was premature – Crayford carried Steed's bullet in his heart for a decade, before it finally moved far enough to kill him; Kartovski is immobilised, but has been kept alive. Lomax's true identity is revealed by certain "tells", such as his penchant for black Sobranie cigarettes and recurring bouts of hay fever, much the way other mind-swapped characters are identifiable via trademark elements of their personalities: in *Who's Who???*, Basil retains his habit of playing with dice; in *Split!*, Kartovski's handwriting is replicated by the people he "possesses"; and in *Three Handed Game*, Juventor's stammer follows him to his new body.

In addition to featuring a suitably *Avengers*-esque plot, *Reincarnation* also hits all of the series' requisite beats, starting with a pre-credits sequence that builds up interest and intrigue, before transitioning into a first act that sets up the threat and introduces the characters, and then segueing into an investigation that sees Chris and Sam making inquiries. Their interviewees include trademark *Avengers* eccentrics, such as Freddy Weir, a man who fervently believes in reincarnation, and wigmaker Thatcher Arkwright, who bases all of his creations on weaves more commonly used for cottage roofs. After making their inquiries, Chris and Sam eventually wind up at the hospital at which Lomax is receiving his brain transplants, freeing an imprisoned scientist and defeating the mastermind behind the plot in the process, before rushing off to save Steed from Lomax number three, though Steed deals with him on his own. On the whole, it feels like an *Avengers* episode, perhaps not one that would rate amongst the best the show had to offer, but a middle-of-the-road effort that could sit quite comfortably next to what had come before, specifically the Peel / King episodes. The resemblance of this story to episodes from those eras of the original show was not accidental, as Clemens was aiming for a return to the series' most successful incarnation with this new project: "We are going back to grass roots, and it will be far more like the old *Avengers* than *The New Avengers*." (*Broadcast*, 15 March 1985) Other Peel / King era throwbacks include a requisite reference to "diabolical masterminds", and Sam's description of herself as a "talented amateur", a phrase used to describe her mother-in-law, Emma Peel, in the series' American title sequence. However, despite this focus on the later years of the original show, there are also elements of *The New Avengers* in the new series, namely in the form of touches of realism. After Weir's demise, Sam telephones her department (presumably the vaguely defined "The Ministry") and requests a "clean up squad" to "take care of things" at the house. Later, Chris does the same at the hospital. Presumably, the squad is responsible for removing bodies, taking criminals into custody, processing scenes for evidence, and ensuring that the public is kept from seeing anything it should not. It is a small detail, but one that was frequently omitted in the original series, in which Steed and his partners would leave the villains unconscious, imprisoned, or dead, seemingly without any concern for the mess they had left behind or the possibility that the villain of the piece might regain consciousness or free themselves and make their escape. Of course, this was part and parcel of the series' surreal universe, in which mundane details were eschewed lest they ruin the fantasy. *The New Avengers*, in contrast, was far more likely to show bodies being taken away or teams processing crime scenes, with such scenes appearing in the likes of *The Midas Touch* and *Cat Amongst the Pigeons*. This was part of the overall clearer picture the series provided of the leads' employer, something that was also achieved by depicting agents and other staff members going about their work, establishing the organisation's headquarters, and spelling out the department's procedures for internal investigations and agents going on leave. References to the "clean up squad" may be relatively minor nods to Sam and Steed's department's operations in comparison, but they still provide more of an insight into the organisation's inner workings than many original series episodes did, and hint that Clemens may have intended to include more *New Avengers*-ish realistic elements in this series than his comments indicate.

After writing *The First Avengers Movie* as a foursome, Clemens apparently came to the conclusion that four avengers were a crowd, and, for this script, reduced his principal cast down to a more manageable, *New Avengers*-esque triumvirate. However, the majority of the script focuses on Chris and Sam, while Steed takes a back seat. Clemens described the character as being "more avuncular" in the script, suggesting that, by 1985, he had seen the writing on the wall and knew the likelihood of a 63-year-old Macnee being either unwilling or unable to take on a major, action-heavy role in the series was high, and made the creative decision to reduce his role. (*Broadcast*, 15 March 1985) It is therefore unsurprising that Steed's primary purpose in the story is to bring Chris and Sam together and serve as the script's MacGuffin, the impetus behind Chris and Sam's investigation and pursuit of Lomax. He features heavily at the beginning and end of the story, but very little in the middle, garnering perhaps as much screentime as Patrick Newell would in a particularly Mother-heavy Tara King episode. The episode ends with Steed informing Chris and Sam that they will be working together as a permanent team before the trio rides off on horseback, with Chris and Sam riding side by side and Steed ahead of them, (symbolically) separate and apart. Macnee had speculated while working on *The New Avengers* that it would perhaps be better if he dropped out, leaving Gareth Hunt and Joanna Lumley to continue as a twosome. If *Avengers International* had made it to the screen, this may have been how things unfolded, with Steed putting in appearances in early episodes to connect the new series with its forebears and ensure that it was considered a legitimate successor to the sixties incarnation, then being phased out once the new characters were sufficiently established to stand on their own. The series could then grow and evolve without Steed, ensuring its longevity.

The Characters

Like any show, the new series' success or failure would have depended on the audience's reception of its characters. Unfortunately, it is in the script's characterisation that its most significant problems arise.

Mrs. Samantha Peel

Sam's name alone should give one an inkling as to what those problems might be. Clemens was determined to return to the series' glory days with this new show, and seemingly decided that one good way to roll back the decades was to resurrect Emma Peel. Of course, Diana Rigg likely would not have reprised her role even if approached to do so, so the script gives us the next best thing: a virtual Emma clone in everything but (first) name. Sam might be one of several daughters of an English lord as opposed to the heir of the founder of Knight Industries, but, that detail aside, Emma and Sam's backstories are more or less identical. Sam is Emma's daughter-in-law, the wife of Emma's son with Peter Peel, who is also called, rather unimaginatively, "Peter". As if it did not stretch the bounds of credulity enough to have Steed working with yet another Mrs. Peel who describes herself as a "talented amateur", it transpires that Peter Peel II inherited his father's rotten luck along with his name. As Sam tells Chris, her husband was an agent who let her tag along on his missions – until he went to Eastern Europe on assignment and never came back. Four years on, Sam, just like Emma before her, does not know if she is a widow. To make matters worse, Sam has also been gifted Emma's Lotus Elan, which she drives just as fast and expertly as her mother-in-law. Even the character's first name is an Emma cast-off. "Samantha", or "Mantha" for short (to emphasise her masculine qualities), was the original name mooted for Emma before Marie Donaldson had her "Man Appeal / M-Appeal / Emma Peel" brainwave. Sam also looks like Emma, described as tall and slim. Aside from lacking in originality, this casting of Sam as "Emma Peel, Mark II" factors rather uncomfortably into her relationship with Steed, with whom she shares a "special bond", to the point that she calls him "John" when she is deeply concerned about him; describes him as carefree, courageous, and "not a bit long in the tooth"; gazes fondly after him when he departs; and kisses him affectionately on the cheek. At best, Steed could be seen as a father figure and mentor to Sam. At worst, depending on the viewer's interpretation of the nature of Steed and Emma's relationship, his relationship with Sam could come across as vaguely incestuous.

What Sam does not borrow from her namesake, she cribs from her other predecessors. Like Cathy Gale before her, she studied anthropology (in her case, at Oxford). Other characteristics of Sam's are shared by one or more previous *Avengers* women: she is very intelligent, is kind and empathetic (she treats Ginger Douglas, Lomax's ex-lover, with great sensitivity), mixes a good martini, is cool and beautiful in the "Hitchcockian mould", is proficient at riding, and is a natural clothes horse who wears an array of action / fighting outfits, "mannish" suits, and youthful, wild, "punkish" clothes. Ironically, Sam's combat skills, which are immune to any criticisms regarding originality as all *Avengers* women are expected to be able to fight, are given short shrift. Sam's most notable action scene is not a fight, but her successful boarding of a moving train in her introductory scene. She also seems to rely on a gun far more than her predecessors – which she carries with a two-handed grip borrowed from Mike Gambit – and, while she has excellent combat skills, she is not afforded many opportunities to use them, save to kick down a door and Lomax out a window. In one instance, she forgoes combat altogether and knocks an assailant out with anaesthetic.

The only really original thing about Sam is her abode. As she likes ships and having a lot of space, she resides in a vast converted warehouse east of Tower Bridge that overlooks the industrial part of the Thames. The open-plan living area features painted girders, a motif of dark wood and reds, floor-to-ceiling bookshelves (complete with library-style ladders), and a set of plaster heads charting man's evolution. It is a set that would have looked fantastic onscreen, and is a rare standout in Sam's otherwise unoriginal characterisation. Overall, however, with so much borrowed history behind her, it is difficult to see Sam as anything more than a cipher for Emma, a placeholder where the viewer would undoubtedly rather see either the real thing or a completely new character.

Ghosts of Avengers Women Past

If Clemens was so keen to play on the fans' affection for Emma in order to attract viewers to the new series, he would have been better off letting his female lead be her own woman and confining himself to fan-pleasing references to the Emma Peel character. The script is rife with references to

Emma as it is, even beyond her connection to Sam. Over the course of the episode, we learn that Emma has been made a Dame (Clemens showing a certain amount of prescience, as Diana Rigg was made a Dame nine years later), and that Steed packs a framed photo of Emma in his luggage when he goes on holiday. Emma is also mentioned by Bobby Lomax, who reminds Steed that, while they both vied for her affections (shades of Prendergast from *The Joker*), Steed always had the upper hand, and references one particularly memorable evening at "Quaglino's – recall that night when we each of us drank from her slipper?"

Emma is not the only *Avengers* woman to be namechecked, however. Cathy Gale is referenced obliquely when Steed mentions that "there was once another Cathy in my life." Two references to Purdey come in the form of a repeated in-joke which plays on her namesake, an expensive shotgun. When Steed tells Sam that he was showing Chris "his Purdey" shotgun, the script exclaims "Mrs. Peel reacts to this name!", implying that Sam recognises it as belonging to one of Steed's ex-partners. These references are welcome, as they draw on the show's extensive past to connect the new series to the old, while also hinting at a broader *Avengers* universe that exists beyond the story of the week. The original show could have done with more of these nods to the past, as it was more realistic for Steed's previous partners to be mentioned occasionally rather than rarely or not at all. Such references would also have rewarded longtime viewers who remembered the old characters without interfering with the enjoyment of those unaware of the show's past. The only disadvantage of these nods to what had come before is that they invite comparisons between Sam and her predecessors, which could have further hampered the audience's ability to accept the character on her own terms.

Christopher Cambridge

Compared to Sam, American agent Christopher Cambridge is a more original creation, though he still owes plenty to his predecessors. The script goes so far as to describe the young, tall, attractive, formally attired Chris as Steed's "American alter ego", just as "urbane and immaculate" as Steed himself. He also shares Steed's aversion to guns, expert horsemanship, and tendency to behave with audacity in serious circumstances (he pours himself a drink while searching Gross' office). Aspects of Chris' character also owe something to Mike Gambit. Like Gambit, Chris is quiet and self-effacing, and prefers urban environments. Most notable, however, are his attire and fighting style. The former is described as consisting of well-tailored, expensive, formal suits of a "discreet cut and colour" which allow him to blend into his surroundings. Gambit's wardrobe – particularly his suits – was selected using similar reasoning, i.e., to allow him to blend in wherever his work took him, from the Ministry to the corridors of Whitehall. Chris' fighting style is also described in much the same way as Gambit's was in early production documentation, with Chris bursting from relative stillness into vigorous, deadly activity: "his expert hands fly into a short, sharp blur of action – almost simultaneously: a stiff hand across the throat...a kick...an elbow across [the] jaw". However, he couples this combat style with a Steed-like thoughtfulness, repeatedly insisting that brains are his weapon of choice and only employing violence when absolutely necessary – for example, rather than have Sam shoot Yakoff, he pretends that Yakoff's brother's brain has been transplanted into his body in order to make the man trust him. Even his decision to (infrequently) wear eyeglasses is strategic. He reasons that even the toughest opponent hesitates momentarily when confronted with the prospect of hitting a man wearing glasses, giving Chris a brief window in which to gain the upper hand. The glasses are also symbolic of Chris' penchant for using "camouflage" to elide his true nature, much the way Steed used his gentlemanly look and demeanour to disguise the fact that he was a ruthless professional agent. In Chris' case, this camouflage extends to painting a picture of himself with his comments that is not strictly accurate. For example, after telling Sam that, if he gets into trouble, he fights with his feet, Sam queries whether he means he uses karate. Chris replies "I run!" Similarly, when confronted by Gross, Chris claims to be "puny" and "a coward". However, after Weir is shot, Sam observes that Chris runs toward the shooter, rather than away. Chris counters that he "must have lost [his] head", demonstrating that he is reluctant to let his true abilities and personality be known, even by those he works with. When Sam continues to press him on the issue, he quits denying that he is capable of holding his own in a fight, and instead deflects further discussion of the topic by expressing the hope that both he and Sam have the sense to stay out of trouble. Chris also displays contradictory behaviour when, in spite of his insistence that brains are the best means by which to tackle obstacles, he uses force to solve problems that have non-forced-based solutions – for example, rather than pick a lock, he uses his elbow to deliver a karate blow to it, and, while he keeps the enemy from firing at him by strategically leaning against an aquarium, he still uses violence to ultimately take them down. He is also happy to talk up his combat skills, rather than play the coward, if it is to his advantage – when cornered by the enemy, he warns them that he is "mustard at close quarters". There is no doubt, therefore, that, as the script says, Chris is "ruthless, efficient [and] highly trained", even if he uses Steed-like deception to try to conceal his abilities. The fact that he gets the best of the fight / action sequences in the story is a testament to this, albeit a rather ironic one given his oft-stated anti-violence stance.

Despite inheriting numerous attributes from Gambit and Steed, Chris, unlike Sam, is differentiated from his predecessors by certain personal details. Other than being American, Chris went to Harvard, favours martinis over other drinks, is a fan of jazz, and does not believe in out-there concepts like reincarnation (Gambit, in contrast, is willing to entertain the possibility that Victoria Stanton is psychic in *Medium Rare*, and Steed does not dismiss the possibility that ghosts may exist in *The Living Dead*). Chris' trademark unnerving frankness also makes him feel like his own character, his blunt, direct lines distinct from Gambit's wry grimness and Steed's blithe understatements (though he does make a pun about only needing brains while standing in front of a tank full of the same that Gambit would appreciate).

The Chris/Sam Relationship

Like some aspects of Chris' characterisation, the dynamic between Chris and Sam is a novel one and helps to set this episode apart from its forebears. Chris periodically makes his interest in Sam known through startlingly frank comments — when she tells him that she does not know if her husband is alive or not, Chris observes that that means she does not know if she is widowed or available while regarding her with an intent, meaningful stare. He deploys the stare and the forward comments again when Sam reveals that she studied anthropology, commenting "The study of Man. That's encouraging," and once more when he tells Sam that he held off on providing her with information because he "was enjoying talking to" her. Sam, for her part, is disconcerted by both his stares and extremely forward attempts to get close to her, and that disconcertment, coupled with her uncertain marital status due to her missing husband, results in her being emotionally unable to entertain his advances and causes her to rebuff them. She also refuses to let him call her anything but "Mrs. Peel" (a character choice likely motivated by Clemens' desire to resurrect that infamous moniker; the script also specifies that she eschews her aristocratic title in favour of using "Mrs.", likely for the same reason). The fact that Sam discusses and struggles with her marital status more than Cathy or Emma did, and is "sad" and "emotional" when talking about her husband, suggest that Sam would have been allowed to display a vulnerable, human side more regularly than those women, just as Purdey was frequently allowed to do in *The New Avengers*, be it by contending with her ex-fiancé (*Obsession*) or the potential deaths of her partners (*Faces, K is for Kill: Tiger By the Tail*). Sam's obviously unresolved grief also suggests that Clemens planned for her character to have a development arc throughout the series, which would have found her attempting to move past her husband's disappearance and becoming increasingly open to a relationship with Chris.

In the pilot, however, that relationship is often abrasive. Indeed, it begins with the pair engaging in a physical fight in Steed's sleeper car after Sam sees Chris pointing a gun at Steed and attacks him. The bout spawns a verbal set-to later on, during which they disagree about who was winning before Steed broke them up. Chris' trademark bluntness does not help matters. He breaks Sam's reverie when he catches her gazing after Steed by querying "What will you wear to his funeral?", and is openly critical of Sam's way of operating. When she kicks Lomax out of a window to save Steed, Chris tells her that she was not using her brains, asserts that they do things "better" in America, and declares that he would have "taken the gun, not the man". He also points out that Sam jumped to conclusions about the situation, not bothering to work out if Lomax was truly threatening Steed or merely examining Steed's shotgun, as Chris himself had been when Sam attacked him. He also calls Sam "Sam" without her permission, even though it is a nickname that only a select few people are allowed to call her, leading her to irritably instruct him to refer to her as "Mrs. Peel" instead. Their encounters can also be awkward. Chris asserts that he is "surprisingly well educated. For an American" after Sam assumes that he does not know what a damehood is, while Sam returns the favour when Chris feels the need to explain that "rug" is American slang for "toupee". While such conflict was present in Steed's dynamics with Cathy Gale and David Keel, and even arose at times between Purdey and Gambit, Chris and Sam's conflict-habituated moments are marked by much more criticism and wrong-footedness, with the pair trying to work each other out while also cautiously deciding how much to reveal about themselves. There would therefore have been plenty of room for the pair's dynamic to grow and develop throughout the series as they became more familiar with one another's backstories and personalities. Indeed, Clemens has Sam stating at the episode's end that Chris cannot call her "Sam" **yet**, hinting that Clemens planned, at some point, for the pair's dynamic to evolve to the point where that honour would be bestowed. The potential for that evolution is evident in the pair's fleeting moments of affection, which are glimpsed throughout the episode. One such moment finds the pair engaging in a humourous exchange regarding the bizarre nature of the case:

CHRIS: You ever get the feeling you were a character in a painting by Dali?

| SAM: | Picasso. His cubist period! And drunk at the time! |

Watching Sam's personal journey and the corresponding evolution of her relationship with Chris would have been extremely interesting. Such character-based throughlines were largely absent from the original series, and their inclusion in this new show would have added a welcome, enriching dimension to the stories of the week.

John Steed

Turning to the original avenger, we find that he is still on the active list, but, in his own words, does not "go scrambling over the Berlin Wall anymore. Princes, Presidents, and Prime Ministers, they're my forte these days." As a result, he lets others do the leg work, leaving Sam and Chris mostly to their own devices, though he does ask to be kept informed. (A hunting dog at his shoot helpfully delivers an update to him at one point.) He was friendly with Lomax before he was forced to kill him five years before the events of the episode. One of only three people allowed to call Samantha Peel "Sam", he is very fond of her, but still carries a torch for her mother-in-law, Emma Peel – and her photo in his luggage. Three things that scare him at this stage of his life are the Inland Revenue, improperly decanted wine, and a surprise visit from his Aunt Agatha! He owns a pair of Purdey shotguns that were made for his father, which were a gift from "a Maharajar" (sic) and bear crests on the underside of the stock in gold wire. Still attractive to the opposite sex, he eschews the affections of the lovely Lady Laura Cartney because she is married to a man that he admires. He is also acquainted with reincarnation enthusiast Freddy Weir. Still on the same anti-smoking bent he championed during *The New Avengers*, and disturbed by the prospect of hitting a woman, he keeps several homes, including a country estate that allows him to indulge in riding when he is not driving his "beloved" 1927 green Bentley sports. He dons well-cut tweeds for his shoot, implying that he continues to favour impeccable tailoring, and still possesses a refined palette, drinking champagne and looking forward to a "Burgundy of unrivalled excellence". All in all, the episode paints a familiar, faithful portrait of *The Avengers*' cherished central character.

Other Characters

Outside of the leads, the characters in the script are something of a mixed bag. The most significant is the man whose reincarnations provide the inspiration for the episode's title: Bobby Lomax. Lomax is described as a legendary figure, a double agent who worked for the Russians, infiltrated MI5, rose to the level of deputy controller, and forged friendships with the likes of Steed and Emma Peel, to the point that he went out to dinner with them and vied with Steed for Emma's affections. Unfortunately, very little of Lomax's depiction in the episode lives up to the legendary, reverent status that he is accorded by both the heroes and villains of the piece. If anything, Lomax appears to be ridiculously accident- and incident-prone. Over the course of the story, he is dropkicked out of a window by Sam after failing to react quickly enough to defend himself, accidentally shoots himself during a scuffle with Chris, and fails to shoot Sam and Chris while they are in her car because she makes an unexpected turn. We also learn that his original death came at Steed's hands after Steed caught Lomax with purloined top-secret papers and shot Lomax with Lomax's own gun. The result is that Lomax, when resurrected, does not inspire the fear and awe that one would typically associate with a villain who has become almost immortal. Instead, Lomax's many deaths and resurrections render him almost comedic, like a cartoon character who is forever being run over or crushed before springing magically back into shape. At the very least, his low success rate in killing or fighting anyone off runs counter to the picture painted of him as a legendary double agent who is so wily and skilled that he managed to avoid being caught for nine years. The only person he manages to kill is Weir, and his sole escape is only achieved after he has accidentally shot himself during a fight with Chris. All three of his attempts to kill Steed fail, the last of which is foiled by Steed himself after he identifies his would-be assassin via his hay fever and preference for black Sobranie cigarettes. These tells also undermine Lomax's image as a top agent, as they indicate a certain sloppiness on his part. The advantage of being in a new body is that one cannot be recognised. Why, then, would a so-called master spy like Lomax effectively negate his disguise by continuing to smoke a brand of cigarettes that is favoured by few people other than him and doing nothing to treat his hay fever?

Of course, if there were other interesting facets to Lomax's character, they might have diverted attention from his blunders and sloppiness and made him seem like a more well-rounded person. Unfortunately, Lomax has a collection of characteristics rather than a personality: he suffers from hay fever, favours black Sobranie cigarettes, and loves a particular brand of Scotch.

These preferences are presumably highlighted to allow the audience to spot Lomax no matter which body he is currently occupying, but they tell us little about the man himself, save that he has discerning tastes. The one aspect of Lomax's backstory that provides a more complex, human dimension to his character is his relationship with Ginger Douglas, which seems to have been a genuinely affectionate one marked by moments of whimsy – for example, after Lomax mistakenly sent Ginger eleven red roses and one daffodil the first time he gave her flowers, he sent her the same erroneous order every year on the same day as a private joke. This gesture, coupled with the loving way Ginger talks about him, suggests that Lomax was not always ruthless and cutthroat, but could be tender and thoughtful as well. Unfortunately, the fact that Lomax was also actively pursuing Emma while he was seeing Ginger makes the reader question the genuineness of this otherwise humanising relationship. In addition, while Lomax may have once been tight with Steed, his knowledge of Steed's shotguns and reminiscences about having dinner with him and Emma do not effectively convey a sense of closeness. Furthermore, his bitterness at having been killed by Steed lacks the visceral tang of betrayal that one would expect to accompany such a catastrophic end of a close friendship. Steed, for his part, returns the favour, and is not particularly moved by Lomax's reappearance other than by being surprised that he is still alive. Their dynamic is a pale copy of Steed's relationship with his childhood friend Mark Crayford in *Dead Men are Dangerous*, which was infused with real feeling in the form of Steed's sadness at the turn the relationship had taken and Crayford's seething, bitter rage. In contrast, one never really buys into Steed and Lomax's history as being particularly deep or meaningful, and the plot and Lomax as a character are the poorer for it.

Fortunately, there are characters in the script who are more interesting and memorable than Lomax, though they garner considerably less screentime. One such character is Freddy Weir, a formally tough agent in his late sixties who has turned into a delightful eccentric in the classic *Avengers* mould in his retirement. Weir steadfastly believes that he has been reincarnated several times, and shows a bemused Chris and Sam a long line of portraits depicting Greek senators, Roman emperors, Elizabethans, 17th century dandies, officers from the Napoleonic wars, and people in the 1900s, all of whom he claims are him. When they address him as "Mr. Weir", he insists they call him "Freddy" instead, as everyone has over the years, even when his name was Ferdinand (when he lived in Spain in 1216), Firenza, or Frederica. Weir also keeps a number of animals that he believes are his reincarnated friends and family. His ex-wife Sylvia is a (cold) fish, as is his brother George, who was always "deep". He ensures that his old friend Tony Watson, who he believes is now a mouse, has a good supply of oats, and delights in making his old headmaster, Dr. Polfrey – of whom he was not fond – run on a wheel as part of his new life as a hamster. He also keeps birds that he believes are his mother and dear friends. Weir goes on to tell Chris and Sam that he, too, came back as an animal – an elephant – in 1812 or 1813, but was felled by a hunter before coming back as a soldier in Wellington's army at Waterloo. He then spins elaborate tales about wooing Nell Gwynne, and spending time with Caesar and Dr. Johnson. He goes on to explain that he is convinced that Lomax has been reincarnated, and will attempt to kill him because he was the one who uncovered Lomax's treachery. He muses that he does not understand why Lomax is so upset with him, as he felt no animousity toward Queen Elizabeth after she beheaded him when he was Dr. Livingstone and he came back as Sir Walter Raleigh. There is so much bizarre, amusing, and delightful detail in Weir's comments and stories that one cannot help but feel a great affinity for this cheery oddball, and subsequently mourn his demise. Even dying cannot bring Weir down, however, as he spends his final moments anticipating coming back as a Pomeranian dog. As he fades, he tells Sam that he is hoping to receive the love and affection that he often sees lavished on Pomeranians, as he has not received much in the way of such affection since his "secretary turned into a gerbil". Sam's sighting of a Pomeranian dog running up the drive toward Weir's house a little while later is a brilliant (possible) final "appearance" by Weir, a surprise that perfectly caps his brief but memorable part of the story and leaves us wondering if, like psychics and man-eating plants from space, genuine reincarnation is a feature of Avengerland.

Thatcher Arkwright is the story's other featured eccentric. In classic *Avengers* fashion, he subverts expectations with his wig maker's establishment, which features a "pink and plush" foyer set up to look like a high-end hairdresser's, complete with "before" and "after" shots of bald men wearing wigs and an attractive female receptionist. However, when Chris and Sam are admitted to Arkwright's workroom, they discover that it is an unglamourous space filled with models of thatched houses and cottages. Even more surprisingly, Arkwright is revealed to be a "big, red-faced, raw-boned, rubicund, bucolic man" who is clad in a farmer's smock and bears absolutely no resemblance to the "fancy-pancy hairdressing folk" (as he describes them) who typically have a foyer like his fronting their businesses. He goes on to tell Chris and Sam that his business is a literal "cottage industry", with every wig woven using the same weaves that adorn the roofs of the various model cottages in his workshop and have been passed down to him by his roof-making ancestors. The *Avengers* bizarreness increases when Arkwright reveals that he is experimenting with making wigs from straw, thereby taking the roof-weave concept one step further, though he admits that the material has its drawbacks, particularly when the wearers are part of the farming community, citing one female farmer who had an "unpleasant incident involving her prize bull". With his homespun aesthetic and accent, and drive to create wigs that are unique to their wearers, Arkwright is endearing and calls to mind countless other *Avengers* eccentrics who were passionate about their careers or hobbies and went to extreme lengths to create the best possible end product, such as B. Bumble, who produced 365 unique varieties of honey by treating the bees making it like his children (*Honey for the Prince*), or Piedi, who made shoes using plaster moulds of the wearer's feet (*Quick-Quick Slow Death*). All in all, Arkwright is a welcome addition to the script that bolsters Clemens' efforts to resurrect the flavour of the Emma Peel era.

Lomax's ex-lover of ten years, Ginger Douglas – described as slim, in her late forties, attractive, and with a mop of ginger hair – is another endearing character. While cheerful and good-humoured – she calls her school "Gingerbread" and her dancers "Ginger Broads" – she is also capable of deep feeling. Ginger conveys her sadness at the loss of Lomax in her few scenes, her melancholy evident when she speaks of how Lomax resisted marriage because of the nature of his work. Moments later, she exudes warmth and nostalgic brightness when recalling how Lomax sent her a bouquet containing eleven roses and one daffodil on the same day every year, a secret that Lomax kept even as he sold state secrets to the enemy. Despite her brief appearance, Ginger feels like a fully formed, complex woman who understood Lomax's flaws, but loved him nonetheless. She is one of the best realised and most likeable characters in the episode.

Most of the other characters are fairly thinly drawn. Gross, the surgeon responsible for Lomax's reincarnations, is described as "cadaverous" (perhaps fitting given that he is forever transplanting brains into new bodies), but is otherwise a fairly generic evil scientist with no notable personality traits. He is simply concerned with keeping Lomax alive so he can use him as proof of concept of the surgery technique, which he wants to persuade visiting Russian delegates to employ to keep their great thinkers alive. As a result, unlike many of the original series' villains, he is unmemorable. Topski is a stock Russian VIP, a plot propeller who gives Gross someone to explain the surgical procedure to for the benefit of the audience; is used to bolster the procedure's credibility by confirming that his old schoolmate, Ivan Nevsky, is now in a new body; and serves any other function the story requires. Nevsky himself is nothing more than proof of concept of the surgery and, when he collapses into a coma, evidence that it is not the miracle that it seemed to be. Yakoff, a heavy, is even less significant, only there to deliver messages to

Gross, menace people, be knocked out by Chris, and amp up the suspense by having a brother whose brain Gross decides to transfer into Chris. Ministry doctor Pinner earns a description – an "acidulous looking man" – but does very little aside from tell Chris and Sam that the dead Lomax had a head injury in addition to being shot. Gross' intern is only there for Gross to argue with about Lomax's chances of survival and various surgical procedures. Arkwright's receptionist and Elga, who works at the hospital front desk, have few lines and even fewer characteristics, other than their looks and, in Elga's case, a slight accent that ensures she is identifiable as a Russian. Russian VIPs Maragin and Nunovski are only included to marvel at Gross' surgical endeavours. A male nurse does not even require a name to go about his work and menace Chris. Professor Wyndham does little more than serve as a lead for Chris and Sam to investigate and provide Gross with the information he requires to undertake his surgeries, though he does add an interesting, morally ambiguous wrinkle to his ostensible characterisation as a victim with his scientific interest in Gross' plan to put Lomax's brain in a female body. A Duke and a myopic man named Thornton at Steed's shoot are merely used to add humour, with the Duke promising Thornton that a number of large birds will appear at the shoot, and Thorton mistaking Chris and Sam's helicopter for one of said birds and firing at it, leading the Duke to chastise Chris for ruining the day's shoot. Lady Laura Cartney, a tall and leggy ex-model, only serves to establish Steed's continued attractiveness to the opposite sex and scruples in choosing not to bed her, and as the messenger who tells Chris and Sam that Steed left with Lomax. *The Avengers'* guest characters and villains typically stood out no matter how small their role, so it is disappointing that so many of the more minor characters in this episode are neither interesting nor memorable.

Trivia Points

- Despite Emma's "I'm not Mrs. Peel" line in *K is for Kill: The Tiger Awakes*, she is always referred to by her married name in the script, and clearly her marriage to Peter Peel lasted long enough for her to have a son. Presumably she is still with Peter, but the script gives no indication as to her marital status.

- At one point, Sam mentions that she studied at Oxford. Given that she and Chris have a (sometimes) friendly rivalry, can it be coincidental that Chris' surname is "Cambridge"?

- Chris and Sam exchange dialogue that is very reminiscent of an exchange between Purdey and Gambit in *K is for Kill: The Tiger Awakes*:

    CHRIS: Would have been nice to have taken him
                alive.

    SAM: Keeping Steed alive was my prime
                concern.

    Compare this to Purdey and Gambit's exchange:

    PURDEY: Gambit, we wanted him alive.

    GAMBIT: Conflict of interest. I wanted you
                alive.

- Some of the character names are recycled from past *Avengers* episodes. There were characters called Lomax in *Concerto*, *The Undertakers* and *Take-over*, though none of these episodes was scripted by Brian Clemens. Lady Laura Cartney shares her surname with John Cleverly Cartney from Clemens' *A Touch of Brimstone*. Wigmaker Thatcher Arkwright brings to mind Arkwright of the Arkwright Knitting Circle in *The Girl from Auntie*. Freddy Weir recalls Freddy Mason in *Medium Rare* and the ill-fated Freddy in *The Midas Touch*.

- Chris' struggle with Lomax's second incarnation leaves him holding Lomax's wig. This is reminiscent of Gambit discovering that his deceased opponent wore a toupée in *The Eagle's Nest*.

- Sam slides down a ladder "circus style", just as Tara did in *Super Secret Cypher Snatch*.

- Sam arrives just after Chris has finished a fight, and finds him leaning calmly against an aquarium tank with his defeated opponents sprawled around him. This echoes a scene in *The Town of No Return*, in which Emma arrives to find Steed surrounded by a similar tableau after engaging in a fight off-screen.

- Ginger Douglas' studio is described as the "home of terpsichore", which brings to mind the Terpsichorean Training Techniques dance school in *Quick-Quick Slow Death*.

Verdict

Steed's final lines in the script indicate that Chris and Sam's investigations would have taken place in Britain, Europe, and the United States, so presumably some American and European episodes of the show would have been in the offing in exchange for American and European funding (hence the "international" in the title). Supporting this hypothesis is Brian Clemens' implication that the financial backing for the series would have come at least partially from American and British sources when speaking about the project in 1992: "I got paid but it all depended on the show being picked up by an American network and that didn't happen. Michael Grade was in there and he was interested in the project before he left to join the BBC." (Anthony McKay and Michael Richardson, "The Avengers Man", *TimeScreen*, Autumn 1992, Number 19) Given that *The New Avengers*' forays into France and Canada garnered, at best, a lukewarm reception, the wisdom of filming the show outside of the United Kingdom would have been questionable, but such a development was perhaps inevitable given the series' ongoing reliance on non-British funds. Still, regardless of where it was set, there is nothing to suggest that the show could not have been at least moderately successful, though it likely would never have reached the heights that the original series did at its peak. By the 1980s, *The Avengers* had been around long enough that its DNA had been incorporated into many detective / spy series, with bizarre plots and male / female partnerships becoming more and more omnipresent. *Avengers* alumni even had involvement in some of these series, with Brian Clemens writing episodes for *Remington Steele*, and Ray Austin directing several episodes of *Hart to Hart*. This would have left *Avengers International* struggling to break new ground in order to differentiate itself from these series while still attempting to remain recognisable, and a lack of confidence in its ability to strike that difficult balance may have prevented it from being commissioned. If that was the case, then the show was a victim of its predecessors' past successes, but perhaps it was for the best that, in the end, *The Avengers* continued, not with a new series, but subtly, through its substantial legacy, which continues to make itself felt in television series and films made around the world to this day – *The Avengers* made truly international.

STEED AND MRS. PEEL
THE ACME PRESS / ECLIPSE COMIC BOOK SERIES

J Z FERGUSON

Project Type: Limited Series Comic Book
Date: 1990-1992

Synopses

The Steed and Mrs. Peel *comic book series comprised two stories:*
The Golden Game *and* Deadly Rainbow.
However, as the second story is set prior to the first, we have elected to present their synopses in reverse order to preserve the flow of the narrative.

Deadly Rainbow

A series of pictographs tells the story of the Leopard People of the Amazon and their leader, Picchu. The tribe sees test pilot Peter Peel and his plane fall from the sky. The Leopard People take in the injured Peter, who has lost his memory in the crash, and nurse him back to health. Three years later, the Leopard People are dying from a disease spread by men who are cutting through the jungle in search of gold. Picchu restores Peter's memory and asks him to return to the outside world and advocate on the Leopard People's behalf. Peter returns to England and does just that, using the press interest in his miraculous reappearance after being presumed dead to draw attention to the cause.

John Steed watches Emma Peel drive off in a Bentley with Peter. Seeing the nattily dressed and bowler-hatted Peter, Steed comforts himself with the knowledge that Emma married someone just like him. Unfortunately, Steed has fallen prey to Peter's practical joke – he has dressed up like Steed and rented the Bentley to add a "twist of surprise" to the good-bye and make it more palatable. Peter takes Emma to Pringle on Sea, the place where they spent the first night of their honeymoon, and outlines his plan to stay there overnight and then go to the Amazon to help the Leopard People. The pair are greeted by the local pub landlord, who remembers them from their first visit and allows them to stay in their old room. After they leave, the landlord makes a call and tells someone that the Peels have arrived. He is so short that he has to stand on a box to see over the top of the bar.

Peter and Emma wonder why their room, which was immaculate during their first visit, is so dusty, and why the bar is empty of regulars. Emma senses that something is wrong, but Peter reminds her that it is no longer her job to investigate strange things.

Steed meets with Mother, who tells him that people, including two agents, have disappeared in Pringle on Sea. He sends Steed to investigate.

Emma is still discomfited by the town, wondering where the locals are and why there are rainbows everywhere. They visit the local church, where the vicar blessed their wedding, but are attacked by a hoard of Leopard People in gold masks and rainbow sweaters.

Mother receives a message via carrier pigeon that reads "Not us – Picchu". He does not understand what it means.

Emma is bound to the church altar and menaced by one of the Leopard People. He lifts a gold dagger and seemingly intends to drive it through her heart!

Emma awakes in her and Peter's room at the pub. Steed is watching over her. While visiting the church as part of his investigation into the missing people, Steed found her strapped to the altar, barely conscious and screaming. There was no sign of Peter. Emma tells Steed about the Leopard People, and takes him to the church when he disbelieves her story. Emma points out the stained glass windows in the church that feature rainbows, but Steed does not understand their significance. Emma finds camera film containers on the floor of the church. Steed suggests they visit the vicar.

The vicar is in a wheelchair, his legs covered by a blanket. He claims to remember Emma from her visit to the town during her honeymoon, but refutes Emma's claim that he saw her and Peter in the church earlier that day. Emma asks what the connection is between the village and the Leopard People. The vicar again claims ignorance, but is startled when Emma picks up a box with a rainbow symbol on it and shows him the miniaturised workmen and carousel rides it contains. The vicar pulls a gun and stands up, revealing that he has been shrunk to half his size. He tells Emma and Steed that the workmen have been shrunk by the power of the Inca crystal, and that people will be shrunk and held hostage until the Leopard People take over the world. Emma knocks out the vicar, gathers the rainbow boxes, and runs off in search of Peter. She turns back to see if Steed has followed, dropping a box in the process, and discovers that he has been knocked out by the pub landlord. Steed is then shrunk and joins the Leopard People in their pursuit of Emma. While fleeing, Emma encounters some workmen and fairground rides – they are from the box she dropped. After they were freed from the box, they returned to their regular size. Emma holds off the Leopard People while the workmen escape, but is captured.

The shrunken vicar returns Steed and the kidnapped Peter to their regular size, and casts aside another rainbow box. He explains to Emma that they can shrink people to half their size, miniaturise them, or brainwash them to think like Leopard People. The Leopard People tie down Steed and Peter and drive a steamroller toward them, then tell Emma that she must choose which one of them survives. While this scene is unfolding, the press arrives and documents Emma's distress. Before Steed and Peter are run over, the Leopard

People stop the steamroller and tell the journalists that the situation they have just witnessed is a warning of what is to come. The journalists duly depart and report what they have seen, splashing the front pages with sensationalist stories about the havoc the Leopard People are wreaking.

Steed, Emma, and Peter are miniaturised and placed on the table in the vicarage. Peter tells the others that the Leopard People cannot shrink people or control minds. Some American men enter the room and begin to celebrate. They are the men searching for gold in the Amazon jungle. They have devised the shrinking / brainwashing tool and are using it on ordinary people to wreak havoc and discredit the real Leopard People so that no one will oppose the bulldozing of their land. Emma, remembering that an eclipse occurs in the village every hundred years and believing it is due at that moment, uses it as a distraction so that she can access the dagger containing the shrinking crystal. She uses the dagger to return the trio to full size. She then smashes the crystal, returning all of the controlled and shrunken people to normal, including the missing Ministry agents. Peter and Emma plan a photo opportunity to reveal the American businessmen's scheme, then discuss returning to the Amazon to sort out the Americans' comrades. Steed asks Peter how there can have been an eclipse when it is the fifth and the eclipse was not due until the seventh. Peter replies that Picchu has power over such things. While Peter makes plans to march through the jungle to reach the Leopard People's home, Steed feels hurt that Emma chose to marry someone as unlike him as she could find.

The Golden Game

Tara King is waiting in a waterside pub. A radio news report plays in the background, informing the occupants of the pub that the murder of London jeweller Evelyn Glass two days earlier is still being investigated. Tara checks her watch irritably – the person she is meeting is late. Some of the other people in the pub are playing a dice game called Crown and Anchor, which is also the name of the pub. A man in nautical dress approaches Tara and introduces himself as Admiral "Foggy" Fanshawe, the person Tara is waiting to meet. Tara tells him he is late for their rendezvous, and Fanshawe replies that he is "[l]ater than you think", before escorting Tara from the pub. Tara tells Fanshawe that the department he runs at the Ministry has been leaking information and probably has a mole. Fanshawe offers to take Tara to his department right away so that they can sort things out. Before they leave, Fanshawe tosses a Crown and Anchor die into the water. It comes to rest beside a dead man strapped to an anchor. He is also in nautical dress and looks somewhat similar to the man Tara believes is Fanshawe...

John Steed meets with his superior, Mother, in his new headquarters in a waterworks, which is accessed via a public washroom stall. Mother, attended by his faithful assistant / bodyguard Rhonda, tells Steed that they have a mole in their midst and the only person he trusts to investigate is Steed. Mother is also worried about Tara. She has been missing since she went to meet Fanshawe, who has now been found dead, strapped to an anchor in the water, close to the agreed rendezvous point. Mother instructs Steed to investigate Fanshawe's death, but warns him to trust no one. He also gives Steed the Crown and Anchor die found by the real Fanshawe's body.

Steed returns to his flat at 3 Stable Mews, and finds a package waiting for him. It contains a book entitled *The Golden Game: Reynard's Riddles*, which features a cartoon fox on its cover. Steed pages through the book and looks at some of the illustrated riddles, then ponders what to do next. As he is unable to trust anyone at the Ministry, Steed telephones Mrs. Emma Peel – who is no longer associated with his department – to ask for assistance.

Steed and Emma attend Fanshawe's funeral. Steed expresses surprise that Emma returned to England to assist him, but Emma replies that she is keen for some excitement after six months in the Amazon with the Leopard People, the tribe her husband, Peter, lived with while he was missing. Steed asks after Peter, and Emma reveals that he stayed on in the Amazon for a ceremony, but will be back in time for Christmas. Steed tells Emma that she is the only person he can trust, and prepares to brief her on the situation. They depart the funeral under the watchful eye of a sexton.

Steed and Emma visit Fanshawe's nautical- and game-themed home. The inebriated butler who greets them assumes that they are members of the Palamedes Club, a games enthusiast organisation that the Admiral was heavily involved with. The butler takes them to the bottle-shaped conservatory and leaves them to search the ship within, which served as the Admiral's office. Emma finds a discarded letter from Fanshawe written to Doris Storm, the agony aunt for *Metropolitan* magazine. In it, Fanshawe asks for advice about foxhunting.

Emma visits the magazine's office and asks where to find Doris Storm. The editor tells her that Storm is donating blood. In the back of an ambulance, one of the nurses injects Storm with something, then flees while her colleague calls for help. Emma arrives on the scene and tackles the murderous nurse, who mumbles gibberish when Emma attempts to question her. Emma rushes to Storm's side, but the dying woman only manages to say "rooks and ravens" before she passes, leaving Emma puzzled.

Steed arrives at the Palamedes Club in time to see the doorman turn away a would-be member. Steed tries to enter the club, but is told by the doorman that only members are admitted and that membership is limited to the designers and inventors of games. Steed claims to have invented a game, but the doorman states that he must be nominated by an existing member in order to be considered for membership. Another member, Simon Bird, arrives and proposes Steed for membership, gaining him entry into the club. Steed recognises Bird from Fanshawe's funeral. Bird requests a meeting with Steed at the Hare and Hounds pub after Doris Storm's funeral.

Back at Steed's flat, Emma tells him that Doris Storm died from being injected with digitalis, and that the nurse who administered the injection is in a confused state and cannot remember why she killed Storm. Emma also mentions that Storm invented the Lonely Hearts board game. Steed chimes in that Storm was also a member of the Palamedes Club. Emma ponders whether Storm's dying words, "rooks and ravens", refer to a game. Steed receives a call from Mother, who tells him that Fanshawe was working on "Hangman", a wargame program that gave him control of the country's nuclear missiles. The leaks Tara was investigating concerned Fanshaw's office and, therefore, this program.

Steed and Emma attend Doris Storm's funeral, where Bird subtly confirms his rendezvous with Steed. Steed and Emma remark that, like Storm and Fanshawe, Bird is a charter member of the Palamedes Club. They also discuss Bird's nightclub, The Rookery. The sexton looks on.

Bird arrives for his rendezvous with Steed and waits in the street outside the pub. A man dressed as the King of Clubs appears and attacks Bird. Steed arrives and listens as the dying man recites a rhyme about a fox in a henhouse. The next day, Steed tells Emma that Bird's rhyme reminded him of the book of riddles he received in the mail. Steed shows Emma riddles in the book that refer to the deaths of Fanshawe and Storm. He also shows her the Crown and Anchor die found by Fanshawe's body, the symbols of which correspond with the people involved in their investigation: Fanshawe (anchor); Tara King (crown); Doris Storm (heart); Simon Bird (club); and the murdered jeweller Evelyn Glass (diamond), who was also a charter member of the Palamedes Club. They wonder who the final symbol, the spade, symbolises.

At Bird's funeral, Steed makes the connection between the sexton and the spade symbol. The sexton runs and Steed and Emma give chase, but lose him. The sexton leaves behind pieces of paper with games of Hangman scribbled on them.

Steed is interviewed for Palamedes Club membership by the club secretary, Chance, and another member, Wollow. In order to determine his suitability for club membership, Chance and Wollow have Steed toss dice to see how lucky he is. Steed tosses a double six, which impresses them greatly.

They tell Steed to visit Waddington Hall to take part in an inauguration ceremony, and provide him with a commemorative dartboard. They ask Steed the name of his game, and are alarmed when he replies that it is Rooks and Ravens.

Back at his flat, Emma tells Steed that *The Golden Game* was never published, and that his copy is the only one. While hanging up his commemorative dartboard, Steed wonders how the book connects to the "Hangman" nuclear defence program. Emma accidentally drops the book, but when she and Steed bend to retrieve it, an arrow crashes through the window, hits the centre of the dartboard, and unfurls a flag with a spade on it. Steed and Emma interpret it as a warning.

Steed visits Waddington Hall for the inauguration ceremony, and meets Chance and the other club members on a giant chessboard. Chance says they have seen through Steed's deception, as [1] another person applied for membership with a game called Rooks and Ravens. The applicant was rejected, but Steed recognises his name: Hilary Fox, an old classmate of Steed's from Eton, whom he knew as "Four-eyes". Chance pulls a gun on Steed.

Back at Steed's, Emma solves a riddle in *The Golden Game*. The answer is "Waddington Hall". Realising that Steed is in danger, she sets off to help him.

While climbing a very long ladder, Steed deduces that Fox had the charter members of the Palamedes Club killed because they rejected his application for membership. Chance reveals that the club is working for Fox because its members fear for their lives. He confesses that the club was responsible for the Fanshawe impersonator, kidnapping Tara, and printing the riddle book. Chance then pushes Steed down a giant fake snake.

Steed lands in a massive pinball machine. He is greeted by the disembodied voice of Fox, who calls Steed a "cheat" and bristles at being called "Four-eyes". While Steed explores the pinball machine, Fox gripes about how Steed has never taken anything seriously, treating life as a game in which he was always the winner. Fox, in contrast, was a loser who was always picked last for teams at school. Fox then launches a giant pinball that Steed narrowly escapes from. Steed exits the pinball machine and enters another room, where he is forced to shoot targets that shoot back. Fox continues to talk while Steed endures these trials, telling Steed that, because he recommended Fox to the Ministry, Fox was able to gain access to Fanshawe's department.

Emma is at the Fox and Geese pub, seeking directions to Waddington Hall from the landlord. A trio of undertakers in the pub overhears her inquiries and pursues Emma's Lotus Elan on a trandem bicycle. Emma takes evasive action, but the trio shoots at her car.

Back at the hall, Fox tells Steed that, after being rejected by the club, he devised a game to end all games. Steed asks what that has to do with the

"Hangman" programme. Fox ignores him and makes Steed engage in a game of jackstraws in order to retrieve a key, which gives Steed access to a room containing a pool of acid. Fox forces Steed to cross the pool using stepping stones while playing a game of Statues, which requires him to freeze whenever the music Fox is playing stops.

Meanwhile, the undertakers approach Emma's crashed car, certain that they have killed her. Emma appears and defeats them after a brief scuffle, then asks one of them where to find Steed.

Steed's game of Statues takes a deadly turn when the stones begin to move apart – Fox is cheating. Steed is rescued by Emma in the nick of time. Emma has already defeated all of the Palamedes Club members, so the pair look for Fox. They find him presiding over a giant roulette wheel, and he proceeds to tell them his plan: he will detonate a warhead over London, then proclaim himself the master of the Golden Game – the game of life and death. In essence, he plans to take over the world. First, however, Fox forces Steed to play one more game: Hangman. Tara and an executioner are revealed, standing at the foot of a gallows. Fox tells Steed that he must guess a six-letter word before Tara mounts all of the steps; otherwise, she will be hanged. Steed's guesses bear no fruit, but he sees the reflection of the word in Fox's glasses and correctly guesses that it is "rhythm". Fox throws a tantrum, accusing Steed of cheating, and tries to hang Tara anyway. Tara frees herself from the noose and fends off the executioner, whom Emma renders unconscious. The women exchange pleasantries while Emma unties Tara's hands.

Fox attempts to set off a warhead, but Steed throws his bowler at him and knocks him off his feet. Fox counters by throwing a small, spherical bomb at Steed, who passes it to Tara, who passes it to Emma, who returns it to Fox. Fox is killed in the explosion, and the trio flees the hall as it collapses around them. The trio heads home on the undertakers' trandem, with Emma asking Steed if he cheated at Hangman, an accusation he cheekily denies.

Analysis

After *The New Avengers* completed production in 1977, numerous efforts were made to keep the *Avengers* flame alive. Mooted 1980s projects included a series of television movies beginning with *The First Avengers Movie*, and a new television show, *Avengers International*. These projects were intended to be continuations of the original series, just as *The New Avengers* had been, and would have featured Patrick Macnee as John Steed. News about these endeavours therefore lent a sense of currency to the sixties incarnation of the series, as a revival of the adventure that began in 1961 always seemed to be just around the corner. However, none of these projects came to fruition, and, as the eighties turned into the nineties, The Avengers slipped from being a "current" programme on the cusp of revival to a vintage one recalled nostalgically. It was in this new era of the series' life that the infamous 1998 Avengers movie premiered, the lack of box office success of which was more than made up for by the publicity surrounding it, which thrust the series back into the popular culture spotlight and undoubtedly factored into the creation of new merchandise, such as VHS and DVD releases of the original series by A&E in the United States. However, there were two significant nineties Avengers releases that pre-dated the workings of the film's publicity machine: 1990's original novel Too Many Targets, penned by John Peel and Avengers expert Dave Rogers (see Two Against the Underworld – The Collected Unauthorised Guide to The Avengers Series 1, Hidden Tiger, 2015); and Steed and Mrs. Peel, a three-issue comic book series produced by British comics publisher Acme Press and released at a rate of one issue per year from 1990 to 1992. Like Too Many Targets, the comics were something new in the world of Avengers tie-ins, as they were created several years after the original and sequel show ceased production, and therefore were tasked with striking a delicate balance between capturing the shows' zeitgeist and offering something new and innovative that appealed to nineties sensibilities. This was a tall order for the creative team behind the comic, which included esteemed comics writer Grant Morrison, who penned lead story The Golden Game, and comic newbie Anne Caulfield, who took on the writing duties for back-up story Deadly Rainbow. Ian Gibson, best known for his work on The Ballad of Halo Jones and Judge Dredd, produced the art for both stories. The result of their collective efforts is a combination of innovation and nostalgia that excels in some respects, but is wanting in others.

Plot

For ardent Avengers fans, the plots of both stories should elicit a feeling of déjà vu. The Golden Game, unsurprisingly, is reminiscent of the Tara King episode Game (1968) in many respects. In Game, people are forced to play games based on their professions that result in their deaths – for example, a military man is killed while playing a wargame, a man who plays the stock market dies while playing a stock-market game, and a professor expires after failing to win a word game. In The Golden Game, the game aspect of each murder is more subtle, with each death symbolised by one side of the die used in the dice game Crown and Anchor: Admiral Fanshawe is strapped to an anchor, as befits his nautical background; jeweller Evelyn Glass is stabbed with a chandelier crystal, which is symbolised by the diamond; the heart is embodied by agony aunt Doris Storm, who deals with people's love lives and has her own heart stopped with a digitalis injection; and the club is Simon Bird, who owns a nightclub and is killed by a man dressed as the King of Clubs. The sides of the die are rounded off by the kidnapped Tara King (the crown) and the ominous sexton who lurks at the murder victims' funerals (the spade). In both instances, the mastermind behind the killings is a person from Steed's past who feels wronged by the murder victims and Steed himself. In *Game*, it is Monty Bristow a.k.a. Sergeant Daniel Edmund, who is killing the people who court-martialled him in 1946 for black marketeering. In *The Golden Game*, it is Hilary Fox, an Eton classmate of Steed's who hates Steed because he is lucky in life, does not take things seriously, and was popular at school, and the Palamedes Club members because they rejected his application for club membership. Both Bristow and Fox make Steed play a number of dangerous games that make use of elaborate sets and props, and are angry when Steed cheats at said games – in *Game*, he uses a gun given to him to play a game to free Tara from an hourglass so she can help him defeat his opponents; in *The Golden Game*, he sees the word that is the solution to a game of Hangman reflected in Fox's spectacles. Both villains are also hypocrites, cheating when it suits them – Fox moves the stepping stones that Steed is using to cross an acid pit while playing a game of Statues, and Bristow hides a cannon in a wargame and uses it to kill the player even though he has won and should therefore be spared. Both Fox and Bristow are killed when the game-themed weapon they lob at Steed is turned against them, with Fox blown up by a marble-like bomb, and Bristow impaled by a razor-sharp playing card. While the two stories are not identical in every respect, the game theme and personal grudge against Steed nursed by the villains suggest that *Game* served as an inspiration for *The Golden Game*. Morrison also seems to have taken inspiration from *Death at Bargain Prices* (1965), in which Horatio Kane, like Fox, plans to use a bomb to gain power over a populace he feels has wronged him – Kane is angry about being dismissed as old-fashioned and out of touch with modern methods, while Fox resents being unpopular. The Palamedes Club, meanwhile, recalls other clubs whose members used their organisation for sinister ends, such as the RANSACK club for intellectuals in *The Master Minds* (1965) and the British Venusian Society in *From Venus With Love* (1967).

Morrison is not alone in cribbing plot points from episodes, as writer Anne Caulfield does the same in *Deadly Rainbow*. The story finds Emma and Peter Peel paying a visit to Pringle on Sea, a town rife with suspicious happenings, a premise that is very reminiscent of that of The Town of No Return (1965). The town's name, Pringle on Sea, is also similar to that of The Town of No Return's setting, Little Bazeley (by the sea). In both cases, people in the town have been disappearing, with four agents having gone AWOL in The Town of No Return, and two agents and a number of other people having vanished in Deadly Rainbow. In both stories, Emma and her partner seek lodging at the local pub / inn, but receive an insincere welcome from the landlord, who is clearly hiding something, and are placed in rooms that have clearly not been cleaned or slept in for some time. In both stories, Emma holds up a towel with a large hole in it to illustrate the poor state of the accommodation. The town has also been taken over by a hostile force in both instances. In The Town of No Return, the townspeople have been imprisoned and / or killed by a foreign power, which has replaced them with its own people and is using the town as a staging ground for an invasion of the whole country. In Deadly Rainbow, people in the town have either been miniaturised or brainwashed and shrunk to half their size by American businessmen seeking to discredit the Leopard People. Mission: Highly Improbable (1967) was clearly also an inspiration when writing this story, as it featured technology capable of miniaturising people. Mind control, brainwashing, and hypnotism also featured in countless episodes, including The Master Minds, Return of the Cybernauts (1967), Split! (1968) and My Wildest Dream (1969), and it is quite likely that Caulfield drew inspiration from one or more of these episodes, as well. While The Avengers recycled plots and ideas, and even remade whole episodes, it did so because of time and budgetary constraints. Given that they did not have such constraints, it is slightly disappointing that the comic writers resorted to similar levels of recycling when plotting their stories.

A familiar aspect of The Golden Game's plot that does not work against it is its general structure, which adheres to the formula of a colour Peel episode. It begins with a teaser sequence, albeit one given a novel twist by being split into two parts and featuring lead characters in each part (the leads typically did not appear in episode teasers). Tara King appears in the first teaser which, like many episodes' teasers, ends with a shocking "sting" image: the sight of the drowned Fanshawe tied to an anchor. The second teaser finds Steed receiving instructions from Mother to investigate Fanshawe's death and Tara's disappearance. It ends with Steed calling on Emma for assistance with his trademark "Mrs. Peel, We're Needed" line, as he did in many colour Peel post-teaser sequences, but this familiar element is also rendered novel by the fact that Steed is requesting Emma's help after she has quit working with him. The story then segues into a two-page spread that acts as a replacement for an episode title card, and comes complete with a trademark colour Peel byline: "In which Steed breaks the rules and Emma gets a full house". After this, the story closely follows the oft-criticised colour Peel episode formula. Many fans believe this formula rendered the episodes repetitive, but it also made them extremely accessible, allowing new viewers to quickly pick up on the show's format. The formula serves the same purpose in the comic, enabling *Avengers* fans who are not avid comic book readers to follow the story. In keeping with that formula, Emma and Steed begin their investigation by looking into the first murder victim, Admiral Fanshawe. They visit Fanshawe's home, where, as in the episodes, they find clues that suggest other lines of inquiry, discovering that Fanshawe was a member of the Palamedes Club and had attempted to contact Doris Storm. As in the episodes, they then split up to follow different leads. Emma visits Storm's magazine just in time to witness her death, an event also in keeping with the formula, as deaths often guided the leads in their investigation. Steed, meanwhile, visits the Palamedes Club and arranges a rendezvous with Simon Bird, who claims to have information to impart. As in countless episodes, Bird is killed before he can tell Steed what he knows, and instead leaves a cryptic clue behind. Still adhering to the episode template, Steed and Emma put the clues they have gathered together and identify the organisation behind the killings, in this case the Palamedes Club. As in many episodes, Steed infiltrates the organisation, asking questions of the club's members in order to gather information or elicit a reaction, but is ultimately rumbled by the villains. With one avenger in danger, the story follows the formula by having the other (Emma) work out that Steed needs help and, after being attacked herself, come to Steed's rescue. A twist on the formula emerges when the story reaches its climax, with the leads not engaging in a fight, but instead rescuing Tara and foiling diabolical mastermind Fox by turning his own weapon against him and destroying Waddington Hall (which, in typically *Avengers* winking fashion, is clearly a nod to the famous British board game manufacturer Waddingtons). A different formula is adhered to at the story's conclusion, with Steed, Emma, and Tara riding off on a trandem bicycle, a moment that harks back to Steed and Emma setting off on some form of transportation at the end of each Series 4 episode.

Deadly Rainbow, in contrast, does not conform to the template of any episode – save for depicting Steed, Emma, and Peter travelling toward a bright horizon on a paddle boat at the story's end, in classic Series 4 fashion – breaking the mould with everything from its pictograph opener to the surreal sight of the faux Leopard People attacking Emma and Peter in the church, but especially with Emma's investment in the events unfolding around her. While the plots of some episodes – such as *Wish You Were Here* (1969), which finds

Tara attempting to rescue her uncle from confinement; *Take Over* (1969), which revolves around Steed paying his annual visit to his friends, the Bassetts; *The House That Jack Built* (1966), in which Emma is menaced by an ex-employee; and *Murdersville* (1967), in which Emma contends with the death of her childhood friend, Paul – were personally significant to the leads, this story is a departure from what came before. It is more intimate, at its core an exploration of Emma's relationships with Steed and her husband and her attempts to reconcile the two. The result is a refreshing tale that explores a different side of Emma and Steed, both individually and in the context of their partnership.

Turning away from structure, both plots feature some strange creative choices and un-*Avengers*-ish elements. *The Golden Game* finds Steed and Emma attending a number of funerals. Funerals did have their place in Avengerland, but there was often some twist to them – see *The Gravediggers* (1965), in which Steed attends Emma's funeral while fervently hoping that she has used the hidden trapdoor in her coffin to escape before being buried alive, and other funerals act as cover for the burial of radar jamming devices; or *Epic* (1967), in which Emma finds herself confronted with a hyper-stylised version of her own funeral. It was rare for the characters to be shown attending actual funerals, and rarer still for overtly religious readings to be included in the proceedings, as they are in the comic. The depiction of funerals as sombre events also runs counter to the, by now tongue-in-cheek, series' tendency to treat death as a minor inconvenience. The funerals do allow for the introduction of the sexton, who is symbolised by the spade on the Crown and Anchor die, but, as we never learn the sexton's identity, the sense of intrigue cultivated by his presence at the funerals is not paid off in any meaningful way. There are also some plot holes. Why do the dying Storm and Bird make cryptic comments – Storm murmurs "rooks and ravens", a reference to the game Fox used to apply for Palamedes Club membership, while Bird recites a rhyme about a fox in a henhouse – rather than simply say "Hilary Fox is behind this"? It is very *Avengers*-ish for people to die with a cryptic comment on their lips, but typically the connection between what is said and the mystery is not so wilfully obscure. Having the dying opt to hint at Fox's identity rather than say his name suggests that the writer is either being deliberately obtuse or attempting to draw out the plot.

Deadly Rainbow also has some issues. Where is Tara King in this story? It begins at the end of *The Forget-Me-Knot* (1968), which closes with Tara entering Steed's flat and announcing that she is his new partner. Why, then, does she not accompany Steed when he is briefed by Mother and visits Pringle on Sea, given that both events occur later the same day? It cannot be that

Steed does not want Emma to see him with her, because he does not know Emma is in the town until he finds her in the church. Tara's absence therefore seems like a major oversight given that the story is supposed to sit within existing continuity. The story also unfolds in a rather disjointed way. While Morrison's comic book background results in a story that flows logically from panel to panel, Caulfield's apparent lack of experience with the medium (no other story credits for comics can be found for her) results in narrative leaps that make her story difficult to follow. These issues arise from the outset, with the story opening with a series of pictographs detailing the history of the Leopard People and their relationship with Peter Peel. This sequence, while visually interesting and unique, is introduced with no context, leaving the reader in the dark as to what they are reading until Peter appears and it becomes apparent that it is a prelude about his time in the Amazon. This issue was exacerbated in the comic's original printing, which did not indicate where *The Golden Game* ended and *Deadly Rainbow* began, making the pictograph sequence initially appear to be some strange interlude in *The Golden Game*. The splash page in the story's second part is also confusingly laid out, with Emma depicted holding one of the rainbow boxes above an image of fairground rides and workmen surrounded by clouds. The page is intended to convey that the workmen and rides are inside the box, but, save for appearing in the same image, there is no apparent connection between them. By the time the connection is more explicitly made later in the story, the reader has likely all but forgotten about the boxes and must flip back to connect the dots. The faux Leopard People's pursuit of Emma is also confusingly laid out, with so much going on that important details – such as Emma putting the boxes in her bag and inadvertently releasing the miniaturised workmen when she drops one – are lost in the shuffle. Steed's transformation into a faux Leopard Person is also confusingly conveyed, with Steed lying unconscious in the vicarage in one panel, and shrunk and chasing Emma a few panels later, leaving the reader struggling to work out when Steed's transformation occurred. The disjointedness continues when Emma encounters the workmen. Even if the reader manages the difficult feat of recognising them as the occupants of the box, they are left wondering why the workmen seem to be carrying on with their work as normal after experiencing such a strange event, only to be wrong-footed once more when Emma's presence seemingly reminds the workmen that they are angry about being shrunk and they walk off the job. Emma's take on Sophie's choice, with the Leopard People forcing her to decide whether to save Steed or Peter, is also confusingly executed. Emma is not shown making any effort to save either man, and instead stands on the sidelines yelling "stop!" while the press, inexplicably, arrives, takes photos, and departs. Steed and Peter are then freed. Again, the audience is left feeling as if it has missed something – not only is there no pay-off for Emma's predicament, but an explanation is not provided for Steed and Peter being spared and the press' presence until the audience has already moved on. Elsewhere, Emma's use of the eclipse as a diversion requires the reader to cast their mind too far back, to her and Peter's conversation about an eclipse being Pringle on Sea's sole claim to fame at the beginning of the story, in order to understand her reasoning. The workings of the shrinking crystal are also confusing. Emma hits it with a spoon to return her, Steed, and Peter to full size, which suggests to the reader that she has destroyed it, but it is soon revealed to be intact. Emma then destroys it to return everyone to normal. Why did Emma not smash the crystal in the first place and return everyone to normal in one fell swoop? Other questions also spring to mind. Why did the faux Leopard People leave Emma strapped to the altar for Steed to find, an act that jeopardised their plan? Where did the Americans get their miraculous brainwashing / shrinking technology? They do not seem to be creative or technologically sophisticated enough to come up with either the scheme or the shrinking device, suggesting that they hired someone to develop the technology and cook up the plot. Unfortunately, there is no indication as to who that mastermind might be, leaving a sense of unfinished business as the reader waits in vain for the brains of the outfit to appear.

Another aspect of the plot that may give *Avengers* fans pause is the supernatural nature of Picchu, the leader of the Leopard People, who is over a century old and able to form psychic connections (he physically reacts to the injured Peter's pain and picks up on Emma's desire for an eclipse to happen at a precise moment), see into the future (he senses that Peter will crash before it happens), and manipulate celestial events (he moves an eclipse up by two days). Do Picchu's powers push *The Avengers*' sci-fi and fantasy elements a step too far? It is true that the series typically offered logical explanations for seemingly inexplicable events, revealing that the ghosts in *The Living Dead* (1967) were people kept captive underground, and that the invisible man in *The See-Through Man* (1967) was achieved using practical tricks. However, not every explanation was grounded in reality, with *Man-eater of Surrey Green* (1965) featuring a mind-controlling, man-eating plant from space, and *Too Many Christmas Trees* (1965) depicting genuine psychics. Picchu's abilities therefore do not feel like a bridge too far for a series that had already featured "out-there" elements.

Art

Given that this is an adaptation of a television series, the translation of the leads from screen to page is a major consideration when assessing the comic's art. Ian Gibson's depictions of the series' characters, however, can best be described as vague likenesses, though, admittedly, Gibson is in good company on this front. While faithful depictions of Steed, Keel, Cathy, Emma, Tara, Purdey, and Gambit can be found among the series' various comic tie-ins, more often than not, Steed was represented by a generic man in a bowler and his female partners by a generic woman with the appropriate hairstyle. Gibson's depiction of Macnee, Rigg, and Thorson's likenesses is in the same vein. Of the three, he fares best with Steed, offering a reasonable approximation of Patrick Macnee's rounded, aristocratic features. Unfortunately, Gibson makes a habit of using Steed's bowler to cast his face in shadow, an aesthetic choice that lends Steed a decidedly sinister air. While Steed was unquestionably a ruthless, devious agent, for the most part, he hid that steeliness beneath a sunny, gentlemanly demeanour. Even when the bowler is nowhere to be seen, Gibson often depicts Steed as angry looking. In one panel, Emma tells Steed to answer his phone, and Steed is shown glaring at her while lifting the receiver, as though he is extremely annoyed at her for telling him what to do. This act would seem like a profound overreaction regardless of the context, but is particularly out of character given Steed and Emma's typically warm relationship. Why Gibson was so keen to depict Steed as a glowering, threatening individual lacking the amiability that characterised Macnee's winning depiction is difficult to understand. His habit of rendering Macnee's tailored suit jackets as boxy rectangles is equally unfathomable, and indeed borders on sacrilege given Steed's status as a well-dressed fashion icon.

While many artists had a modicum of success in capturing Steed's likeness, they typically struggled with Diana Rigg's kittenish features, and Gibson is no exception. At times, he captures Emma's spirit, intelligence, and personality, even when the likeness itself is far from perfect – one panel, in which Peter tells Emma that she would be "hopeless" at being a demure, hanky-embroidering housewife, finds Emma reacting with a wide-eyed, mock-hurt expression that perfectly replicates Rigg's oft-employed look of exaggerated dismay. For the most part, however, Emma's look in the comic is variable. She is, by turns, a haughty sophisticate, pudding-faced, generically attractive, sharp featured and exotic, a watercolour-tinged lovely, thin lipped and pallid, hard bitten and no nonsense, and wide eyed and innocent. A panel showing Emma sprawled on the ground while watching the sexton flee casts her as a glamourous old Hollywood actress, complete with extra-long eyelashes, beauty spot, and mouth hanging open seductively. When a dart embeds itself in Steed's commemorative dartboard, she is meek and mousy looking, but in the next panel she looks like a clever, curious cat. All this leaves aside Gibson's predilection for gifting Emma with the overly muscular, Amazonian, busty physique possessed by practically every female superhero, a body type that is the antithesis of Rigg's catlike litheness.

Tara garners far fewer appearances in the comic than Emma or Steed, but, while her rounded face and large eyes give her a passing resemblance to Linda Thorson, she falls afoul of the same occasionally pudgy cheeks and angular features that plague Emma. To make matters worse, when the two women are shown sitting behind Steed on a bicycle built for three, they possess near-identical visages, which is perhaps the best indication of how little effort was made to capture the actors' likenesses.

Compared to the leads, Peter Peel was something of a gift for Gibson, as his face was never shown onscreen, meaning Gibson could essentially create his look from scratch. However, as in the case of the leads, Gibson has trouble keeping his creation's look consistent. Peter is sometimes depicted as a tall, athletic, floppy-haired thirtysomething, the prototypical dashing air ace with strong, square-jawed features. On other occasions, however, Peter looks much older, resembling a tired, middle-aged, slightly overweight history professor. The latter look is mostly confined to the flashbacks to Peter's time in the Amazon, in which Peter is bearded, but re-emerges at unexpected intervals, with Gibson somehow managing to make Peter look like he has facial hair even when he is cleanshaven. There is also the small matter of Gibson choosing to make Peter blond. While this hair colour suits Peter's devil-may-care, slightly brash characterisation, it directly contradicts one of the few aspects of his appearance that was established onscreen: that he had dark hair. Peter was played by Patrick Macnee and stunt double Paul Weston, and, while he is only shown from a distance, Macnee's dark hair is readily apparent to the viewer. An insignificant detail, perhaps, but one that – in combination with the fact that Gibson draws Peter wearing a brown suit rather than the black overcoat and matching suit he wears in the episode and driving a vintage Bentley rather than the grey-silver sports car he drives in the episode – makes it difficult to believe that the Peter depicted in the comic is the same character seen at the end of *The Forget-Me-Knot*. (Gibson is at least consistently inconsistent when depicting this scene, drawing Emma in an orange outfit instead of the yellow one that she wore in the episode.)

Outside of the character likenesses, another issue with the art is the regularity with which it features images that are grotesque or evoke a feeling of nausea. The Peel / King era of The Avengers eschewed graphic images, such as blood or dead bodies with visible wounds, and also avoided the killing of female characters. *The Golden Game*, in contrast, features the shocking sight of the dead Fanshawe tied to an anchor as if crucified, his eyes wide open and distressed, within the first few pages. For someone settling into the comic and expecting the usual innocuous trappings of Avengerland, this extreme and malicious depiction of a dead body comes as an unwelcome, nasty shock. The discarded bicycles, barrels, tin cans, and the like scattered around Fanshawe on the floor of the Thames only add to the very un-*Avengers* grubbiness of the scene. Elsewhere, the murder of Doris Storm not only breaks the series' "no women killed" rule – though this was violated by the likes of *The £50,000 Breakfast* (1967) – but is made worse with a close-up of Storm's distressed face, which provides a prime view of her bloodshot eyes and the spit flying from her mouth as she gurgles horribly. A few panels later, we see beads of sweat being flicked from her contorted, claw-like hands as her body twists in a death spasm. The depiction of Simon Bird's demise is even worse, with drops of blood sent flying when he is struck down, and gore pooling by his body as his hands contort in the same manner as Storm's. Worst of all are the close-ups of Bird's face that provide the reader with a prime view of the bloody sweat running down his cheeks. These images are the antithesis of *The Avengers*' sanitised deaths.

Other panels are less graphic, but still feel distasteful given *The Avengers*' sophisticated environs. *The Golden Game* opens with Tara King in a seedy-looking pub filled with less than auspicious characters, a setting that is the polar opposite of the glamorous locales that one would expect Tara to frequent. The intention seems to be to impose a nineties grunge aesthetic on the series' technicolour sixties wonderland. Steed's introduction reinforces this ill-suited, grungy vibe. He is shown entering a public bathroom where a seedy-looking janitor is smoking a cigarette and mopping the floor with a steaming bucket of lurid green water. The scene appears to have been taken from the series' first season. Is Dr. David Keel waiting outside, clad in a raincoat and smoking a cigarette of his own? Is a drug deal taking place in one of the bathroom stalls? To make matters worse, we are subjected to the indignity of seeing Steed sitting on a toilet (with the seat down, mercifully), before it is revealed that the stall he has entered is the secret entrance to Mother's latest hideout. Perhaps Gibson intended the image of Steed on a toilet to be amusing, but, while *The Avengers* was more than capable of laughing at itself, this upfront acknowledgement of bodily functions shatters the series' illusion of fantasy. The trend continues with Fanshawe's butler, who is inebriated and red-faced, and belches and spits when he talks. Another drunk is present during Bird's murder, tackily dressed in a pink shirt (untucked), yellow tie (loosened), and brown suit (rumpled), and spitting as he speaks while yellow dots symbolising his inebriation dance around his head. While *The Avengers* did depict drunk characters, it did not go out of its way to make them so viscerally repulsive. While more minor, the red eyes of the nurse brainwashed to kill Doris Storm and the lurid green colour of the steaming pool of acid add to the story's very un-*Avengers* queasiness quotient.

Another disconcerting, though far less unpalatable, aspect of the art is the sense that Gibson, at times, forgets that the series is set in the sixties. While Emma and Tara's fashions correspond with a sixties aesthetic, this seems to be a result of Gibson using their wardrobes from the series as a reference rather than an attempt to depict a particular time period. Otherwise, there are no overt signs that the comic takes place in the sixties. This is not necessarily a bad thing, as the series strived to be timeless, shunning overt references to current events to prevent episodes from becoming dated. However, while it is fine for the art to not signal that the comic takes place in the sixties, it should not, as it does in some instances, suggest that the comic takes place in another decade. The most egregious example of this is a panel depicting the street outside the Palamedes Club, which features a number of passersby who appear to be dressed as either seventies punks or in the boxy, wide-shouldered fashions of the eighties. Elsewhere, magazine editor Ms. Manchester's desk is kitted out with an eighties computer and printer. Whether the inclusion of these visuals was intended to be tongue-in-cheek, or was simply an oversight on Gibson's part, their non-correspondence with the series' setting pulls the reader out of the story.

The art is not without its merits, however. While the later seasons of *The Avengers* were well-funded, they did not possess unlimited budgets, and finances had to be carefully marshalled to ensure there were sufficient resources for the whole season. As a result, large-scale sets were unaffordable. The comic, in contrast, had no such budgetary constraints, enabling Gibson to create elaborate settings on a grand scale. The most notable of these is Admiral Fanshawe's home, a stately manor with the bow of a large ship sticking out of the front and a bottle-shaped conservatory that contains a full, life-sized ship. The reader is provided with plenty of opportunities to relish the intricacies of the ship and the conservatory's high ceilings, plant life, and decorations. Fanshawe's residence also features life-sized game pieces and an elaborately decorated, game-themed foyer. These beautifully rendered locations look fantastic on the page, possessing both a huge sense of scale and an *Avengers*-ish quirkiness factor, and would have been beyond the reach of the series' budget. The same is true of Fox's giant game sets, which include an enormous pinball machine – complete with huge metal ball – and a massive snake and ladder that are descended and ascended, respectively, by Steed in scenes that showcase their enormity. A target range that shoots back, an acid pit with moving stepping stones, and an enormous roulette wheel are also in the mix, and outstrip the game-based sets in the episode *Game* in both scale and intricacy. In *Deadly Rainbow*, the limitless "budget" goes toward the cast, with a bevy of extras in the form of faux Leopard People and journalists inflating the story's headcount far beyond that of an *Avengers* episode. However, while the lack of budgetary constraints is unquestionably an asset, it also robs the comic of some of the series' signature feel, the grand sets lacking the series' intimacy and atmosphere, and the larger casts not in keeping with the creative decision to sparsely populate the series' universe.

Issues aside, the comic's overall aesthetic is aligned with the look of the Emma / Tara era Avengerland. The colour palette is bright and lively, and the settings are ones that either featured, or could have featured, in actual episodes: old-fashioned pubs, Mother's waterworks and boat headquarters, graveyards, grand houses, glitzy office blocks, parks, country lanes, a church, and a quaint village. The art is also brimming with the colour episodes' energy, with fights, chases, and action sequences aplenty. More sedate panels depicting conversations, meanwhile, tap into the series' predilection for visually interesting shots, mixing up angles and utilising innovative layouts to create a dynamism that keeps the audience engaged.

The Characters

Emma

As *Deadly Rainbow* takes place on the day Emma leaves Steed, and *The Golden Game* picks up roughly six months later, the comic provides a rare insight into Emma's life after working with Steed. While fans have been speculating about Emma's post-series existence for decades, the series and its licensed tie-ins have, remarkably, rarely explored her "afterlife". The sole onscreen indication as to where Emma's life has taken her comes in *The New Avengers* episode *K is for Kill: The Tiger Awakes* (1977), in which Emma (depicted using recycled footage) telephones Steed and reveals that she is "not Mrs. Peel anymore", suggesting that she and Peter have divorced. While onscreen depictions of Emma after her time with Steed were obviously limited by the fact that Diana Rigg was uninterested in reprising the role beyond her unofficial forays in West Germany and Spain in the late sixties, it is surprising that the character's story has not been explored more in other forms of media. Other than *Steed and Mrs. Peel*, the sole licensed appearance of a post-*Forget-Me-Knot* Emma comes in the novel *Too Many Targets* (John Peel and Dave Rogers, St Martin's Press, 1990). *Steed and Mrs. Peel* therefore fills an interesting niche, providing insights into Emma's post-espionage life and using them to reveal new aspects of her characterisation, though the comic's depiction of her does not always ring true.

In terms of what the comic gets right, Emma's sense of style is generally retained, as she dons a number of looks that are in keeping with her onscreen wardrobe. These include a red minidress with a blue overcoat; a similar red dress worn with a tan coat; catsuits in black, white, black with white trim, and white with black trim (though, unlike her onscreen Emmapeelers, these feature overly sexualising v-necks); a tan long-sleeved shirt and red trousers; a red coat worn with a teal minidress; a tan shell and orange trousers; a black sleeveless catsuit worn with a white blouse and boots; and an orange skirt suit. The comic Emma also replicates some of her onscreen counterpart's mannerisms, such as brushing her hair back from her face and putting pens to her lips. In *The Golden Game*, her willingness to engage in a slightly humiliating game of hopscotch at Fanshawe's home in order to appease his butler is in keeping with her decisions to (reluctantly) perform undignified acts for the sake of an investigation, such as dressing in a harem outfit and performing the dance of the seven veils in *Honey for the Prince* (1966). As in the show, she is depicted as being knowledgeable about many subjects, including who Doris Storm is and which magazine she works for; what digitalis is made from; Pringle on Sea's eclipses; and how to solve riddles. She continues to be formidable on the action front, tackling the sexton and the nurse who attacks Doris Storm; overpowering the trio of undertakers with karate chops, kicks, and throws; defeating the whole of the Palamedes Club single-handed; and knocking out the brainwashed vicar with a karate chop and disarming him with a kick. She continues to expertly drive her powder blue Lotus Elan, and remains a good shot, shooting a gun out of reach of one of the undertakers. As in the series, she rescues Steed, pulling him out of the acid pit in the nick of time in *The Golden Game*, and returning him to full size after he is miniaturised in *Deadly Rainbow*. She continues to take bizarre happenings in her stride, making plans for tea after defeating a number of faux Leopard People in *Deadly Rainbow*. Her sense of humour has also remained intact, with Emma suggesting that Peter truss the Americans behind the faux Leopard People scheme up on a merry-go-round to attract the attention of the newspapers.

However, Emma's depiction in the comic is also inaccurate or out of character at times. Her nails are sometimes painted red or pink, but Emma did not wear coloured nail polish in the series. Her fighting style is also sometimes incorrectly portrayed. In *Deadly Rainbow*, Emma is shown kicking back with one leg while aiming a downward punch at another opponent, a balletic pose more akin to Purdey's dance-inspired mode of fighting than Emma's kung fu and karate. She also seems oddly uneasy about the possibility that Steed cheated at the game of Hangman to save Tara. In the series, Emma was well-aware of Steed's tendency to bend rules and the truth, and therefore should not be shocked that he would cheat to save Tara — if anything, she should approve of him doing so, as it was for a good cause. She is also oddly preoccupied with people's weight in both stories, a topic she never discussed onscreen. In *The Golden Game*, she notes that Tara has lost weight, while *Deadly Rainbow* has her complaining about her captors placing her by fattening food. This was likely an attempt to make Emma a relatable character by giving her a stereotypically female area of concern, but it is a demeaning to reduce a highly educated, intelligent, and accomplished woman to fretting about peoples' waistlines.

Other aspects of Emma's characterisation are not inaccurate, but instead provide new insights into Emma as a person. Emma's decision to return to England without Peter in order to help Steed demonstrates her independence within the parameters of her marriage. Furthermore, her description of the Leopard People ceremony that Peter stays on for as "gruesome" indicates that she does not feel she has to like the same things her husband does. We also learn that Emma believes she does not have the "temperament" for modelling (though she did model for a case in *The Bird Who Knew Too Much* [1967]). Most notably, we discover that she is capable of behaving rashly. When Peter goes missing, Emma rushes off to find him without stopping to listen to Steed's suggestions as to what to do or carefully consider her next move. The only time we see Emma's logic and reason evaporate in the face of her strong emotions onscreen is in *Murdersville*, in which she nearly kills a man as revenge for the murder of her friend Paul. Even her brief moment of panic regarding her predicament in *The House That Jack Built* was not as intense and ill-judged. Furthermore, neither of those episodes found her actively disregarding an external voice of reason or endangering innocent parties with her recklessness. In *Deadly Rainbow*, in contrast, she not only disregards Steed's advice, but leaves him vulnerable to capture and winds up having to go on the run to avoid being captured herself, resulting in more desperate decisions that cause further damage: she knocks out a workman to steal his steamroller, then drives said steamroller straight into a greenhouse. When she finally returns to her senses and fights off the faux Leopard People to allow the workman and his colleagues to escape, she is quickly outnumbered and captured. This reckless Mrs. Peel, blinded by fear for her husband's well-being, is far from the cool, collected individual shown in the series, who relied on reason even when her or Steed's life was on the line. Later, we see Emma's emotions get the best of her again when the faux Leopard People present her with a quandary – save either Peter or Steed from being crushed by a steamroller, or lose them both. Still shaken by her earlier distress at Peter's disappearance and faced with losing at least one person she cares deeply about, Emma's logical mind abandons her and she is paralysed, reduced to crying out for the faux Leopard People to stop the ordeal and unable to come up with a plan to rescue Steed and Peter. This situation therefore not only demonstrates that Emma cares about both men equally and that her decision to leave Steed was far from an easy one, but, like the rest of the story, it humanises her by providing insights into her psyche and revealing that that even an intelligent, logical woman such as she does not have all the answers when faced with a choice that any human being with normal emotions would find impossible to make. These revelations about Emma do not weaken her, but make her a richer, more relatable character whose accomplishments are all the more impressive for having been achieved while overcoming very human foibles.

The Emma/Steed Relationship

The placement of the two stories vis-a-vis the series' timeline also allows for a unique exploration of Emma's relationships with other significant characters. The way she and Steed relate to one another in these stories is particularly fascinating, as it is clear that Peter's return has fundamentally changed their dynamic. In *The Golden Game*, Steed hints at this change when he meets up with Emma at Fanshawe's funeral, admitting that he was not sure she would respond to his call for assistance, and therefore implying that he is uncertain as to whether he can still rely on her as a friend and ally. Emma attempts to allay his fears by telling Steed that he is "irresistible", thereby indicating that Peter's return has not negated their friendship. The fact that Steed has her South American contact information supports her assurances, as she would not give it to him if she did not want him to stay in touch. At the same time, Emma acknowledges that they are no longer as comfortable and familiar with each other as they once were, and that this is the first time they have communicated to any extent since her departure, by asking Steed if he still likes his tea stirred anti-clockwise. Sandwiched between these two interactions is a brief-yet-meaningful exchange that identifies the source of the pair's awkwardness. Steed, quite casually, asks after Peter. A brilliant, wordless panel – possibly the best in the whole of *The Golden Game* – follows, in which

Emma's face is shown in close-up as she gives Steed a knowing look that indicates that she is not fooled by Steed's feigned casual politeness and senses Steed's jealousy at being supplanted by Peter. Rather than confront Steed about his passive-aggressive comment, however, Emma chooses to take the question at face value, telling Steed that Peter is still in the Amazon. Steed then tries to smooth things over by telling Emma she is the only person he can trust, thereby signalling her importance to him. Emma graciously responds that she is "touched" by the sentiment, but hints at some jealousy on her part by asking what happened to "new girl" Tara, which suggests that, like Steed, she is not entirely happy about being replaced, even though it was she who decided to leave. Steed skirts over the question by telling her that he will explain everything and laying out his plan for them to solve the mystery and then have dinner at the Ritz, "just like old times". However, the fact that he feels the need to evoke a sense of cheerful nostalgia indicates that there is still tension between them. The entire scene is brilliantly done, conveying Steed and Emma's awkwardness as they dance around each other, admitting to hurt and jealousy while trying to work out which parts of their old dynamic can be salvaged. Steed's statement about "old times" is also an acknowledgement that their previous relationship is, indeed, in the past. No matter what new dynamic they establish and how close they remain, things will never be quite as they were when they were working together. This sense that they are attempting to find their footing while dealing with their respective feelings continues throughout the story. When they search Fanshawe's home, attend Doris Storm's and Simon Bird's funerals, discuss the case over a picnic, and converse about the specially printed book and Steed's Palamedes Club inauguration, they work together as seamlessly as they did in the series. On other occasions, the tension resurfaces, such as when Steed gives Emma an angry look when she tells him to answer the phone. However, it is notable that their relationship warms up the longer they work together. After Emma rescues Steed from the acid pit toward the end of the story, she smooths his lapels in a very intimate way and promises to buy him a new umbrella to replace one that was destroyed. One senses at this point that their warm, trusting friendship has been reestablished, albeit in a different form.

If the pair come a long way over the course of *The Golden Game*, they come an even longer way between the beginning of *Deadly Rainbow* and the end of *The Golden Game*. In *Deadly Rainbow*, Emma awakes from being attacked by the faux Leopard People to find Steed at her bedside. When Steed smugly describes how he heroically rescued Emma, who was strapped to the church altar, Emma responds by tetchily demanding to know where Peter is. Steed replies by patronisingly asking Emma if Peter is a "good influence" on her, as she was screaming and barely conscious when he found her. "You didn't behave like that when you were with me," Steed finishes, relishing the opportunity to cast aspersion on Peter for "weakening" Emma and on Emma herself for choosing her "inferior" husband over him. The entire scene is extremely antagonistic, the antithesis of the pair's typically warm relationship. Steed goes on to question Emma's sanity when she tells him about the faux Leopard People and points out the town's obsession with rainbows. Emma, in turn, is short with Steed, and ignores his advice about how to proceed with her search for Peter. Their willingness to listen to each other and work together has evaporated. By the end of the story, the hostility seems to have abated, but, with Peter on the scene, there is still a distance between them. It is easy to see why, in *The Golden Game*, Steed was worried that Emma would not respond to his call for help – his hostility toward her and her relationship with Peter would have been enough to drive anyone away. While it is unpleasant to see the pair at odds, this glimpse of a heretofore unseen side of their relationship is fascinating.

Steed

There are, unsurprisingly, parallels between Steed's personal journey and the evolution of his relationship with Emma over the course of the two stories. *Deadly Rainbow* finds him trying to cope with Emma's departure in the final moments of *The Forget-Me-Knot* by consoling himself with the fact that Emma seemingly married someone exactly like him. Despite his attempts to comfort himself, however, it is clear that Steed views the end of their working relationship as being akin to a death. The comic cleverly conveys that Steed is in mourning via a panel showing him holding a large, heart-shaped balloon in a hue best described as "funereal black". The symbolism continues in the next panel, in which Steed releases the balloon, just as he released Emma, before turning his attention to Mother's latest briefing – he has chosen to throw himself into his work rather than dwell on his personal pain. However, the fact that Steed chooses not to involve Tara in his Pringle on Sea investigation, despite her being assigned as his partner at the end of *The Forget-Me-Knot* – and therefore at the beginning of this story – suggests that Tara's presence would only remind him of Emma's absence and undermine his attempt to use work to distract himself from his heartache. Other heart-shaped balloons, including a large black one, appear during Steed and Mother's conversation, reinforcing the message that Steed's heartache continues to linger in the background, despite Steed's attempts to distract himself. Mother, notably, does not force the issue by requiring Tara to be involved in the investigation, instead allowing Steed to do what is best for him. When Steed reunites with Emma in Pringle on Sea, however, the pain he felt upon their parting bubbles to the surface and manifests in pointed, petty jabs about Peter and Emma and a flippant attitude toward Peter's disappearance. It is only when he and Emma are attacked by the local vicar and discover the miniaturised workmen that he puts his feelings aside and attempts to offer Emma wise counsel regarding her next move. Emma responds by disregarding his advice and barreling off to search for Peter. The thoughtful expression on Steed's face as Emma leaves him behind is interesting, as it suggests that Steed is surprised to see Emma behaving recklessly and has realised, for the first time, that they are pursuing different objectives. It is also the moment that he seems to understand that their relationship was fated to irrevocably change as soon as Peter reappeared, regardless of whether Emma chose to continue working with him or not. Steed's acceptance of the fact that he, Peter, and Emma have all been influenced by events beyond their control leads him to realise that neither Emma nor Peter is to "blame" for his unhappiness and causes him to change his behaviour. For the rest of the story, he does not treat Emma and Peter with hostility, but instead works with them to solve the mystery and graciously bows to Peter's superior knowledge of the Leopard People. By the end of the story, Steed's bitterness and anger have been replaced by wounded pride at the realisation that Emma married someone so unlike him.

By the time of *The Golden Game*, Steed is more like his old self, but there are hints that the events of *Deadly Rainbow* have left their mark on him. When he finds the injured Bird, he seems extraordinarily alarmed and instructs a nearby drunk to call an ambulance, and removes his hat when the man dies, all signs that violence and death, which he is regularly exposed to in his line of work, are affecting him more than usual because his emotions are closer to the surface since Emma's departure. He is also very protective of Tara, looking at her picture after she is kidnapped with clear concern and subtly blaming Mother for her disappearance by agreeing when Mother says he should not have let Tara meet Fanshawe solo. He also makes a rather odd comment in response to Mother's instruction to trust no one, describing himself as being "like an abacus". While Steed is a highly skilled, ruthless agent, he also experiences and expresses intense emotions, whereas one would expect a person who described themselves as an "abacus" to be cold, clinical, and driven only by logic. Whether this is an indication that Steed is trying to keep his emotions at arm's length, or simply a poor piece of characterisation, is unclear.

Steed's analytical mind, however, remains unaffected by Emma's departure, as he is able to decode the riddles in Fox's book. He is depicted as being as effortlessly charming as ever, using his gentlemanly persona to counter the hostility of the Palamedes Club's doorman and his aristocratic authority to brush past the man when Simon Bird grants Steed entry into the club. He also deftly handles Palamedes Club members Wallow and Chance, using his friendly demeanour to extract information about the club's history and workings, while making a provocative comment about hoping his luck is better than that of the club's (deceased) charter members and telling them his game is called "Rooks and Ravens" – the phrase that Doris Storm uttered as she was dying – to goad them into reacting. He still has a nice line in clever quips, telling the doorman that he is "not just playing games, you know," and reacting to an arrow narrowly missing his head with typical understatement: "And I thought dropping a fork meant visitors." He also remains defiant and unruffled in the face of danger. Surrounded by sinister Palamedes Club members, he expresses the hope that he is not late, claims that the fact that Fox also submitted a game called "Rooks and Ravens" is a coincidence, and refers to Fox as "Four-eyes", a "poor loser", and "unsufferable [sic]". Even when Fox is making attempts on his life, he keeps his composure while playing one deadly game after another. When he is about to tumble into a pool of acid, his composure slips, but he quickly regains it when Emma rescues him, quipping "Fancy meeting you here" and, when he sees that Emma has defeated all of the club members, "You seem to have made quite an impression." He is also still crafty, winning the game of Hangman by seeing the word reflected in Fox's glasses. All in all, the picture of Steed painted in the comic is a familiar one, but Emma's departure and reappearance in his life allow us to see flashes of vulnerability and emotion beneath the polished demeanour.

The Emma/Peter Relationship

Deadly Rainbow's depiction of Emma and Peter's relationship is another welcome byproduct of the story being set shortly after the end of *The Forget-Me-Knot*. Their marriage has been the subject of numerous fan works, most of which depict it as unhappy and ending in divorce or with Peter's death, and Peter himself as uncaring, unfaithful, or even evil. This animosity toward Peter is understandable, as his reappearance directly caused the break-up of Steed and Emma's much-loved partnership, but such negative depictions of Peter and his marriage to Emma do both characters a disservice. The idea that Emma – a strong, self-confident, and independent woman who knows her own mind – would return to a husband she did not love merely because she felt obligated to do so is a ridiculous one that casts aspersion on Emma's judgment and intelligence. Furthermore, it is difficult to believe that a woman who took the helm of her father's company at the age of 21 would be naïve enough to go on to marry a horrible man and stay with him for four years until his disappearance. As Emma's characterisation does not indicate that she would tolerate being in a relationship with someone who did not treat her with love and respect, was not her intellectual equal, and was threatened by her accomplishments, it is logical to conclude that Emma genuinely loved Peter and considered him to be worthy of her.

Steed and Mrs. Peel, to its credit, follows this logic when depicting the pair's relationship, while also wisely differentiating it from the dynamic Emma shares with Steed (though one wonders if Emma's decision to call her husband "Peel" is a case of both character and writer imposing her way of referring to Steed on this relationship). Emma relates to Peter in a very wifely way, relegating traditionally masculine tasks, such as carrying suitcases up the stairs, to him and fussing over his bleeding lip. She is also depicted as being more openly flirtatious with her husband than she was with Steed, pressing her hand to Peter's chest while leaning into him, touching his mouth, and curling an arm around his shoulder. This erotic body language suggests that the pair's relationship has always been a passionate one, and remains so despite the years they spent apart. They also share a wry, playful sense of humour. When Emma sarcastically expresses a desire to be a demure housewife who spends her time embroidering hankies, Peter quips that she would be hopeless at it. Emma later picks up on this running joke when Peter asks for a hanky for his bleeding lip, quipping "With embroidery, or without?" They even manage to joke about Peter's memory loss and the time he spent missing, with Emma wryly pointing out that Peter said he would be gone for three days and disappeared for three years, to which Peter replies, "I promise I'd have sent you a postcard...if I'd known what name to sign." Emma is also depicted as being supportive of Peter's drive to help the Leopard People, countering "Try and stop me" when Peter queries whether she is willing to spend their second honeymoon in the Amazon. She also trusts Peter implicitly, referencing her espionage work on more than one occasion without worrying that he will betray her confidence.

However, the marriage is not depicted as lacking in conflict. Peter pushes Emma to ignore her instincts about suspicious goings-on in Pringle on Sea, telling her it is not her job to investigate such things and reminding her of her self-imposed mantra: "I'm closing my eyes... I see nothing strange." When Emma continues to insist that something is wrong, he gently mocks her for what he believes is paranoia by saying that the vicar at the local church has probably been "kidnapped by sinister masterminds". While Peter is likely only trying to remind her that her old life is over and to look to the future, pushing

Emma to ignore her instincts when there is tangible proof that something is wrong comes across as patronising. Similarly, Peter's executive decision to return to the Amazon, which he presents to Emma as a fait accompli, casts him as a selfish individual who expects others to go along with his wishes. On the other hand, Peter does ask Emma if she wants to go to the jungle after telling her his plans, suggesting that, if she refused, he would accept that decision. There are also indications that Emma wants to move on from her old life – she tells Peter, "I think the jungle will be very good for me – it'll keep me away from diabolical masterminds," and tries to forget about Steed – meaning that, by urging her to ignore strange happenings, Peter may simply be attempting to help her achieve this goal. He also admits that Emma was right to be suspicious after they are attacked by the faux Leopard People. Elsewhere, Peter not taking issue with Emma returning to England to help Steed in *The Golden Game* indicates that he has no desire to control her and that he supports her pursuing espionage work, just as she supports his work with the Leopard People. It also indicates that they are perfectly capable of leading independent lives and maintaining a long-distance relationship, and therefore trust each other implicitly. They also make a good team on the action front, fighting the faux Leopard People side by side, with Peter even asking his wife for combat pointers. All in all, the picture that is painted of the Peels' marriage is one of two strong-willed people who are in love and have the capacity to compromise.

Peter

Despite having a prominent role in *Deadly Rainbow*, Peter himself remains something of a mystery, with virtually nothing revealed about his background. What we do learn, however, paints him as a multi-dimensional human being, neither a saint nor the demonised caricature that he is often depicted as by fans. The splash page featuring countless newspaper headlines that show that Peter is using the publicity surrounding his miraculous return as a platform to draw attention to the plight of the Leopard People (who cared for him after his crash) casts him as a man of principle and honour who is loyal to his friends. He also demonstrates his dedication to the Leopard People's cause by returning to the jungle shortly after he and Emma are reunited and remaining there for many months. Peter is also portrayed as a romantic, bringing Emma back to the place where they spent the first night of their honeymoon, but is not jealous or possessive. He shows no sign of being threatened by Steed, instead working with Steed to neutralise enemies, asking Steed to accompany him and Emma to the jungle to help the Leopard People, and happily letting

Emma return to England to work with Steed without him. Peter also possesses a wry, grim sense of humour, which he deploys in dangerous situations. Upon realising that his plane is malfunctioning, he quips, "I think killing the test pilot counts as a design failure." When attacked by a horde of faux Leopard People, he tells Emma that he "didn't cover this in flying school", but proves more than capable of handling himself and dispatches an opponent with the humourous parting shot "I'm sorry, I'm an easygoing man, but... I hate those sweaters!" However, his sense of humour also runs to the callous or cruel at times. It is his idea to pick Emma up at Steed's flat while dressed like Steed and driving a vintage car. Emma expresses regret at taking part in the joke, as she knows that Steed will likely be shocked to see that she has apparently married his doppelganger, but Peter argues that adding a "twist of surprise" makes "dreadful" good-byes more palatable. However, it is hard not to think that Peter's joke is an underhanded way of discomfiting the man his wife spent three years with, an act that paints him as mean spirited. Peter is also depicted as an adventurer and a thrill seeker – we learn that he participated in a round the world helicopter race – who keeps his head in the face of danger, whether contending with a crashing plane, fighting faux Leopard People and their American controllers, or finding himself tied down in front of a steamroller. He also thinks nothing of conducting a route march through the Amazon jungle. While the comic does not tell us Peter's life story, therefore, it provides plenty of information about who he is as a man.

The Tara/Emma Relationship

If we do not learn much about Peter's background, we learn even less about Tara King, as her participation in *The Golden Game* is very limited and she is completely absent from *Deadly Rainbow*. Nevertheless, the comic does an excellent job of developing a dynamic between Tara and Emma in the few scenes they share. Like Peter, Tara's portrayal in fan works is often less than flattering, with her often depicted as being at odds with Emma and competing with her for Steed's affections. However, these depictions overlook the fact that Emma and Tara's sole onscreen interaction in *The Forget-Me-Knot* is not antagonistic, but marked by kindness and mutual respect. Rather than ignoring Tara when she asks for directions to Steed's flat or treating her with hostility, Emma provides the directions and offers Tara a piece of friendly advice, telling her that Steed likes his tea stirred "anti-clockwise". The gesture is Emma's way of conveying that she feels no ill will toward her successor. Tara, in turn, accepts the advice with a small smile, acknowledging that she recognises both Emma herself and the kindness and graciousness of her gesture.

The Golden Game picks up on this goodwill between the women, with Emma concerned for Tara's well-being and attempting to help Steed save her. The women then collaborate to defeat a henchman before exchanging friendly greetings. Even Emma's out-of-character comment about Tara having lost weight does not result in animosity, with Tara merely quipping, after her acrobatic swing from the hangman's noose, that she tries to exercise. Later, the women work together to defeat Fox, with Tara passing his bomb to Emma, who then passes it back to Fox. At the story's close, they are shown amiably sharing a trandem with Steed while making wry comments about the man himself. The most meaningful moment they share, however, is a small, subtle one. After Steed uses his bowler to attack Fox, Emma retrieves it, but, rather than give it to Steed herself, she gives it to Tara, who returns it to Steed while Emma looks on. It is a wonderfully understated, poignant moment that beautifully illustrates Emma's acceptance of the fact that she is no longer Steed's partner and that Tara has taken the place in his life that she willingly gave up. Though seeing Steed and Tara interact is undoubtedly painful for her, the gesture speaks volumes about Emma's kindness, maturity, and selflessness, and is the ultimate proof that she bears Tara no ill will. It is a refreshing creative decision on Morrison's part to depict Emma and Tara as sharing the same amiable relationship they did onscreen, rather than resort to the stale trope of women regarding each other as rivals.

Tara

Outside of her dynamic with Emma, Tara is, unfortunately, largely relegated to being the damsel in distress. She is kidnapped early in the story and only reappears near the end, when Fox casts her as the victim in a game of Hangman in order to torment Steed. However, she does redeem herself by single-handedly escaping the hangman's noose and using it as a swing to launch herself at the man acting as her executioner. She is also depicted as a competent agent when conversing with the faux Fanshawe, brushing off his attempts to flirt and chiding him for being late for their meeting and not taking the Ministry's security concerns seriously. After her disappearance, Mother regrets letting Tara meet Fanshawe on her own because he believes her to be rash and impetuous, but that assessment is not borne out by her behaviour in this story. There is little she could have done differently when dealing with the faux Fanshawe – even if she had asked for identification, he likely would have produced a convincing forgery. Instead, the fact that she is shown working solo demonstrates that she has grown as an agent and is able to operate independently from Steed. Mother's concern for Tara's well-being is therefore somewhat infantilising and results from an unfair assessment of her abilities.

Other Characters

The depictions of the other players populating this literal comic strip Avengerland are something of a mixed bag. *The Golden Game*'s rough and ready occupants of the Crown and Anchor pub would feel more at home in the grittier, Keel- and Gale-era Avengerland, in which seedy settings and seedier characters were a common sight, than in the comic's more fantastic, Peel / King-era setting. The fake Admiral Fanshawe, a larger-than-life presence in a blue double-breasted captain's jacket and hat who doles out an endless stream of nautical analogies, in contrast, is more akin to the eccentrics of the era in which the story is set. He also delivers a subtle example of the series' trademark wit, responding to Tara's accusation that he is late by telling her that he is "later than you think", an allusion to the murder of the real Fanshawe. Leaving aside his drunkenness, Fanshawe's pirate-garbed (complete with eyepatch and earring) butler is a classic *Avengers* eccentric who thinks nothing of asking guests to play hopscotch in the corridor and injects humour via his keenness to return to his "work" in the wine cellar. Ms. Manchester, the editor of *Metropolitan* magazine, makes an outsized impression as Edna Mode's predecessor, resplendent in a magenta ensemble, cat's eye glasses, and oversized heart earrings. Her single-minded campaign to persuade Emma to take up modelling, which involves waxing lyrical about Emma's bone structure, is classic *Avengers* obsessive behaviour. Doris Storm and Lesley the nurse appear too briefly to leave an impression beyond as victim and killer, respectively, but Lesley's nameless nurse colleague at least uses her fleeting appearance to provide a little humour via her concern about her boyfriend's stash of Hungarian national dress. Bradford, the doorman at the Palamedes Club, and Fox's executioner are thugs that exude the hulking menace of Saul in *The Town of No Return*. The nameless wannabe Palamedes Club member is a prototypical *Avengers* obsessive who views the rejection of his Chutes and Serpents board game as akin to a criminal act, but murder victim Simon Bird is a generic character who only adds to the body count. The King of Spades assassin, decked out in his playing card finery, would have looked fantastic onscreen and been a worthy addition to the series' rogues' gallery, but the drunk who witnesses his work is too distasteful for the series' fantasy realm. Chance, the Palamedes Club's secretary, in contrast, is a perfect fit for the show: lean, sharp-featured, oozing sophisticated menace and arrogance, he is the prototypical *Avengers* baddie. Palamedes Club member Mr. Wollow is also a familiar *Avengers* character type: the reluctantly dishonest man who is in over his head. The trio of undertakers who attempt to turn Emma into their latest customer, however, slip too far into parody, their ridiculously tall hats and nearly identical appearances rendering them Tweedledee and Tweedledum-alikes who are too cartoonish even for this era of the series. The same, unfortunately, is true of diabolical mastermind Hilary Fox. His features are so ridiculously caricatured that it seems unlikely he could exist in real life, even in *The Avengers'* surreal universe, and, as a result, it is difficult to take him seriously as a threat. However, Fox's motivation for his crimes and personality are suitability *Avengers*-ish, even if his appearance is not, as he has much in common with Mark Crayford, the villain in *The New Avengers* episode *Dead Men are Dangerous* (1977). Both Crayford and Fox are old schoolmates of Steed's who hate Steed because of his luckiness and popularity and stoop to cheating in order to best him, with Fox moving the stepping stones in the acid pit while Steed is using them and attempting to hang Tara even after Steed wins the game of Hangman, and Crayford cheating to best Steed during a childhood race. Steed treats both of these envious individuals with kindness, recommending Fox for a position at the Ministry and allowing Crayford to think he was unaware of his cheating, but receives little gratitude in return for his efforts. Instead, both men are poor losers, in every sense of the word.

Similarities to The Avengers TV Series

In addition to the aforementioned familiar plot points, there are plenty of touches and in-jokes referencing particular elements and episodes of the series scattered throughout the comic. In *The Golden Game*, Tara wears a green skirt suit and black shirt ensemble that is nearly identical to one of her outfits from *The Forget-Me-Knot*. In the photo on Steed's desk, she appears to be wearing her orange t-shirt with white piping from *Whoever Shot Poor George Oblique Stroke XR40?* (1968), albeit with a green coat instead of the yellow one she wears in the episode. As in the Emma Peel episodes, Steed is shown driving a green Bentley. However, this transportation choice is incorrect from a continuity standpoint, as Steed drove a yellow Rolls Royce Silver Ghost when working with Tara. As in the series, Mother's headquarters are in unusual locations, including a hand-propelled paddlewheel boat and an underground water system. The exterior and interior of Steed's flat, 3 Stable Mews, are faithfully recreated, and his address is also correctly written out on an envelope. Steed places his bowler and umbrella on a table in his flat in an arrangement similar to the one featured in the colour Peel titles. The splash title page shows Steed pointing his umbrella like a rifle, a pose he struck in the colour Peel opening titles, and also features profile silhouettes of Steed, Emma, and Tara that are akin to those featured in the colour Peel titles. The target with a heart in the centre on the splash page calls to mind the man- and woman-shaped targets with hearts at their centres from the orange Tara King titles. A red carnation in a vase in Steed's flat recalls Emma placing a red carnation in Steed's buttonhole in the colour Peel titles and the large bunches of carnations contained in the suits of armour in the outdoor Tara King titles. Steed is shown drinking brandy, as he so often did during the series, and both Steed and Emma drink champagne, with one panel showing a close-up of their hands clinking their glasses in a recreation of a moment from the colour Peel titles. During a picnic, Steed spreads out a checkered tablecloth that recalls the chessboard from the Peel titles made for the American market. Later, at Waddington Hall, Steed pulls the lever of a slot machine to gain entry, a mechanism reminiscent of the one on the time machine in *Escape in Time*. Another reference to the chessboard titles comes via the life-sized chessboard and chess pieces at Waddington Hall. Steed is forced to pass a test to be admitted to the Palamedes Club, something he was also required to do to become a Hellfire Club member in *A Touch of Brimstone* (1966). The Palamedes Club members' red cloaks are also reminiscent of Hellfire Club garb. The trio of undertakers call to mind other examples of their profession in *The Gravediggers*, while one of the undertakers' warning to his colleagues that Emma is no pushover recalls a similar conversation between the villains in *Dead Man's Treasure* (1967). Emma straightens Steed's lapels after rescuing him from the acid pit, recalling the image of her resting her hand on the same in the colour Peel titles, while Steed's umbrella has the same Whangee bamboo handle that he favoured in the series. Emma defeats the Palamedes Club members offscreen and they are shown strewn about in a tableau similar to the one featuring Steed's unconscious victims in *The Town of No Return*. As in many an episode, Steed tosses his steel-rimmed bowler to disarm a villain. Emma namechecks the titles of the Tara King episode *Love All* (1969) and *The New Avengers* episode *House of Cards* (1976). In *Deadly Rainbow*, Emma is shown wearing a black and white op-art outfit, complete with beret, that recalls many of her season four John Bates ensembles. She wears this while fighting some scientists in a small laboratory or control room, a scene which appears to be a take on the fight at the end of *The Thirteenth Hole* (1966), though, in the episode, the scientists watch the fight via a monitor rather than engage in it.

Verdict

Steed and Mrs. Peel is an interesting 1990s experiment. It had a difficult balance to strike between being a nostalgia piece and offering an innovative twist on the material that appealed to fans and new readers alike. The result is a mix of old and new that is successful in some ways, but not others. To its credit, its best quality is an innovation: the setting of both stories post-*The Forget-Me-Knot*, a creative choice that allows readers to see how Steed and Emma's relationship evolves after Peter's return. *Deadly Rainbow* pushes the envelope in further novel directions by including overtly supernatural elements and telling a story that is very personal to Emma and puts her in the driver's seat to an extent that even the most Emma-centric episodes – *The House That Jack Built*, *The Joker*, *Epic*, *Murdersville* – did not. Another positive is the art, which balances innovation with familiarity, capturing the vibrant, colourful, out-there Avengerland and its resident eccentrics, sinister individuals, and diabolical masterminds, while at the same time featuring settings that would have been far beyond the reach of the series' budget.

Unfortunately, some of the innovations go too far. Blood, spit, and belching drunks have no place in the fantasy-based iteration of Avengerland. The almost gothic emphasis on funerals and their associated sermons and Emma's overly muscular, superheroine physique also feel out of place. While some innovation is welcome and in keeping with the show's spirit, such elements go so far against the series' grain that they render the show unrecognisable and defeat the purpose of adapting an existing property. The comic also occasionally feels sloppy, with continuity errors, unclearly conveyed plot points, variable character likenesses, anachronisms, and lines of dialogue that one could never imagine the characters saying onscreen.

Issues aside, there are enough intriguing ideas in *Steed and Mrs. Peel* to make one wish that the creatives had produced further issues and continued to innovate while getting a better handle on the series' parameters. Unfortunately, it would be another two decades before more original comic stories starring Steed and Mrs. Peel made it to print, but these three issues, while certainly not perfect, provide an interesting, if skewed, take on Avengerland.

BEYOND AVENGERLAND

LAS LUCHADORAS VS. EL ROBOT ASESINO
DAS DIADEM/DER GOLDENE SCHLÜSSEL
MINIKILLERS
ESCAPADE

LAS LUCHADORAS VS. EL ROBOT ASESINO

J Z FERGUSON

Project Type: Feature Film
Release Date: January 9th 1969 (Mexico)

Synopsis

A robot – clad in a black coat, trousers, and hat and wearing sunglasses on its silver head – approaches and attacks a homeless man.

Gaby Reyna, national champion wrestler of Mexico, defeats an opponent in the ring, much to the elation of the cheering crowd. Her uncle, the prominent scientist Professor Reyna, who watched the fight, tells her that he was worried she would lose, but a confident Gaby states that her opponent, while a good fighter, was inexperienced. Her uncle adds that Gaby was also more skilled than her opponent, before departing to let Gaby get showered and changed before they have dinner.

The robot carries the unconscious homeless man to the lab of an evil scientist named Orlak, and lays him on a surgical table. Orlak and his assistant, Waldo, perform a surgical procedure on the homeless man that they have performed many times before. Like all of the previous surgeries, this one is a failure, and the frustrated Orlak laments that he cannot work out why his subjects die. Still, he is determined to repeat the procedure until he succeeds. Waldo then warns Orlak that Carfax is angry. They descend into the basement of the lab, and find Carfax in his cell. The product of another of Orlak's surgeries, Carfax is part man, part zombie. The controller that Orlak implanted in Carfax's brain has caused changes to his body, leaving him deformed. Carfax is also mentally unstable, driven by instinct and prone to sudden attacks of madness caused by the controller putting painful pressure on his brain. The only person Carfax obeys is Orlak, because Orlak has put Carfax in a hypnotic state. The surgical procedure has been modified to prevent another Carfax from being created, but since then, all of Orlak's subjects have died. Orlak laments the fact that Carfax is his only "success", but Waldo argues that Orlak should be proud of inventing the robot used to kidnap the homeless man. Orlak, however, is not satisfied – the robot took lots of time and money to build, and he does not have the resources or patience to make another one, let alone several. Instead, he wants to control humans by surgically inserting controllers into their brains. Waldo suggests that the key to overcoming their failures is to bring new scientists onto the project, but admits that the chances of persuading any scientists to work with Orlak are slim to none. Orlak is undeterred – he will force scientists to work for him.

Gaby's uncle, Professor Reyna, invites her to dinner at his place. Reyna then asks his assistant – who happens to be Orlak! – if he would like to join them for dinner. Orlak declines, claiming to have a pressing matter to attend to.

Waldo identifies a scientist who may be able to help Orlak: Professor Reyna. Lefty, who also works for Orlak, has stolen Reyna's cardiogram. Orlak feeds the cardiogram into a slot on the robot. Because each person's heartbeat is different, the robot is able to use the cardiogram to locate its targets.

A nurse working in Orlak's lab brings Carfax dinner, but Carfax attacks and kills her when she releases him from his cell to eat. Orlak investigates when she does not return and finds her body. Orlak uses a whip to corral Carfax back into his cell.

Gaby visits her uncle's lab before dinner, but the pair squabble. Her uncle lectures her, telling her that she should get married instead of focussing on wrestling. While Gaby is in the other room, the robot smashes through the door and knocks out her uncle. When Gaby goes to investigate, she is knocked out as well.

Two detectives, Captain Arturo Campos and his partner Chava Lopez, arrive at the scene of the attack. They look at the shattered door and speculate that the assailant must be very strong. They question Gaby, who laments that she did not see her attacker, who hit her from behind. The trio wonder what has happened to her uncle, who is nowhere to be found.

Waldo and Orlak discuss the unconscious Professor Reyna, whom they have locked in a cell. They muse that the professor will be surprised to discover that he has been kidnapped by his own assistant. Reyna is an anatomy expert, and Orlak asks Waldo if he has chosen an engineer to add to their collection.

Returning to Professor Reyna's lab, Orlak feigns innocence and offers to assist the police with their investigation into Professor Reyna's disappearance. Reyna's secretary interrupts their conversation, telling the police that the professor's cardiogram is missing. Gaby wonders why it would be stolen, but Orlak offers no explanation.

Gaby returns to her wrestling training and is introduced to Gema Nelson, who has just returned from a successful international wrestling tour. Gaby's promoter asks her to show Gema the ropes.

The two detectives report to their superior and confess that they have made no progress in the Professor Reyna investigation.

Gema thanks Gaby for the training session, but can tell Gaby is troubled. Gaby tells Gema that her uncle has been kidnapped, and Gema offers to help however she can. Gaby says that she could use some company, and invites Gema to come stay with her. Gema accepts the invitation.

The robot is programmed using the cardiogram of an engineer, Dr. Roca, and attacks the man in his car. The robot is so strong that it prevents the car from moving just by resting a hand on it. It then rips the car door off of the vehicle and abducts Roca.

Gaby engages in a wrestling match, with the detectives looking on. Arturo tells Chava that they are there to look for clues regarding Gaby's uncle's disappearance, but Chava speculates that Arturo is attracted to Gaby. After the match, the two men invite Gaby and Gema to dinner, but, before they can leave, Arturo receives a phone call alerting him to the abduction of Dr. Roca. Gaby and Gema tag along to the crime scene, and question how someone could rip a door off of a car and why scientists are being taken. Chava theorises that more scientists will be abducted.

Chava is correct. The robot has already been sent after Dr. Agustin Hill. It smashes through his office door and knocks him out. Arturo and Chava's superior is incandescent at the news, telling the two detectives that they must solve the case before they are all forced to resign. Arturo says that they have no leads or clues, but Chava again points out that all of the kidnap victims are scientists. Gema adds that the lack of bodies tells them that the scientists are still alive.

Orlak has a meeting with the abducted scientists, and tells them that he needs their help to create human robots. In exchange, he offers them the wealth and power that will come from controlling the human race. Professor Reyna refuses, appalled at the prospect. Orlak tells him that he can leave, but when Reyna attempts to do so, the robot kills him. Dr. Roca agrees to help Orlak, lamenting that his work has left him impoverished. Dr. Hill also acquiesces, believing he has no choice but to agree to help.

Professor Reyna's body is dumped. Gaby vows to find his murderer. Orlak pretends to share in her grief, while Arturo is left wondering who the next kidnap victim will be.

The robot abducts Dr. Chavez as a replacement anatomy expert, brushing aside the doctor's secretary en route. Gaby and Arturo question her about what the kidnapper looked like. Gaby asks her if the kidnapper struck her with a chopping motion like the one used to knock Gaby herself out, and the secretary confirms that "he" did. Chava and Gema discover that Dr. Chavez's medical records, like those of the other abducted scientists, are missing. Gema wonders who could destroy things with their bare hands, and speculates that the kidnapper is a karate master. Chava suggests that it could be a robot...

A reluctant Dr. Chavez agrees to help Orlak after the other scientists explain the situation.

Gaby and Gema try to take their minds off things by deciding what colour to paint their shared home. Orlak drops by and asks if there has been any progress in the investigation into Gaby's uncle's murder, but Gaby reveals that there has been none. Arturo and Chava also drop by, and Gaby asks if they have located Dr. Rich. Orlak recognises the name and claims to have read about him. Rich is an expert in automation and cybernetics, and Arturo explains that they want to talk to him because they believe the abductor of the scientists is a robot. Orlak laughs the suggestion off as preposterous, then quickly excuses himself.

Orlak calls Waldo and tells him that the detectives and female wrestlers are going to see Rich. Orlak says if they find out that he has a deal with Rich regarding cybernetics, he will be revealed as the kidnapper. Waldo feeds the cardiogram of Dr. Rich into the robot.

Dr. Rich's daughter scolds him for not eating because he is so busy working, then leaves him. The robot arrives via a car driven by Waldo and Lefty, and attacks Rich's daughter. It then comes for Rich, who shoots the robot in vain before being attacked. The detectives, Gaby, and Gema arrive a short time later and discover Rich and his daughter, both dead. The robot is still in the doctor's office, and the foursome attack it, but they are all knocked out. When they regain consciousness, they realise that they are indeed up against a robot.

Dr. Chavez, an explosives expert, creates a device that explodes and sends up smoke. He uses it as a diversion to escape Orlak's lab, but the robot is sent after him. He arrives at Gaby's and begs her to call the police. The robot is right behind him, and smashes its way through Gaby's door. It knocks both her and Dr. Chavez out and takes the doctor.

Hill and Roca come up with a way to turn humans into robots: a bracelet made of a material that works with the conductivity of the skin. Orlak is pleased, and tells them to get to work. The finished product disturbs the brain and seizes the will and nervous system, turning people into puppets. Orlak demands that Hill and Roca demonstrate how the bracelet works, and forces them to use Chavez as a human guinea pig. Orlak puts the bracelet on Chavez, and Dr. Roca uses the controller to make Chavez walk around and raise his arms. An excited Orlak grabs the controller and presses several of the controls at once, stopping Chavez's heart. Hill and Roca are horrified, but Orlak does not care that the man is dead – he now understands the limits of the device and plans to construct many more bracelets in order to enslave the human race.

Over a meal at Gaby and Gema's, Arturo theorises that the robot is directed by cardio impulses, hence the missing cardiograms. Gaby laments that they were unable to learn anything from Dr. Rich before he was killed. Arturo has an epiphany, realising that it was not a coincidence that Dr. Rich was killed seconds before they arrived. Arturo points out that Orlak was present when they discussed visiting Rich, and concludes that Orlak orchestrated Rich's death to prevent him from talking to the foursome.

The group travels to Orlak's to confront him. Lefty lets them into the house and leads them to the lab, where Orlak awaits them. Arturo tells Orlak that they believe that he is behind the disappearance of the scientists, and orders Orlak to come to police headquarters. Orlak is prepared, however, and has one of his men pull a gun on the foursome, while another releases the robot. Gaby asks Orlak why he betrayed her uncle. Orlak responds that every action he has taken has been in pursuit of his dream, which has now been achieved. Orlak has a bracelet put on Gema and demonstrates how it can be used to control the nervous system. Gaby is horrified and calls Orlak a murderer. One of Orlak's men attempts to put a bracelet on Gaby, but she fights him off and puts the bracelet on the robot's wrist instead. The robot goes haywire and begins to attack Orlak's men. Gaby removes Gema's bracelet while Arturo fights Orlak and Chava attacks some of the other men. The robot crushes one man to death before Gaby destroys the bracelet controller, causing the robot to explode in a shower of sparks. Orlak escapes and takes Carfax with him. The robot and various pieces of broken equipment set the lab alight, and the women and detectives flee as the building is engulfed in flames. They assume that Orlak has been killed in the inferno.

Orlak is not dead, however. Instead, he is plotting his revenge against Gaby, Gema, Arturo, and Chava for ruining his plans. To that end, he sends Carfax to abduct one of Gaby and Gema's fellow female wrestlers.

Gaby's promoter asks her and Gema if they know the whereabouts of the kidnapped wrestler, Berta Reyes, who disappeared without a trace two days earlier. Gaby and Gema know nothing about the disappearance, so the promoter departs to call the police.

Orlak transfers Carfax's brain and physical strength into Berta, then puts a bracelet on her to control her. He plans to use Berta to kill Gaby in the wrestling ring, then direct her to kill Gema and the detectives. He dresses Berta in a protective wire mesh suit, and covers her face with a mask to prevent her from being recognised. Orlak dubs his new remote-controlled killing machine "Elektra", and markets her to the wrestling world as an American champion wrestler. Elektra defeats countless opponents and is eventually challenged by Gaby.

Gema has a bad feeling about Elektra and warns Gaby to be careful during their fight, but Gaby is confident that she will win. The detectives are in the audience for the fight, as is Orlak, who is armed with his controller. Gaby initially seems to be winning the bout, but then Elektra fights back, using illegal moves and knocking out the referee. Gema spots one of Orlak's men in the crowd and puts him in a headlock, then forces him to tell her about Orlak's plan. She takes him to a policeman working security, then jumps into the ring to try to help Gaby. Gaby is knocked out and Gema alerts the detectives to the danger. With Arturo and Chava in hot pursuit, Orlak flees and calls Elektra to him.

The detectives mount a search of the building, preventing Elektra and Orlak from escaping. In desperation, they ascend a flight of stairs that leads to the area above the ring. Gaby, Gema, Arturo, Chava, and several policemen and bystanders congregate at the bottom of the stairs. Arturo goes up the stairs to apprehend Orlak and Elektra, and the gathered crowd hurries back to the ring to watch Arturo tangle with his two opponents in the gantry above. Arturo attempts to reason with Orlak, but Orlak sets Elektra on Arturo and she pushes Arturo over the gantry railing. Arturo dangles above the wrestling ring while Elektra attempts to loosen his grip. Chava tries to shoot Elektra, but the wire mesh in her costume protects her from the bullets. Gaby tells Chava to shoot Orlak instead, since he controls Elektra. Chava shoots both the bracelet controller and Orlak. Elektra tumbles onto the mat below, followed by Orlak. Arturo hurries downstairs and steps into the ring to check on them, but they are both dead. A grim Gaby, Gema, Arturo, and Chava depart. The lights above the ring are switched off, leaving Orlak and his dead dream in the dark.

Cast

Joaquín Cordero (Arturo Campos), Regina Torné (Gaby Reyna), Héctor Lechuga (Chava Lopez), Malú Reyes (Gema Nelson), Carlos Agostí (Dr. Orlak), Genaro Moreno (Waldo), Pascual García Peña (Professor Reyna, Gaby's uncle), Gloria Chávez (Berta Reyes / Elektra), Gerardo Zepeda (Carfax), Victorio Blanco (Vagrant) with Leo Herrera, Eduardo MacGregor, Sally Winters and René Barrera

Production

Story and Adaptation – Alfredo Salazar
Producer – Guillermo Calderón
Director – René Cardona
Music – Antonio Díaz Conde
Cinematography – Raúl Martínez Solares

Film Editing – Jorge Busto
Assistant Editor – Joaquín Ceballos
Production Design – José Rodríguez Granada
Set Decoration – Carlos Arjona
Makeup Artist – María del Castillo
Head of Production – Enrique L. Morfín
Production Manager – Alfredo Salazar
Assistant Director – Manuel Alcayde
Sub-Director – Valerio Olivo
Dialogue Recordist – Eduardo Arjona
Sound Supervisor – James L. Fields
Sound Editor – José Li-ho
Sound Re-recordist – Galdino R. Samperio
Colour Technician – Rafael Leal

Produced by Cinematográfica Calderón S.A.
Filmed at Estudios Churubusco Azteca, Churubusco, Mexico City

Analysis

Over the course of its run, *The Avengers* became a truly international phenomenon, sold to dozens of countries and translated into a host of languages: in France, it became *Chapeau Melon et Bottes de Cuir*; in Spain, *Los Vengadores*; in the Netherlands, *De Wrekers*. Unsurprisingly, the series was adapted for different mediums in a number of countries in an effort to capitalise on its global success. South Africa produced an *Avengers* radio series, adapting Emma Peel and Tara King episodes for audio. Tie-in novels were translated into everything from Dutch to Portuguese. Comic strips, published in the pages of *Tele Poche* in France and by Gold Key in the United States, followed Steed and Emma as they embarked on brand new adventures. In Germany, Diana Rigg was persuaded to reprise her Emma Peel role in the short film *Das Diadem*.

Of course, not everything bestowed with a touch of the *Avengers* magic was sanctioned by the rights holders. Bootleg *Avengers* merchandise has been produced since the sixties, and the pirating of episodes of the show became common practice with the advent of VHS. In addition, many properties, from *Wonder Woman* to *X-Men*, have blatantly "borrowed" elements of Avengerland and its characters. However, the series was not only exploited by well-known properties, as evidenced by a copyright-flouting curiosity that emerged at the end of the sixties. *Las Luchadoras vs. el Robot Asesino* (*The Wrestling Women vs. the Killer Robot*) is a 1969 Mexican wrestling movie that borrows liberally from the colour Emma Peel episode *Return of the Cybernauts*. The film reuses the basic premise of, and lifts entire scenes and lines of dialogue from, the original episode, then mixes them with elements of the grindhouse and wrestling movie genres and a few innovations of its own to create arguably the most bizarre concoction inspired by the series, albeit one that serves as an indicator of just how influential the series had become by 1969.

Aside from its mere existence, the film is surprising in a number of ways. As a low-budget, somewhat schlocky movie that flagrantly rips off the original episode, one would expect it to be chock full of gratuitous, pulpy sex and violence, a prime example of the grindhouse or exploitation genre of cinema. Instead, the film subverts expectations when it comes to both sex and violence by failing to include significant examples of either. (There was, apparently, a more lurid version of the film that included more sexually explicit and violent material and was released under the title *El Asesino Loco y el Sexo* (*The Mad Killer and Sex*), but that version was not the one viewed for this analysis.) Indeed, the film's sexual or sexualised content is minimal. Dr. Rich's daughter wears a modest dressing gown, while the nightgown worn by Berta Reyes, Gema and Gaby's fellow wrestler, is only slightly revealing and receives very little screentime, appearing in only one brief close-up, after which the camera does not linger on her form. Gaby and Gema are also not overly sexualised. Their everyday wear consists of shirt and trouser ensembles, as well as sixties dresses and miniskirts, but the latter are paired with tame tops to form colourful, attractive outfits that flatter and are fashionable without being gratuitously revealing. Their wrestling outfits are similarly tame, consisting of leotards that, while figure hugging, cover the whole body and seem to be designed more for ease of movement than to put the actresses' figures on display. (Gaby and Gema's wrestling opponents wear what are, essentially, one-piece swimsuits; they are somewhat revealing, but not overwhelmingly so.) Even a scene in which Gaby and Gema converse while showering in the locker room is framed so as not to be voyeuristic, with the women in neighbouring high-walled cubicles with only their heads and shoulders visible. The most overtly sexualised moment in the film begins with Orlak's nurse lifting the hem of her uniform to adjust her stocking's attachment to its suspender belt while Carfax (who possibly takes his name from the abbey in Bram Stoker's *Dracula*) looks on. The nurse then releases Carfax from his cell, and, foolishly, turns her back on him. Carfax attacks her and tears open the top of her uniform, but very little flesh is shown before the camera cuts away. Later, when Orlak finds her body, her uniform does not seem to be significantly disturbed at all, the primary evidence of the attack being bloody scratches on her face and neck. The entire sequence is completely at odds with the rest of the piece and feels shoehorned in, as if the creatives were told that it was mandatory that some sort of sexualised scene be included.

Violence of any consequence is also in short supply. The attack on the nurse is a rare extreme example, and is also one of the few scenes that features blood, the other being when the robot squeezes one of Orlak's men to death, causing him to bleed from the mouth. Another violent moment comes shortly after Orlak discovers the nurse's body, when he uses a whip to force Carfax back into his cell. However, the whip is not even shown striking Carfax, with the camera focusing on Orlak cracking the whip while Carfax himself remains off-screen. The violence in this scene is therefore mostly implied. Elsewhere, the robot's attacks are so tame as to be laughable. The blows it lands have so little force behind them that, in reality, the robot would not even be able to knock its victims over, let alone kill them or render them unconscious. Gaby and Gema's wrestling bouts, meanwhile, consist of a series of holds and throws that are more technical than aggressive. They serve to demonstrate that Gaby and Gema are capable, skilled fighters who can handle themselves in the ring, but are not gratuitously violent or framed as sexualised catfights. Indeed, aside from Gaby's fight against Elektra, during which Elektra attempts to kill Gaby, the bouts do not even evoke a sense of peril.

In addition to the sparing use of sex and violence, another surprise comes in the form of Gaby and Gema's relationship. Given that both women are competitive wrestlers and the film is inherently schlocky in feel, one automatically assumes that the pair will develop a bitter rivalry that culminates in a climactic catfight. This result seems inevitable from the moment Gaby's promoter introduces Gema as a wrestler who has just finished a successful international wrestling tour, and asks Gaby to help train her. After the promoter departs, the viewer waits for the pair to start sizing each other up while exchanging veiled catty remarks and smiling brittlely at each other, but the pleasantries and smiles the pair trade are genuine, lacking any undercurrent of jealousy or hostility. Gaby then offers to start training Gema immediately, and the women get into position on the mat, but where the audience expects the first catfight to ensue, the film instead switches to a new scene, completely subverting expectations. We do not return to the duo until the training is over and they are in the locker room. There, the sense of goodwill between them continues, with Gema thanking Gaby for her help and Gaby demurring that she was happy to be of assistance. Gema then follows up her gratitude with kind concern, noting that Gaby seems sad and asking her if she is all right. Gaby explains that she is worried because her uncle, her only living family member, is missing. Gema expresses sympathy for Gaby's plight, and offers to assist in whatever way she can. Though Gema has no personal connection to the mystery, true to her word, she assists Gaby throughout the investigation. She also looks out for Gaby's wellbeing, cautioning Gaby to be careful in her fight against Elektra, before spotting one of Orlak's henchmen in the crowd during the fight and questioning him about Orlak's plot. She then assists Gaby in the ring against Elektra at great personal risk to herself. The gestures of kindness go both ways, with Gaby inviting Gema, who is from out of town and knows no one, to stay with her. A gracious Gema says the offer sounds wonderful, but initially declines because she does not want to impose. She only accepts Gaby's offer when Gaby says that, with her uncle missing, she could use the company. Once Gema moves in, the pair are depicted as happy roommates, with Gaby inviting Gema to help choose a colour to repaint their shared home, and the pair cooking meals for visitors. Gaby also saves Gema's life by freeing her from Orlak's control, removing the will-suppressing bracelet before any harm can come to her. The women's lack of rivalry even extends to the men in their lives, with each woman pairing off with one of the male detectives with nary a hint that either woman covets what the other has. All in all, it is a very amiable relationship marked by kindness and goodwill, the expectation that the women would compete with one another never fulfilled. Given that female characters are often pitted against each another, it is a refreshing surprise to see the pair form a warm, mutually supportive friendship.

The depiction of the women is also surprising in other ways. When Arturo and Chava are introduced as the detectives in charge of investigating the kidnappings, one assumes that Gaby and Gema will be sidelined, left to wait upon events while the men solve the case. In a delightfully unexpected twist, however, the inclusion of the detectives instead enables the women to directly participate in the investigation. Arturo and Chava bring Gaby and Gema along to survey the sites of the abductions of Drs. Roca and Chavez. At the latter site, Arturo allows Gaby to join him in questioning Chavez's secretary, during which she asks what the abductor looked like and if he struck the secretary with the same chopping motion used on Gaby herself. Meanwhile, Gema searches Dr. Chavez's files with Chava and discovers that the doctor's medical records are missing, just as the other kidnapped scientists' records were, then posits that the abductor could be a karate expert. The women also accompany the detectives on their visit to the home of Dr. Rich, with the women clearly intending to take part in the questioning of Rich. The women are also included when the detectives visit their superior and confront Orlak about his crimes. While it is unrealistic that the detectives would let two civilians attend crime scenes and actively participate in a police investigation, Gaby and Gema's involvement subverts the expectation that the detectives would fill Steed and Emma's investigative roles and turn the movie into a primarily male-dominated one. The film also allows all of the characters to play a role in solving the mystery and / or defeating the villain. Arturo makes the connection between Orlak's presence when the foursome announced their plan to visit Dr. Rich and the attack on Rich seconds before they arrived, which allows the group to identify Orlak as the villain of the piece. Gaby works out the robot's mode of attack (chopping blows), prevents the group from being put under Orlak's control by placing a bracelet on the robot to make it malfunction and attack the villains, and saves the day – and Arturo's life – at the movie's climax by telling Chava to shoot Orlak rather than the armoured Elektra, reasoning that taking Orlak out of the equation will neutralise both Elektra and Orlak in one fell swoop. Gema spots Orlak's man in the crowd at Gaby and Elektra's wrestling match and forces him to tell her everything about Orlak's plot, then alerts the detectives to the peril. Even Chava, the slapstick comedy character, ultimately kills Orlak and has some "eureka" moments, predicting that there will be a string of scientist abductions and suggesting that the kidnapper is a robot, a theory that initially invites ridicule, but which is proven to be correct.

The film also does not undermine the women's established characterisation for the sake of the story. Television and films of the period often made a habit of turning capable female leads into helpless incompetents or having them behave illogically at choice moments in order to serve the plot or create a sense of peril. The film, refreshingly, resists this urge. When Gaby is knocked out by the robot, it is either because the robot hits her from behind before she is even aware of its presence, or because it is supernaturally strong. Elektra's superhuman strength also gives her the upper hand in her fight against Gaby. These encounters do not undermine Gaby's status as a champion wrestler, but instead demonstrate that her opponents are powerful enough to overcome any opponent, no matter how skilled. The same logic applies to Gema, who also comes out the worse for it in her tangles with the robot and Elektra, but whose lauded prowess is backed up by her ability to subdue one of Orlak's goons and her own victory in the ring. Rather than have the women's fighting skills suddenly abandon them to create suspenseful action sequences, therefore, the film instead allows their skill level to remain constant, and ratchets up the tension by pitting them against opponents that are impossible for any human being to defeat.

Gaby's characterisation is also a pleasant surprise. The film portrays her as a kind, generous person who looks out for her uncle and warmly extends the hand of friendship to Gema. She also has a lively sense of humour, teasing her uncle and exchanging banter with others in scenes that demonstrate that she does not take herself too seriously. However, Gaby's good-naturedness should not be mistaken for meekness. Cast in the *Avengers* mould, Gaby is a strong heroine, and her goodwill evaporates when people abuse it. When her uncle nags her to quit wrestling and get married, she does not allow her affection for him to prevent her from giving as good as she gets in response, stating that she likes wrestling and pointing out that her uncle is a bachelor who has not taken his own advice. This exchange also demonstrates Gaby's independence – she does not need or want a husband to support her, but instead prefers to make her own way with her wrestling career, which is financially lucrative enough to allow her to afford a spacious abode and a wardrobe of on-trend fashions. She is also extremely confident, and refuses to undersell or minimise her skills in order to make others feel better about themselves. She frankly states that one opponent was too inexperienced to beat her, and is equally certain that she will be able to defeat Elektra, in spite of the mystery woman's unbeaten record. Gaby's record in the ring over the course of the film proves that she is not bragging about her abilities when she makes these claims, and she manages to hold her own against Elektra until the woman's superhuman strength is activated. She is equally capable of holding her own during the investigation into the missing scientists, going along to crime scenes and questioning witnesses with the same confidence she displays in the ring. However, Gaby's independence and confidence do not render her too proud to seek or receive support, be it by allowing Arturo to help her to her feet after being attacked by the robot, or asking Gema to keep her company when she is feeling upset about her uncle's disappearance. Gaby also does not believe that her wrestling career requires her to sacrifice her femininity – she enjoys dressing up in colourful clothes and accessorising her looks with jewellery, handbags, and fashionable shoes. Gaby is also unafraid to show a range of emotions. She is tough in the ring, sad and vulnerable (but never hysterical) when her uncle is missing, and righteously angry and vengeful when she discovers that he has been killed. The film therefore depicts Gaby, not as a one-note character, but as a multi-faceted human being, one who is capable, likeable, and sometimes vulnerable; does not tolerate disrespect; and refuses to adhere to anyone's beliefs regarding how she should look or behave as a woman or competitive wrestler.

Gema is more thinly drawn than Gaby, but is still an endearing character. Like Gaby, she is kind and empathetic, picking up on Gaby's distress regarding her missing uncle and offering to help however she can. She is playful and has a sunny disposition, qualities that are established when Chava asks for a demonstration of her wrestling skills and Gema cheerfully obliges by putting him in a hold, implying that she does not take herself or her skills so seriously that she will not indulge in what could be interpreted as a frivolous request. Gema is not all sweetness and light, however. She is formidable in the ring, and, if she is pushed too far, her temper frays and her goodwill drains away, to the point that even friends and allies find themselves on the receiving end of her cutting words, as Chava does when he asks her why she did not protect him from the robot. Gema, also a bit worse for wear, sarcastically replies that she was drinking margaritas on the beach while Chava was being attacked, and later elbows him in annoyance. Gema's harder edge also comes to the fore when Gaby's life is on the line. Putting Orlak's underling into a headlock, she mercilessly interrogates him until he tells her about the true nature of Gaby's opponent, then drags him to a policeman and dives into the ring to help Gaby. Despite sharing some of Gaby's qualities – such as strength and empathy – Gema therefore feels distinct, her lighter, more playful sense of humour and fierier temper setting her apart from the more composed, poised Gaby.

Interestingly, the strong and positive portrayals of Gaby and Gema may be attributable to their film being part of director René Cardona's series of five female wrestler films, which began with 1963's *Las luchadoras contra el médico asesino* (English title: *Doctor Doom*) and concluded with this film. These films were the feminine counterparts of the popular "lucha" or "luchador" films that starred male wrestlers, but were more than an attempt to cash in on the trend. The women wrestlers featured in the films were unable to wrestle in Mexico City due to a ban on female wrestling in the capital, meaning they were forced to miss out on the country's largest audience and compete elsewhere in their homeland. The films therefore served as a way for the starring female wrestlers to flout the ban and be exposed to a larger audience. If these films were intended to up the profile of the starring female wrestlers and their sport, the people behind the films would hardly want to portray the female wrestlers as weak, ineffectual, or unable to hold their own in the ring, and this may explain why Gaby and Gema are depicted as surprisingly well-rounded and formidable characters.

Captain Arturo Campos and his assistant Chava Lopez round out the investigative foursome. The two men supposedly work for the "secret service", a creative choice likely made in an attempt to replicate *The Avengers*' espionage format. However, for all intents and purposes, they operate like ordinary police detectives and report to a superior who complains about their lack of results after reading a newspaper article that asks why the "police" – which is clearly intended to be a reference to Arturo and Chava, begging the question as to why no one picked up on the inconsistent terminology used to describe them – have done nothing to stop more scientists from being kidnapped. Like Gema, the detectives are more thinly drawn than Gaby, with Arturo the handsome, serious, competent one, while Chava is cast as the comic relief – he is easily subdued by Gema, nearly faints at the sight of a dead body, attacks the robot by jumping on its back and punching it, and delivers lines that could have been written for a cartoon character: after he has been attacked by the robot, he groans, "Did anyone get the licence plate? ... A truck passed over me". Chava's silliness and slapstick qualities are at odds with the movie's overall tone, which skews toward drama rather than broad comedy. As a result, the character of Chava often feels out of place, as though he has wandered in from another, very different film. However, as previously discussed, Chava is also responsible for some breakthroughs in the case and ultimately kills Orlak, actions that go some way toward making him seem like a credible character who is necessary to the plot, rather than a comedy act shoehorned into the movie for cheap laughs.

Predictably, the two detectives are attracted to Gaby and Gema, with the poised Gaby paired off with the serious Arturo, and the bubblier Gema placed with the comedic Chava. The people behind the movie clearly deemed some sort of romantic element to be essential to the film's success, but the romances are unnecessary to the plot and completely at odds with the film's thriller tone. As a result, like Chava's broad comedy moments, the romance feels shoehorned in, a by-the-numbers story component that smacks of unoriginality. There is also an element of improbability at work in one of the romances, as the reasons for Gema's attraction to the goofy Chava are somewhat difficult to divine. Presumably, he appeals to her lively sense of humour, and she also seems to have an urge to look after him, wincing in sympathy at the size of the robot-inflicted bump on his head. However, improbability aside, it must be said that the relationships between the men and the women are extremely respectful. At no point do the male detectives condescend to the women regarding their physical or intellectual capabilities. Instead, they include them in their investigation as much as possible, and any suggestions that the women offer are given the same amount of consideration as the men's. (Indeed, Arturo probably gives the women's ideas more credence than anything Chava has to offer!) The men also seem unthreatened by the women's wrestling abilities, and do not make any derisive comments about their decision to pursue a wrestling career rather than settle down. Instead, Chava asks Gema to demonstrate some wrestling moves and relies on her to protect him from the robot, and both men cheer Gaby on in the ring. Gaby and Gema, in turn, do not attempt to frame themselves as "superior" to the men, and instead are more interested in an equal relationship. Even the sharing of meals is respectful and marked by a sense of equality, with the men asking the women out for dinner, and the women reciprocating by hosting the men at their home. Overall, therefore, while the fact that the women and the detectives pair off is painfully predictable, the mutually respectful nature of those romances comes as something of a pleasant surprise.

The antithesis of Arturo and Chava's refreshing attitudes toward the women is Professor Reyna's opinion of Gaby's life choices. Though he is Gaby's only living relative, and she obviously has great affection for him, his treatment of her does not seem to warrant that affection. In the handful of scenes in which he appears, he tells Gaby that he doubted whether she would be able to beat her opponent in the ring and invites her for dinner, only to inform her that she will be the one cooking it. He also asks her to complete a small task at his lab before dinner, prompting Gaby to quip about being put to work, then uses derisive terms to describe the art of wrestling and proceeds to lecture her about getting married. While Gaby gives as good as she gets in their exchanges – she points out his hypocrisy in telling her to get married when he has remained a bachelor – and seems to dismiss some of his views as the harmless rantings of a member of the older generation, Professor Reyna's conversations with Gaby make him a rather unlikeable character. He is somewhat redeemed later in the story, when he is the first of the scientists to show any moral turpitude, flatly refusing to work with Orlak or assist in his plans for world domination in any way, a stand that ultimately costs him his life. Gaby is visibly upset by both his kidnapping and death and vows to avenge him, the strength of her emotions speaking to the depths of her affection for him. However, Gaby's affinity for her uncle and his moral stand against Orlak still somehow fail to negate the negative feelings evoked by his sexist lecturing of his niece.

Another (intentionally) unlikeable character is Orlak, the villain of the piece (who possibly takes his name from the 1924 horror film *The Hands of Orlac*, or, alternatively, the 1960 film *Orlak: El Infierno de Frankenstein* (English title: *The Hell of Frankenstein*), which featured Arturo's portrayer Joaquín Cordero in the title role). In addition to being unlikeable, he is also less interesting than his *Return of the Cybernauts* counterpart, Paul Beresford. Beresford kidnaps the scientists because he wants them to devise a way to punish Steed and Emma for the role they played in the death of his brother, Dr. Clement Armstrong, in the previous Cybernauts story, *The Cybernauts*. Unlike the episode, the film is not a sequel, and therefore does not have this backstory to draw upon in characterising its villain. Nevertheless, the film makes a stab at replicating the personal connection between the villain and the heroes that features in the episode. Initially, it does this by making Orlak the assistant of Gaby's uncle, Professor Reyna. This personal connection allows him to share friendly scenes with the heroes, and fires Gaby's anger when she discovers that someone her uncle trusted and relied upon was responsible for his death. The personal connection is strengthened when Orlak plots to kill the heroes with his latest creation, Elektra, as punishment for foiling his plans.

However, Orlak's quest for vengeance only emerges toward the end of the film, and therefore, unlike in the case of Beresford, revenge is not the impetus for Orlak's drive to create and use the will-controlling bracelets. The film is therefore forced to find another motivation for Orlak's diabolical plans, and opts for a creatively bankrupt spin on the "take over the world" trope, with Orlak seeking a way to turn the human race into puppets that he can control. While many films and series feature villains with a similar motivation, they typically embellish that motivation to create a richly characterised villain and provide a more engaging entertainment experience. The film, in contrast, provides no explanation as to why Orlak has chosen this particular means of world domination or what drove him to dedicate his life to controlling the human race. Compared to Peter Cushing's wonderfully mannered, yet viciously sinister and vengeful, Beresford, therefore, Orlak is a generic cartoon villain. As such, he is not very interesting or unique, and certainly does not give any of The Avengers' signature "diabolical masterminds" a run for their money. Indeed, his only notable villainous moments occur when he delivers a burst of maniacal laughter with such gusto that one genuinely believes him to be completely unhinged. His mild-mannered "Assistant Orlak" persona, in contrast, is fairly well realised. To achieve it, the actor merely dons a pair of glasses and adopts a more submissive demeanour, but these minor changes render Orlak almost unrecognisable, the audience only reminded of who he is when the character's name is spoken. Counterintuitively, the character is more interesting and nuanced when he is wearing his "disguise" than when he is himself, and one wonders if Orlak, and the film, would have been more engaging if the emphasis had been on the assistant incarnation rather than the mad scientist.

However, even the relatively thinly drawn Orlak seems nuanced when compared to Lefty, Waldo, and Orlak's other henchmen and assistants, who are so generic as to be barely distinguishable from one another. The flatness of these characters becomes even more apparent when one compares them to Beresford's assistant, Benson, whose presence alone enriches the episode by providing another connection to its predecessor, The Cybernauts. However, even if one sets aside Benson's status as a rare example of continuity in The Avengers, Frederick Jaeger's performance as the grim-faced, morally bankrupt, and slightly nervous character is one that Orlak's helpers cannot hope to match, though, admittedly, the script gives them little in the way of material to work with.

Despite containing several examples of fairly weak characterisation, the film does, surprisingly, evoke bursts of real emotion. Though they only interact in one scene, the relationship between Dr. Otto Rich and his daughter is imbued with genuine warmth. The daughter's concern for her father's well-being after he fails to eat because he is so wrapped up in his work rings true, as do their exchanged "I love yous" and Rich's affectionate reference to his late wife; the latter comment suggests that the pair's closeness has developed because they have had to rely on each other alone for a long time. After witnessing the pair's mutual affection, one cannot help but care enough about Rich and his daughter to mourn their demises. Later, the reactions of Gaby, Arturo, Gema and Chava to the daughter's dead body effectively convey their horror and revulsion at the sight, emotions that they pass on to the audience. Elsewhere, the fate of Gaby and Gema's fellow wrestler, Berta Reyes, adds an element of tragedy to the film's final act. Abducted by Orlak, infused with Carfax's strength and madness, and controlled by one of Orlak's bracelets, Berta's entire personality and sense of identity is subsumed and destroyed, replaced with the mindless killer drone that is Elektra. When she falls to her death at the film's conclusion, along with Orlak, none of the lead foursome seems to feel a sense of triumph at either person's demise. Instead, Arturo checks the bodies to confirm that they are dead, and the group departs, grim-faced and subdued. Collectively, they seem to be reflecting on the loss of life resulting from Orlak's plot. Episodes of adventure and telefantasy series made toward the end of the sixties often ended with a quip and a smile, all the havoc and death that filled the preceding fifty minutes seemingly forgotten. The film, in contrast, refuses to sweep the tragedy of Berta and the scientists' deaths under the carpet, ending on a reflective, sombre note, rather than a heroic or humourous one, a creative choice that encourages the audience to ponder the price of the leads' victory.

The film also manages to innovate amongst the plagiarism. The cardiograms used by the robot to locate its targets are inserted into a slot in the robot itself, rather than a separate computer, as in the episode. This innovation allows the viewer to see the inner workings of the robot, which are classic examples of sixties sci-fi design, all bright lights and whirring mechanisms. While cheesy by today's standards, the robot's inner workings are at least visually interesting and serve to differentiate it ever-so-slightly from a Cybernaut.

While exceeding expectations in many ways, the film also has many weaknesses, some of which have already been discussed. One additional weakness comes in the form of the long scenes devoted to Gaby and Gema's wrestling bouts. While these serve to establish their credentials as expert wrestlers whose skills are more than a match for any (human) opponent, they are also long and drawn out and bring the plot to a standstill (with the exception of the climactic final fight against Elektra). Of course, this is a wrestling movie, and it is safe to assume that such sequences are par for the course for the genre and would be appreciated by its fans. For the average viewer, however, these sequences quickly become tedious – one can only watch Gaby / Gema flip her opponent onto the mat so many times before the urge to skip to the next scene becomes unbearable.

The movie also quite obviously lacked the budget and skilled crews boasted by the colour Emma Peel episodes. Many of the sets are clearly very inexpensive: the same medicine cabinet appears in both Orlak and Professor Reyna's labs, suggesting that props and furniture were recycled to save money, while other sets, such as the female wrestlers' locker room and training area and the detectives' superior's office, are fairly bare bones, containing the minimum number of furnishings and props needed to convey their purpose. The mask used to depict Carfax's disfigured face is extremely fake looking, and the wardrobe, outside of Gaby and Gema's colourful fashions, consists mainly of a series of drab suits modelled by the male characters and forgettable ensembles worn by the female ones. The investigating foursome's escape from Orlak's clutches is also very badly staged. Threatened with having a bracelet put on her, Gaby knocks out the man carrying said bracelet, runs across the room to put it on the robot's wrist, then runs back across the room to push the controlled Gema out of Lefty's line of fire, all without encountering any resistance from Orlak or his men. Orlak's men then attempt to tame the robot as it goes haywire, and the camera cuts to Orlak, who has apparently been standing by and watching the scene unfold without making any attempt to stop Gaby. Arturo then attacks Orlak, and Gaby and Gema stand around while the pair fight and the business with the robot carries on in the background. Arturo then tells Gaby to destroy the bracelet controller, which explodes spectacularly (and ridiculously) at the slightest kick. The controller's destruction then, rather illogically, causes the robot to explode in a shower of flames and sparks. More sparks fly when Orlak and two of his men are pushed against some pieces of equipment during the fight. The sparks are presumably meant to signify that the people pushed against the equipment are being electrocuted, but while said electrocution seemingly kills his men, Orlak inexplicably survives. Orlak then runs away, but, despite being close by, Arturo makes no attempt to pursue him. The entire sequence is clearly intended to be a spectacular, climactic fight scene featuring all of the characters, but those choreographing it were apparently unable to co-ordinate more than one or two pieces of action at a time. The result is that, at any given moment, some of the characters are standing around instead of assisting their allies in the fight. Overall, the sequence is an unrealistic, illogical, and unengaging mess that is the antithesis of *The Avengers*' slickly choreographed fight scenes, and is perhaps the best indicator of the relative lack of professionalism at work in the production of the film.

Similarities to Return of the Cybernauts

The extent of the film's plagiarism of Return of the Cybernauts is evident from the number of elements that it has "borrowed" from the original episode. First of all, the robot itself is an obvious Cybernaut rip-off, virtually identical in appearance to the Cybernauts that appear in The Cybernauts and Return of the Cybernauts. As in the series, the film's robot is dressed in a black coat, trousers, gloves, hat and shoes, has a silver head with a molded face, and wears sunglasses. Like the Cybernauts, the robot has a stilted gait and attacks its victims by bending its arm at the elbow, raising it, and straightening it to unleash a slicing, karate chop-like blow. (Unlike in the series, however, the robot's blows are not accompanied by a whooshing sound.) Like its forebear, the robot makes a habit of smashing holes in doors to get to its victims and locks onto its targets using their cardiograms, with the film reiterating that a person's heartbeat is as unique as a fingerprint. The cardiogram cards themselves are also reminiscent of those in the episode, with a photo identifying the person on one side and a squiggly line representing the pattern of the person's heartbeat on the other. Like Steed and his associate Conroy, the investigating foursome of Gaby, Gema, Arturo and Chava notice that the missing scientists' medical records and / or cardiograms are missing, having been stolen for use with the robot. Arturo and Chava also admire the damage that the robot leaves behind, much the way Steed and Emma do in the Cybernaut episodes.

The basic plot of the episode is also replicated in the film, as are certain scenes and lines of dialogue. In both cases, the villain of the piece is using the robot to abduct scientists who possess the requisite expertise to help him achieve his goal. One abduction scene in the film is virtually identical to one in the episode, with the scientist attempting to escape the robot by car, only for the vehicle to be held in place by the incredibly strong robot. The scientist is then pulled from the car by the robot. In the episode, the Cybernaut smashes the vehicle's roof open and pulls the scientist (Dr. Neville) out through the slashed opening; in the film, the robot rips the driver side door of the car off and drags the scientist (Dr. Roca) out. In both cases, the villain abducts a trio of scientists, who are placed in separate cells. The villain then tells the kidnapped scientists that he will make them wealthy men if they assist him in his cause. In each case, one scientist agrees to assist the villain because he wants the money (Professor Chadwick in the episode; Dr. Roca in the film), another agrees because he believes that he has no choice (Dr. Neville in the episode; Dr. Hill in the film), and the third refuses to help the villain (Dr.

Russell in the episode; Professor Reyna in the film). In both instances, the refusing scientist (Russell / Reyna) is told by the villain that he is free to go, but when he tries to make his exit, the robot is revealed and kills him. In both cases, the death of their colleague serves as the final impetus for the other scientists to agree to help the villain with his scheme.

In both the episode and the film, another scientist (Dr. Garnett in the episode; Dr. Chavez in the film) is kidnapped to replace the one that has been killed. In each case, the robot arrives while the replacement's secretary is on the telephone with a friend, and stops in front of the replacement's office door. The secretary in both cases flirts with the robot, having not seen its face and believing it to be a tall, attractive man. In both instances, the secretary admiringly touches the robot's shoulders while complimenting it, and the robot responds by striking her with such force that she is thrown across the room and collapses. In both the episode and the film, the secretary is questioned about the incident, but is more interested in getting her picture in the paper than talking about the attack, asking if she can change into a revealing bikini that she has almost been arrested twice for wearing, and expressing disappointment when she is told that there will be no press. As in the episode, the film's secretary perks up when asked to describe the robot, rhapsodising about how big it was and claiming that the robot's eyes were misty with "his" desire for her. Gaby and Arturo split Steed's interrogative role in this scene, with Gaby asking (as Steed does) if the secretary's reference to eyes means that the secretary saw the robot's face, to which the secretary reluctantly admits, as in the original episode, that she did not. Gaby, like Steed, then replicates the robot's chopping motion and asks the secretary if the robot did not respond to her charms, but instead struck her in a similar way. As in the original episode, the film's secretary grudgingly confirms that that is what happened. Arturo then chimes in to respond to the secretary's comment that she is sure the robot found her very attractive, agreeing that the robot probably did, albeit ironically. Steed's response to the same comment, in contrast, indulges the woman's pride and self-flattery.

A scene in which the other two scientists tell the villain that they have explained the situation to Garnett / Chavez and persuaded him to assist in the scheme also appears in both versions. Garnett / Chavez, who in both instances is an explosives expert, then requests materials to build a prototype device. Garnett / Chavez is groused at by Benson / Waldo for requesting expensive materials, but counters that he understood that he had access to unlimited resources. Garnett / Chavez then builds a small explosive device in the shape of a box with the requested materials, before asking to see the villain. In another recycled scene, Garnett / Chavez holds the box out to the villain, who asks what it does. Garnett / Chavez then throws the box on the floor, which causes it to explode and release smoke, and escapes in the confusion. In both cases, the escaped scientist seeks refuge with one of the leads – in the episode, Emma; in the film, Gaby – but is retaken by the robot when Gaby / Emma goes to the kitchen to get him some water / a damp cloth for his head. Hearing the commotion, Emma / Gaby returns to the living area, but is knocked out by the robot. Gaby and Emma both complain about having a sore head after being attacked (Gaby to Gema, Arturo and Chava; Emma to Steed), and are reminded not to tangle with a robot / Cybernaut. The escaped scientist in both cases is returned to his cell, at which point the villain notices that one of the other two scientists has left his cell to work with the third scientist in his enforced abode. This prompts the villain of the piece to ask if the other two scientists are abusing his hospitality, but they reveal that they have come up with a means of achieving the villain's goal. In both cases, the two scientists (Neville and Chadwick in the episode; Hill and Roca in the film) create a device that they present to the villain: a bracelet that, when placed on a person, uses the conductivity of the skin to disrupt the brain and seize the will and nervous system, turning the person into a human puppet who can be directed by remote control. In both cases, the villain asks for a demonstration, and forces Chadwick and Neville / Roca and Hill to put a bracelet on Garnett / Chavez and move him around using the remote control. In both instances, the villain then grabs the remote control and uses multiple controls at once. This puts too much of a strain on Garnett / Chavez's heart, and kills him. The more moral scientist of the pair (Neville / Hill) runs over to check on the dead man, and is horrified to discover that he has been killed. The villain, however, is unperturbed, declaring that it is good to know the limits of the device and deeming the test a success. The villain of the piece then puts a bracelet on Gema / Emma and moves her around. He then attempts to put a bracelet on Gaby / Steed, who fights back. Steed / Gaby places the bracelet on the robot instead, which causes it to go haywire. In the ensuing fight, a character is crushed to death by the robot – in the episode, it is Beresford; in the film, it is one of Orlak's minions. The robot is only stopped when the bracelet's remote control is kicked / crushed underfoot by Gaby / Emma. Orlak's survival of this encounter allows him to plot another attack against the leads, which plays out in a wholly original segment that extends the film's running time well beyond the 50 minutes allotted to the episode. However, the number of scenes and elements that appear in both the episode and the film leaves no question as to how heavily the episode was plagiarised.

Similarities to The Avengers TV Series

The film also features a number of *Avengers*-ish elements outside of its similarities to *Return of the Cybernauts*. Like the series, the film generally eschews blood, showing it only twice: once in the form of the scratch marks on the dead nurse's body, and again when the man crushed to death by the robot is shown bleeding from the mouth. Gaby is also vaguely Emma Peel-like. The actress' reddish-brown, shoulder-length hair recalls Diana Rigg's auburn tresses, and Gaby tosses her mane in a very Emma-like way during her wrestling scenes. Gaby's fighting outfit – a blue bodystocking worn with silver ankle boots – recalls Emma's Emmapeeler catsuits, particularly the blue example worn in *Something Nasty in the Nursery* and *Mission: Highly Improbable*, which was dyed a similar shade and also paired with silver ankle boots. Like Emma, who donned catsuits in a variety of colours, Gaby wears another bodystocking in the film, this one in pink. Despite being a wrestler, rather than a karate / kung-fu expert like Emma, Gaby throws the odd karate chop into her routine in what appears to be a conscious effort to replicate Emma's fighting style. Orlak, meanwhile, has many 'mad scientist' equivalents in *The Avengers*, from *The Cybernauts*' Dr. Armstrong to Dr. Cresswell in *The Positive Negative Man*.

While the film was obviously produced with a much lower budget than the one allotted to *The Avengers* in 1969, the general look of the film's sets is in keeping with the aesthetic of sets in *The Avengers* and other contemporary sixties series. Orlak's lab is equipped with the requisite oversized pieces of high-tech equipment of indeterminate function, which were essential to any sixties television series lab set, including those featured in *The Avengers*. Professor Reyna's lab, meanwhile, comes equipped with a test tube set-up that recalls the one in Emma's flat in *The Positive Negative Man*. The wrestlers' training room, complete with large mat, is akin to Olga's training area in *The Correct Way to Kill*, while Gaby's airy, neutral-toned home recalls Emma's studio flat, which was equipped with a couch, a piano, and little else, save for her current project (e.g., science experiment set-up or in-progress abstract sculpture).

Certain plot elements also call to mind particular episodes of the series. Gema's theory that the abductor of the scientists is a karate expert echoes Emma's theory regarding the killer's identity in the original entry in the Cybernaut trilogy, *The Cybernauts*. Given that the film chose to draw on the trilogy's second instalment for inspiration, it seems likely that the creatives were aware of the original episode, and borrowed this theory from it for

Gema to posit. Furthermore, there is a scene in the film that is reminiscent of one in the original Cybernaut episode, in which the robot is shot several times by one of its victims, but the bullets (naturally) have no effect. Gaby's desire to avenge a loved one, i.e., her uncle, meanwhile, calls to mind Dr. David Keel's drive to avenge the death of his fiancée in The Avengers' first episode, Hot Snow, though it must be acknowledged that The Avengers was far from the only series to feature a character motivated by revenge. The film's surgery scene, which features repeated shots of a piece of equipment measuring milliamperes, recalls discomfiting scenes featuring the use of unusual equipment during a surgical procedure in the likes of Whoever Shot Poor George Oblique Stroke XR40? and The Gravediggers. Orlak's creation of a "human robot" in the form of Elektra, meanwhile, anticipates the man-machine hybrid Felix Kane, who features in the Cybernaut trilogy's final entry, The Last of the Cybernauts...??

Verdict

A low-budget production that shamelessly lifts its plot and entire scenes from Return of the Cybernauts and mixes them with elements of the wrestling and grindhouse genres, this film nevertheless manages to be more than the schlocky piece that one might expect. Its depiction of its heroine and her dynamics with her male and female co-investigators is surprisingly progressive, and "shocking" examples of sex and violence are kept to a minimum. The film's liberal reuse of material and elements from Return of the Cybernauts, meanwhile, demonstrates the extent of The Avengers' sphere of influence, which, by 1969, clearly stretched well across the pond to Mexico. If imitation is the sincerest form of flattery, then this shameless rip-off of Avengerland is proof positive that the series' plots, sci-fi and fantasy stylings, and physically formidable heroines were considered to be part of a formula that, if replicated, guaranteed success. The film should therefore raise a smile from any Avengers fan who recognises that its very existence tacitly reaffirms that the show was a titan of popular culture, influencing projects in ways big and small. As a film in and of itself, it is an interesting curio rather than an essential watch for Avengers fans, but those who give it a look will likely be pleasantly surprised that there is enjoyment to be had beyond spotting the copied elements.

DAS DIADEM /
DER GOLDENE SCHLUSSEL

ALAN HAYES

Project Type: Short Film Series
Release Date: 1968-69 (West Germany)

Synopses

While essentially one film, this production was released in three different editions. Synopses follow for each of the variants.

Das Diadem (The Tiara)

A 17 minute 30 second short film, issued in monochrome

Emma Peel descends in her Piper Cherokee PA-28 light aircraft and lands on the tarmac runway of an airfield. We see, in extreme close up, an eye – she is being spied on. She removes her headset and exits the plane, picking up a small vinyl-finished case. She walks the short distance to her Mercedes-Benz 250SL Automatic sports car which is parked up just inside a hangar. She drops the case on the back seat of the car before driving off. As she disappears from view, we see the dark-trousered legs of a man wander into the foreground...

Mrs. Peel arrives at her destination, and drives the Mercedes down a suburban road lined with residential properties. She brings the car to a halt on the paved driveway of one of the houses, presumably the one in which she lives. As she retrieves the case from the back seat and closes the car door, a heavy-set man with shaven hair is reflected in the side-view mirror. Unaware of the man's presence, Emma skips merrily around to the back of the property, and enters the house via large wooden double doors.

In her lounge, she places the case on an occasional table next to the sofa. She sits down and removes her necklace, on which, rather than a jewel, hangs the golden key to her case. She ensures that the case is locked before hanging the necklace around her neck once more. She goes over to the bookcase and deposits the case in a cupboard at its centre which she also locks.

At the front of the house, the heavy-set man watches from behind the perimeter wall as Emma picks up her diving suit and breathing equipment. She takes them around to the back of the car and places them in the boot, slamming it shut. She then reverses the car out of the driveway and heads off down the road, taking the first left turn.

The scene cuts to the nearby Dolphinarium where Mrs. Peel is swimming in the pool with dolphins, and taking photographs with an underwater camera. Unbeknownst to her, the golden key drops from her neck to the bottom of the pool. It also escapes her attention that the man with shaven hair has followed her there and is watching from cover. After she has climbed from the water and left, her pursuer – wearing a wetsuit and dive mask – jumps into the pool and searches for the dropped necklace and golden key.

Mrs. Peel returns home in her sports car. Inside, she emerges from her darkroom and studies one of the photographs that she took at the pool. She notices something alarming about it and realises that she has dropped the necklace and golden key in the Dolphinarium pool. She dashes outside to the car…

At the pool, the man with a shaved head pulls himself up out of the water just as Mrs. Peel enters and runs down the stairs towards him. He drops beneath the surface and swims off, closing an underwater gate behind him. Emma attempts to follow him on dry land, but finds the door leading in the same direction is locked. She inserts a small charge into the keyhole. It explodes and the door swings open invitingly.

Beyond it, she finds a maintenance room filled with pipes, valves and gauges. She looks around, but cannot see her foe. He is working his way around the pipes, seeking a way to make his escape. A cat and mouse chase ensues, with it not being entirely clear who is chasing whom. Eventually, he finds a pressure valve, which he turns, releasing gas vapour into the room.

Emma is nearly overcome by the fumes. Holding a handkerchief to her nose and mouth, she eventually discovers ladder rungs built into the tiled wall. She appears to collapse, but gets a second wind and climbs them, exiting through an inspection hatch in the ceiling. This leads out onto the forecourt, right next to where she has parked her sports car. She drives off and returns home, where she sits on the sofa and consoles herself with a glass of Champagne.

The scene changes to a nightclub, where the man with the shaved hair is sitting on a bench by the entrance, next to a telephone. He dials a number. At home, Mrs. Peel answers the call. They have a brief conversation, presumably to arrange a meeting at the club, the caller playing with the golden key and chain in his hand as he talks. Mrs. Peel appears pensive, but soon decides what to do – she must get the golden key back. She runs outside to the car.

Emma arrives at the nightclub and the man with the shaved head leaves furtively a few seconds later. She takes in the scene: there are people at tables and sitting at the bar. They are smoking, drinking, winking at her suggestively, watching... She feels uneasy, as if all eyes are upon her. Not seeing the man from the pool there, she realises that she has been duped and makes a swift exit...

Back at Mrs. Peel's house, the shaven-haired man has broken into the cupboard and takes out the little case. He is trying to open it with the golden key when Emma enters and advances upon him from his blind side. She gives him a kick, taking him by surprise. They fight, but his is a losing battle against Mrs. Peel's karate blows and vicious kicks. He draws a revolver but is disarmed, Emma kicking it away out of reach. He tries grabbing her arms, but she breaks free and deals out the final blow. He collapses, unconscious, his head knocking against the case.

The case falls open, revealing its bounty: a ceramic piggy bank.

With her adversary lying prone on the lounge carpet, Emma treats herself to another glass of Champagne. After this little breather, she smashes open the piggy bank and finds it contains a somewhat crumpled map, with a route marked to what appears to be a castle. She drives through the night to this destination.

Outside her house, Mrs. Peel's unfortunate opponent has recovered consciousness and makes a radio call from his car, warning his confederate to expect a visitor. He sets off after her.

One of the gang places a diversion sign on the route, in the hope of throwing Mrs. Peel off the scent, but she ignores it and continues on the route indicated on the map. Seeing that this has happened, the shaven-headed man radios through again, with the result that his accomplice at the castle releases a snake from a basket – an added peril for Mrs. Peel to face.

Emma arrives at the castle in her Mercedes. She pulls up by a small bridge over the surrounding moat and walks across it to the front door. As she does, she notices a light go off inside the building, turned off by the accomplice of her defeated opponent. She finds the door is not locked and enters.

The entrance hall is lit only by a candle, the flickering light of which barely penetrates the gloom. She takes hold of the candlestick and searches the room. The flame picks out an ornate clock face, relief sculptures and various paintings, but Emma does not spot the snake which is slithering around her feet. She finds a mirror – only to see an adversary appear behind her in the reflection! This man carries a revolver and wears a stocking over his face to disguise his features.

The snake is about to attack when Mrs. Peel blows out the candle flame, drops the candlestick to the floor, and engages the stockinged man in combat. She throws him to the floor. He quickly leaps back up and resumes the contest, but it is soon concluded when she karate chops him and renders him unconscious.

A moment later, a second stocking-faced man enters carrying a diamond tiara on a felt cushion. He is quickly despatched by Mrs. Peel, who floors him by pulling a rug from under him. She then takes the tiara and descends a spiral staircase.

The second gang member comes to his senses alongside her other victim and they descend the stairs in search of their quarry. At the same time, their shaven-headed accomplice pulls up outside the castle in his Citroën.

Mrs. Peel runs along a narrow, painting-lined corridor and hides herself in one of two large chests placed against the left-hand wall. The stocking-faced hoodlums burst in. One of them carries a submachine gun, and he takes great pleasure in firing it at the chest in which Emma is hiding. He then fires off a second burst just for kicks.

Meanwhile, their shaven-headed confederate enters the castle and falls victim to the snake, which bites him on the ankle.

Making sure to load fresh cartridges into the machine gun, the other two gang members investigate the chest. Instead of containing the bullet-riddled body of Mrs. Peel, they are shocked to find it is actually the entrance to a staircase which leads down into the dark bowels of the castle. They investigate.

Emma has, by now, found her way out of the castle. She stands on a second bridge that stretches across the moat and, watched by a swan, studies the tiara.

In the castle entrance hall, the shaven-headed man lies dead, eyes staring into eternity, as the snake slithers across his corpse.

Emma makes for the main entrance of the castle. When she reaches the bridge there, she realises that she is faced with gang members on both sides, cutting off her retreat. She takes them on. They have little hope against her. She outnumbers them one to two! She despatches both with a series of devastating karate chops – and both end up in the moat.

Mrs. Peel smiles at the swan, which seems nonplussed, as if this is an everyday occurrence. She drives off into the night as the defeated gang members – those that are still alive – drag themselves from the cold waters.

Der Goldene Schlüssel (The Golden Key)

A 6 minute 47 second truncated version of Das Diadem, *issued in colour*

Emma Peel lands her Piper Cherokee PA-28 light aircraft on the tarmac runway of an airfield. She removes her headset and exits the plane, picking up a small yellow case. She walks the short distance to her flame red Mercedes-Benz 250SL Automatic sports car which is parked up just inside a hangar. She drops the yellow case on the back seat before driving off in the car. As she disappears from view, we see the dark-trousered legs of a man wander into the foreground. Her arrival has not gone unnoticed...

Mrs. Peel has parked the Mercedes in the drive of a suburban house, presumably her home. As she retrieves the yellow case from the back seat and closes the car door, a heavy-set man with shaven hair is reflected in the side-view mirror. Unaware of the man's presence, Emma skips merrily around to the back of the property, and enters the house via large wooden double doors.

In her lounge, she places the case on an occasional table next to the sofa. She sits down and removes her necklace on which, rather than a jewel, hangs the golden key to her yellow case. She ensures that the case is locked before hanging the necklace around her neck once more. She goes over to the bookcase and deposits the case in a cupboard, which she also locks.

The scene cuts to the nearby Dolphinarium where Mrs. Peel is swimming in the pool with dolphins, and taking photographs with an underwater camera. Unbeknownst to her, the golden key drops from her neck to the bottom of the pool. It also escapes her attention that the shaven-headed man has followed her there.

Back at the house, Emma emerges from her darkroom and studies one of the photographs that she took at the pool. She notices something alarming about it and runs outside.

At the pool, Mrs. Peel's pursuer – wearing a wetsuit and dive mask – pulls himself up out of the water just as she enters and runs down the stairs towards him. He drops beneath the surface and swims off, closing an underwater gate behind him. Emma attempts to follow him on dry land, but finds the door leading in the same direction is locked. She inserts a small charge into the keyhole. It explodes and the door swings open invitingly.

Beyond it she finds a maintenance room, filled with pipes, valves and gauges. She looks around but cannot see her foe. He is working his way around the pipes, seeking a way to make his escape. A cat and mouse chase ensues, with it not being entirely clear who is chasing whom. Eventually, he finds a pressure valve which he turns, releasing gas vapour into the room. Emma is nearly overcome by the fumes. Holding a handkerchief to her nose and mouth, she eventually discovers ladder rungs built into the tiled wall. She appears to collapse, but gets a second wind and climbs them, exiting through an inspection hatch in the ceiling. This leads out onto the forecourt, right next to where she has parked her sports car. She drives off.

Back at home, she sits on the sofa and consoles herself with a glass of Champagne. She receives a telephone call. The caller has the necklace and golden key and is telephoning from a nightclub. They have a brief conversation, presumably to arrange a meeting at the club. Emma appears pensive, but soon decides what to do. She runs outside to the car.

Mrs. Peel arrives at the nightclub and the man with the shaved hair leaves furtively a few seconds later. She takes in the scene: there are people at tables and sitting at the bar. They are smoking, drinking, watching... She feels uneasy, as if all eyes are upon her. Not seeing the man from the pool there, she realises that she has been duped and makes a swift exit...

Back at Mrs. Peel's house, the shaven-headed man has broken into the cupboard and takes out the little yellow case. He is trying to open it with the golden key when Emma enters and advances upon him from his blind side. She gives him a kick, taking him by surprise. They fight, but his is a losing battle against Mrs. Peel's karate blows. He tries grabbing her arms, but she breaks free and deals out the final blow. He collapses, unconscious, his head knocking against the yellow case.

The case falls open, revealing its bounty: a pink, ceramic piggy bank.

Das Diadem - In Color

A 3 minute 26 second truncated version of Das Diadem, *issued in colour*

A snake slithers across the floor in the entrance hall of the castle.

Outside, Emma Peel has just arrived in her Mercedes-Benz 250SL Automatic sports car. She closes the driver's door and walks across the small bridge over the surrounding moat that leads up to the front door. She notices a light go off inside the building. She finds the door is not locked and enters.

The entrance hall is lit only by a candle, the flickering light of which barely penetrates the gloom. She takes hold of the candlestick and searches the room. The flame picks out an ornate clock face, various paintings and relief sculptures, but Mrs. Peel does not spot the snake which is slithering around her feet. She finds a mirror – only to see an adversary appear behind her in the reflection. This man carries a revolver and wears a stocking over his face to disguise his features.

The snake is about to attack when Mrs. Peel blows out the candle flame, drops the candlestick to the floor, and engages the stockinged man in combat. She throws him to the floor. He quickly leaps back up and resumes the contest, but it is soon concluded when she karate chops him and renders him unconscious.

A moment later, a second stocking-faced man enters carrying a diamond tiara on a felt cushion. He is quickly despatched by Mrs. Peel, who floors him by pulling a rug from under him. She then takes the tiara and descends a spiral staircase.

A shaven-headed gang member pulls up outside the castle in his Citroën, while his two confederates, now recovered from their encounters with Mrs. Peel, negotiate the spiral staircase in their pursuit of this infuriating woman.

Emma runs along a narrow, painting-lined corridor and hides herself in one of two large chests placed against the left-hand wall. The stocking-faced hoodlums burst in. One of them carries a submachine gun, which he takes great pleasure in firing at the chest in which Mrs. Peel has concealed herself.

Meanwhile, their shaven-headed confederate enters the castle and falls victim to the snake, which bites him on the ankle.

Making sure to load fresh cartridges into the machine gun, the other two gang members investigate the chest. Instead of containing the bullet-riddled body of Mrs. Peel, they are shocked to find it is actually the entrance to a staircase which leads down into the dark bowels of the castle. They investigate.

Emma has, by now, found her way out of the castle. She stands on a second bridge that stretches across the moat, and, watched by a swan, studies the tiara.

In the entrance hall, the shaven-headed man lies dead, eyes staring into eternity, as the snake slithers across his corpse.

Mrs. Peel makes for the main entrance of the castle. When she reaches the bridge there, she realises she is faced with gang members on both sides, cutting off her retreat. She takes them on. They have little hope against her. She outnumbers them one to two! She despatches both with a series of devastating karate chops – and both end up in the moat.

Emma smiles at the swan, which seems nonplussed, as if this is an everyday occurrence.

Cast

Diana Rigg (Emma Peel)

All other cast members were uncredited and remain unidentified.

Production

Photography – Klaus Benser
Camera Assistant – Heiner Bauhoff
Musical Score – Jonny Teupen
Producers – H.G. Lückel and Dieter Nettemann
Director – Uwe Beetz
Film Printing – Eclair-Paris
Produced by Accentfilm GmbH International,
Mülheim an der Ruhr, West Germany

Analysis

Der Goldene Schlüssel and *Das Diadem* were the earliest entries in a mooted ten-episode short film series produced for the home cine projector market in West Germany by Accentfilm GmbH International, and distributed by Revue Films. The film series was produced in response to the success of *The Avengers* on West German television's second channel, Zweites Deutsches Fernsehen (ZDF), which aired it with German dubbed soundtracks as *Mit Schirm, Charme und Melone*. The series debuted with *The Cybernauts* on Tuesday 18th October 1966 and transmissions continued until Tuesday 7th May 1968, when *Who's Who??* brought the run to a premature close. Fourteen episodes were skipped across the black-and-white and colour series, with these omitted episodes finally being dubbed into German in the 1990s. Despite its abbreviated run, *The Avengers* found a considerable audience: *Mit Schirm, Charme und Melone* regularly gained around 55 per cent of the viewing audience. The *Frankfurter Allgemeine Zeitung* newspaper heaped praise upon it, suggesting it was "the best entertainment series in Germany ever," and the weekly journal *Die Ziet* seemed to agree, declaring it "the most intellectual of all crime-series."

The series' success in West Germany not only served as the impetus for the short film series, but also for Accentfilm GmbH International to make an audacious move to secure the services of one of the show's stars, Diana Rigg. The company – which had previously released short features on natural world subjects and cut-down episodes of Gerry and Sylvia Anderson's *Thunderbirds*, amongst other things, on 8mm film – was set up by two employees of a West German camera shop, H.G. Lückel and Dieter Nettemann. Wolfgang von Chmielewski, who worked with Lückel and Nettemann on *Minikillers*, remembered them fondly when speaking to the author in September 2010: "Lückel and Nettemann were salesmen for Mr. Mengede, who had a large and highly successful photo store in Mülheim an der Ruhr, Photo Mengede. I don't remember how I met them, but they dreamt of Hollywood and I had been there, first as a student (Art Center College), and later as an actor, going by the stage name Charles De Vries in productions including Stanley Kramer's *Ship of Fools* (1965). When we met, I was a young and upcoming director at Westdeutscher Rundfunk (WDR), part of ARD television network. These were the 1960s when some creative producers had offered Elizabeth Taylor the outrageous sum of half a million US dollars to host a TV show about London, and then sold the idea for a million to an American Network. Only then did they sign Taylor and made a fortune. Well, Lückel had the same mindset, and came up with a similar concept. In many ways, he was also a true pioneer of the home video market! There were department stores in Germany, like Neckermann, and chains like Photo Porst, photo stores that sold home movies on 8mm and Super 8. In partnering with his colleague Nettemann, Lückel figured if they could sell films perhaps starring someone like Diana Rigg for ten German Marks a copy, the chains would order hundred of thousands, and they would make millions. If I remember correctly, Photo Porst made a contract with them for 200,000 copies, if they did a series in Spain, as they had proposed." This proposal would come into being as *Minikillers* in 1969.

Diana Rigg took the starring role in *Der Goldene Schlüssel* and *Das Diadem*, although the character that she played was never named on screen. The packaging, however, is quick to note her connection to *The Avengers*, suggesting that she is "known as Emma Peel" (with the words 'Emma Peel' given the greatest weight). Another statement appears on the underside of the access flap, and could not be more clear: "Diana Rigg as Emma Peel appears every eight weeks in a new thriller for your home cinema." These films, for all intents and purposes, depict the same character that Diana Rigg played in *The Avengers* and this is why the synopses presented over the previous pages refer to the character as "Emma Peel". The use of the *Avengers* character was important to the marketing of these films, but there is no evidence to suggest that the makers cleared the rights through official channels, and certainly the boxes and on-screen credits make no mention of the British copyright holders.

Diana Rigg aside, the cast and crew of *Das Diadem* were all amateurs. One unidentified participant, who featured as a gang member, later revealed during a 2000s television appearance that Diana Rigg's involvement owed as much to chance as it did to planning. Apparently, one of the people involved had been travelling home from London when he bumped into a former school friend on a train. This person was working in London as a journalist and was able to supply an address through which Diana Rigg's management could be contacted. Negotiations reputedly went back and forth, and in the end she travelled over to Germany and received a payment in the region of 10,000 Deutschmarks for the work.

The actor's memory is borne out by a report in the *Hamburger Abendblatt* newspaper of 28th August 1968: "Diana Rigg, hard-hitting Emma Peel from *The Avengers*, wants to deliver a new film series into the living rooms of German citizens. Her shrewd manager Jeremy Banks decided to sidestep television for his star this time, and gave permission for a ten-episode series on Standard 8 and Super 8 formats so that anyone with a cine projector could screen it in their homes. Filming of the series will begin in early September in Mülheim an der Ruhr. Emma, who prefers theatre to television and cinema, has been persuaded by her manager to play a reporter... All episodes are individual films and are being shot in colour."

However, the films were shot silent and music and sound effects were added in postproduction. There have been many theories for this approach over the years, with most suggesting it was a cost-cutting exercise or a sign that the films had next to no budget assigned to them. One suggestion that seemed so elaborate that it might possibly be true concerned petrol stations. This subject was raised by the gang member actor during his television interview – he recalled that the films were made at a time when it was still common for people to remain in their cars at filling stations while their vehicle was refuelled or checked. Dialogue-free films of about five minutes duration would be played so as to entertain them during this time, but, speaking in 2010, Wolfgang von Chmielewski dispelled this theory, at least regarding *Der Goldene Schlüssel*, *Das Diadem* and *Minikillers*: "There were no gas stations or any of that, Lückel was much smarter than that! It was pure arithmetic that silent movies had to be made for the home market. If I remember correctly, 80 per cent of the prospective buyers had silent projectors in those days, and Photo Porst was too conservative to push the sale of sound projectors. All they wanted was some easy money and to keep people with silent projectors happy. Hence, we shot silent movies, but recorded fancy musical soundtracks and included occasional sound effects for those with sound equipment."

Of course, another clue is in the production company's name, Accentfilm GmbH International – they had an eye on foreign sales. As film companies discovered in the early decades of the 20th century, it was relatively straightforward to market silent films internationally without the language problems that the sound era had to negotiate – insert dialogue intertitles in local languages and it didn't matter one jot if your screen stars were monolingual. *Der Goldene Schlüssel*, *Das Diadem* and *Minikillers* even eschewed caption cards, relying on mime, facial expressions and an emphasis on action.

The decision not to record live sound had a further benefit, in that German viewers could imagine Emma Peel's voice in their head while watching the films and it would be the one they were used to, that of dubbing artiste Margot Leonard. Diana Rigg's own voice had not been heard in Germany. Coincidentally, Leonard had previously dubbed Honor Blackman for German prints of the James Bond film *Goldfinger* (1964).

Although the fullest version of the film is the variant that goes by the title *Das Diadem* (*The Tiara*), it was not the first released. Instead, *Der Goldene Schlüssel* (*The Golden Key*), a colour film comprising of, essentially, an alternative edit of the first seven minutes of the full film, was issued very shortly after filming. The *Hamburger Abendblatt* newspaper report of 28th August 1968 notes that the "first films will be available on September 28th at Photokina Köln," a biennial photographic trade fair held at the Koelnmesse Trade Fair and Exhibition Centre in Deutz. It is not known for certain that *Der Goldene Schlüssel* hit this tight deadline, but *Bravo* magazine of 28th October 1968 states that "you can now buy an individual Emma-film for home use: an 8mm movie that was filmed in Duisburg and Mülheim an der Ruhr with Diana. It lasts five minutes and is called *The Red Key*." [sic] The two known variants of *Das Diadem*, one full-length in monochrome running to just under 17 minutes, and another in colour with a duration of about three and a half minutes, appear to have been issued in the winter months of early 1969. This seems to be confirmed by *Bravo* magazine's 13th January 1969 issue, the back cover of which noted that, "If you like Diana Rigg for your home theatre, you can buy the movie in the photo shop soon." (This short report also suggested, erroneously, that Rigg would be "handling heavy weapons" in the film, something which Mrs. Peel does not do in *Das Diadem*.)

The *Bravo* report was illustrated with a photograph of Diana Rigg brandishing the submachine gun used by one of the gang members in the film. Another image from this shoot appeared, somewhat misleadingly, on the front of the cardboard boxes containing *Das Diadem* film reels.

Filming Locations

The September 1968 filming for *Der Goldene Schlüssel* / *Das Diadem* is reputed to have lasted four or five days according to sources close to the production. The Spanish excursion – scheduled for production in 1969 as part of the deal with Photo Porst – with all its attendant sunlight and glamour, must have seemed like a pipe dream to the cast and crew when the cameras began rolling in Accentfilm's locality during the dying days of summer.

Using Mülheim an der Ruhr as their production base, the filming unit worked cheaply, using properties, vehicles and possessions belonging to the cast and crew where possible, and travelling no further than 15 km (9.3 miles) from Mülheim.

There was no in-studio filming conducted, with all scenes shot in real locations:

- Mrs. Peel lands her Piper Cherokee light aircraft at Essen/Mülheim airport, a small airport located 6 km (3.7 miles) southwest of Essen and 3 km (1.9 miles) southeast of Mülheim. There are no scheduled passenger flights to or from the airport – it is mainly used for private flying and business charters.

- The sequences centred around Mrs. Peel's home were filmed in the suburbs of Mülheim an der Ruhr. It is thought that the property was owned by a party involved with or close to the production.

- The scenes where Mrs. Peel swims with the dolphins and later chases one of the gang members in the pipe room and tunnels were shot at the Duisburg Zoo dolphinarium, situated on Mülheimer Strasse. The dolphinarium remains open and has changed little since the filming took place in 1968. Copies of *Der Goldene Schlüssel* included a small, printed insert which included the following statement from the producers: "The images in the dolphinarium were taken with the kind permission of the Duisburg Zoo."

- *Das Diadem*'s other showpiece filming venue was in Kettwig, which was then a town in its own right, but was merged in 1975 as a borough of the city of Essen. It was here in the south west of the town that all the sequences outside and inside the castle were filmed, at the picturesque Schloss Hugenpoet (pronounced Hugenpoot). The name translates as "toad puddle", a reference to the marshy landscapes there in the Ruhr valley. There has been a castle on the site since at least the year 778 and the current structure, one of the architectural treasures of the region, dates back to the 17th century. Built in the northern German style, Schloss Hugenpoet belongs to the von Fürstenberg family and has been open to the public as a high-class hotel-restaurant since 1955.

Similarities to The Avengers TV Series

As might be expected for a film that features Diana Rigg as Emma Peel – even if Accentfilm's right to use the character was questionable – there are a good few *Avengers*-ish touches. The first of these is that Mrs. Peel drives an open top sports car. However, she seems to have traded in her powder blue Lotus Elan for a left-hand drive, flame red Mercedes-Benz 250SL Automatic that carries a German (D) country sticker on its boot door and the registration number XY-25689. During the night scenes, in something of a continuity error, she trades this in for another Mercedes, a 300SL with the registration number V7-4797X. Earlier on, Emma pilots a Piper Cherokee PA-28 light aircraft, demonstrating a skill that one could well imagine being part of her repertoire.

Mrs. Peel's fighting style – which is heavily featured in Der Goldene Schlüssel / Das Diadem – is very reminiscent of the one she used in The Avengers, with karate chops, kicks and swipes abounding. Close-ups are also shot in much the same way as they were in the series.

As in The Avengers, the fights are bloodless, though possibly the shot of the snake biting into the gang member's ankle is one that the British producers would have avoided and left to suggestion. Despite Mrs. Peel's proficient use of karate, the only opponent to be fatally injured is killed by the snake, not her.

Emmapeelers are not to be seen here, but Diana's wardrobe is still somewhat Avengers-inspired, and the wetsuit is undoubtedly kinky...

Steed may be absent, but Champagne is definitely present – and imbibed on two occasions in the full-length film.

The film's musical soundtrack by Jonny Teupen consists of one long piece of Avengers-ish music that is reminiscent of the Avengers Series 5 tag scene theme composed by Laurie Johnson. This theme is also referenced in the Minikillers score by Jonny Teupen and Hans Rettenbacher.

Jonny Teupen (1923-1991) was a popular German harpist and composer of music in the Jazz and Easy Listening genres. He had studied with Max Saal at the Akademische Hochschule für Musik Berlin. After working with the Theater des Volkes and the Staatsoper Unter den Linden, he became solo harpist of the Nordwestdeutscher Rundfunk (Northwest German Broadcasting – now WDR Köln), to which he belonged until 1985. He also recorded several jazz-oriented albums. In the sixties and early seventies he was generally considered to be the pre-eminent harpist in Germany.

The film's big climax takes place not in suburban Mülheim but in the opulent, if slightly decaying surroundings of a country mansion seemingly in the middle of nowhere. It offers candlelit rooms, creepy paintings, secret tunnels... and a snake! These elements are most definitely inspired by the milieu of The Avengers, particularly that of the Series 5 episode The Joker.

Trivia Points

- Copies of Der Goldene Schlüssel included a small, printed insert naming some of the people who worked on the film, also giving their city of origin: Uwe Beetz (Berlin), Klause Benser (Düsseldorf) and Jonny Teupen (Köln).

- Diana Rigg enjoyed a short stay in West Germany four months prior to the filming of *Das Diadem*. She arrived at Düsseldorf airport on 6th May 1968, where she was met by autograph hunters. The purpose of the two-day visit was reportedly to make television appearances, presumably to publicise her forthcoming film *On Her Majesty's Secret Service*, and to take part in fashion photography. She had earlier visited Hamburg with Patrick Macnee in 1966 on a publicity junket for *The Avengers*.

Verdict

It must be said that these films do not have a particularly good reputation in *Avengers* fandom. Their amateur nature – outside of the casting of Diana Rigg – could well be a part of this, not least because the films give off an air of exploitation cinema, despite the fact that they are not actually salacious. The amateur feel extends to the direction which at times is eccentric to say the least, the two cut-down colour versions being somewhat more competent. The lack of dialogue does not help this and in some edits it is not clear exactly what is going on – notably when the action in *Der Goldene Schlüssel* cuts from Mrs. Peel's home to a pool where she swims with dolphins; as she has not been seen travelling there, the viewer initially thinks this is another area of her house.

Being essentially a silent film, it is hardly the most intellectual or witty of productions, but it does have some memorable sequences – the shot of the snake slithering over the gang member's corpse is genuinely chilling, and who wouldn't want to spend an exciting evening in what must be the dullest nightclub ever committed to film? It is populated with people who are interacting only with their drinks and cigarettes and no one seems to be getting off with anyone else! It has a remarkably sullen atmosphere – like death's waiting room. I suspect that this was not intentional. It also has to be said that the film's McGuffin, the diadem / tiara, looks distinctly cheap and cheesy – and why one of the gang members walks in with it on a presentation cushion will confuse me until my dying day. Maybe presentation really matters to him? But he gets thumped, and deservedly so. What a fool...

Despite all this, I must confess to having a great affection for *Der Goldene Schlüssel / Das Diadem*. It's a slice of 1960s kitsch and the sort of thing you imagine a serious actress like Diana Rigg would not have considered being a party to in a million years – but she threw herself into it and looks to be thoroughly enjoying herself. If I had a choice between watching a low-grade *Avengers* episode, such as *Homicide and Old Lace*, and this, then West German amateur hour entertainment would win out every time, with it offering further adventures of Mrs. Emma Peel – or perhaps those of an Emma Peel from a different, slightly twisted dimension where the acting of those around her is not entirely convincing.

MINIKILLERS

ALAN HAYES

Project Type: Short Film Series
Release Date: 1969 (West Germany)

Synopses

Minikillers *was serialised in four unnumbered parts.*
Synopses follow for each episode.

Operation: Costa Brava

Accentfilm's Description:
"The elegant American at the swimming pool dropping off his chair while dying... The people present – being horrified – are jumping up. A beautiful woman (DIANA) disappears and with her the mysterious weapon – right in front of dangerous Jack... The MINIKILLERS in action!"

The Punta d'en Rosaris, a rocky outcrop on the Costa Brava with a winding stone stairway, affords breathtaking views of the Mediterranean. The nearby beach of Lloret de Mar offers views of a different kind: sun-loving tourists relaxing in swimming trunks and bikinis. Other holidaymakers lounge above and away from this summery scene, taking in the sun around the outdoor swimming pool of one of the town's hotels. José, a moustachioed middle-aged man looking stylish in a fawn-coloured suit, strides out onto the hotel terrace, descends the steps and heads towards the balcony. He prepares to light a cigarette and looks out to sea. Close by, on the roof of a tall building, several men are keeping watch on the hotel. One looks through binoculars, while another works with a radio set set stored inside a slim briefcase. José, the men's boss, sends a radio signal to another of his employees: Jack, a Hawaiian-shirted, well-built, bald man who has been waiting in his vehicle near the hotel. Springing into action, Jack exits his vehicle carrying a large, rectangular box and makes his way to the hotel. He crosses paths with Diana as she emerges onto the terrace wearing sunglasses, a purple bikini and an orange top piped in blue. She is carrying a small towel and a book and means to get some serious sun.

Diana passes José. He turns slowly, taking a short drag on his cigarette as he follows her movements with a steady, admiring gaze. As she sits on a lounger and starts to read, an elegant, professional-looking American man seated next to the pool looks up from his English-language newspaper and appears to approve of his new poolside neighbour. Soon, another empty lounger is filled by Jack, who is no longer carrying his box. José retreats. A waiter brings drinks to the tables of Jack and Diana, and shortly afterwards the former takes a fob watch from his shirt pocket and begins to adjust the time on it.

On the rooftop of the building overlooking the hotel, the goings on are being surveyed through binoculars by a fair-haired man. He lowers his spyglasses and picks up a rifle, aiming it at the American by the hotel pool. Meanwhile, Jack stops the hands of his watch when they read one-thirty. He smiles a cold smile.

While she cradles her orange juice, something captures Diana's attention and raises a warm smile – a small, blonde doll, wearing a dark blue dress over a red and white striped jumper. It is walking along the poolside, controlled by Jack's watch. As it passes the people who are by the pool, they look on in curiosity and amusement. When it arrives at his feet, the American picks it up and studies it, a wide smile spreading across his face. He looks across at Diana, who smiles back.

The gunman also smiles as he views the scene through his gunsight. His smile is mirrored on Jack's face before he depresses the crown of his watch decisively.

Instantaneously, streams of liquid squirt from the centres of the doll's eyes, spraying directly into the American's face. Surprised, he recoils, wipes his face with his hand and then laughs. Diana laughs, too, but her reaction quickly changes when the American suddenly clutches his face in agony and falls to the ground. Poison!

Their curiosity and amusement having suddenly turned to terror and concern, the holidaymakers gather around the unfortunate American. Jack, however, seems unperturbed and remains seated.

On the rooftop, the sniper, realising that a shot will not be necessary, lowers his rifle. Job done.

An elderly tourist examines the motionless victim and gestures that there is nothing that can be done for him – the doll has claimed its victim. Diana, in turn, claims the doll, removing it from the scene. As she makes for her hotel room with it, Jack is angry – this was not part of the plan.

Jack meets with a thick-set accomplice with a buzz-cut hairstyle and instructs him to attack Diana and leave a piece of paper and a pocket watch behind, both of which he hands over to the accomplice. The thick set accomplice lies in wait for Diana in an arched walkway at the side of the hotel, but, as he is not particularly well trained, she spots him. She turns the tables and surprises him, defeating him with ease, employing karate moves, and finally throwing him to the ground below. Remembering his instructions, her assailant leaves the piece of paper and the watch where Diana will spot them. He then stumbles off, nursing his aching back as the soundtrack riffs on the Laurel and Hardy signature tune. Diana smiles broadly as her unequal opponent staggers away. She then sees that he has dropped two items and goes to retrieve them, not knowing that the killers mean for her to have them.

Back in her hotel room, with the doll sat on the dressing table before her, Diana opens the back of the pocket watch and discovers that its inner workings are not what she expected – instead of clock mechanisms she finds complex, electronic circuitry inside. She theorises that the watch was used to control the doll and activate the poison spray. While she is lost in her thoughts, a door is opened behind her and a second doll is placed in the room. José's men intend to deal with Diana in the same way as they did the ill-fated American by the pool. The doll starts to walk towards her, closing in on her step by tiny step. Diana is blissfully unaware of its presence...

Diana plays around with the pocket watch, adjusting the time. As she does so – out of her eyeline – the second doll reacts, stopping and starting as she moves the watch's hands. The doll is being controlled by the watch! Not having seen the second doll, Diana is confused as to why the watch is not having any effect on the doll that she appropriated from the poolside.

She decides to turn her attention to the piece of paper that she found with the watch. It is a flyer for a club. She rises from her chair, picks up her bag and leaves the room, moments before the second doll squirts liquid from its eyes, its intended victim having saved herself without even knowing it.

Heroin

Accentfilm's Description:
"A mysterious beach... DIANA in a dangerous trap... On a mysterious yacht the gangsters and... the MINIKILLERS!"

Diana is relaxing on the sands, stretched out on her beach towel and reading her book. She notices several scuba divers entering the water nearby and takes a couple of photographs of them. She also fires off a few shots of a motor yacht which is hovering close to the shore. Aboard it, two men are watching Diana through binoculars and it soon becomes apparent that the three tower block spies and José, the moustachioed man from the hotel, are on board; the latter is clearly the man in charge. The blond-haired man wears a headset and is checking his radio equipment, and the would-be sniper is making sure his rifle is in good working order. On the deck, three beautiful, brunette women in bikinis are each working on one of the killer dolls.

Diana begins to peel an apple with a small knife, but then comes to a sudden, shocking realisation: the other people on the beach around her are not real – they are all life-size mannequins! On the yacht, José instructs the radio operator to activate the trap. The blond man duly presses a red button. On the beach, the mannequins begin to fall, pulled into a large net that rises from beneath the sands and encircles Diana. The net draws in tighter and tighter, ensnaring Diana and the lifeless mannequins. As the net is dragged down the beach towards the waiting boat, Diana realises she still has the fruit knife and begins frantically sawing at the netting. She struggles as the net reaches the water's edge.

When the haul is brought aboard the boat, there is no sign of Diana, just useless mannequins in various states of dismemberment. Having escaped in the nick of time – and now wearing just a pink bikini, her wrap seemingly lost in the tumult – Diana swims over to the back of the yacht where she boards a small wooden dingy that has been roped to the stern for ship-to-shore journeys. From there, she climbs aboard the yacht, unseen, and sneaks below deck. As the crew try to work out where she has got to, José orders the captain to head back. The boat turns and speeds off.

Below deck, Diana looks around and finds a black-and-white photograph of two men. It is marked with the word 'INTERPOL' and the face of each of the men is crossed through with an 'X'. She does not recognise the first man, but the second is the American who was killed by the doll at the hotel.

Diana tries a door. It leads to sleeping berths below. Taking the photograph with her, she conceals herself inside – grabbing a yellow oilskin jacket on her way – just as José walks in. He carries one of the dolls and looks around, suspecting Diana's presence, but eventually leaves. She then re-emerges wearing the oilskin jacket.

As the crew busy themselves on deck, Diana finds a doll inside a red refrigerator. She checks it over and finds two plastic-wrapped sachets inside a hole in its back. They appear to contain a white powder – heroin, she concludes. She wags her finger at the doll reprovingly. She puts the sachets back inside the doll and places it on top of the fridge.

The yacht draws into port and prepares to dock. On the shore, a black Mercedes 600 W100 (registration: MO-AD 995) comes into view and approaches the yacht as it is being moored up. It is driven by Jack, the bald henchman, and carries three young women as passengers.

As the crew begin to disembark, Diana pulls back a hatch and goes up on deck. At first, the going is good – she appears to be undetected – and she sees that José has gone ashore and is warmly greeting the girls who have arrived by car. Unfortunately, the henchman sitting in the Mercedes spots her on the boat and springs into action, raising the alarm. Two of José's men confront her, but she deals with them quickly. The henchman, armed with an automatic pistol, works his way along the starboard side of the cabin, but Diana evades him by entering the cabin from the port side and exiting behind him to the starboard side.

Diana gets into the Mercedes, waves to the exasperated José – who was about to join the hunt – and drives off. She travels a short way down the road and deliberately pulls up next to a white-uniformed traffic warden standing by a 'no parking' sign. She gives the warden a friendly wave, and skips over to her waiting black Jaguar E-Type sports car (registration: D-LT 688). As she drives off, the warden places a parking fine notice under the windscreen wiper of the Mercedes.

Macabre

Accentfilm's Description:
"A car across the dusty mountain road is blocking the way. DIANA stops... In the rear view mirror of her car she sees four men... Where are the MINIKILLERS!"

Diana is relaxing at an outdoor café on the Lloret de Mar seafront, taking in the scene while she sips at a cup of black tea. Unbeknownst to her, she is being spied on from above – José and two of his accomplices are keeping watch on her from a balcony at the top of the nearby Banco Zaragozano building. Jack, the bald henchman, is waiting below in the Mercedes, which is parked up a short distance from the seafront.

José takes out a cigarette and puts it in his mouth. He gestures to his two accomplices to depart and brings up to the cigarette what, at first, appears to be a match. In reality, it is the aerial of a radio device. He uses it to signal Jack, who, upon receiving the notification, discards his own cigarette and picks up a doll. He fits it with a compact explosive attached to a timer device and walks to Diana's sports car. He furtively places the doll behind the passenger seat.

He retreats, unseen by his intended victim who is seated nearby. Atop the Banco Zaragozano building, José inhales smoke from his cigarette and smiles. Most satisfying – everything is going to plan.

Having finished her tea, Diana rises from her table and strolls over to the E-Type. She drives off for the hills, with the black Mercedes close behind. As she reaches the higher ground to the east of Lloret de Mar, she realises that she is being pursued and both cars increase their speed, skidding around the dusty, winding roads, their tyres complaining at the heavy braking.

Diana has to brake abruptly when she encounters a broken-down car blocking the narrow mountain road. As she screeches to a halt with one wheel up on the cliffside pavement, the passenger seat is thrown forward and the concealed doll is revealed. She picks it up and notices that there is a ticking sound coming from inside it. The Mercedes draws to a halt a safe distance behind, and Diana spies it in the side-view mirror. A pleasing idea comes to her...

Five henchmen get out of the Mercedes. Four of them walk towards Diana and the Jaguar, while Jack stays back by the car. She kisses her finger and affectionately anoints the doll's forehead with it, then hurls the Minikiller backwards towards José's men. Jack recoils in fear as the doll explodes. The explosion accounts for the four men, but Jack – who was standing clear of the blast – advances on Diana. They tussle on a precipice, but he is no match for her and she throws him over the edge after a brief contest. He lies prone at the foot of the cliff. She picks a yellow flower from the clifftop, gives it a little kiss and tosses it after her defeated opponent. It lands on his chest. He stirs and begins to slowly, dazedly pull himself up. He has a long and difficult climb ahead of him. Diana smiles and leaves.

Back at the hotel, with the sharp-suited José watching, barely concealed, from a doorway, Diana gets into her Jaguar sports car. Just as she does this, a waiter walks over and hands her a black-edged card that he has brought to her on a silver platter. Diana raises an eyebrow and her face betrays the hint of a smile at the card's contents. José also smiles in anticipation of the next move in their game as he watches the Jaguar disappear into the distance.

The information on the card leads Diana to the nearby Modernist Cemetery. She parks up outside the ornate gates and enters the cemetery grounds. She wanders around for a while, eventually chancing upon an old-fashioned horse-drawn hearse, complete with its equine powerhouse. She goes over to the beautiful creature and gently strokes its head. As she does this, she realises that she has other, less friendly company.

Three men stand before her, ranged around an open coffin by a mausoleum: José and Jack, now both attired in black suits, and the thick-set man who had previously attacked and been defeated by Diana in the hotel grounds. José gestures grandly towards the coffin, inviting Diana to try it for size.

Two more nattily dressed henchmen appear behind Diana and drag her towards the coffin. As they descend a set of steps, she puts them off balance and quickly despatches them with a throw and a karate chop respectively. The thick-set man and Jack try to restrain her, but the result is the same – she is too proficient and quick for them.

Diana jumps up into the driver's seat of the hearse, grabs the reins and spurs the horse into action, escaping from the clutches of her foes in fine style. The frustrated José grimaces and puts his bowler hat on dejectedly as Diana and the hearse disappear into a burning orange sunset.

Flamenco

Accentfilm's Description:
"Slowly the many tons lifting jack is approaching DIANA, who is lying captivated. DIANA is desperately looking for a way out of this situation... However, the heavy piece of concrete is coming near inexorably... An action of the MINIKILLERS?"

Diana is attending a flamenco show at the El Relicario nightclub, wearing a sequinned dress divided into horizontal gold and white stripes. She sips from a glass of Champagne at a small table close to the raised stage. The celebrated dancer El Sali is bringing his nightly act at the venue to a close, pounding the floorboards with his lightning-fast feet.

The gang of drug smugglers are also present, keeping a wary eye on Diana's activities, but they have a second, more important purpose. José – effortlessly stylish in a striking white tuxedo – has left the surveillance to Jack as he is busy entertaining his beautiful, young girlfriend at one of the dining tables up on the inner courtyard balcony. Their table is packed to the rafters with expensive food and drink, and they are enjoying themselves enormously. Jack comes over, taps his employer on the shoulder, whispers in his ear and then joins the couple at the table. He reaches for a serviette and appears to be settling down to eat.

A waiter comes over to Diana's table and refills her Champagne glass. When he leaves her, she takes a look at the photograph she removed from the yacht showing the two Interpol agents. Her hunch was right – the man to the left of the picture is undoubtedly El Sali. She concludes that El Sali was the dead American's Interpol colleague, and that the cross over his face on the photo means that El Sali has also been marked for death by the smugglers.

With a final flourish, El Sali completes his flamenco routine to riotous applause from the audience. Diana claps appreciatively, as does José, his girlfriend and even the surly Jack. José gestures to Jack that it is time for action, and the bald man leaves the table as El Sali encourages the audience to applaud the musicians. Diana sees Jack leave and decides to follow.

While the public area of the nightclub is colourful and opulently decorated, the basement, with its plain, white, unevenly painted walls, looks tired and rundown. The sort of place a man could get killed...

El Sali enters his dressing room, which is situated in a drab basement corridor. He sits at his dressing table and, with the aid of the mirror, begins to remove his stage make-up. He is horrified when he sees, in the reflection, that one of the killer dolls is in the room, advancing on him. It is being controlled from the corridors, where Jack is adjusting a pocket watch. Suddenly, twin sprays of poison squirt from the doll's eyes and the flamenco dancer grasps at his face in sheer terror and pain.

Very soon afterwards, Diana walks down the steps at the end of the basement corridor. She has come to see El Sali. However, the moment that she enters his dressing room, Jack comes up behind her and chloroforms her.

Meanwhile, José and his girlfriend continue to revel in their lobster dinner. José is doubly pleased when Jack reappears from the basement and signals that everything went like clockwork. Jack appears calm and contented. He lights a cigarette and notes that the stage, which the late El Sali had danced on only minutes before, is now descending into the floor.

Directly underneath, Diana regains consciousness and finds herself tied hand and foot beneath the descending concrete rostrum. She is laying where the base of the stage will sit. Her future looking somewhat two-dimensional, she tries to find a way to extricate herself or halt the descent of the stage. She spies the operating mechanism, a series of interlocking cog wheels. She reaches her hands out towards them... and shortly afterwards, upstairs, Jack notices that the rostrum has stopped descending, about one foot above floor level.

Concerned, Jack goes to see what has happened. In the under-stage area, he finds the severed cords that had held Diana, and a ring that has been wedged in between two of the metal cogs. Diana watches, amused, from behind a stack of wine boxes. Jack removes the ring and holds it in his fingers, studying it, seemingly oblivious to the fact that the stage has now resumed its descent. He gets out from under it at the last second, but somehow manages to trap his right hand under it. He struggles in pain, but cannot move...

Diana returns to El Sali's dressing room and finds him dead, slumped across the dressing table. She notices that he died with one finger pointing at the mirror. Calculating the angle indicated in the reflection, she investigates a large black-and-white photographic poster on the wall. It depicts the late, great dancer in full flow beneath the word 'FLAMENCO'. Diana feels along the word and finds that the 'F' twists to unlock a door behind the poster. It reveals a brick wall. Her initial confusion subsides when the brickwork slides away to the right. A light turns on beyond it. Diana has found a hidden storeroom.

Upstairs at his gallery table, José has received a whispered message from one of the waiters. He makes his apologies to his girlfriend, kisses her hand and makes for the basement.

In the secret room, Diana finds a significant number of killer dolls, concealed in a series of Cava boxes.

Meanwhile, in El Sali's dressing room, José pepares to inject a doll with a syringe, which he fills from a vial. He wears rubber gloves while he performs this operation and covers his face with a gloved hand while he squirts the syringe to clear air from the needle.

At the same time, Diana is finding more heroin sachets in the concealed recesses in the backs of the dolls. She replaces them and studies a pocket watch that she also discovered.

The preparation of the doll now complete, José cradles it in his arms as he removes the rubber gloves. He smiles at the doll, stroking its blonde hair. He sits down with the doll in his hands, facing him.

Diana places one of the dolls on the floor of the storeroom and tries to operate it using the pocket watch. Nothing seems to happen. She shakes the doll, thinking it might trigger it into action. Nothing. She tries the watch once again.

In the dressing room, two fine lines of liquid arc from the doll's eyes, splashing into José's face. Terror-stricken, he tries desperately to clear the poison from his skin, but to no avail. Mere moments later, he is dead, open-mouthed and staring wide-eyed as he faces his maker.

Oblivious to the deadly effect of her fiddling with the watch, Diana abandons her attempt to make the doll work.

A little later, Diana has alerted the police, who have arrived to take control of the situation. She sips Champagne at the nightclub bar as policemen haul Jack out in handcuffs – they have freed him from his crushing predicament. As he struggles against their hold and is bundled past her, she gives a cheeky wink to the camera.

Cast

Diana Rigg (Diana), José Nieto (José, the Boss of the Smuggling Ring), Moisés Augusto Rocha (Jack, the Bald Henchman [as Jack Rocha]), H. Coscollin (Henchman with Rifle), Mme. Million (José's Girlfriend), El Sali (Self, the Flamenco Dancer), Richard Kolin (American Interpol Man – uncredited)

Other cast members were uncredited and it has not been possible to identify them.

Production

Writers – Mark von Chmielewski and Wolfgang von Chmielewski (*)
Photography – Josef Kaufmann
Camera Assistant – Gerd Weiss
Musical Score – Jonny Teupen and Hans Rettenbacher (**)
Vibrophonist – Dave Pike (***)
Production Assistant – H. G. Tienemann
Script Girl – Ulrike Kercher
Unit Manager – Virgilio Valle
Photographer – John Kelly (***)
Film Editor – Erika Winter
Make-Up – Ingrid Hartkopf and Waltrand Winkler
Technical Assistant – Luthar Büscher
Title-Mirrors – Vittorio Bonato
Producers – H.G. Lückel and Dieter Nettemann
Director – Wolfgang von Chmielewski (*)

Produced by Accentfilm GmbH International,
Mülheim an der Ruhr, West Germany
in association with Aries Film, Spain

(*) Wolfgang von Chmielewski's work on the script was uncredited. Mark von Chmielewski is generally credited as Michael in online sources. The brothers were credited as "M. von Chmielewski" and "W. von Chmielewski", and it is this choice that later led to confusion over the writer's name.
(**) Hans Rettenbacher was more often credited as Johann Anton Rettenbacher.
(***) Uncredited.

Analysis

Minikillers was a four-part entry in the short film series produced for the home cine projector market in West Germany by Accentfilm GmbH International, and was distributed by Büscher Films (rather than Revue Films, who had handled the earlier Diana Rigg films).

The first two faux *Avengers* films – *Der Goldene Schlüssel* and *Das Diadem* – were notable successes for their producers, H.G. Lückel and Dieter Nettemann, who are believed to have negotiated the sale of 200,000 film copies through the Photo Porst chain. (Indeed, it was reported in the issue of *Bravo* magazine dated 18th August 1969, that, up to that point, 130,000 copies had been sold in department and specialty stores – and that this was considered "a huge success".) The deal had reputedly been swung on the promise of a follow-up being made in Spain. That promise was fulfilled with *Minikillers*, suggesting that production of the four-parter was already a part of Lückel and Nettemann's long-term plans. Additionally, the same issue of *Bravo* magazine (18th August 1969) reported that the producers had negotiated a lucrative international deal: "The Americans, sensing the success, have already bought the license to sell them." Anecdotal evidence suggests the Americans did indeed take the title and that *Minikillers* films were offered in bondage boutiques, including one on Times Square in New York.

Buoyed by their success, Lückel and Netteman called on an up-and-coming director, Wolfgang von Chmielewski (1940-2021), who was, at the time, working for the West German broadcaster Westdeutscher Rundfunk (WDR) in Düsseldorf, feeling that this would benefit the end result. Von Chmielewski had spent much of the previous ten years studying at the American National Theatre and Academy under Francis Lederer (1959-63) and the Art Center

College (1960-62) in Los Angeles, before dropping out to pursue a career in filmmaking. During his time in the United States, he acted under the pseudonym Charles De Vries in an array of television series – including *Combat*, *77 Sunset Strip*, *Desilu Playhouse* and Bob Hope's *Chrysler Theatre* – and films such as Bernard Wicki's *Morituri*, Stanley Kramer's *Ship of Fools* (both 1965) and Luchino Visconti's *Witches* (1967). During this time, he worked with Vivien Leigh, Joan Fontaine, Marlon Brando, José Ferrer, Yul Brynner, Lee Marvin, Richard Basehart, Silvana Mangano and Simone Signoret, among many others. His desire to make films led him back to his native Germany, where he worked for WDR, mostly in live television, news and children's programming. Seen as a rising star, WDR also commissioned him to make documentaries, and these projects took him to Africa, Asia, Israel and France. He also travelled to New York to direct *Pop Art USA*, which he also co-produced with artist Willoughby Sharp in 1966, and which featured interviews with the likes of Andy Warhol and Roy Lichtenstein. *Minikillers* saw him branch out into entertainment, and subsequently he directed the feature film *Held des Tages* (*The Hero of the Day*, 1971) in Germany, produced and directed the award-winning industrial film *Thema Geld* (First German Industrial Film Prize, 1972) and wrote episodes of the detective series *Sonne, Wein und harte Nüsse* (*Sun, Wine and Tough Nuts*, 1977), which he also co-produced in Southern France. In later years, Von Chmielewski settled in Spain and then, in the 1990s, in the United States of America, where he dubbed movies and video games into German, French and Spanish. This led to him founding Voicegroup, a casting and voice direction service. The company started by focusing on Automated Dialogue Replacement (ADR) for movies and later came to specialise in adding actors' voices to video games for software companies such as Dreamworks, Activision and Ubisoft. Wolfgang also worked as a personal language consultant for Steven Spielberg on *Schindler's List* (1993) and James Cameron on *True Lies* (1994), and added his own voice via ADR to many major movies.

Along with Von Chmielewski, Josef "Joshi" Kaufmann (1936-2017), a highly gifted Israeli cameraman who was also working at WDR, was brought on board. Among his early work as a cinematographer was the second television series of *Tim Frazer* (1964), adapted into German from the works of celebrated British crime writer Francis Durbridge. As with director Von Chmielewski, his contribution to *Minikillers* would raise production standards over and above those of the previous Accentfilm productions.

Wolfgang von Chmielewski recalled the *Minikillers* commission when he spoke to the author in 2010: "They hired me to create an extravaganza in Spain, in silent 8mm, delivered silver plates of Catalan cuisine on location and Krug Champagne, which was Diana Rigg's favourite. I remember clearly that *The Avengers* was over. I also heard that Diana was grossly underpaid there, while Lückel threw money at her! I wrote this stuff with my brother Mark in Los Angeles, which was a lot of fun for guys in their twenties. Lückel and Nettemann paid well for our script, and then hired me to direct in Spain, where Lückel had vacationed quite often and had all the local contacts. In fact, the Costa Brava was firmly in German hands in those days, and it was a major sales point that the series was filmed there! Germans work hard all year, even in the coal mines, and dream all year about the three to four weeks in Spain, where they spend all their money in the summer and act like big shots. Lückel was a bit like that when we were there, and the silver platters with gambas (prawns) kept coming, and Krug Champagne for Diana, when we were shooting. Slightly intoxicated, Diana was great to work with, and her limo blasted *(I Can't Get No) Satisfaction* by The Rolling Stones all day. Too bad it didn't impress me much, because I was a bit in the other camp, a Beatles fan.

"We shot in 35mm, 24 frames per second, and that was reduced to Normal-8 [referred to as Standard-8 in the United Kingdom] and Super 8 at 18 frames per second. The sound was added on a tiny magnetic stripe. The original may be in the vaults of Hadeco in Neuss, near Düsseldorf, but I also recall that Aries Film in Barcelona was involved. We also recorded and edited sound effects like explosions in Barcelona. As an aside, Lückel and I met a German girl in a Barcelona bar. She was 100 per cent bilingual, and he hired her on the spot. She shared the hotel room with the director during the entire production, and he (I) married her in the early 1970s and moved to Spain with her. Great memories in every way!" (There are unconfirmed reports that the late Josef Kaufmann owned 16mm prints of *Minikillers*, though it is unclear whether they still survive.)

Wolfgang von Chmielewski's writing partner, his younger brother Mark von Chmielewski (d. 2020), received the sole on-screen credit for scripting *Minikillers* – perhaps due to Wolfgang also being the film serial's director. In common with his brother, Mark acted in the United States in the 1960s, and also went by the same stage surname – De Vries. His earliest screen credit as Mark De Vries dates back to 1963, for the first of four appearances in episodes of *Combat*, a series that centred on the adventures of a squad of US infantrymen in World War II France. He also featured in episodes of several well-known television series including *The Girl from U.N.C.L.E.* (*The Danish Blue Affair*, 1966), *I Spy* (*The Honorable Assassins*, 1967), *Ironside* (*Check, Mate; and Murder* – Part 2, 1970) and Rod Serling's *Night Gallery* (*The Devil is Not Mocked*, 1971).

Trade information for *Minikillers* made some bold statements about the film, suggesting that it was "the most elaborate film production the world has ever seen for an 8mm film... An 8mm film that differs from normal cinema film only in its frame size. Starring the world's stars: Diana Rigg (in a few weeks in the new James Bond film 007 as Lady Bond in cinemas all over the world), José Nieto, Jack Rocha, H. Coscollin, as well as the most famous flamenco dancer El Sali and the mysterious Minikillers. Under the direction of Wolfgang von Chmielewski, Josef Kaufman, a television cameraman who has won several international awards, has conjured up a film that will turn home cinema into an experience. What will particularly interest you is the unprecedented sales support for an 8mm film."

The same source seems to indicate that there was a significant push to advertise *Minikillers*, with Accentfilm taking out three months of aerial advertising in the form of three planes flying over every city in the West German federal territory, and an additional four months of on-car advertising. Additionally, one million balloons carrying the message "*Minikillers* 8mm Spielfilm" were launched, and there was information about the film and advertising appearing on television and radio, and in daily newspapers, illustrated magazines and trade journals.

When offered for sale, the films' cardboard packaging carried a series of colour photographs taken by John Kelly, who was also responsible for the pictures from the *Minikillers* shoot that appeared in *Bravo* magazine in August 1969. The text on the film boxes is trilingual, with information in German, English and French. The *Minikillers* title was not translated into French or German.

Accentfilm had been quite up front in pushing the *Avengers* / Emma Peel connection in the packaging for *Der Goldene Schlüssel* and *Das Diadem*, making it clear that those films were intended to depict Diana Rigg as Emma Peel, even if this was not explicitly mentioned on screen. However, *Minikillers* is less forthright in this regard, with the packaging calling the character 'Diana'. This suggests that the producers had received a 'cease and desist' notice from rights holder the Associated British Picture Corporation, which was reportedly in the know about these unofficial German productions, as the well-respected *Avengers* author Dave Rogers confirms: "Patrick Macnee informed me that the production company was fully aware that Di had filmed the movies."

The musical score does, however, employ the same 'tag scene homage' that was sprinkled through the first films, notably to introduce the character Rigg plays, suggesting that we are watching the same character seen in *Der Goldene Schlüssel* and *Das Diadem*: Emma Peel. Despite this, the author has chosen to refer to the character as 'Diana', as per the packaging, in the synopsis presented earlier in this chapter.

Speaking to a journalist during filming, Diana was at pains to distance her character from that of Emma Peel, describing the plot in this way: "It's an 8mm – a detective story. I'm playing a nosy journalist who finds out about an international gang of drug dealers. They smuggle their substances by hiding them in dolls who are little killers. The poison comes out of their eyes. That's where the title *Minikillers* comes from." (*Bravo* magazine, 18th August 1969)

Whereas in *Der Goldene Schlüssel* and *Das Diadem*, Diana Rigg had been the solitary professional actor involved, there was a notable improvement in the quality of casting for *Minikillers*, particularly for the central roles. Wolfgang von Chmielewski comments: "My brother Mark and I cast the main actors, José Nieto and Jack Rocha. The rest were amateurs, except for the flamenco dancer who performed in Lloret de Mar and was hired by us."

Both Nieto and Rocha are names recognisable from Spanish cinema, particularly in the horror and exploitation genres. When *Minikillers* was filmed, Nieto (1902-1982) was fresh from working on Paul Naschy's *La Marca del Hombre Lobo* (*The Mark of the Wolfman*, 1968). He had been active since 1925, debuting during the cinema's silent era – experience that would have served him well on *Minikillers* – and would go on in later years to appear in the British films *Tommy the Torreador* (starring pop star Tommy Steele, 1959) and *Black Beauty* (1971). Born in Portugal in 1927, Rocha enjoyed a film career that was less centre stage than Nieto's, but he did feature in supporting roles in many productions including Jesús Franco's *Count Dracula* (1970), *The Devil Came from Akasava* (1971), *The Corpse Packs His Bags* and *The Vengeance of Dr. Mabuse* (both 1972). His final screen work came in 1978, when he appeared in the exploitation drama *Alicia en la España de las maravillas* (*Alice in the Spain of Wonders*), an erotic fantasy based upon Lewis Carroll's *Alice in Wonderland*. Perhaps mercifully, his role in this film went uncredited.

Although professional actors had been hired for the main roles, this practice did not extend to the stunt performers, and this was something that Diana Rigg found frustrating. The 18th August 1969 edition of *Bravo* magazine described how this decision affected filming and also its star: "At 7 in the morning, [Diana] gets a wake-up call. At 8.30, her driver Horst Schnittger and 'his' precious star speed to Blanes, which is 20 kilometres away [sic], and where scenes are being shot on a motor yacht. An hour later, they're already shooting. Diana has to bear with a clumsy, untrained stuntman. Patiently, she explains the karate kicks to him: 'It's not the hitting that's important, but the pulling back of your hand as quickly as possible. Good stuntmen barely touch their partners when they're pretending to hit them.' By the time the stuntman understands that, the leading lady is already black and blue. They continue to shoot the fight and, during the first rehearsal, Diana slips on the wet deck boards and almost falls overboard. In an attempt to save her, a helper pushes Diana against the capstan with such force that she ends up with a ten centimetre long abrasion of the skin right over her hip bone. All of this would be enough to put any actor in a bad mood, but Diana tries to calm down the horrified director Wolfgang Chmielewsky: 'It's alright, we can continue to shoot.' Later, she tells me why she puts up with all of this: 'I can't let all of these people down. Everyone is so nice, and they're trying to make my stay as comfortable as possible."

Diana Rigg's remuneration for her work on *Minikillers* was not disclosed, but it was clearly a substantial payment as Rigg claimed in *Bravo* magazine of 18th August 1969 that, "The salary is not less than what I got for the James Bond movie *On Her Majesty's Secret Service*." Reports put her 007 salary at £50,000 (approximate comparative value in 2024 according to the Bank of England: £695,577).

Although *Minikillers*, unlike the previous Accentfilms, credited production crew and principal actors on screen, it did not list character names. Similarly, over the course of approximately forty minutes of screentime, it is not revealed what any of the characters' names are, an omission that also plagued *Der Goldene Schlüssel* and *Das Diadem*. One notable exception is El Sali, the flamenco dancer, who is playing himself and whose name is shown on screen in publicity posters for his shows. This somewhat unusual situation has meant that, for instance, some sources credit Diana Rigg as 'Karate Journalist', José Nieto as 'Smuggler Boss with the Deadly Dolls' and H. Coscollin as 'Henchman with Rifle'. This is to say nothing of Moisés Augusto ('Jack') Rocha's Internet Movie Database credit, which for many years was 'Bowled Henchman', which suggested he was a failed cricketing henchman as opposed to one who was simply follicularly challenged. However – unbeknownst to people who are watching modern transfers of *Minikillers* – two characters are named on the outer packaging of the physical films: Diana Rigg's character is referred to as 'Diana' and the bald henchman character is revealed to be called 'Jack'. Since, in both cases, these are the actors' real names, the author has elected to use these in the synopsis presented earlier in the chapter and has taken the liberty of christening 'the Boss' character 'José' after actor José Nieto.

Minikillers is thought to have been made available through photo retailers from autumn 1969, with each film retailing at 29.99 Deutschmarks. In a change of strategy from the first wave of films, there was no monochrome option offered, only colour prints in Standard 8 and Super 8 formats. It is not known whether all four films were released simultaneously or given a staggered release.

A tie-in 7-inch single record by the Johnny Teupen Orchestra was issued in November 1969 by Accentfilm, and distributed by Golem Music. The single featured an alternative, extended version of the main theme (designated *Minikillers I*, duration 2 minutes 24 seconds) as well as a B-side (unsurprisingly, *Minikillers II*, 2 minutes 4 seconds) which was concocted from sections of the score with an added vocal element.

When talking to the author in 2010, director Wolfgang von Chmielewski recalled that, in addition to Jonny Teupen and his occasional collaborator Johann Anton 'Hans' Rettenbacher, Dave Pike, a well-known American vibrophonist, also featured on the musical soundtrack of *Minikillers*. Von Chmielewski supervised the soundtrack recordings, and he and Pike went on to become good friends.

The outer sleeve that came with the single suggested that there was a vinyl record available for each film, comprising the synchronous film soundtrack. The thinking behind this was that it would enable purchasers with silent projectors to watch *Minikillers* with sound. It is unclear whether these discs were ever released. If they were, they are exceptionally scarce today.

One of the most memorable aspects of *Minikillers* is the distinctive opening title sequence which features Jonny Teupen's theme music accompanied by a series of trippy visuals featuring the Minikiller dolls. These were the work of Cologne-based visual artist Vittorio Bonato (1934-2019), who used distorting mirrors to achieve an effect that sits somewhere between kitsch and the outright disturbing. Bonato's most famous artworks include a series of experiments with glass mirror deformations, which he commenced in 1969 and through which he confronted traditional ways of seeing and questioned customary behaviour. The result was that the observer saw the familiar in a completely new form, and Bonato's creative discovery appears to have fed directly into his striking *Minikillers* visuals. Three years earlier, Bonato had co-founded the Cologne artist collective K-66 with his friend and collaborator Joachim Bandau, with whom he later created the celebrated Troisdorf City Gates that have stood at either end of the pedestrian zone in Alt-Troisdorf since 1984. Working in later years as Victor Bonato, he remains well respected in art circles for works such as *Grosse Glas-Spiegel-Verformung* (Large Glass Mirror Deformation, 1970), *Welle Konvex-Konkav* (Convex-Concave Wave, 1976) and *Geteilte Konvexstörung* (Split Convex Disorder, 1981). The *Minikillers* sequence – and indeed Teupen's theme – features only on the first and third instalments, *Operation: Costa Brava* and *Macabre*. The remaining films open with live action footage of Diana Rigg, first sunbathing on a secluded beach (*Heroin*) and then watching El Sali's flamenco dancing act at El Relicario (*Flamenco*).

For many years, it was only possible to view *Minikillers* either by projecting the physical films or by tracking down the unofficial home video reissue produced by the French *Avengers* fan club, Steed & Co. Unfortunately, while the fan club's ambition and desire to make the films available for those interested is to be applauded, their transfers were made at too fast a speed (24 frames per second rather than the correct 18). A consequence of this is that many internet references to these films state incorrect, shorter running times and sometimes erroneously complain that the vinyl versions of the *Minikillers* theme play at too slow a speed. It was only in 2011, when StudioCanal UK employed BBC Resources – and, specifically, technical wizards Tim Emblem-English and Jonathan Wood – to make professional transfers of film prints held by Alan and Alys Hayes that these films were finally viewable as filmed (albeit not from 35mm or 16mm sources), and officially issued on *The Avengers: The Complete 50th Anniversary Collection* and as part of a separately released special features disc. Of course, these new transfers were sourced from Super 8 and Standard 8 prints, rather than the original 35mm masters, which remain lost. (For the record, the running times of the *Minikillers* episodes are 10 minutes 20 seconds, 10 minutes 5 seconds, 10 minutes exactly and 11 minutes 30 seconds respectively.)

So, what happened to the mooted ten-episode series? *Minikillers* accounts for four instalments, and even if the three variants of *Das Diadem* are generously accepted as another three episodes, there were still at least three episodes that went unproduced. When talking to a journalist during the filming of *Minikillers*, Diana Rigg revealed that her contract with Accentfilm was for "more than six movies." (*Bravo* magazine, 18th August 1969)

Wolfgang von Chmielewski supplies the answer: "Lückel and Nettemann went broke a few months after production wrapped on *Minikillers*. Everyone was happy and got paid, and I have no idea how Lückel and Nettemann failed. Maybe they had counted on another sale of 200,000 copies that didn't come through? All I remember is that Mengede took them back, kind as he was. They were salesmen at his camera store again, and had a great adventure to remember and talk about for the rest of their lives. I vaguely remember that a man near Düsseldorf, a bit primitive and in the heating business, bought or bailed out Accentfilm and produced some 'sex films' for the home market. I vaguely remember directing a couple, which was really great fun. Nothing really about sex, only girls in precarious situations that resulted in their exposure. Like swimming naked in a lake and a peeping Tom steals their clothes, and they escape by hitching a ride – naked – with an older – and happy – guy in a Bentley." John Steed? Stranger things have happened...

Filming Locations

The location work for *Minikillers* is believed to have been undertaken in June 1969, following on almost directly from Diana Rigg's filming on the James Bond thriller *On Her Majesty's Secret Service*, which was concluded early in the month. The film unit were based in Lloret de Mar, the largest resort on the Costa Brava, Spain, and the great majority of the filming was conducted in its immediate vicinity. The filming was scheduled to be completed over a six-day period, with daily shoots generally commencing before nine in the morning and lasting as long as twelve hours. At least one of the filming days involved a night shoot, for the *Flamenco* instalment. There was no in-studio filming conducted, with all scenes shot in real locations:

- The hotel seen in the first episode – *Operation: Costa Brava* – is the Hotel Roger de Flor, 9, Carrer Turó de l'Estelat, Lloret de Mar. This 4-star hotel with outdoor pool is built on a hill, raising it above the level of taller buildings at sea level, and offering magnificent panoramic views of the resort and the Mediterranean. It is possible that some of the cast and crew stayed at this hotel during filming. Diana Rigg, however, is known to have stayed at another Lloret de Mar hotel – the Hotel Santa Marta, to the west of the resort – in apartment 112.

- The high-rise tower block from which the goings on at the hotel are monitored is the Normax-Torremar building on the sea front road at 18, Passeig de Camprodon i Arrieta. Known locally as "the skyscraper", it has 18 floors, was built in 1963, and remains the tallest building in Lloret de Mar.

- The second episode – *Heroin* – opens on a small, 250 metre beach, Cala sa Boadella, Lloret de Mar. Framed by rocky outcrops and forest, this secluded beach is situated approximately 3 km (1.9 miles) to the west of the main Lloret de Mar resort and, in *Minikillers*, was the spot where Diana becomes ensnared in a large fishing net, along with a number of creepy mannequins.

- José's yacht docks at Port de Blanes, some 5.3 km (3.3 miles) southwest of Lloret de Mar. At the end of the episode, Diana parks the Mercedes outside 18, Carrer Esplanada del Port, Blanes, and goes over to her own car, which is parked across the road.

- At the beginning of the penultimate episode – *Macabre* – we see Diana enjoying a cup of tea at an outdoor café. This location is on the pedestrian pavement that splits the parallel roads Passeig d'Agustí Font and Passeig de Jacint Verdaguer (where her Jaguar E-Type is parked) on the Lloret de Mar seafront.

- We also see José and his men spying on Diana from the top of the Banco Zaragozano building, which is at 9, Passeig de Jacint Verdaguer, Lloret de Mar. In later years, this bank was taken over by Barclays, but today the building has been remodelled as a bed and breakfast hotel, with the ground floor given over to an Italian restaurant.

- When Diana heads off into the hills around the resort, she follows the Cami Cala Trons A road. At the time of filming, this area was undeveloped and the road merely a dirt track. Today, it is home to several luxury hilltop properties and the road has been tarmacked and paved.

- The second half of the episode is set at a cemetery, the Cementiri Modernista (Modernist Cemetery) at 1, Avinguda Vila de Blanes, Lloret de Mar – hence its title, *Macabre*. When the cemetery was conceived in the 1890s, its intended location was strongly disputed, as the Church did not agree that a cemetery should be constructed on the outskirts of the town. Today, with the expansion of Lloret de Mar, it is very much integrated within the town, but back then the distance to the inhabited urban centre was significant. However, construction went ahead, supported by 'Indiano' investors – a group of wealthy families who had largely made their fortune through overseas trading with the Americas. These backers purchased large plots in the cemetery in order to build their own mausoleums, thereby displaying their wealth. The first stone was laid in 1896 and the cemetery was officially inaugurated in 1901. It was reputedly inspired by the idea of a village of the dead, complete with streets and house-like mausoleums. The mausoleums are particularly noteworthy, designed and built by esteemed architects and sculptors such as Antoni M. Gallissà Soqué, Vicenç Artigas Albertí, Bonaventura Conill Montobbio, Ismael Smith, Eusebi Arnau and Josep Puig i Cadafalch, who also designed the striking entrance gates. It is also worth noting that, at the time of filming, the roads around the cemetery were dust tracks, whereas today they have tarmac surfaces and pavements, a sign of the town's expansion.

- The final episode – *Flamenco* – is set in a single location, a nightclub where El Sali performs his flamenco routine. This was filmed at the El Relicario nightclub situated at 3, Carrer de Marina in Lloret de Mar, one of the venues where El Sali regularly appeared. (It is more than likely that El Sali's dressing room required minimal decoration for filming.) The public area seen in *Minikillers* was actually open air, with filming being undertaken only after night had fallen. Today, the open courtyard has been roofed over, but the building remains.

- *Bravo* magazine (18th August 1969) reveals that, "At 3am, Diana's 'day' is finally over. The final scenes are being shot at the Gran Hotel Monterrey in Lloret." It is possible that the sequence in Diana's hotel room in *Operation: Costa Brava* was shot at this location (27, Avenida Vila de Tossa, Lloret de Mar).

Similarities to The Avengers TV Series

As might be expected for a film that features Diana Rigg, readily identifiable as Emma Peel, there are several *Avengers*-ish touches in *Minikillers*. The first of these is that Mrs. Peel drives an open top sports car, having eschewed both her powder blue Lotus Elan (*The Avengers*) and her flame red Mercedes-Benz 250SL Automatic (*Der Goldene Schlüssel / Das Diadem*) in favour of a black Jaguar E-Type, which, it must be said, is a fine choice of vehicle for the glamorous, jet-setting heroine.

Diana's fighting style, as seen in *Minikillers*, is very reminiscent of her fighting style in *The Avengers*, with karate chops, kicks and over-shoulder throws aplenty.

Another comparison that can be drawn between *The Avengers* and *Minikillers* is that, in both, the central protagonists are not terribly good at saving those that they are trying to protect. The avengers have a reputation for arriving "just too late". In *Minikillers*, the first Interpol agent is killed in Diana's presence, and she singularly fails to intervene in time to save the life of the second, the flamenco dancer El Sali. As Steed and Mrs. Peel sometimes appear to be, Diana here is reactive rather than proactive when it comes to the crunch.

As in *The Avengers*, the fights are clean and bloodless, though some of the deaths by poison spray are a little graphic compared to those in the British series, particularly that of the Boss in the *Flamenco* episode. The sight of El Sali's dead body in the same episode – the distorted reflection of which appears in his dressing room mirror – is positively chilling, and would definitely have felt out of place in the filmed *Avengers*.

In the third instalment, *Macabre*, Diana and Jack fight on a clifftop and the tussle ends with Jack being thrown over the edge. He lands at the foot of the cliff and, as he slowly recovers his wits, Diana picks a yellow flower from the clifftop, gives it a little kiss and tosses it after her defeated opponent. Emma Peel performs a similar action in the Series 4 *Avengers* episode *Silent Dust*, in which she picks a flower and drops it on her poleaxed foe, Omrod (William Franklyn). One wonders if Diana's gesture in *Macabre* was perhaps inspired by this moment or was remembered and suggested by Diana Rigg.

Diana's wardrobe is varied and very much of the era. It must be said, though, that the predominance of bikinis is perhaps not the most *Avengers*-ish of elements. However, for a part of *Operation: Costa Brava*, she is attired in a blouse, trousers and Chelsea boots (or similar), all in black, which she accessorises with a black belt with a large, squared silver clasp. This is the nearest that Diana gets to wearing an archetypal *Avengers* fighting outfit, and she puts it to good use.

As with the earlier films, in true *Avengers* style, we see Diana enjoying glasses of Champagne, notably while she is watching El Sali's flamenco act. However, it is something of a faux pas that when she finds the dolls in the secret storeroom, they are concealed within Castellblanch Cava boxes, not Champagne ones!

One *Minikillers* sequence might arguably owe a debt of inspiration to *Epic*, a fifth series episode of *The Avengers*: the funerary events of the *Macabre* instalment. It is notable that, in both *Macabre* and *Epic*, Diana Rigg comes across a hearse (horse-drawn in one, motorised in the other) and is then faced with her own mortality (an open coffin in *Minikillers*, a series of gravestones with her character's name on them in *Epic*). It also has to be said that the descending stage / ceiling idea witnessed in *Flamenco* – a favourite of chapter serials, fantasy television and even *Star Wars* (1977) – would not have been out of place amongst Z. Z. von Schnerk's directorial machinations in the same episode, and indeed conjures up memories of Emma Peel's predicament beneath the wine press in *A Surfeit of H$_2$O* (1965, but not shown in Germany until 1998).

Finally, the Series 6 *Avengers* episode *They Keep Killing Steed* (1968) was initially meant to be filmed in Zaragosa, Spain. It was ultimately rewritten and filmed in the UK, due to budgetary constraints. When the story was adapted for South African radio in the early seventies, it was based on a draft script and went out as *Too Many Olés*, a story set in Zaragosa!

Trivia Points

- Diana Rigg certainly took to the Spanish climate and way of life as, around the time that she made *Minikillers*, she purchased a farmhouse property on the island of Ibiza. Journalist Gordon Moore visited Diana at her Spanish retreat and described her acquisition in the 17th December 1969 edition of *The Australian Women's Weekly*: "The building is a typical Ibicenca farmhouse. Countless washings with lime have given the walls a blinding white simplicity that makes you screw up your eyes. It is this clarity of light and the reflections from the white dwellings that make Ibiza and the other Balearic Islands a mecca for artists and photographers. From the blinding sunlight, you enter the limpid cool of the farmhouse interior, all stone floors and low ceilings. The house has nine rooms wandering over the land with small windows overlooking the rolling hills to the sea."

- Diana Rigg spoke to *Bravo* magazine (published 18th August 1969) and revealed her immediate plans after completing work on *Minikillers*: "I will be staying at my idyllic house in Ibiza for a while to relax. My agent says that a real star doesn't do something like that, but I don't mind turning down a couple of offers once in a while. I find my life wonderful. I know who I am, I know what I do and why I do it. And I have the right friends. I have all of that. What more could I possibly want?"

- The *Ogden Standard-Examiner* (Utah) of 24th December 1969 also printed a story about Diana's Ibiza property: "She purchased a small house on one of those still-untouched-by-tourists islands off the coast of Spain, where she goes when she wants to be alone with her thoughts. 'It's actually impossible for my agent to reach me there,' she explained. 'I have no phone and although there is a telegraph office, nobody volunteers to deliver messages. But the tourists are starting to creep in...' This summer [1970]... she intends to make a film but on her island, using her own property as the principal setting and with a company of her own so it will be fun. She has the script and hopes to have the financing before the first summer tourist reaches Spain." During this time, she was splitting her time between London, where she was living in Augustus John's old studio off Finchley Road, and Ibiza, to which she came for holidays and sun.

- The black Mercedes 600 W100 that the character Jack drives in *Minikillers* – and which Diana briefly appropriates to escape from José and his henchmen at the harbour – was made available for Diana Rigg to drive while she was filming at Lloret de Mar. It is this car that Wolfgang von Chmielewski referred to as her "limo", in which she often listened to The Rolling Stones. *Bravo* magazine reported that it had been driven all the way to Lloret de Mar from Mulheim an der Ruhr in Germany (a distance of 1,353 kilometres) and that a chauffeur – Horst Schnittger – was on hand to drive her if she wished.

- The scene in which 'Diana' swims up to the motor yacht, climbs into the dingy and sneaks on board involved Diana Rigg being in the water for an hour, according to *Bravo* magazine (18th August 1969). The sequence required eight takes before director Wolfgang Chmielewski and cinematographer Josef Kaufmann were happy with the shot.

- The Minikiller dolls, dubbed 'Baby First Step', were 18 inches (46 centimetres) tall and made by Mattel Inc. The Mattel publicity machine declared it "the world's first walking doll" when they launched the product in 1965. The doll's walking mechanism was powered by two 'D'-size batteries (inserted in its back, in the cavities where Diana finds the heroin sachets) and was sold complete with roller skates – this talented little lady could skate as well as walk! The model seen in *Minikillers* appears to be the 1965 original, as the facial features were changed a year later to give the doll a "happy smile" – as the commercials put it – to go with its brand new voicebox feature. Perhaps the *Minikillers* producers got a good deal on the dolls, as they had been superseded by a new version that could talk and did not have a spine-chilling expression on its face!

- The *Bravo* magazine journalist who wrote the feature that appeared in its 18th August 1969 issue accompanied Diana Rigg to the Moef Gaga club – at 14, Carrer de Santa Cristina, Lloret de Mar – with the pair arriving at around midnight. The reporter was impressed with Diana's professionalism when their table was surrounded by locals and American, British and German tourists eager to meet the *Avengers* star. Asked by many of these people for her autograph, Diana reportedly signed patiently, made eye contact and didn't stop smiling. "A wonderful woman! She makes a lot of money, and how hard she has to work for it," the reporter comments.

Verdict

In common with the earlier Accentfilm productions, *Minikillers* is not particularly well regarded. I can't help but think that it gets rather unfairly dismissed. Many ratings are based on the washed out, soft transfers that play one third faster than they should and don't show Wolfgang von Chmielewski's direction or Josef Kaufman's distinctive and classy cinematography to their best advantage.

Admittedly, forty minutes is a long time to string out a dialogue-free drama, particularly when there are no intertitles to help things along, but watched as intended – in its individual ten minute chunks – it's genuinely enjoyable. There are plenty of memorable sequences: the surprising sight of the remote control doll strolling poolside and the subsequent murder of the American Interpol man; the surreal scene on the secluded beach, with Diana surrounded by mannequins before the smugglers' trap is sprung; the equally creepy sequence at Lloret de Mar's modernist cemetery (which seems well worth a visit in itself); the beautifully photographed last episode which features flamenco dancing, another side to José's character as he wines and dines his girlfriend, and the chilling deaths of El Sali and José himself. That these are all backed up by a wild, kitsch and frankly bonkers but brilliant musical score by Messrs. Teupen and Rettenbacher is icing on the cake.

The Spanish setting and the warm colours brought out by the Mediterranean sun also afford *Minikillers* some added glamour. It looks expensive and alluring despite the 8mm format. It's ironic that *The Avengers* proper couldn't afford to film in Spain, as planned, for what became *They Keep Killing Steed*, but two Germans, who, not long before, had been salesmen in a photographic shop, managed to!

There are flaws, of course. Not least of these is that we have a band of drug smugglers whose operation seems more geared toward killing people with dolls than it is toward smuggling. Furthermore, if you're smuggling heroin in children's dolls, then surely you package them in boxes for children's dolls, rather than boxes for wine? Also, if you're going to kill a couple of Interpol men, who are presumably on the gang's trail (but that's never made explicit; one of the drawbacks of a silent film!), then surely you don't kill them with the exact same things you're hiding the heroin in? Maybe I'm overthinking it.

It must be said that the *Minikillers* thugs are more dim-witted and ineffectual than henchmen in other television and films. Here we have a henchman with a rifle that he aims a few times, cleans up a lot... but never fires, not once. We have henchmen who can't defeat Diana, even if two of them take her on at once. One of them receives a musical comment in the form of a snatch of the Laurel and Hardy theme for his efforts, and it couldn't be more appropriate. Jack, the cool-looking Hawaiian-shirted henchman, is a much more interesting character, but even he is about as good in a fight as Woody Allen. I can forgive his comedy moment towards the end of *Flamenco*, but when he gets caught in his own trap out of sheer stupidity, it really does drive the final nail into his henchman credibility rating. It also reflects on Diana. To slightly misquote the 7th Doctor Who, "You can always judge a woman by the quality of her enemies." How could she *not* defeat these fools?

Overlooking these problems, *Minikillers* is a marked improvement on the amiable amateur hour of *Der Goldene Schlüssel / Das Diadem*. In every department, it is a step up in quality: script, casting, acting, location choices, direction, music, style and cinematography (that final shot in *Macabre*, where Diana drives into the sunset on the horse-drawn hearse, and the camera focuses on the hearse, then the sun and, finally, on the grass seeds, is top drawer).

The Accentfilms are interesting for *Avengers* fans in that – to all intents and purposes – they show Emma Peel (or at least a character that can be imagined to be Emma Peel) independent of John Steed. Although the character was seen in a similar situation for the greater part of both *The House That Jack Built* and *The Joker* in *The Avengers*, in each of these episodes Steed turns up at the end to offer his support and a lift home in his Bentley. Here, Emma is completely self-sufficient. However, Steed's absence does rob *Minikillers* of one of *The Avengers'* key ingredients: the contrast between his traditionalism and Mrs. Peel's modernism, though perhaps this is something that makes *Minikillers* interesting in its own right and not simply a straight copy of *The Avengers*.

A word about Diana Rigg. She famously never spoke of these Accentfilm productions in later life, and one can perhaps understand why. It was the nearest that Diana came to working in exploitation cinema and, while clearly the money was good, it was a means to an end – if she could make a (mini)killing for a few weeks' filming in Germany and Spain, then maybe she could take a poor-paying theatre production that was more professionally fulfilling off the back of it? As with the earlier films shot in Germany, Diana seems to have had a great time making *Minikillers* on the Costa Brava, judging by her demeanour on screen and her comments in the press at the time. And it has to be said that Josef Kaufman's camera gets the very best out of Diana Rigg – her warmth of character and sense of fun just glow through the screen in his work.

Maybe *Avengers* fandom doesn't love *Minikillers*, but I'm completely smitten.

ESCAPADE

J Z FERGUSON
with thanks to Michael Richardson and Anthony McKay

Project Type: Television Series Pilot
Transmission Date: 19th May 1978 (USA)

Synopsis

Act One

It is a dark San Francisco night. Two women are lowered from a helicopter and begin to navigate a training course. The two women are agents Paula Winters and Suzy. Suzy times Paula as she approaches a house, disables a facsimile of a guard, and breaks into the house. Inside the house, Paula finds and blows up a safe, which triggers the sensor alarm that she failed to deactivate in advance. Paula looks to Suzy in panic, but Suzy encourages her to keep going. Paula takes the contents of the safe and rejoins Suzy. The pair hook themselves up to the helicopter and are pulled heavenward.

Later, in the locker room, Paula asks Suzy how she did. Suzy replies that she finished running the course in time, but would have been "dead" if she had taken ten seconds longer. Paula explains that she got confused, and Suzy warns her that she cannot get confused during the actual mission, for which the course was a trial run. The mission is set to take place on Saturday, and Suzy reminds Paula that it will require her to face real guards and real danger. Paula admits that she is nervous, but Suzy reassures her by telling her that she was nervous about her first assignment, too. Suzy advises Paula that her nerves can give her a "fine edge" during the mission that will help her to succeed. Paula says that her mind went numb during the trial run, and that she worries that she will forget the code that she has been required to memorise for her mission. Suzy runs through the code with Paula and tells her to relax.

On Saturday, the day of her first assignment, Paula goes for a run, but a car follows her. Her jogging route takes her past the home of Joshua Rand, who has just stepped outside to retrieve his morning paper. Paula stops to talk to Rand and laments that she has to jog to stay in shape, whereas Rand looks great despite seemingly never exercising. Rand quips that he stirs his own martini every night, implying that this keeps him fit. Paula tells Rand that it is the day of her first assignment, and Rand assures her that nothing will go wrong. Paula resumes her jog. The car continues to shadow her until she returns to her apartment, at which point a darkhaired man — Arnold Tulliver — gets out and follows her into her building. In her apartment, Paula turns on the shower and begins to change out of her jogging clothes. Tulliver listens outside her door.

On his drive to work, Rand spots a Volkswagen Beetle in the ditch, then sees a woman collapse in the middle of the road. He stops just short of her prone body and gets out to investigate, only to discover that it is Suzy. When

Rand checks her pulse, Suzy opens her eyes and grins. Rand tells her if she needed a ride, she could have found a less dramatic way to get him to stop, like sticking out her thumb. Suzy quips that if she had done that, he probably would have driven right by. Rand teasingly agrees that he probably would have. He observes that her car has broken down again, and asks her why she does not get rid of it. Suzy counters that there is nothing wrong with it – she thinks it is "in love" after being "kissed" by a truck. Rand recognises that this is her way of telling him she has had another car accident, but Suzy merely quips that it is not her fault that she parked next to a sex-mad truck.

The two agents arrive at an old house. The front door is guarded by two men, and one of the guards scans a pass to admit them. They are escorted upstairs by another two guards, who bring them to a door that is manned by a third guard. They enter a well-furnished study, and put their hands on a palm reader. The bookcases in the study pull back and a large computer, Oz, slides out from behind them. Oz is the pair's superior, who provides them with their instructions. Oz informs them that its sex-delineation circuits are currently on the blink, meaning it cannot determine which of the agents is Rand and which is Suzy. Suzy quips that they know the difference, and that is all that matters. The computer reminds the agents that it does not like to be called "Oz", but Rand points out that it is easier to say than "Computerized Security Initiator MK. V/K7". Oz complains that it does not understand what "Oz" means, but Suzy casually replies that that is only because Oz never saw the movie. The pair tell Oz that they are there for the special briefing, but Oz points out that Paula has not arrived yet. Oz is unimpressed that Paula is late for her first assignment, and asks Rand and Suzy to remind it to reprimand Paula. Suzy quips that, with all of its memory circuits, they should not need to remind Oz of anything. Oz self-consciously confirms that this is the case, and then begins to giggle, explaining that it was recently installed with a chuckle track and is having trouble getting the hang of it. It then gives them their daily briefing via its videoscreen, which it describes as its "eye". The footage is from the previous day and shows passengers disembarking from the 11:15 flight from Istanbul. Rand identifies one of the passengers as Arnold Tulliver, a freelance agent who steals secrets and sells them to the highest bidder. Rand tells Suzy and Oz that he has tried to catch Tulliver, and Tulliver has returned the favour by trying to kill him. Oz reminds them that Tulliver has a Class "A" danger rating. Suzy surmises that Tulliver is in town to do something devious. Oz then wonders where Paula is, and Suzy suggests that Oz call her. Oz does. The phone rings in Paula's apartment, where the shower is still running, but Paula is not standing beneath the stream. Paula answers, but sounds disoriented, blearily saying that she "can't".

Suzy and Rand go to Paula's apartment, and pull up just in time to see Paula's car drive away with someone who looks like Paula at the wheel. Suzy notes that the car was heading south, but Rand points out that, if it was Paula in the car, she should have been heading north to see Oz. The pair go to Paula's apartment and stop outside the door. A passing neighbour tells them that he just saw Paula drive away. However, Rand can hear the shower running and kicks the door open. Suzy checks the shower, but there is no one inside. The kettle then starts boiling, and Rand finds a cup has been laid out for the water. Rand surmises that Paula left in a hurry. Suzy wonders if Paula lost her nerve because she was nervous about her first assignment. They check Paula's closet for her jogging outfit, and discover that it is missing. Since the person they saw in Paula's car was wearing the jogging outfit, Suzy concludes that it was Paula they saw driving away.

Meanwhile, a woman clad in the jogging outfit alights from Paula's car (which is parked across the water from the Golden Gate Bridge) and runs off. We cannot see her face.

Rand contacts Oz and tells it to send out a description of Paula and her car. Suzy tells Rand that she now believes that it was not Paula in the car. A necklace that she lent to Paula has been left behind in the apartment, and Suzy claims that the real Paula would have been wearing it when she left. Rand is surprised that Suzy kept the necklace – he describes it as a cheap trinket that he bought for her in Albuquerque. Suzy calls it a prized possession, and tells him that she researched its providence – it is the Navajo equivalent of an engagement ring! Rand stammers that he had no idea, but forgets about his faux pas when Suzy shows him a suitcase full of teddy bears on Paula's bed. Rand regards it with bafflement.

Act Two

Rand and Suzy dissect the teddy bears, with Suzy complimenting him on his sensitive hands and telling him he should have been a surgeon. Rand counters that he has a sensitive palate, too, and Suzy takes the hint, asking if he wants a drink. Rand tells her not to drown it like she always does. In one of the teddy bears, he finds a photo of a boy standing in front of a distinctive obelisk, and asks Suzy if there were any men in Paula's life. The boy has red hair, like Paula, and Rand speculates that it could be Paula's son, but Suzy believes Paula would have told her if she had a child. Rand suggests that the boy could be a young relative of Paula's. A call comes in alerting them that Paula's car has been located. Rand and Suzy search it and find Paula's jogging outfit in the trunk. Rand spots the obelisk that was behind the boy in the photo across the water from the location of Paula's car. They discover the obelisk is in the middle of a graveyard, and search the area. Suzy discovers another teddy bear beside a grave belonging to a man named Edward Malone, who died more than twenty years before Paula was born. While the pair is puzzling on this, Rand sees a redhaired woman in a floaty dress running away. The pair give chase, but lose her. Suzy wonders why Paula never told her about the original chiffon dress she is wearing, which Suzy thinks is beautiful. Unbeknownst to Rand and Suzy, they are being watched by Tulliver.

Rand and Suzy break for lunch, then continue to puzzle on the mystery. They discuss the fact that Oz has delayed Paula's assignment and plans to send another operative in her place. Suzy wonders if she might be the replacement. Rand speculates that the strange business with Paula may have been instigated to delay her assignment, which involved stealing the Alpha papers, but Suzy cannot see the connection between the papers and the teddy bears in the graveyard. Rand believes Tulliver may be involved, and that the whole business with Paula is a false trail intended to distract them from Tulliver's true plan. Still, he intends to follow it, not for Paula's sake, but because it might get them some answers. They pass a photography shop, and spot a photo in the window of Paula dressed in a wedding gown and with a groom by her side. The shop owner tells them that the picture is of a Mr. and Mrs. Malone, the same surname written on the tombstone where they found the teddy bear. Suzy spots what looks like Paula running past the shop and again comments on her dress, speculating that it was made in Europe and wondering where she got it. They follow the woman in the dress to an apartment and find the dress in a closet. Suzy confirms that it is from Paris. Running feet send them out into the corridor, and they chase a man with a gun down the stairs. He runs out onto the fire escape and tumbles off of it to his death. Suzy asks Rand why he did not shoot the man to disable him and keep him from running. Rand replies that he hates carrying a gun – he hates the noise guns make, and the fact that carrying a gun ruins the drape of his jacket. He also points out that, sooner or later, someone with a bigger gun takes your gun away and uses it against you.

Act Three

Oz tells Rand and Suzy that the dead man was Bartholomew "Bart" Danzik, a small-time crook, and that he was carrying another teddy bear. Oz also tells them that Edward Malone was no one significant, and that no Malones ever married Paula Winters. Rand decides to dig deeper into Edward Malone, who was a sea captain and ran a small boat. Rand and Suzy go to the docks and stop in at a local bar. Suzy comments that the pink chiffon dress does not suit a redhead like Paula, and Rand admits that this suggests that the person in the dress may not be Paula. A sailor in the bar teases Rand for carrying the teddy bear found on Danzik. Suzy tells the sailor to back off, and that Rand could easily beat him in a fight. This provokes the sailor, forcing Rand to fight and defeat the man. The sailor's shirt splits open in the scuffle, revealing a tattoo of Paula on his chest. Tulliver passes by the bar's window as the pair question the sailor. The sailor tells Rand and Suzy that he found the tattooist who did the tattoo by old Malone's boat. Rand and Suzy visit the boat and discover it is the *Paula*. They then spot a redhaired woman in Paula's jogging outfit. They chase her and she jumps into the water, where she is hit by a speedboat. The body is too badly mangled to make a positive identification, but is later revealed to be that of Jill Carter, a small-time criminal, not Paula.

At what appears to be Paula's apartment, an unconscious, drugged Paula lies on the bed while Tulliver and another man discuss their scheme. The other man says that the deaths of Jill and Bart were not part of the plan, but Tulliver argues that the deaths will work in their favour by adding to the confusion. They drug Paula further.

Back at Rand's, an amorous moment between him and Suzy is interrupted when someone who looks like Paula runs past his house.

Tulliver is busy questioning the drugged Paula about the code she learned for her first assignment. He sends his henchman to make a call.

Act Four

Suzy and Rand are playing cards when they get a call from Paula asking for help. They travel to the location she gives them, and arrive at a lake. They see a boat with what looks like Paula lying unconscious in it. Rand swims out to investigate, and is nearly run over by a motorboat. The prone figure in the boat is revealed to be a dummy wearing what appears to be Paula's jogging outfit, but Suzy observes that it is not in Paula's size. Rand concludes that everything that has occurred is part of a plan conceived by Tulliver to lead them away from Paula's apartment.

Tulliver is recording Paula's drugged responses to his questions. He plans to use the codewords she is providing to gain access to her employer's secret transmissions, then sell information from the transmissions for large sums of money. Rand and Suzy arrive, but there is no one in Paula's apartment. Suzy sees the neighbour who told them Paula was out the morning of her disappearance, and recognises him from the footage of Tulliver disembarking from the plane. Rand concludes that Tulliver mocked up another apartment to look like Paula's in order to make her think that she was still at home. They break into the apartment of the "neighbour" Suzy recognised from the footage, who is actually Tulliver's henchman, and defeat Tulliver after a stand-off. Paula, still drugged, mumbles that "teddy bear" is the keyword.

Suzy and Rand tell Oz that it was the code that Tulliver wanted, not the Alpha papers. Suzy then delivers the Alpha papers – which were acquired by Paula and Suzy – to Oz, and queries whether the computer's sex-delineation circuits have been fixed. She then asks Oz if it is a boy or girl computer, which confuses it greatly. Suzy asks Rand about the state of his sex-delineation circuit. He replies that it is in need of an overhaul, before leading a smiling Suzy away.

Cast

Granville Van Dusen (Joshua Rand), Morgan Fairchild (Suzy), Len Birman (Arnold Tulliver), Janice Lynde (Paula Winters), Alex Henteloff (Wences), Gregory Walcott (Sailor), Dennis Rucker (Paula's Neighbour), Charlie Webster (Bart – uncredited), Jonathan Harris (Voice of Oz – uncredited)

Production

Director – Jerry London
Writer – Brian Clemens
Producer – Brian Clemens
Executive Producer – Philip Saltzman
Music – Patrick Williams
Director of Photography – Jack Swain
Editor – James Gross
Art Directors – George B. Chan, David Marshall
Set Decorator – Ralph Nelson
In Charge of Production – Fred Ahern
Unit Production Manager – Tom Foulkes
Production Manager – Dick Gallegly
Postproduction Supervisor – Don Hall
Assistant Director – Bob Bender
Special Effects – Chuck Dolan
Executive Editorial Supervisor – Richard Brockway
Music Supervisor – John Elizalde
In Charge of Talent – John Conwell

A Woodruff Production in association with A Quinn Martin Production

Analysis

In the autumn of 1977, *The New Avengers* wrapped production. Though the series' cast made a promotional trip to the United States in June 1976, an American sale of the show failed to materialise in time to save it from its unreliable French financing, which eventually had to be propped up by Canadian interests. Stateside airings of the show did not occur until 1978, but those airings, while belated, led many to hope that American funding could be acquired to bring the series back for a third season. Unfortunately, the amount offered by the show's American broadcaster, CBS, fell short of what was required to fund the series' production, even when coupled with additional funding offered by London Weekend Television, and no other backer was secured to make up the difference. However, before *The New Avengers'* potential U.S. revival was even on the table, another American-funded foray into Avengerland was mooted. In late 1976, *New Avengers* producer and writer Brian Clemens was contacted by the American production company Quinn Martin – responsible for major 1970s television series including *The F.B.I.*, *Barnaby Jones*, *Cannon* and *The Streets of San Francisco* – with a request for him to assist with the creation of an *Avengers*-esque series, to be shot on 35mm film. Clemens was amenable to the idea, and joined the project as a producer and writer. After a period of development – during which the show's title was changed from *The Avengers USA* to *Escapade* for copyright reasons – a report on the filming of the show's 50-minute pilot, *I Thought It Was Someone I Knew*, surfaced on 9th March 1978. Unfortunately, Clemens already had reservations about the production, as the series' two leads had been cast without his knowledge or input. (Anthony McKay and Michael Richardson, "The Avengers Man", *TimeScreen*, Autumn 1992, Number 19) Nevertheless, Clemens fulfilled Quinn Martin's request to write a second script for the series and brainstormed a full season's worth of story ideas. Executive producer Philip Saltzman also wrote a number of scripts for the series, and the pilot itself received an airing on CBS on 19th May 1978. However, no series was commissioned that year or the next, despite 1979 bringing reports of San Francisco locations being scouted for the filming of further episodes, likely because the Quinn Martin production company was sold later in 1978. *Escapade* was finally aired in the UK in the 1980s, but, by that time, the project was well and truly dead. Brian Clemens attributed the series' failure to its leads, stating "The first one was shot but it didn't work and I think the problem was in the casting." (Anthony McKay and Michael Richardson, "The Avengers Man", *TimeScreen*, Autumn 1992, Number 19) However, given the lack of success in getting more seasons of The New Avengers made, was the failure to continue with Escapade a missed opportunity to continue the Avengers legacy in some form? Did the show live up to the pedigree of its forebear? Laying the Avengers mantle aside, could Escapade at least have served as an entertaining entry in the adventure / espionage genre? An analysis of the pilot episode provides answers to at least some of these questions.

As one would expect from a script penned by Brian Clemens, the plot of *I Thought It Was Someone I Knew* is very much in the Emma Peel / Tara King / New Avengers mould, to the point that it lifts story elements from episodes from all three eras. Suzy and Rand following a trail of clues while in pursuit of fellow agent Paula Winters calls to mind episodes in which the leads were chasing something or someone, such as *The Tale of the Big Why*, in which Steed, Purdey, and Gambit pursue ex-con Burt Brandon, then retrace his steps and attempt to decipher clues he left behind in order to find evidence that he has hidden away; *Dead Man's Treasure*, in which Steed and Emma decode the clues in a car rally treasure hunt in order to recover top secret documents that have been hidden with the rally's prize; and *Take Me To Your Leader*, in which Steed and Tara follow an oft-exchanged briefcase in order to identify the leader of an espionage courier network. Suzy and Rand's speculation that Tulliver is attempting to stop Paula from acquiring the Alpha papers – when, in fact, he is laying a false trail to keep them busy while he pumps Paula for information – calls to mind the villains' misdirection scheme in *Hostage*, which hinges on Steed and his department assuming that the villains are after the Allied Attack Plan, when, in fact, they only want Steed to steal the plan so they can frame him as a traitor. The use of a Paula lookalike also recalls *Hostage*, in which one of the enemy henchmen dresses up like Steed in order to frame him, but also draws on the series' penchant for doppelgangers and impersonators, who feature in the likes of *Man with Two Shadows*, *Two's a Crowd*, *The Girl from Auntie*, *They Keep Killing Steed*, and *Faces*. In addition, the teddy bears found in the graveyard, at Paula's apartment, and on the body of one of the villains recall the teddies in the Cathy Gale episode *Mr Teddy Bear*, and the stuffed animals used to gain access to an escape route for fleeing criminals in *Escape in Time*.

Like any Peel / King Avengers story, the episode also contains plenty of eccentric touches and surreal moments: the Paula lookalike fleeing, spectrelike, across the graveyard in a flowing dress; the suitcase of teddy bears on Paula's bed; the lone teddy by a grave in the graveyard; the ghostly Paula lookalike's reappearance in the incongruous setting of an urban street; Paula's faux wedding photo displayed in a shop window; Suzy collapsing in the middle of the road; Rand and Suzy apparently occupying Paula's apartment at the same time as Paula and the villains without them seeing each other. The false trail left by Tulliver also makes for a diverting, offbeat plot thread that encourages the audience to use the various bizarre clues encountered by the leads to work out the villain's objective. However, while the surreal and quirky touches are intriguing, some of them strain credulity in their attempt to wrongfoot and baffle. Paula would only agree to pose for her fake wedding photo while in a drug-induced haze, so why does she look bright and alert in the photo? How did Tulliver get the photo into the shop's window without the owner noticing it and wondering where it had come from? How did Tulliver manage to persuade the sailor to have Paula's face tattooed on his chest? It is a large tattoo, but the sailor clearly has no idea who Paula is and does not appear to be working for Tulliver or to have received any compensation from him for receiving the tattoo. And yet, seemingly for no reason, he has consented to have a tattoo that facilitates Tulliver's plan, a scenario that strains the bounds of credulity. Furthermore, how could Tulliver have known that the sailor would accost Rand and be provoked into fighting him? Again, there is no indication that Tulliver made the sailor fight Rand. Indeed, the sailor only notices Rand because he is carrying a teddy bear, but Tulliver would have no way of knowing that Rand would bring the teddy with him to the bar, that he would visit the bar at all, or that that particular sailor would mock him for carrying the teddy. Even if Tulliver could have foreseen Rand's presence and his possession of the bear, the sailor only becomes violent when Suzy begins telling the sailor about Rand's fighting prowess – if Suzy had not been present, a fight likely would not have broken out and the tattoo would not have been revealed. Even if Tulliver could, somehow, have been certain that the fight would occur, he still could not have ensured that the sailor's shirt would rip open during the scuffle to reveal the Paula tattoo. If that had not happened, Suzy and Rand would never have questioned the sailor about the tattoo's origin, and therefore would not have been led to Malone's boat, the *Paula*, or seen the Paula lookalike at the marina. And yet, Tulliver is shown passing by the window of the bar while Suzy and Rand are questioning the sailor, as if he had somehow foreseen that every one of these coincidences and improbable events would not only occur, but happen in the exact order and at the exact time that he needed them to for his false trail to continue. This elevates Tulliver from mastermind to omniscient being, blessed with a remarkable prescience that allows him to flawlessly predict the future. Tulliver also seems to be psychic in that his use of the teddy bears suggests that he knew "teddy bear" was a keyword for the code, something that the drugged Paula reveals. However, if Tulliver did not know this phrase until he drugged and questioned Paula – as evidenced by the fact that he is shown pressing Paula for the keyword – then how could he have incorporated teddy bears into the false trail he left for Rand and Suzy? If he already knew that "teddy bear" was a key phrase, then why did he need to abduct Paula and ask her about the code in the first place? Along with these plot holes, Tulliver's ultimate goal is something of a letdown after the episode's drawn-out chase. He is not attempting to execute any grand scheme, but simply wants the codes so he can listen in on Suzy and Rand's department's communications for an hour and sell the secrets he gleans from them. After a promising start, therefore, Tulliver's plan and the episode's plot ultimately seem unnecessarily complex for what is a relatively small payoff for villain and audience alike.

The theme tune for *Escapade* is a catchy one. It begins with a rapid-fire tempo (played on guitar) that engenders tension and suspense, before transitioning into a loping, jaunty rhythm that suggests that the two leads approach their dangerous espionage work with an unconcerned, confident attitude, and defeat their adversaries without breaking a sweat. At the same time, the jazzy brass element of the jaunty sections evokes a sense of mystery and intrigue, and also possesses a smouldering quality that reflects Rand and Suzy's sexually charged relationship. The tense and jaunty segments alternate throughout the theme. The result is a piece that ploughs its own furrow and is unlike any of the *Avengers* themes. Instead, the jazz / brass elements anticipate the saxophone-tinged compositions of the 1980s, such as the theme for the series *Moonlighting*, while various electronica-inspired touches scattered throughout – a nod to the leads' computer boss, Oz, the console of which features heavily in the opening titles – predict the eighties' love of synths. Variations on the theme play throughout the episode, and are a fitting accompaniment to the action, the more leisurely portions serving as the perfect background for transitions between plot points and physical locations, while the up-tempo segments add extra tension to action or suspense-driven sequences.

As evidenced by the mixed reception received by *The New Avengers*' French and Canadian episodes, successfully transplanting a series as quintessentially British as *The Avengers* to foreign soil is a difficult feat to achieve. However, *Escapade*'s task was made slightly easier by the fact that, *Avengers* influence or no, it was an American series being made in the United States, rather than a British one relocated to American soil and forced to negotiate its new surroundings while attempting to maintain its flavour. On the other hand, if *Escapade* was going to have any hope of embodying *The Avengers*' signature charm and offbeat nature, its setting had to be chosen with a certain amount of care. The likes of New York and Los Angeles, while the settings of many a successful series, lack the all-important *Avengers* "quirk" factor, a fact that *Escapade*'s producers, to their credit, seemed to recognise, as they plumped for San Francisco. With the world's crookedest street, the legendary Haight-Ashbury scene (providing some sixties connections to this American corner of Avengerland), and the iconic trolley cars – on which passengers have to be firmly seated or possess a strong grip to prevent themselves from being accidentally ejected before reaching their stop – there is plenty of whimsy, originality, and eccentricity to be found in the city to give the series a distinctly *Avengers*-ish flavour. In addition, one could imagine such iconic locations as the Golden Gate Bridge, Fisherman's Wharf, and Alcatraz playing some role in future plots and creating a sense of place, just as London locations did in *The Avengers*. Furthermore, San Francisco is a large enough city to be believable as a base of operations for an intelligence organisation, and its location in the same state as Los Angeles means that the characters would have access to the resources of a larger centre, if required. Overall, therefore, San Francisco is, quite possibly, the best choice of location for an American Avengerland in the whole country.

The locations featured in the pilot are also well chosen. The episode capitalises on its San Francisco setting early on – Paula's jog sees her powering up the city's iconic steep streets while bracketed by classic examples of San Francisco homes. Elsewhere, Rand's waterfront drive is interrupted by Suzy collapsing in the middle of the road, and he comes to a stop with the Golden Gate Bridge in the background. The bridge re-emerges as the backdrop for Paula's abandoned car, shown both when the faux Paula flees from it and when Rand and Suzy discover it. The pair's exploration of a marina, through which they chase the faux Paula, is a good use of the city's maritime connections. Other settings are less unique to the city, but are *Avengers*-ish and therefore well chosen. The graveyard, with its all-white motif, is a surreal, unearthly place. Aesthetically, it looks like a ghost city, an impression reinforced by the sight of the faux Paula running through it in her diaphanous gown, like a spectre newly raised from one of the graves. Its layout, with mausoleums, trees, and graves – behind which the faux Paula frequently disappears – seemingly arranged at odd angles to one another, adds a disorienting, mazelike element to the place. There is a sense that anyone and anything could disappear into the graveyard's ether at any time, as though the very nature of its purpose has thinned the walls of reality within its borders. Later, Rand and Suzy stroll down a charming street clad in raincoats, while Rand shelters them from the rain with the quintessential Steed accessory: an umbrella. The wet weather, quaint streetscape, and raincoats lend the scene a British flavour that transcends its Pacific coastal location. The episode's only truly poorly chosen location is the rather swampy lake at which Rand and Suzy discover a Paula dummy in a canoe. It is visually uninteresting, lacks a surreal feel despite serving as the setting of an odd tableau, and fails to capture the whimsy that typified rural areas in The Avengers. Overall, however, the episode's locations serve the plot and help to establish the look and feel of this new, American Avengerland

The Characters

Joshua Rand

While *Escapade* was originally conceived as *The Avengers USA*, in some respects, it would be more accurate to describe it as *The **New** Avengers USA*. While *Escapade*'s flavour is clearly intended to evoke the surreal / bizarre feel that characterised *The Avengers* in the Emma Peel and Tara King eras, it is *The New Avengers*' influence that is felt most strongly when it comes to the characterisation of the two leads. It is therefore unsurprising that Rand owes something to *The New Avengers*' male protagonists, John Steed and Mike Gambit, though his resemblance to the latter is more obvious. As a younger man – Granville Van Dusen was about to turn, or had just turned, 34 when he shot the pilot, coincidentally the same age Gareth Hunt was when he began portraying Gambit – Rand is more readily identifiable as an American Gambit than a trans-Atlantic Steed. In addition, Rand displays a number of characteristics that are more in Gambit's wheelhouse than Steed's. He drives a Mercedes-Benz 450SL convertible (registration: 865 PCE), a more modern vehicle that calls to mind Gambit's Jaguar XJS, rather than Steed's classic cars, or even his more stately "Big Cat" Jaguar. Rand also makes a habit of kicking doors down, as Gambit was wont to do, and Suzy comments that a destination is "a long way, even the way you drive", suggesting that she believes he drives recklessly, a comment that Purdey, or even Gambit himself, could have easily made about Gambit's driving given his penchant for high-speed chases and past career as a racing driver (who crashed a lot). As a thirtysomething man living in 1978, Rand is also separated from Gambit's last produced onscreen adventure in 1977 by a matter of months, and therefore dons trendy seventies fashions that could have just as easily been modelled by Gambit, and, in some cases, had Gambit-worn equivalents: a tuxedo worn with a large black bowtie and boots with a significant heel is akin to Gambit's own tux, donned in the likes of *Three Handed Game* and *K is for Kill: Tiger by the Tail*; cream trousers and a jacket worn with a black turtleneck, and a similar white turtleneck, cream trouser, and brown jacket ensemble, are reminiscent of Gambit's tan corduroy trousers and jacket worn with a white turtleneck in

Dirtier by the Dozen and *Gnaws*, and his white turtleneck with brown jacket and trousers ensemble in *To Catch a Rat*; a cream double-breasted Macintosh calls to mind Gambit's example in *Trap*; and a checked shirt reminds one of Gambit's own in *Dead Men are Dangerous*. Like Gambit, Rand is not always portrayed as suave, but finds himself beleaguered and / or embarrassed in certain situations. In one instance, Rand, having swum out to a boat in his clothes, finds himself standing shivering on the dock, soaking wet, with a blanket around his shoulders, and sans trousers, having given them to Suzy to dry. He receives no sympathy from Suzy for his humiliating plight; instead, she unabashedly stares at him trouserless, to the point that he is forced to ask her to turn around to give him some privacy while he puts his trousers back on.

Other similarities between Rand and Gambit include their tendency to rely on instinct. Gambit follows his instincts in *Angels of Death* when identifying a potential traitor, while Rand comments that his instincts and experience tell him that, despite appearances, Paula was not in the car that he and Suzy saw departing from her apartment. Rand also employs a piece of Gambit phraseology, telling Suzy he got a double "A" for observation (Gambit awards Purdey an "A for observation" in *Faces*), and humourously confirms to Suzy that he knows she is a woman, just as Gambit does to Purdey in *K is for Kill: Tiger by the Tail*.

While the similarities between Gambit and Rand are numerous, there are undeniable similarities between Rand and Steed, as well. The most obvious of these is Rand's reluctance to carry a gun – he tells Suzy "I don't like the noise, and, also, it would ruin the drape of this jacket, and, also, carry a gun and sooner or later somebody comes along with a bigger gun and takes your gun away and uses it against you." This recalls Patrick Macnee's oft-stated hatred of guns and desire to avoid carrying them as Steed, resulting in him using his umbrella, steel-rimmed bowler, and wits to defeat opponents. Rand also seems to want to avoid violence, if possible. When a sailor taunts Rand for carrying a teddy bear, Rand's first instinct is to ignore him and not engage. He only reluctantly agrees to fight when Suzy goads the sailor into attacking. This avoidance of violence is in keeping with Steed's *modus operandi*, which found him refraining from engaging in outright combat unless absolutely necessary, preferring instead to find clever, devious solutions to get out of trouble. Gambit, in contrast, while not spoiling for a fight, engaged in combat more readily. Rand also has some of Steed's ability to bluff his way out of unusual situations with complete composure. One instance of this occurs after Suzy implies that she will provide sexual favours to a store owner if he agrees to provide her with information. The store owner provides said information, but, when he asks when he and Suzy can meet up, she tells him to ask her husband.

The flustered store owner turns to Rand and asks if he is Suzy's husband. In response, Rand adopts a serious, authoritative expression and widens his eyes to reinforce the gravity of the situation, before informing the man that he is Suzy's psychiatrist and leaving before he can be questioned further. Steed employed a similar wide-eyed, sombre expression on many occasions while acting as though his own strange behaviour, or that of others, was not worthy of comment (see his performance as an overenthusiastic, intense, and eccentric wine merchant in A Surfeit of H_2O, during which he discomfits and flusters Sue Lloyd's Joyce Jason with his antics). Like Steed, Rand is also capable of bluffing his way out of high-risk situations, as he does in the episode's climax, when he pretends to have a gun in his pocket, only to reveal that it is actually a piece of one of the teddy bears. In the same moment, he reveals a Steed-like concern for the integrity of his attire, telling Tulliver that he will shoot him through his jacket pocket if he has to, even though he hates "to ruin a $200 coat". His Steed-inspired sartorial concern also emerges via his aforementioned unwillingness to carry a gun because it ruins the drape of his jacket.

While Rand owes something to both Steed and Gambit, he is, in other ways, his own distinct character. First of all, Rand is very businesslike. While both Steed and Gambit were professional agents who took their jobs very seriously when warranted, they also found plenty of opportunities for witty quips and had boyish senses of humour and mischief, with Steed coupling his playfulness with beaming bonhomie and eccentricity, and Gambit delighting in corny puns and gags and the odd practical joke. Rand, in contrast, tackles his duties with a stoic, earnest professionalism, remaining focussed on the problem at hand, forever engaging in logical deduction, and constantly turning evidence over in his mind. Rand reveals this single-minded approach to the job when Suzy assumes that his drive to follow the false trail laid by Paula's kidnapper stems from a reluctance to abandon a damsel in distress. Rand refutes her assumption, attributing his doggedness to being "calculating" – he not only wants to help Paula, but to discover the identity of the person behind the false trail and their reason for laying it. Even after he is certain that Tulliver is the one behind the trail and is using it to divert attention from his true purpose, Rand remains determined to follow it, believing that he will be able to glean clues from it that will reveal Tulliver's plan. He is also a practical man, scolding Suzy for continuing to drive a malfunctioning car and dismissing her theory that Oz is controlled by a mysterious person, telling her that he has seen for himself that it is connected to a large bank of computers. This lack of frivolity also extends to his relationship with Suzy. Unlike Steed and Gambit, who delighted in flirting with their female partners, Rand has drawn a strict line between business and pleasure and resists Suzy's overtures – with a will he describes as being made of "tempered steel" – because he does not believe in having romantic dalliances with people he works with. While Suzy's constant overtures do wear down his defences – he kisses back when Suzy kisses him, and acquiesces when Suzy asks if she can keep one revealing outfit in his closet – he makes far more of an effort to keep her at arm's length than Steed and Gambit did with their female partners, whom they were happy to romance. This is not to say that Rand is not interested in romance – Suzy comments that she saw a list of 14 women in his file, a number Rand describes as a "lean year" – but, unlike Steed and Gambit, he prefers to confine it to his leisure time rather than conflate it with his work.

Rand is not driven, focused, and disciplined at all times, however. In the morning, he is shown wandering around lethargically in his bathrobe, seemingly uninterested in doing anything more strenuous than retrieving his newspaper. Catching a glimpse of Paula mid-jog, he tells her that just watching her exertions makes him feel tired. Paula responds by observing that she never sees him exercise. Rand replies that he mixes his own martini every night, framing himself as a man of leisure who does not exert himself when he is not working. While Steed also exuded a "gentleman of leisure" vibe, and Gambit was capable of sprawling on the couch, both were generally energetic, or, at the very least, not lethargic. Rand, in contrast, would seem to be content to spend his time between assignments napping and relaxing, given the opportunity.

The episode also introduces a few personal facts about Rand that further define his character and differentiate him from his British predecessors. He voices his love for deep sea fishing and the Portland Trail Blazers basketball team, two pieces of information that cast him as the quintessential outdoorsy, sports-loving American male. In addition, Rand's love of the Trail Blazers suggests that he has roots in the state of Oregon, and possibly grew up there before moving down the coast to San Francisco. Rand also mentions that he loves his mother, implying that she is not only alive, but that he is still close to her and willing to discuss her in casual conversation. Perhaps she is back in Oregon and Rand visits her occasionally, something he might have been depicted doing had a full series been commissioned. This filling out of Rand's biography contributes to his development as a distinct character, rather than an Americanised Steed / Gambit hybrid.

Suzy

As in the case of Rand, *The New Avengers*' influence is evident in the characterisation of Suzy, which owes something to that of Purdey. The most obvious similarity between the two is their one-name mode of address. Unlike

Cathy, Emma, and Tara, there is no "Miss" or "Mrs." honourific appended to Suzy's name, nor do we learn her surname – like Purdey, who instructed others to address her as "just Purdey", Suzy is simply referred to as "Suzy" by Rand, Oz, and Paula. There is also a vague physical resemblance between Suzy and Purdey. Suzy, like Purdey, is blonde and slim with a broad, toothy grin, and wears fashions similar to those donned by her predecessor. An orange trouser suit calls to mind Purdey's orange ensemble from *Dirtier by the Dozen* and the trouser suits she wore in *To Catch a Rat* and *Medium Rare*. Suzy's blousy lilac top and matching skirt, worn with a purple scarf with white polka dots, call to mind a white and purple button-up top with bloused sleeves and a matching white and purple layered skirt worn by Purdey in *House of Cards* and *The Midas Touch*. A brown velvet culotte overall worn with a black turtleneck and high brown boots is reminiscent of Purdey's culottes, calf-high velvet boots, cardigan, and striped turtleneck ensemble in *To Catch a Rat*. If these outfits of Suzy's were transferred from her closet to Purdey's, therefore, they would blend seamlessly into the latter's wardrobe.

One outfit that would definitely not have a place in Purdey's closet, however, is the ensemble modelled by Suzy in the episode's final scene. Consisting of a pair of shiny, electric blue short shorts and a matching tank top with an "S" sewn onto it, this ridiculous ensemble is akin to the bright green short shorts and t-shirt worn by the woman supervising Tony Fields' laps at the racetrack in *Three Handed Game*. With her cloudlike blonde hair and platform wedge heels, that woman is more cheesecake than substance, and that same insubstantial image is cultivated by Suzy in her shiny blue quasi-cheerleader ensemble. While Purdey donned short shorts in *K is for Kill: Tiger by the Tail* and *Trap*, in both instances she paired them with a long-sleeved top, and, in the latter instance, wore a leotard under the shorts, resulting in a smarter, classier look. As a result, perhaps the only detail of Suzy's outfit that truly recalls any of Purdey's is the "S" for Suzy, which is in the same vein as Purdey's personalised motorcycle jacket in *The Tale of the Big Why*. Otherwise, Suzy's outfit is symbolic of Purdey and Suzy's most significant point of divergence: their approach to their interactions with the opposite sex. While Purdey enjoyed the attentions of men, she generally kept them at arm's length with humourous and eccentric comments that made her true feelings very difficult to discern. This behaviour was amplified in her dynamic with Gambit, with Purdey opting to respond to Gambit's romantic interest in her with teasing mixed signals, sometimes pulling away when he attempted to demonstrate his affection (*The Last of the Cybernauts...??*, *Faces*), while on other occasions offering encouragement by kissing him (*Sleeper*), mouthing the word "love" in "I love you" (*Target!*), and leaning seductively over him (*Dirtier by the Dozen*). These teasing moments were augmented by more serious ones, in which a crisis pushed Purdey to express genuine emotion. For example, in *Faces*, Purdey wept openly at Gambit's apparent death, ranted angrily about how the real Gambit was "a thousand times better" than his supposed murderer, and admitted that she cared about Gambit. In addition, Purdey had a habit of indirectly revealing her feelings for Gambit by becoming jealous whenever he brought up his little black book of telephone numbers (*Faces, Sleeper*), mentioned or appeared with a date (*Dead Men are Dangerous, The Last of the Cybernauts...??, K is for Kill: Tiger by the Tail*), or expressed interest in other women (*House of Cards, Three Handed Game*). However, Purdey's actions generally spoke louder than words, with her preferring to subtly insinuate her feelings rather than spell anything out explicitly.

Suzy, in contrast, is about as subtle as her electric blue short shorts when it comes to sex and romance. Best described as "man hungry", she is forever eyeing up members of the opposite sex – spotting Paula's faux neighbour, she immediately compares him to Robert Redford. Similarly, even though she has no intention of performing sexual favours for the store owner, it is notable that she implies that she frequently employs this empty promise in order to get what she wants. While the *Avengers* women would flirt with men to get information relating to an investigation, they would not, even via a veiled comment, offer to perform sexual favours in exchange for that information. Suzy's go-to information-gathering tactic is therefore reflective of her general sexual boldness, which is amplified when it comes to Rand. He is unquestionably the focus of Suzy's interest, as evidenced by the fact that Suzy claims she is "saving" herself for him. This comment also sets Suzy apart from her predecessors. None of the *Avengers* women would have felt the need to "save" themselves for anyone, let alone discuss their willingness to do so, and they certainly would not have addressed the topic of their sex life so directly. This is merely one example of how Suzy takes on the role of pursuer vis-à-vis Rand, and performs it by making extremely forward, unsubtle comments and gestures that leave no room for interpretation. Other examples of Suzy's forwardness in her pursuit of Rand include pressing Rand to admit that he loves her; massaging Rand's shoulders; kissing him; telling him that she wants to join his legion of lovers; revealing that a piece of jewellery he purchased for her is akin to an engagement ring; interpreting Rand's comments about playing "a few games" and "be[ing] had" as being sexual in nature; and describing her revealing clothing to him. All of this happens over the course of a single episode, whereas Gambit, in the same "pursuer" role, made his interest in Purdey known in fewer, and generally more subtle, ways, or did not make that interest known at all, in any given story. In addition, the Purdey / Gambit flirtations almost always involved an element of humour, typically in the form of quips and playful sparring, whereas Suzy's advances, while sometimes amusingly framed or eliciting a humourous reply or reaction from Rand, are more straightforward and earnestly made, and therefore not particularly entertaining. Instead, they become rather tedious in their frequency, and evoke a feeling of irritation toward Suzy as the episode progresses and it increasingly seems as though she has a one-track mind and is incapable of thinking about anything other than Rand and her libido. (It should be noted that the exasperation evoked by Suzy's unrelenting pursuit of Rand is unrelated to the fact that the pursuer is a woman – if the positions were reversed, Rand making such frequent overtures toward Suzy would become equally tiresome.) In addition, the frequency with which Suzy and Rand's conversations inevitably loop back to her attraction to him comes at the expense of them discussing other topics, and therefore prevents the viewer from gaining an insight into other aspects of their relationship. Gambit and Purdey, in contrast, discussed an array of topics, none of which concerned Gambit's attraction to Purdey in any way, shape, or form. These interactions cemented the sense that, beyond being potential lovers, Purdey and Gambit were professional partners who worked well together, as well as good friends who enjoyed each another's company. In contrast, any sense of friendship and camaraderie in Rand and Suzy's dynamic is too often subsumed by Suzy's tendency to sexualise their relationship. Interestingly, in a July 1978 edition of the *Daily Record* newspaper, Morgan Fairchild herself indicated that she was unhappy with Suzy's innuendo-laden exchanges with Rand, and would have preferred that the nature of the Rand / Suzy relationship be more ambiguous. Presumably she would have voiced those concerns had a full series been commissioned, in which case it would have been interesting to see how the dynamic between the two lead characters was retooled.

An aspect of Suzy's characterisation that does owe something to Purdey is that she is something of an eccentric. In Purdey's case, her quirks often contributed to her success as an agent. For example, in *Dirtier by the Dozen*, Purdey used clever, offbeat quips to charm a group of soldiers into giving her information while keeping their amorous advances at bay, refuting one soldier's comment that women go for men in uniform – "No, that's dogs... they go for postmen." – and removing another's hand from her thigh while responding to his assertion that she likes a touch of danger – "The danger, not the touch." After being taken prisoner by the men's leader, Colonel "Mad Jack" Miller, Purdey uses her particular brand of quirkiness to neutralise his threats and rob him of the satisfaction of intimidating her – Miller: "I'm afraid we have no facilities for the imprisonment of young women." Purdey: "You mean you haven't got a hairdryer?" Purdey uses the same offbeat humour to disarm her jailer in *The Eagle's Nest*, countering his suggestive comment about "fancying things" by telling him that she fancies "a *steak au poivre*, preferably at the George V in Paris". In *The Midas Touch*, she wrongfoots the villains after being captured by cheerfully imparting her newly acquired knowledge about the identity of the director of *The Treasure of the Sierra Madre*: "Most people think Walter Houston directed it. It was John." Purdey's offbeat nature also allows her to pick up on details that those with a more conventional mindset might miss. For example, she locates Suzy Miller in *House of Cards* by examining a photo of the Millers at a cottage, and reasoning that the fact that the Millers are shown tending the garden of the cottage proves that they own it, as no one would tend to a garden at a rental property. She then identifies the type of church spire behind the cottage, and uses that information to locate the cottage, where she finds Suzy Miller in hiding. Similarly, in *The Tale of the Big Why*, her lateral thinking allows her to work out where secret documents were buried. Decrypting a clue hidden in the name of the episode's titular novel, she works out that the documents were buried in the area covered by the tail of the letter "Y" on a map labelled "SURREY".

Like Purdey, Suzy also uses her eccentric tendencies and unorthodox take on the world to assist her in her work as an agent. First of all, she uses her habit of zeroing in on seemingly irrelevant details that more conventional people would fail to notice to her advantage. For example, her seemingly frivolous infatuation with the dress worn by Paula's double is revealed to not be frivolous at all when Suzy concludes that the woman wearing it cannot be Paula, pointing out that, as a redhead, Paula would not choose such a dress because it does not suit her colouring. Later, she checks a tracksuit found on a dummy of Paula and points out that it cannot be Paula's own because it is the wrong size, implying that Paula was not directly involved in setting up the tableau in which the dummy was used. Her less conventional approach also comes through in her willingness to rely on her personal impressions of Paula, rather than hard evidence, in drawing conclusions. She concludes that the woman seen leaving Paula's apartment cannot be Paula because she did not take the necklace Suzy lent her with her, and also believes that a child in a photo cannot be Paula's, reasoning that Paula would have told her if she was a mother. Even Suzy's intense interest in the opposite sex sometimes proves to be an asset to her cause. Her attraction to Paula's neighbour leads her to recognise him from footage of Tulliver disembarking from a plane, a clue that ultimately allows the pair to work out where Paula is being held. In another instance, Suzy uses her penchant for quirkiness to acquire information from a reluctant source without providing anything in return. Questioning an uncooperative store owner about a wedding photo of Paula displayed in his store window, Suzy implies that she will provide sexual favours in return for information about it. The store owner provides the information, then eagerly tells Suzy that he closes at five. Suzy, in turn, deflects his insinuations with a very Purdey-like, eccentric response: "I'm so glad to hear that. I think most people work much too hard these days." As Suzy turns to leave, the store owner asks about them getting together, to which Suzy delivers the parting shot – "You'll have to ask my husband." – then makes her exit, having got the information she required at no cost to herself. Such scenes establish Suzy as an agent whose unique way of thinking and approach to solving problems complements Rand's strictly logical method.

However, in other instances, Suzy's quirkiness is a hindrance rather than an asset, and affects the ability of the audience to perceive her as a competent, professional agent. While Purdey's quirks and eccentricities did not always contribute to the resolution of the case at hand, they served to flesh out her character without undermining her abilities. In the course of the series, we learn about her habit of initiating conversations about esoteric topics at odd moments, such as the identity of the director of *The Treasure of the Sierra Madre* during a car chase (*The Midas Touch*), and the ability of men to commit during a stakeout (*Forward Base*). We also discover that she has a prodigious appetite, as revealed by her yearning for steak au poivre (*The Eagle's Nest*), her telling Gambit she needs food "now" (*The Tale of the Big Why*), and her affinity for marshmallows (*To Catch a Rat, Three Handed Game*). Other episodes demonstrate that she has a strong constitution when it comes to liquor, downing moonshine (*Emily*) and vodka (*Gnaws*) without so much as blinking, and inventing a stomach-testing concoction of lemonade, vodka, bitters, and gin (*Dead Men are Dangerous*). These quirks are interesting and memorable, and help the audience to get to know Purdey better, but do not render her a ridiculous character who cannot be taken seriously. Suzy's quirks, in contrast, are, in some cases, so over-the-top as to render her a borderline caricature rather than a woman capable of behaving like a professional agent. The best example of Suzy's overcooked daffiness is the setup for her first interaction with Rand. En route to report to Oz, Rand is forced to lurch to a stop when a woman collapses in the middle of the road. Rand brakes just in time to avoid running her over, then discovers that it is a seemingly unconscious Suzy. When Rand attempts to check her vitals, however, Suzy's eyes pop open and she smiles. An irritated Rand exclaims, "Suzy, will you stop doing that!", implying that she makes a habit of such antics. He then tells Suzy that she could have just stuck out her thumb if she wanted him to stop, but Suzy quips that he probably would have driven right by if she had, a comment that Rand wryly agrees with. However, it seems highly unlikely that Suzy would really have to go to such extremes just to hitch a ride with Rand, meaning her behaviour is less endearing and quirky, and more reckless and dangerous. If Rand had not been able to stop in time, he could have killed her. While this moment is perhaps intended to be a signifier of the trust that Suzy places in Rand, as well as an example of her quirkiness, it instead comes across as an irresponsible act on Suzy's part that needlessly puts both herself and her partner at risk. While Purdey sometimes got herself into a tight spot when she chose to investigate a lead on her own (such as in *Cat Amongst the Pigeons* and *The Midas Touch*), she never purposefully endangered her life, and certainly did not take risks merely to attract attention. Suzy displays this reckless streak again when she goads a sailor who is mocking Rand into attacking him by bragging about Rand's fighting prowess, despite Rand's own attempts to defuse the situation and warnings to Suzy to disengage. In the end, Rand winds up having to fight the man due to Suzy's bravado on his behalf. It is another case of her "quirky" personality causing trouble for her partner. Suzy is also something of a liability in the episode's climactic stand-off with Tulliver, during which her unending stream of eccentric comments about how she will tend to Rand should he be injured distract Rand from the situation at hand. While a professional agent's duty is to support and protect their partner, Suzy's behaviour frames her as more of a liability than an asset to Rand's cause. In addition to being a liability, Suzy comes across as unreliable due to her choice of transportation: a Volkswagen Beetle (a car likely chosen to emphasise Suzy's quirkiness) with a penchant for breaking down. When Rand suggests that Suzy get a new car, Suzy counters that there is nothing wrong with her vehicle – instead, she claims that it is simply lovesick after being "kissed" by a "sex-mad" truck. As a professional agent, Suzy should have reliable transportation, lest she need to get somewhere in a hurry. Having a car that is prone to breaking down is therefore irresponsible, rather than endearing, while Suzy's cutesy euphemism for having a car accident suggests that she is something of a liability behind the wheel, a state of affairs that is confirmed by Rand's comment that she has had "another" accident. While Steed was told by Emma to get a new car, and Gambit admitted to a history of crashing on the racetrack (and occasionally crashed during a chase), both were portrayed as having reliable transport and generally being good drivers, as, indeed, were Suzy's *Avengers* women predecessors. Unlike in the case of Purdey, therefore, many instances of Suzy's quirkiness undermine her image as a competent, professional agent.

Also undermining Suzy's image as an agent is her seeming lack of combat skills. Her chastisement of Rand for not carrying a gun suggests that she believes one needs firearms to defend oneself, and, on more than one occasion, she drops into a very unconvincing karate stance. The stance is presumably intended to imply that she is proficient in self-defence, but instead gives the impression that she is simply copying poses that she saw on television. Matters are not helped by the fact that Suzy does not engage in any fights in the episode. In one instance, a fleeing suspect pushes Suzy – who is in her combat stance – down some stairs and into a wall without her offering even the slightest resistance. She therefore seems to be incapable of defending herself or defeating an opponent in combat. While *Avengers* women did not always come out on top in their fights, they at least held their own. Notably, in the aforementioned *Daily Record* article, Morgan Fairchild expressed disappointment that Suzy did not participate in any fights, and revealed that, if the pilot had gone to series, she would have insisted on being involved in the action sequences.

Even small scenes that do not reflect upon Suzy's professional performance are damning for her as a character. Rand's instruction to her to not drown his drink like she always does suggests that she cannot even perform minor tasks correctly. Other moments frame Suzy as a somewhat callous individual, even toward people she claims to care about. She pats Rand's shoulder sympathetically, but slightly patronisingly, when he discusses Tulliver's past attempts to kill him, laments the timing of a call for help from Paula because she had a good hand in the card game she was playing with Rand, and discusses treating Rand for a gunshot wound in a flippant manner, before concluding that it would be easier if he was wounded by a knife. Purdey could also be callous about her colleagues' feelings, but, unlike Suzy, would typically sober up when it came to matters of life and death.

Collectively, these weaknesses in Suzy's characterisation undo the good work fostered by the moments in which her quirkiness leads to breakthroughs in the case, as well as the opening scenes of the episode, which find Suzy supervising Paula as she trains for her first assignment and providing words of wisdom and reassurance when Paula admits to being nervous about going out in the field. Such scenes set Suzy up as an experienced senior agent who mentors and supports others, possessing some of the gravitas exuded by Steed when he instructed Purdey and Gambit on the ins and outs of the job. It is a shame that much of the episode does not support this competent image of Suzy, resulting in an uneven characterisation that portrays her as an asset in some respects, but a liability in others.

The Rand/Suzy Relationship

Given that Rand and Suzy share some of Gambit and Purdey's characteristics, it is unsurprising that Rand and Suzy's dynamic is reminiscent of Gambit and Purdey's in certain ways. First of all, some of their exchanges touch on the same topics that Purdey and Gambit were wont to discuss. One such topic is love. In the case of Purdey and Gambit, any discussion of this subject is undertaken relatively subtly, with Gambit hinting at his feelings for Purdey by quipping "Only that you love me very much" in response to her inquiry as to whether she left anything out in her summary of the Cybernauts (*The Last of the Cybernauts...??*) and voicing his belief in the ability of men to commit (*Forward Base*); Purdey teasingly hinting that she might return his affections by mouthing the "love" in "I do love you" (*Target!*); and both parties saying things that imply their affection when they believe the other is dying or dead (*Target!*, *Faces*). Following in their footsteps, Suzy and Rand also discuss the topic of love as it relates to their relationship, but Suzy, in classic Suzy fashion, takes things one step further by eschewing her predecessors' more subtle approach and outright asking Rand if he loves her:

<u>SUZY:</u>   You love me, don't you? I can tell because you never tell me. You must love me very much.

<u>RAND:</u>   Suzy, I love my mother, deep sea fishing, and I love the Portland Trail Blazers, but I don't love you.

<u>SUZY:</u>   Bet you do.

<u>RAND:</u>   Ten thousand dollars?

<u>SUZY:</u>   Not even a little bit?

> RAND HOLDS HIS FINGERS APART A LITTLE, MUCH TO SUZY'S DELIGHT.

Other exchanges not only touch on topics similar to those discussed by Purdey and Gambit, but also feature lines of dialogue that are reminiscent of those in *The New Avengers*. For example, in *Gnaws*, Purdey says, "I am a woman. Women are allowed their idiosyncrasies," to which Gambit replies, "And nobody knows that better than I." The following exchange between

Rand and Suzy echoes Purdey and Gambit's conversation in subject matter, wording, and rhythm:

SUZY: I changed my mind. It's a woman's privilege.

RAND: I know.

SUZY: And I am a woman.

RAND: I know that, too.

Escapade also features scenes that are akin to those in *The New Avengers* in which a beleaguered Gambit finds himself in embarrassing circumstances, and Purdey either ignores his embarrassment or relishes having the upper hand. *To Catch a Rat* features one such scene, in which Purdey expresses self-satisfaction at having defused an awkward moment instigated by Gambit's drawing of a gun in a church by pretending that Gambit was attempting to force her to marry him. Purdey claims that her performance, which was for the benefit of two women arranging flowers in the church, allowed them to escape the situation without any embarrassment. A red-faced Gambit sarcastically agrees. Similarly, in *Three Handed Game*, Purdey relishes Gambit's humiliation when she walks in on him modelling nude for artist Helen McKay. These scenes are akin to a moment in *Escapade* in which a soaking wet Rand, having swum in a lake with his clothes on, finds himself standing on the dock without his trousers, a sight that Suzy relishes. Having endured this bout of Gambit-like embarrassment, Rand is unamused when an unsympathetic Suzy turns her mind from his plight to other things:

SUZY: They don't fit.

RAND LOOKS AT HIS TROUSERS.

RAND: The label said shrink-proof.

SUZY: No, the tracksuit. It's the wrong size. Paula takes a size ten, and that tracksuit is a size fourteen. Don't you think that's funny?

RAND: Well, Suzy, at the moment I'm soaking wet, I'm approaching terminal pneumonia, and my pants don't fit. I don't think anything's funny.

Another exchange, conducted while the pair are being held at gunpoint by Tulliver, recalls Purdey's habit of making a series of remarks that ignore the issue at hand, causing Gambit to repeat her name with increasing frustration in an effort to make her listen to him (e.g., in *The Last of the Cybernauts...??*):

RAND:	(The bullet) might even go right through me.
SUZY:	If it doesn't, I'll just boil water and cut it out.
RAND:	Thank you, Suzy.
SUZY:	Or I'll rush you straight to the hospital.
RAND:	Thank you, Suzy.
SUZY:	A knife wound would be easier.
RAND:	Suzy!

Other exchanges do not have specific equivalents in *The New Avengers*, but could very easily have been performed by Purdey and Gambit without seeming out of place. One such exchange follows Suzy's revelation that she has been keeping a large portion of her wardrobe in Rand's closet without telling him:

SUZY:	Do you feel compromised?
RAND:	No. Trapped.
SUZY:	That's ridiculous! Now, I let you keep steaks in my fridge.
RAND:	That's different. We ate the steaks.
SUZY:	You want me to get peppermint-flavoured clothing?
RAND:	I don't care what flavour they are. I want them out of my closet.

Suzy's actions smack of the type of liberty Purdey would take, and her justification of those actions employs the same sort of bizarre logic that Purdey frequently employed. Rand's surprise at her revelation and counterargument that keeping steaks in Suzy's fridge is not the same thing, meanwhile, are very Gambit-like.

Other, smaller moments also have a familiar ring to them, harkening back to both the original series and its sequel. Suzy's observation that "It's a big lake" echoes Purdey's "It's a big country" line in *The Gladiators*, while Rand's "Suzy, I know it's a big lake" response is Gambit-like in its slight exasperation at her stating the obvious and echoes his "I know it's a field" line in *House of Cards*. Rand telling Suzy to get a new car, meanwhile, echoes Emma telling Steed to do the same in *Too Many Christmas Trees*, while Suzy patting Rand on the shoulder with mock sympathy when he states that Tulliver has tried to kill him recalls Emma's own indulgent pats on Steed's shoulder in the likes of *The Master Minds*.

Where the Rand / Suzy relationship departs from that shared by Purdey and Gambit, Steed and Emma, or Steed and any of his female partners is in its explicitness. While *The Avengers* and *The New Avengers* were rife with innuendo, none of its characters had overtly sexual (onscreen) conversations with one another. *Escapade*, in contrast, has its characters engaging in exchanges that are startlingly frank in their suggestiveness. Not only does Suzy tell Rand that she is "saving" herself for him, but, in a conversation that would be impossible to misconstrue, Rand explains his rationale for resisting a romantic entanglement with Suzy, i.e., he does not believe it is a good idea to get involved with someone he works with. While series publicity raised this as a possible explanation for Purdey's resistance to Gambit's charms, and the series itself hinted at other explanations (e.g., the traumatic end to her engagement and her fear that Gambit may be killed in the line of duty), at no point did Purdey spell out her rationale in a conversation with Gambit. Instead, the pair opted to dance around the subject. Suzy and Rand, in contrast, delve explicitly into this topic when Suzy brings up Rand's active sex life and her unashamed desire to be part of it:

SUZY:	You know, I got a look at your file once. Just once. But that was enough. There were fourteen women listed there.
RAND:	Must have been '74. That was a lean year.
SUZY:	What is it with you, anyway? Safety in numbers? Or are you just plain greedy?
RAND:	It's my social conscience. I believe in sharing everything. Especially me.

SUZY:	I like to share, too.
RAND:	Suzy, you're very beautiful and desirable, but...
SUZY:	But?
RAND:	We work together.
SUZY:	You don't know that yet. That we "work" together.

SUZY KISSES RAND.

The sealing of the exchange with a kiss is the final touch that tells us we are not in Avengerland anymore. *The Avengers* and *The New Avengers* made a point of not showing Steed and his female partners or Purdey and Gambit lock lips onscreen, except on a few choice occasions that were carefully constructed in order to preserve the ambiguity of the characters' relationships: Steed and Cathy Gale kiss to reinforce Steed's cover story in *The Little Wonders*; and, in *Who's Who???*, enemy agents kiss while their minds are in Steed and Emma's bodies, meaning Steed and Emma themselves are not responsible for the act. The only kiss between two avengers that lacks an alternative explanation is that shared by Purdey and Gambit in *Sleeper*, when Purdey plants a quick goodnight kiss on a surprised Gambit's lips. However, the dim lighting, Purdey's teasing parting comment, and Gambit's lack of opportunity to reciprocate serve to preserve an element of mystery in the pair's relationship in spite of the act. The rarity of onscreen kisses between main characters, and the alternative explanations offered for those kisses, are evidence of *The Avengers*' decision to incorporate sex subtly, via innuendo, double entendre, and meaningful exchanged looks, rather than by showing anything explicit onscreen, a creative choice that allowed the series to appeal to a wider audience – those on the alert for a sexualised dimension to the characters' dynamics were provided with plenty of fodder in the form of teasing clues, while those not seeking out such a subtext were able to watch Steed and co.'s adventures without discomfort. In contrast, it would be very difficult for even the most oblivious or naïve viewer to misinterpret what is being conveyed in the following Suzy and Rand exchange:

SUZY:	When you asked me to stay and play a few games, I thought...

RAND:	I know what you thought.
SUZY:	You must have a will of iron.
RAND:	Tempered steel.
SUZY:	You said I was beautiful. Desirable. You kissed me.
RAND:	You kissed me.
SUZY:	Well, I didn't see you running away. At least, not 'til near the end. And you kissed me back.

Of course, there is nothing inherently wrong with Suzy and Rand's explicit, up-front conversations and behaviour, and whether one enjoys those aspects of their dynamic will be a matter of personal taste. However, on an objective level, their behaviour is the antithesis of The Avengers' subtle approach to sex in its character dynamics. As Brian Clemens wrote for the series throughout its run, he was more than capable of writing Rand and Suzy's relationship in the same playfully ambiguous way he did Steed and Emma's or Purdey and Gambit's. Whether he chose not to in an effort to try something new with Escapade, because he thought an explicit approach would be better received by an American audience, or at the behest of Quinn Martin Productions is unknown, but the overt sexualization of the Rand / Suzy relationship is a definite departure from the Avengers formula.

Oz

Rand and Suzy's superior, "Computerized Security Initiator MK. V/K7", known more familiarly as "Oz", fills the role occupied in The Avengers and The New Avengers by the likes of Mother, Father, One-Ten, Charles, Thomas McKay, and a host of others, as well as Steed himself in certain episodes of The New Avengers. It is unsurprising, then, that, in the scenes in which Oz features, it effectively stands in for Steed and becomes the series' de facto third lead, a status it – though not its voice actor, Lost in Space alum Jonathan Harris – is also accorded in the opening titles, in which it features prominently. Clemens originally envisioned Oz as being contained in an obelisk located in the middle of the desert, which would have rendered Oz a remote, almost alien entity – one can imagine it being unreadable, all knowing, and all powerful, looming over Rand and Suzy as it handed down edicts from on high. Oz's proposed desert location also would have cultivated the same slightly eerie, surreal quality possessed by Avengerland's deserted streets, and been more than a little reminiscent of the empty or sparsely adorned landscapes in which the action took place in *The Avengers*' and *The New Avengers*' title sequences. In addition, Clemens' initial conception of Oz would perhaps have encouraged the audience to question whether it was a completely benevolent entity, or an amoral, unfeeling machine that would have no qualms about sacrificing its agents if "logic" dictated that that was the best course of action. This characterisation would certainly have been in keeping with *The Avengers*' and *The New Avengers*' cynicism about technology and depiction of large, high-tech computers as a means of committing murder in the likes of *The House That Jack Built*, *Killer*, and *Complex*. If Oz was originally intended to be sinister or amoral, that would have had intriguing implications for the series' tone and the types of stories it told.

However, presumably for production reasons, Oz's abode became a stately home, with the computer protected by guards and coming out of hiding when Suzy and Rand placed their hands on a palm reader. In keeping with its very human residence, Oz is anthropomorphised, but not in a sinister or coldly calculating way. Instead, Oz speaks with an amiable, slightly priggish voice, and seemingly experiences emotions such as bemusement, frustration, disapproval, and embarrassment. While depicted as efficient, it is also imbued with a touch of human fallibility via its malfunctions, which include the failure of its sex-delineation circuits – which renders it incapable of distinguishing between Rand and Suzy – and its habit of succumbing to uncontrollable giggling after adding laugh tracks to its repertoire. As well as humanising it, these foibles cast Oz as a comedy character, and thereby inject almost cartoonish humour into the series. In keeping with this humourous bent, Oz also, to an extent, serves as an electronic version of *The Avengers*' trademark eccentrics, right down to its knowledgeability (it speaks 32 languages), tendency to get sidetracked, forgetfulness – Oz tells Rand and Suzy to remind it to reprimand Paula, leading Suzy to suggest that, with all its memory circuits, no one should need to remind Oz of anything, a point that Oz sheepishly concedes – and a penchant for sharing its acquired knowledge with the leads (at one point, it uses the teddy bears Suzy and Rand discover during their investigation as an opportunity to inform them that the teddy bear was named after Theodore Roosevelt). The nickname "Oz", as well as Suzy's speculation that someone is controlling the computer behind the scenes, hints at the possibility that future episodes would have explored Oz's inner workings and whether there was one or more people pulling its strings. Those episodes could have revealed that Rand's dismissal of Suzy's theory that Oz is a mere front – he claims that Oz consists of a bank of computers in the lower levels of the house that is kept under tight security – was a fib intended to keep the identity of Oz's true operator a secret from all but those with the highest security clearance. This speculation about Oz could have made for an intriguing ongoing plot thread, and would have lent Oz a more sinister edge if executed properly. Such a sinister edge would, in turn, have helped to offset Oz's inherent cartoonishness, which likely would have become grating as the series wore on.

Oz's inclusion also signals the series' desire to be perceived as being on the cutting edge of technology. However, while making the leads' superior a computer does add a novel, tech-centric element to the series, there is also a definite cheese factor at work when it comes to Oz, particularly in relation to its appearance. For that reason, Oz's console – a silver terminal adorned with a plethora of blinking lights and reel-to-reel spools – certainly would have had to be updated if the series ran for multiple seasons, to prevent it from becoming a laughable anachronism. In addition, there would have been limitations to what could be done with a recurring cast member who was a stationary piece of technology, as it would be far less versatile than a human being in terms of the situations in which it could be placed. Therefore, while the Oz character offered opportunities for novel plots, it also had the potential to become more of a liability than an asset due to its inherent limitations.

Paula Winters

It is somehow fitting that Paula Winters is an almost-spectral presence in this episode, represented mostly by a faceless, counterfeit Paula. As a character, she has about the same amount of substance as a ghost, which is perhaps unsurprising as she essentially serves as the episode's McGuffin, driving the plot and serving as the other players' main motivation for their actions: Suzy is worried about her friend and wants to find her so she can help her; Rand is tracking her in the hope that, by doing so, he will be able to divine his old nemesis Tulliver's true aims and finally defeat him; and Tulliver kidnaps her in order to extract her department's secret codes from her mind. However, for all that people cannot seem to stop talking about Paula and seeing her wherever they go, Paula is actually absent for the bulk of the story. Her main scenes all occur within roughly five minutes of screentime at the start of the episode, during which Paula is shown conducting a practice run for her first assignment, receiving a pep talk from Suzy in the locker room, going for a jog, and talking to Rand. These early scenes establish Paula as a young, inexperienced agent in the Tara King mould, keen to learn and in awe of the more senior Rand and Suzy, but uncertain of whether she has what it takes to go out in the field. Like Tara, she is also a pleasant, amiable character, and one that the viewer would perhaps be interested in learning more about given that Suzy and Rand seem to be invested in her success as an agent. Unfortunately, after these early scenes, the characterisation of Paula comes to an abrupt halt, as she disappears from the screen and is replaced by a double. When the real Paula reappears, she is drugged, and she remains that way throughout the remainder of her screentime. As a result, the audience is left with a lasting image of Paula as a slightly dozy individual who allows herself to be easily taken captive and pumped for information, and ultimately has to be rescued by Rand and Suzy. Paula is somewhat redeemed at the episode's close, when Rand and Suzy announce that, with Suzy's assistance, she successfully completed her first assignment and acquired the Alpha papers. However, this accomplishment is undermined by the fact that Paula is not shown acquiring the papers, nor does she triumphantly deliver them to Oz in person. The latter task falls to Rand and Suzy, leaving a sense of unfinished business in Paula's arc, which is sacrificed in favour of giving Rand and Suzy the last word and gag and allowing them to depart while exchanging meaningful, suggestive glances that imply that their next stop will be the bedroom. Even when Paula is onscreen, there is the sense that her scenes are constructed to serve other characters rather than Paula herself, be it to frame Suzy as a mentor, Rand as a living legend, or Tulliver as a criminal mastermind. While this is often the lot of guest characters in television series – to serve the plot and leads rather than their own characterisation – one wishes that Paula was slightly more fleshed out, as some of the incidental characters who worked at Steed and co.'s department in *The New Avengers* were. The likes of the exactingly correct Ministry man McBain (*Medium Rare*), naughty file clerk Finder (*To Catch a Rat*), and smug and overconfident agent Larry (*Three Handed Game*) not only facilitated the plot, but were interesting and memorable in their own right. Unfortunately, instead of giving Paula the same treatment, the story reduces her to a cipher. Indeed, Paula is better served in the characterisation stakes by Tulliver than the script itself. The fictional backstory that he invents for her – that Paula married a man named Edward Malone and had a child – would have made Paula a more intriguing character and added twists to the plot if proven to be true. One could imagine Rand and Suzy questioning whether Paula was a double agent, or Paula herself revealing that she disclosed the codes in an effort to protect her secret family from Tulliver. Either scenario would have resulted in a more interesting characterisation of Paula and a more exciting climax to the episode than what was scripted.

Arnold Tulliver

We learn a number of things about Arnold Tulliver over the course of *Escapade*'s pilot. He is a freelance agent who steals secrets and sells them to the highest bidder. A devious man, he delights in using diversionary tactics — such as the false trail he lays for Rand and Suzy in the episode — to distract from his true aim. He is also not a man to be trifled with — he has a Class "A" danger rating and has made multiple attempts on Rand's life. This backstory casts Tulliver in the same mould as Steed's old nemeses in *The New Avengers*, such as his childhood friend Mark Crayford (*Dead Men are Dangerous*), French operative The Unicorn (*The Lion and the Unicorn*), and Russian spy Ivan Perov (*House of Cards*). These characters contributed to *The New Avengers*' "thicker cardboard" characterisation of Steed by providing insights into the senior agent's personal history and demonstrating that his past actions lingered in his mind and had consequences for the present day. In addition, such characters helped to establish a broader *Avengers* universe that existed beyond the confines of the story of the week, their backstories demonstrating that, between their encounters with Steed, they had carried on with their lives. This approach to the characterisation of the series' villains contributed to *The New Avengers*' internal richness, and Brian Clemens clearly wanted to imbue *Escapade* with that same richness, starting with the character of Tulliver. Indeed, with Tulliver, Clemens intended to go a step further than he had in *The New Avengers*. While villains from Steed's past were limited to a single appearance in *The New Avengers*, Tulliver was to be a first: a recurring nemesis for the leads. Though *The Avengers* had, on rare occasions, brought back antagonists — most notably the Cybernauts and their assistant wrangler, Benson (*The Cybernauts*, *Return of the Cybernauts*), and the inept Ambassador Brodny (*Two's a Crowd*, *The See Through Man*) — they were limited to two or three appearances across the whole of the series' run. Tulliver, in contrast, was intended to be a semi-regular character. While it is not known exactly how frequently Tulliver would have appeared, it is telling that Clemens included him in a second script that he penned for the series. Titled "Illusion", the story would have found Tulliver attempting to acquire a device that projected images onto a person's eye, and thereby controlled what that person believed they were seeing. Tulliver would have used this device to gain access to a nuclear installation in order to sabotage it. The fact that Clemens included Tulliver in both of the scripts he penned for the series suggests that he envisioned the character as putting in numerous appearances throughout the show's first season.

However, while the regular inclusion of Tulliver would almost certainly have helped to establish a broader universe for the series beyond the story of the week and deepen Rand's characterisation as the pair's history was gradually revealed, there is one problem: Tulliver is not a very interesting or impressive character. As discussed elsewhere in this piece, the revelation that Tulliver's sole motivation for his elaborate misdirection plot is to extract codes from Paula and use them to gather and sell secrets is something of a letdown. One would expect that Tulliver would only make such a significant investment of time and effort in order to execute a grand, ambitious plot, akin to what he hopes to achieve in the "Illusion" script. That plot would have provided a far more impressive introduction to Tulliver, as well as been in keeping with the formidable status ascribed to him by Rand and Oz. Of course, a more epic and ambitious plot would have been difficult to include in a pilot, as, by necessity, such episodes devote a large portion of their runtime to introducing the series' characters and format. However, the small-scale scheme that the pilot was able to accommodate unfortunately frames Tulliver, not as a clever, devious, dangerous operator who plays for high stakes, but as a slightly grubby individual who plays overly elaborate spy games in order to gain a relatively trifling reward. To make matters worse, he is also depicted as bland and uninteresting. Admittedly, his silent shadowing of Paula, Rand, and Suzy throughout much of the episode is very effective. Oozing quiet menace, he appears to be both omniscient and capable of being everywhere at once. However, that illusion of menace and mystery is shattered toward the end of the episode, when Tulliver finally speaks. His conversations with his henchman reveal that he has no distinct characteristics or mannerisms, and his dialogue is workaday and uninspired. This, coupled with his unremarkable looks, renders him an utterly forgettable, bland baddie who could have appeared in any number of series as a mid-level criminal involved in one illegal money-making scheme or another. He certainly does not appear to possess a personality or intellect that is in keeping with the sense of whimsy and predilection for the bizarre that would seem to be integral to the ability to conjure up a false trail featuring teddy bears in graveyards and a faux Paula running around in a designer dress. Indeed, the disconnect between Tulliver and the strangeness of his diversion is so extreme that one is left to wonder if an unseen "mastermind" character is truly behind the scheme, and Tulliver is simply following orders. Unfortunately, no such mastermind emerges, and we are left with tedious Tulliver. Perhaps Tulliver would have been fleshed out and become more interesting in future installments, but the picture painted of him in the pilot episode is that of a generic criminal, rather than a memorable baddie on par with *The Avengers*' iconic diabolical masterminds.

Other Characters

When examining the minor supporting players in Rand and Suzy's adventure, what is most memorable about them is, ironically, how unmemorable they are. While it is generally true that it is difficult for a two-dimensional role with minimal screentime to make an impact, *The Avengers* turned crafting interesting or entertaining minor roles into something of an artform. Think of the menacing Saul, the almost-wordless henchman in *The Town of No Return*; the sweetly flirtatious Julie, who works at Pinter's food counter and infuses her solitary scene with a playfulness that Steed returns in kind in *Death at Bargain Prices*; or the dour Napoleon in *Honey for the Prince*, who silently departs for his "Waterloo" fantasy, only to return battle scarred and, just as silently, admit defeat. These characters could have played their roles of henchman, person providing information that moves the plot along, and background colour in a much more utilitarian, workaday way, but the script goes the extra mile to make them colourful, endearing, or sinister. In addition, many of *The Avengers'* incidental characters were imbued with the series' signature eccentricity, which rendered them more memorable than the average small role.

Escapade, in contrast, fails to imbue its minor characters with a similar level of colour or interest. Henchman Bart does little more than get chased by Rand and Suzy before falling to his death, while the man pretending to be Paula's neighbour plays his assumed role with bland amiability, and, when he is revealed to be working for Tulliver, acts as little more than someone for Tulliver to explain his plot to for the benefit of the audience. Neither character is interesting or eccentric in any way, shape, or form. The sailor who picks a fight with Rand, meanwhile, is an obnoxious, jumped-up sort, full of bravado and little else. His bemusement when Suzy and Rand query about the tattoo on his chest is vaguely amusing, but, overall, he is more of an irritant, and certainly not on par with *The Avengers'* unique and well-crafted minor players. The photography shop owner, meanwhile, starts off as a gruff, workaday presence, then turns clumsily lascivious when he believes that Suzy intends to provide him with sexual favours in return for his assistance. It is true that he provides some comedy with his nonplussed reactions to Suzy's reference to her fictional husband and Rand's claim that he is her psychiatrist; however, the main source of amusement in the scene is the antics of Rand and Suzy. In and of himself, the shop owner, like the other minor characters, is uninteresting, unlikeable, and unmemorable. Though these are small parts, they feel like missed opportunities to add colour to *Escapade*'s canvas. Perhaps Brian Clemens believed that, if *Avengers*-ish characters filled such roles in an American series, they would seem over-the-top or out of place, but the series feels poorer for the utilitarian nature of its minor players.

Filming Locations

As previously discussed, *Escapade*'s use of San Francisco locations gives this American corner of Avengerland its own unique flavour. Michael Richardson, author of the extraordinary *Avengers* reference work *Bowler Hats and Kinky Boots*, has identified many of the filming locations used for *Escapade*, and very generously passed along his findings for inclusion in this piece. Many thanks to Michael for the following information:

- Paula is initially shown jogging at the Steiner Street and Green Street crossroads, with the St. Vincent de Paul Catholic Church visible in the background.

- Rand's home is located at 2640 Steiner Street. The home has been extensively refurbished since its appearance in *Escapade*, and therefore looks very different today. It was also used in the film *Mrs. Doubtfire* (1993).

- Paula's apartment building, which she approaches from Laguna Street as she finishes her jog, is located at 2192 Washington Street.

- Rand finds Suzy lying in the middle of the road while driving on El Camino Del Mar. After Rand picks Suzy up, they continue on this road before turning left into the Legion of Honor Drive, with the Legion of Honor museum briefly visible in the background.

- Oz's home is the Filoli Historic House and Garden, off Canada Road.

- Paula's car is abandoned by her double on a gravel track between Chrissy Field and a beach. The Golden Gate Bridge is visible in the background.

- The graveyard in which Rand and Suzy search for Paula is the Cypress Lawn Memorial Park, off El Camino Real, Colma. While Cypress Lawn contains a tall obelisk, it was not erected until 1992, meaning the one that appears in *Escapade* was likely a prop.

- Rand and Suzy chase the Paula lookalike to a church before losing sight of her. The church is the Noble Chapel at the Cypress Lawn Memorial Park, Colma.

- The road near the Noble Chapel where Rand and Suzy search for Paula is possibly the El Camino Real junction with Old Mission Road, Colma. It has the same layout as that depicted onscreen and is near the Cypress Lawn Memorial Park.

- After losing the Paula lookalike, Rand and Suzy are shown departing The Delicatessen restaurant, located at 1988 Union Street (now vacant). They then make their way down Union Street, passing Thai Silk (now Extreme Pizza) at 1980 and Wells Fargo Bank (which occupies the same location today) at 1900. A six-storey building, located at 2001 Union Street, is visible behind Rand and Suzy during their journey, the ground floor of which houses the Bank of America (now Comerica Bank). They then make their way to Bayside Photo, located at 1748 Union Street (now vacant). The other side of the street appears to have been partially redeveloped since filming. (With thanks to Anthony McKay, creator of the invaluable location-spotter's website *A Guide to Avengerland* [avengerland.theavengers.tv], for the identification of the Union Street locations.)

- Rand and Suzy walk down 6th Street while being watched by the Paula lookalike from 172 6th Street, the Dudley Apartments. In pursuit of Bart, Rand and Suzy climb down the fire escape of the Dudley Apartments, which is mounted on the side of the building fronting on Natoma Street.

- While searching for information about Edward Malone, Rand and Suzy visit a bar likely located on Pier 35 of the Embarcadero. The Pacific Far East Line barge carrier *Japan Bear / America Bear / John Penn*, the home port of which was San Francisco, is moored in the background. It is difficult to be certain that this is the location that was used for filming, as the area has been heavily redeveloped, but none of the other piers seems to be a suitable match. The interior of the bar was likely filmed in a building on Pier 39, off the Embarcadero, as Pier 35 is visible through the window. Today, there does not appear to be a building that matches the inside of the bar and has a view of Pier 35, but it is possible that the building in which the bar was located has since been demolished and replaced by another building.

- The marina through which Rand and Suzy pursue the Paula lookalike is the Yacht Harbour at Marina Green, off Marina Boulevard. The Golden Gate Yacht Club building and the Marina District Lighthouse also appear onscreen.

- Answering Paula's call for help, Rand and Suzy travel along Harding Road. Their ultimate destination is the North Lake Boat Launch off Harding Road. The lake on which they find a boat with a dummy of Paula inside is North Lake.

Similarities to The Avengers & The New Avengers TV Series

As this was a Brian Clemens story written for a show that was originally entitled *The Avengers USA*, there are, unsurprisingly, *Avengers*-ish elements to *Escapade*. Some of these, such as recycled lines of dialogue, character attributes, and plot points, have already been discussed in this chapter, but similarities can be found elsewhere, as well. For example, there is plenty of *Avengers* influence at work in *Escapade*'s title sequence. The studio segments featuring Rand and Suzy play out against a plain white background, an empty landscape that is nearly identical to the ones that acted as the backdrops to Steed, Keel, Cathy, Emma, Purdey, and Gambit when they appeared in their title sequences. The Tara King era went against the grain by introducing a measure of colour – one of her title sequences plays out against a wash of vivid orange – as well as by venturing into the great outdoors, but, in both cases, the worlds she and Steed occupy are just as empty as those inhabited by the other avengers in their title sequences, with even the outdoor setting consisting largely of green grass, trees, and a blue sky that stretch out, seemingly endlessly, toward the horizon. The stylised, all lowercase font used to spell out the series' title, meanwhile, seems like a response to *The New Avengers*' all-uppercase lettering, which was also written in a decorative font. In addition, the brief clips of Rand and Suzy that shoot them from the neck up and feature them turning toward the camera recall similar clips of Steed, Gambit and Purdey in their animated titles, while the *Escapade* titles' montage of clips calls to mind the montages in the live-action *New Avengers* titles. Another trademark of *Avengers* title sequences was the sparing use of furniture and props, with a few choice items – a life-size chessboard and chess pieces, a table furnished with champagne glasses, a lone streetlamp, etc. – spotlighted.

Escapade's title sequence set is also sparsely furnished, with Oz initially the lone piece of set dressing. The scene becomes a bit busier later on, though not overly so, with the introduction of a tableau that seems to be staged so as to include as many *Avengers*-esque ingredients in a single frame as possible: Rand and Suzy sit playing chess (a game that is something of an *Avengers* motif, as it is featured in the Emma Peel "chessboard" title sequence, many of the leads' surnames have chess connotations – "Gambit", "King", and Emma's maiden name, "Knight" – and it is the theme of the episode *Room Without a View*), with a bottle of champagne (the avengers' beverage of choice, drunk by Steed and Emma in both the "chessboard" and colour Peel titles) close at hand, while a vase containing a lone rose sits on the table between two glasses. A rose in a gun is an iconic image from the colour Peel era titles, and *Escapade*'s rose, and the styling of it, was likely intended to evoke that image. The episode itself features another bloom with *Avengers* connections: a carnation, which Rand and Suzy find with a teddy bear in the graveyard. The carnation was Steed's buttonhole of choice on many occasions throughout the series, and featured prominently in the colour Emma Peel and outdoor Tara King title sequences.

Escapade also features a number of character names that were previously used in Brian Clemens' *Avengers* scripts. Characters with *Avengers* namesakes include Suzy, who calls to mind *House of Cards*' Suzy Miller and Steed's girlfriend Suzy in *Hostage* (and anticipates another would-be American *Avengers* woman, *The First Avengers Movie*'s Suzy Stride); Tulliver, who recalls Dr. Tulliver in *House of Cards*; and Bart, who shares a name with one of the robbers in *Sleeper* and characters in *Brought to Book*, *Brief for Murder*, and the Clemens-reworked Roger Marshall story that became *A Funny Thing Happened on the Way to the Station*.

Verdict

There are two ways to assess *Escapade*: as a continuation of *The Avengers'* legacy, and as a (potential) series in its own right. As a standalone example of a late 1970s adventure / telefantasy / espionage series, it makes for a reasonably entertaining hour of viewing. The runaround plot is diverting enough to hold one's attention, and the intriguing glimpses of the faux Paula, her face always unseen, add an eerie, surreal element to the proceedings. There is humour to be found in Rand and Suzy's interactions, with Granville Van Dusen, in particular, adept at conveying wide-eyed bemusement and twinkling irony in response to developments in the plot and Suzy's antics alike. San Francisco is a fun and visually interesting setting for the pair's adventures, and Suzy's fashions are colourful and (mostly) well-chosen. However, there are also weaknesses, particularly in the case of Suzy's characterisation. If she was to be perceived as a believable professional agent and multi-dimensional human being, rather than a one-note caricature, future episodes would have had to foreground her espionage skills, and tone down her eccentricity and man-hungry pursuit of Rand. The series also would have needed to feature more impressive and formidable foes than Tulliver, and improve Tulliver's characterisation to make him worthy of his planned "arch-nemesis" status, if drama and a sense of peril were to be evoked. However, with these adjustments – which likely would have been made at Morgan Fairchild's insistence and in future scripts by Brian Clemens – the series could have entered the eighties as a light-hearted also-ran in the same vein as the likes of *Remington Steele* and *Hart to Hart*.

As a series in the *Avengers* mould, however, *Escapade*, ironically, does itself a disservice by trying too hard to fill that mould. Yes, there are *Avengers*-ish touches and elements throughout, but, by 1978, many of those elements had been borrowed by countless series. Just about every show with a male / female investigatory duo, bizarre / surreal plot elements and moments, witty humour, and physically and intellectually formidable heroines owes as much to *The Avengers* as *Escapade* does. This widespread *Avengers* influence would have made it difficult for *Escapade* to stand out in the televisual landscape. Furthermore, the most successful of the *Avengers*-influenced series were the ones that found new ways to combine and reinvent the ingredients that made *The Avengers* a worldwide hit. This strategy is in keeping with the series' own innovative spirit, as it was forever tinkering with its formula. *Escapade*, in contrast, borrows the show's character elements, dialogue, dynamic between its leads, bizarre plots, and visuals in an effort to become an American copy of *The Avengers*. Unfortunately, this wholesale replication of elements of the two British series results in *Escapade* coming off as a pale imitation of those series, rather than its own show. If *Escapade* was to have any degree of success, it would have had to quit attempting to copy its predecessors and instead follow the lead of so many other shows by borrowing a few *Avengers* elements, reinventing them, and blazing a new trail. Whether it would have been brave enough to move away from the series that had instigated its creation, however, is another question entirely.

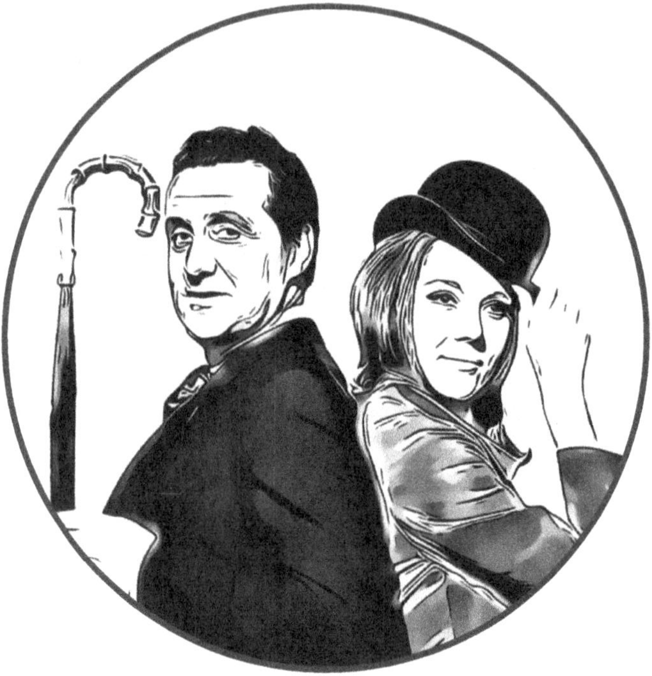

AFTERWORD

We hope that you have enjoyed reading about the weird and wonderful curiosities that we've explored in *Escapades*. We've loved analysing and uncovering new information about these oft-surprising projects. We were also delighted to bring you excerpts from exclusive interviews with some of the people behind these projects: Simon Oates, Donald Monat and Wolfgang von Chmielewski.

Though our journey through *Avengers* escapades is now at an end, yours may just be starting! If so, here are some curious, fascinating, and fun *Avengers*-related artifacts to seek out and explore:

- Curious about *Invitation to a Killing*, the script that became *Have Guns – Will Haggle*? Hunt down the radio serial *Straight from the Shoulder*.

- Fancy burying your head in a fictional biography of our favourite bowler-hatted secret agent? Try *John Steed: An Authorized Biography, Volume I – Jealous in Honor* by Tim Heald.

- Is that John Steed hiding in plain sight in *Assault on the Tower*, a 1978 episode of *The Hardy Boys*? Someone should tell Mother...

- Remember that *Avengers* episode co-starring Jane Birkin? You don't? Get on the trail of the April 1966 issue of *Man's Journal* and take a look at *Strange Case of the Green Girl*, a photo-story featuring Ms. Birkin and Patrick Macnee.

- Want to read a very different version of *The New Avengers – Dirtier by the Dozen*? Seek out Justin Cartwright's *Fighting Men* novelisation.

- What if Peter Peel figured in the 1998 Warner Bros. movie *The Avengers*? Find Don Macpherson's 1995 draft script for the film online and discover just how integral to the plot he could have been!

Plus, there are Boom! Studios comics to discover and Big Finish audios set during several eras of the series available for your listening pleasure. In short, there is an abundance of Extrapades out there, and we hope you seek out and enjoy some of these unique projects.

Wishing you a happy journey through Avengerland and beyond!

ACKNOWLEDGEMENTS

It has been a delight putting together *Escapades – An Exploration of Avengers Curiosities* and that is due in no small amount to the brilliant and talented people who have helped with the book and *The Avengers Declassified* website that has fed into it. We would particularly like to thank the following:

Wolfgang von Chmielewski
Donald Monat and June Dixon
Simon Oates and Jaki Oates
John Wright and Coral Wright

Neil Alsop, The Avengers International Fan Forum (dissolute.com.au/avengersfanforum/index.php), Brandi Bassler, Ian Beard, Ian Beazley, Chris Bentley, The Bela Lugosi Blog (beladraculalugosi.wordpress.com), Anthony Berryman, Roy Bettridge, Rupert Blaise, David Brunt, Tony Buller, Scott Burditt, John Buss (murdersville.co.uk), Beverly Charpentier, Denis Chauvet, Ajay Chowdhury, Barry Clarke, Jane Clarke, Samuel Clemens, Simon Coward, Mike Cunningham, Allen Dace, Matt Dale, Andy Davidson, Rick Davy, Tori Davy, Sam Denham, Anthony Drown, Adrian Egan, Steve England, Frans Erasmus, Simon Exton, Robert Fairclough, Paul Farrer, Elizabeth Feely, John Freeman (downthetubes.net), Ron Geddes, Des Glass, Grant Goggans (tinyurl.com/dimetro), Mitchell Hadley (www.itsabouttv.com), David Hamilton, Robert Hammond, Alys Hayes, Rita Hayes, Martin Holder, Gareth Humphreys, Tony Jay, Piers Johnson (tinyurl.com/mrspeelneeded), Brett Jones, Gary Keaping, Kinky Boots podcast (tinyurl.com/kinky-av), Denis Kirsanov, Rodney Marshall, Dave Matthews, Michael Mayer, Richard McGinlay, Anthony McKay, Ken Moss, Cedric Mueller, Mike Noon, Carlos Pagés, Andrew Parsons, Barbara Peterson, Chris Perry, Michael Scott Phillips, Andrew Pixley, Eileen Pollock, Allard Postma, Jon Preddle (broadwcast.org), Quoit Media, David Richardson, Michael Richardson, Dave Rogers, Joris Royer, David Alain Laich Ruiz, Al Samujh, Sheena Samujh, Andrew Shepherd, Holger Schmitz, David K. Smith, Andrew Staton, Andrew Stocker, Kim Thompson, John Tomlinson, Tim Trounce, David Tulley, Steve Watts, Kevin West, Jason Whiton (spyvibe.blogspot.com), Jaz Wiseman (itc-classics.co.uk), Mark Witherspoon and Jonathan Wood.

J Z Ferguson and Alan Hayes

ABOUT THE AUTHORS

J Z Ferguson is an enthusiast of British popular culture with a particular affinity for television series of the sixties and seventies. She has been a fan of *The Avengers* since 1998, when she discovered the series shortly after seeing the infamous film adaptation. She contributed chapters to all five volumes – and was joint-editor of the last two volumes – of *The Avengers on film* series, which consists of *Bright Horizons*; *Mrs. Peel, We're Needed*; *Anticlockwise*; *Avengerland Regained*; and *Avengerland Revisited*. She has also written for the *Classic British Television Drama* series, penning chapters on shows such as *The Saint*, *Danger Man*, *The Persuaders!*, and *Gideon's Way*. She wrote about sexual liberation and representations of gender in the context of sixties television series for Rodney Marshall's *Swinging TV*; *The New Avengers* and *Zodiac* for the seventies-centric follow-up, *Survival TV*; and *Cuffy* for the eighties-themed volume *New Waves*. She wrote a guest essay for *Man in a Suitcase: A Critical Guide*, and contributed chapters to the Hidden Tiger titles *Avengerworld: The Avengers in Our Lives* and *Tis Magic! Our Memories of Catweazle*. She has also written for the website *The Avengers Declassified*. She lives in Canada.

Alan Hayes has been fascinated by TV since the 1970s, and fell in love with *The Avengers* in 1976 when he was introduced to Steed, Purdey and Gambit – still his definitive *Avengers* team. He has co-written several books with awkwardly long titles including *Two Against the Underworld – The Collected Unauthorised Guide to The Avengers Series 1* (with Richard McGinlay and Alys Hayes) and *Dr. Brent's Casebook – An Unauthorised Guide to Police Surgeon* (with Richard McGinlay). He has edited three charity anthologies, *Avengerworld – The Avengers in Our Lives*, *Tis Magic – Our Memories of Catweazle* and, for Quoit Media, *Playboys, Spies and Private Eyes – Inspired by ITC* (with Rick Davy). He has also produced a series of official reconstructions of lost Series 1 *Avengers* episodes for StudioCanal, lending his voice as narrator to four of these. Alan has also been known to dabble in graphic design, producing book, DVD and CD artwork for Quoit Media and Hidden Tiger. Additionally, he has designed print materials for the theatre group Dyad Productions, which have been displayed at the Edinburgh Fringe Festival and at national and international venues. He lives in St. Albans, England, is very happily married, and both he and his wife are in servitude to a madly skittish but gorgeous cat called Katy.